THE HEROIC LEGEND OF
ARSLAN

STORY BY
YOSHIKI TANAKA

MANGA BY
HIROMU ARAKAWA

6

The Heroic Legend of
ARSLAN

TABLE OF CONTENTS

CHAPTER 35	TWIN-BLADE'S FALCON	3
CHAPTER 36	THE CHARACTER OF A KING	35
CHAPTER 37	FORTRESS OF SANDSTONE	65
CHAPTER 38	TWO PRINCES	95
CHAPTER 39	ROYAL BLOOD	127
CHAPTER 40	THE THREE PRINCIPLES	155

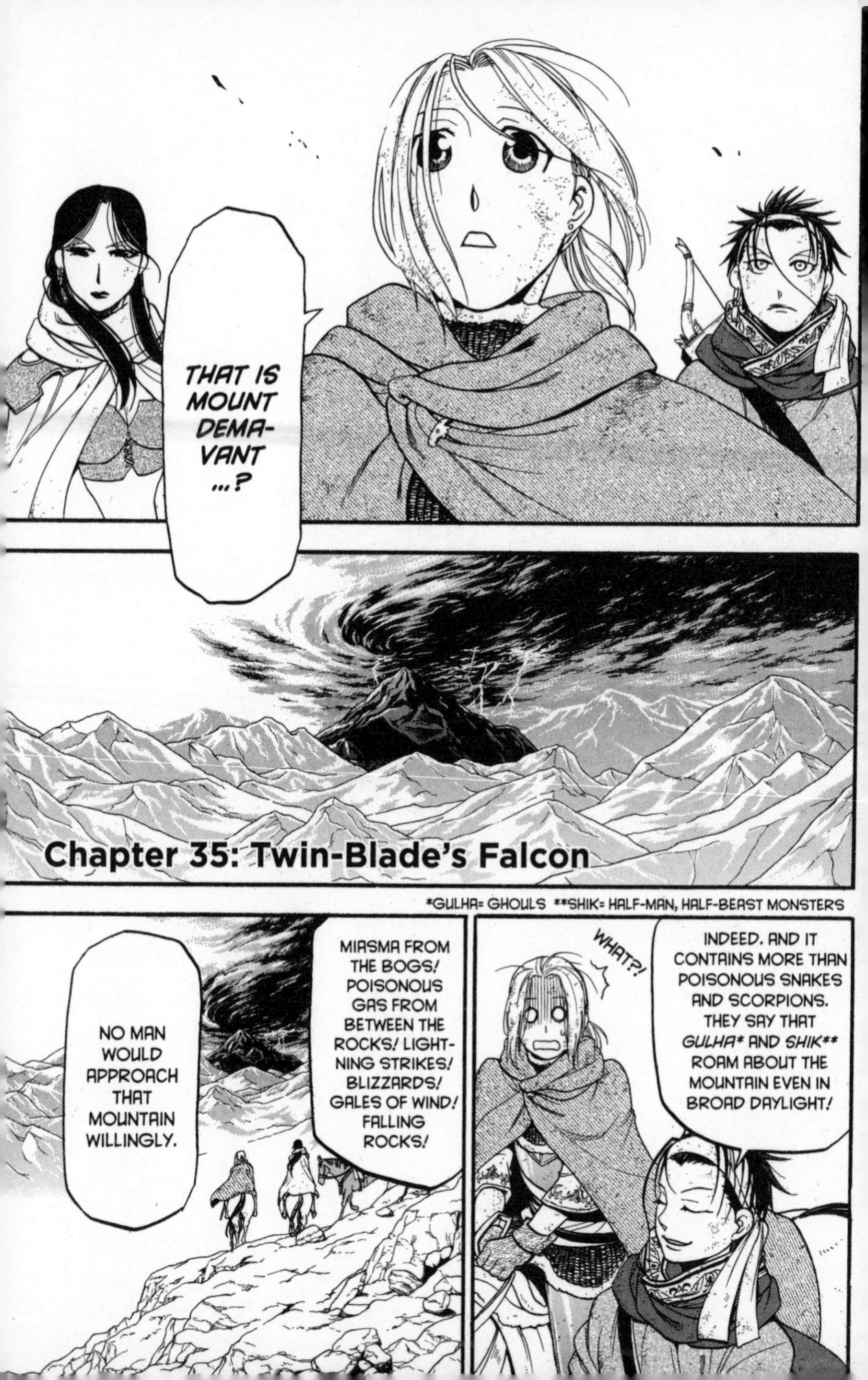
THAT IS MOUNT DEMA-VANT ...?
Chapter 35: Twin-Blade's Falcon
*GULHA= GHOULS **SHIK= HALF-MAN, HALF-BEAST MONSTERS
INDEED. AND IT CONTAINS MORE THAN POISONOUS SNAKES AND SCORPIONS. THEY SAY THAT GULHA* AND SHIK** ROAM ABOUT THE MOUNTAIN EVEN IN BROAD DAYLIGHT!
WHAT?!
MIASMA FROM THE BOGS! POISONOUS GAS FROM BETWEEN THE ROCKS! LIGHT-NING STRIKES! BLIZZARDS! GALES OF WIND! FALLING ROCKS!
NO MAN WOULD APPROACH THAT MOUNTAIN WILLINGLY.

SO THAT IS THE MOUNTAIN OF THE LEGENDS...

I SEE...

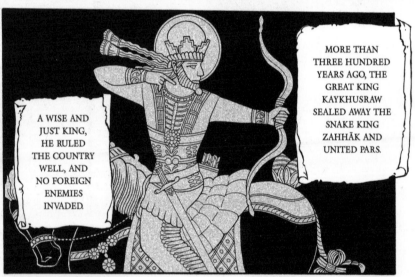

MORE THAN THREE HUNDRED YEARS AGO, THE GREAT KING KAYKHUSRAW SEALED AWAY THE SNAKE KING ZAHHĀK AND UNITED PARS.

A WISE AND JUST KING, HE RULED THE COUNTRY WELL, AND NO FOREIGN ENEMIES INVADED.

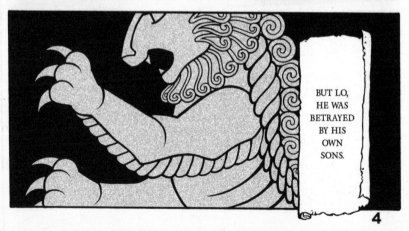

BUT LO, HE WAS BETRAYED BY HIS OWN SONS.

4

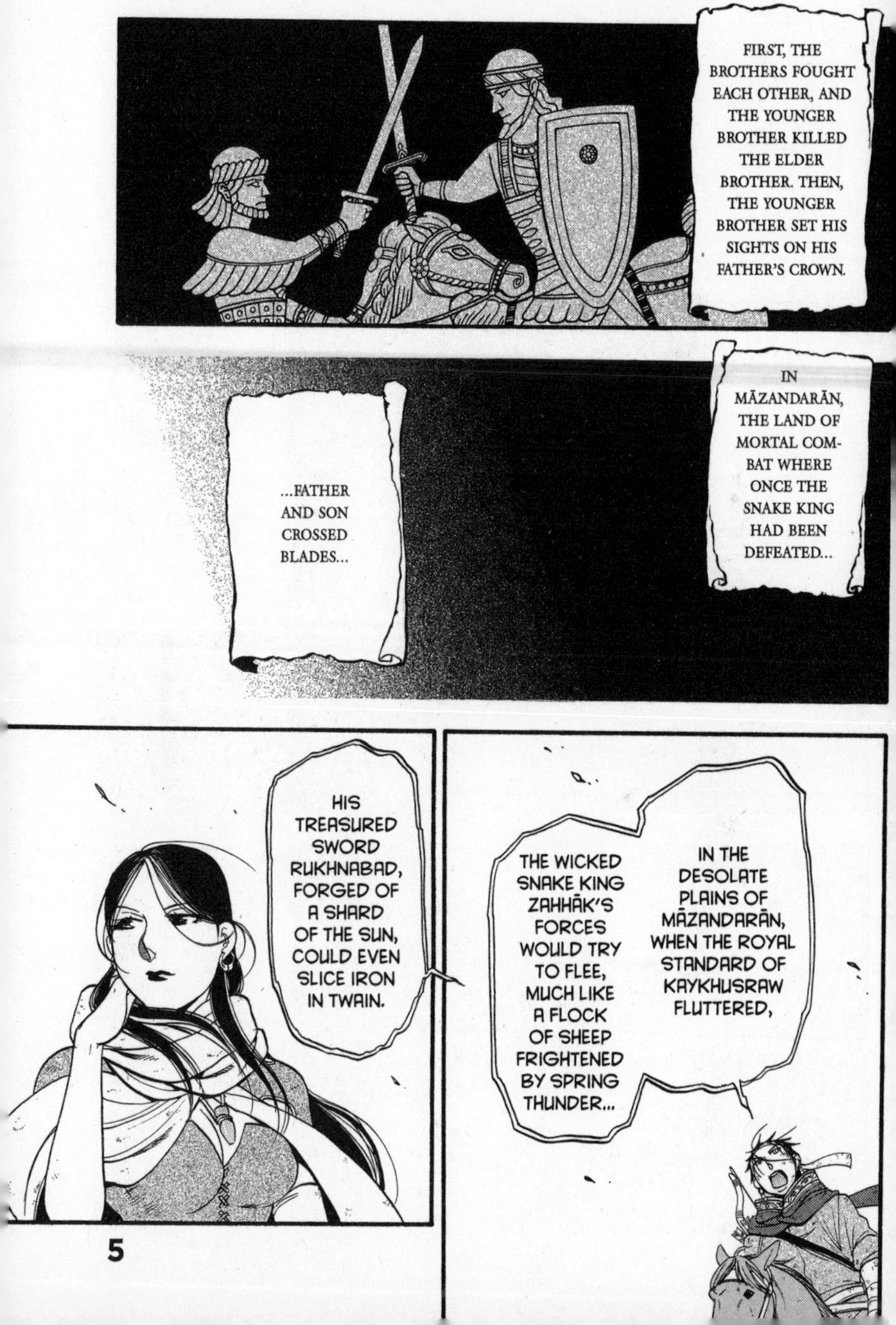
FIRST, THE BROTHERS FOUGHT EACH OTHER, AND THE YOUNGER BROTHER KILLED THE ELDER BROTHER. THEN, THE YOUNGER BROTHER SET HIS SIGHTS ON HIS FATHER'S CROWN.
IN MĀZANDARĀN, THE LAND OF MORTAL COM-BAT WHERE ONCE THE SNAKE KING HAD BEEN DEFEATED...
...FATHER AND SON CROSSED BLADES...
IN THE DESOLATE PLAINS OF MĀZANDARĀN, WHEN THE ROYAL STANDARD OF KAYKHUSRAW FLUTTERED,
THE WICKED SNAKE KING ZAHHĀK'S FORCES WOULD TRY TO FLEE, MUCH LIKE A FLOCK OF SHEEP FRIGHTENED BY SPRING THUNDER...
HIS TREASURED SWORD RUKHNABAD, FORGED OF A SHARD OF THE SUN, COULD EVEN SLICE IRON IN TWAIN.

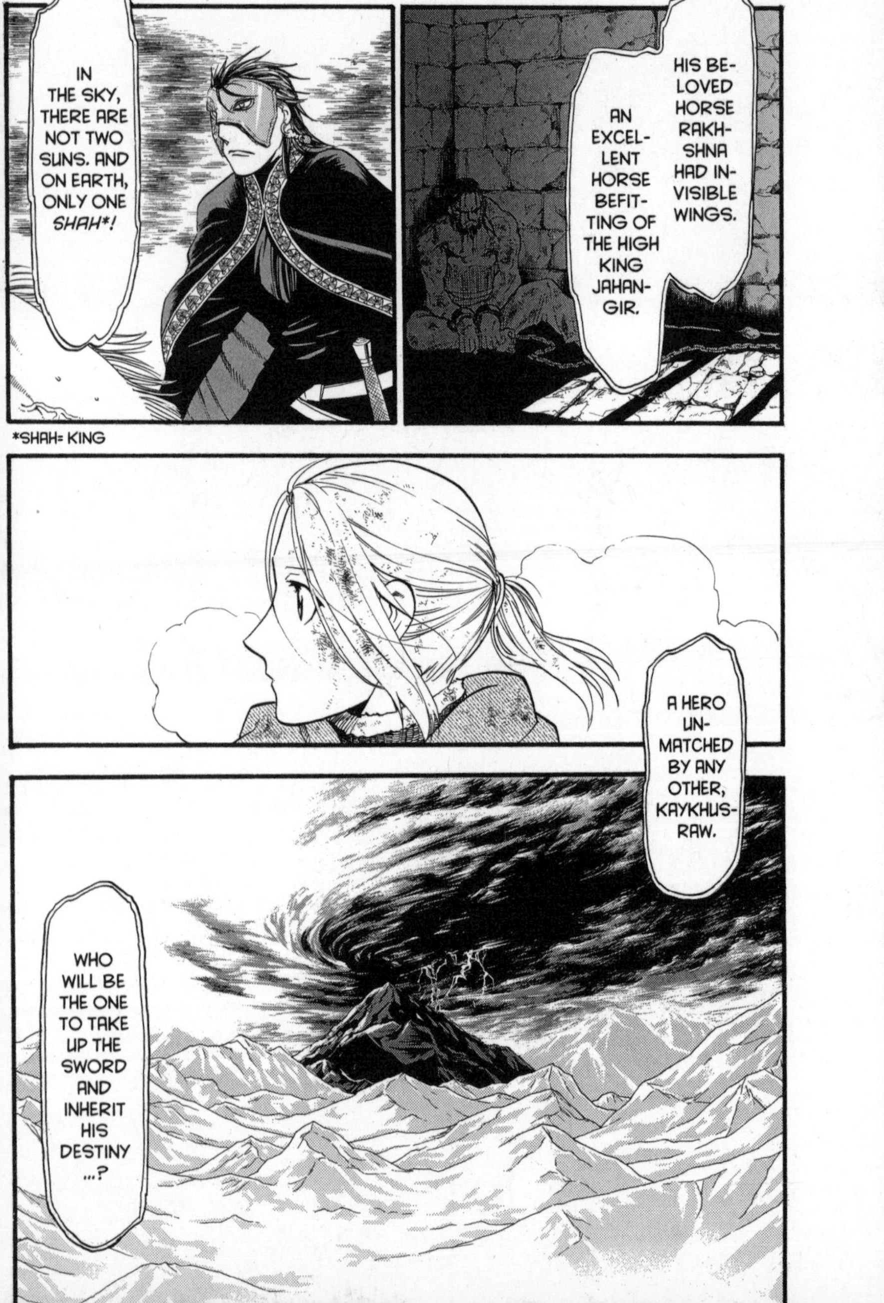
HIS BELOVED HORSE RAKHSHNA HAD INVISIBLE WINGS.
AN EXCELLENT HORSE BEFITTING OF THE HIGH KING JAHANGIR.
IN THE SKY, THERE ARE NOT TWO SUNS. AND ON EARTH, ONLY ONE *SHAH**!
*SHAH= KING
A HERO UNMATCHED BY ANY OTHER, KAYKHUSRAW.
WHO WILL BE THE ONE TO TAKE UP THE SWORD AND INHERIT HIS DESTINY ...?

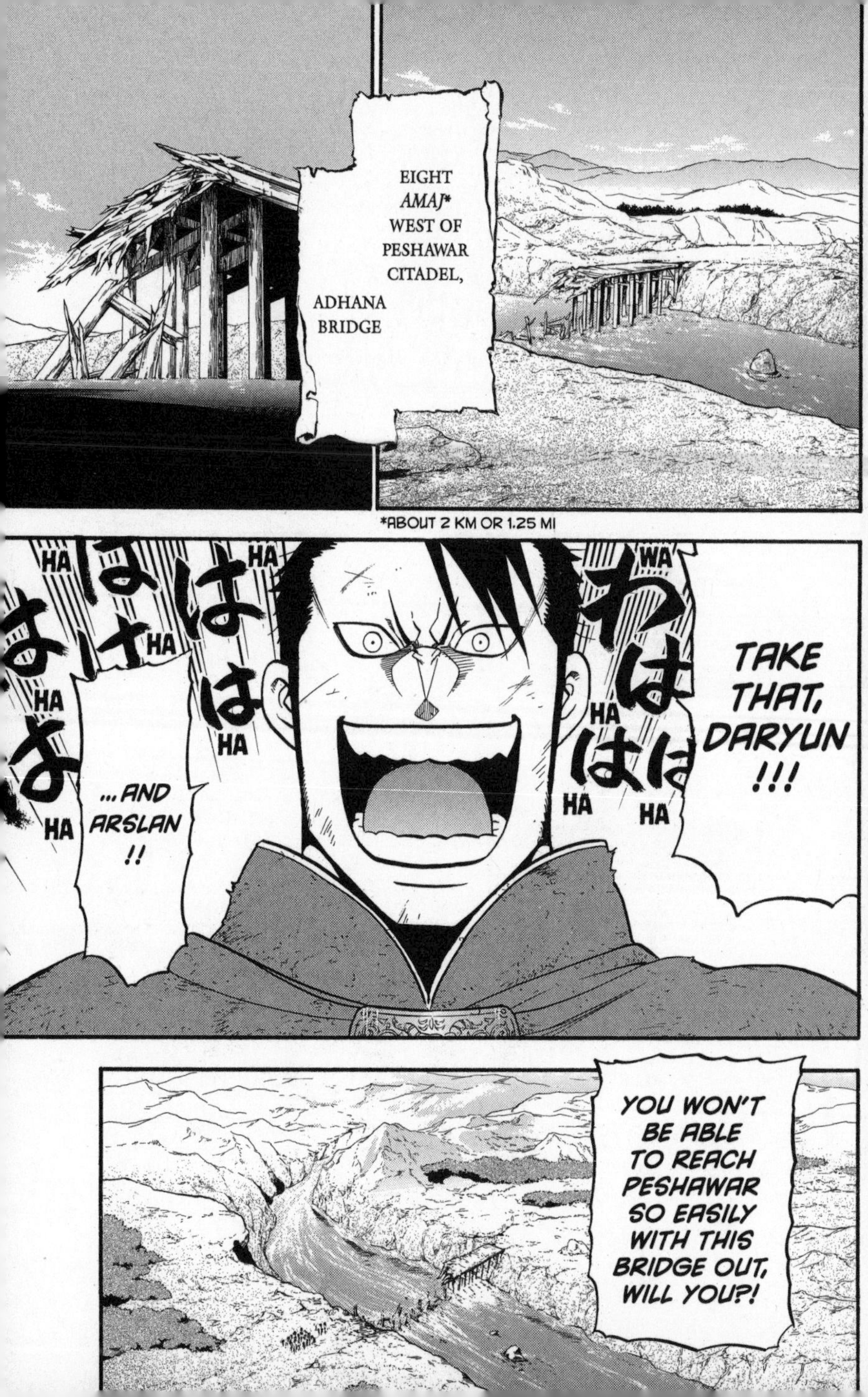
EIGHT *AMAJ** WEST OF PESHAWAR CITADEL,
ADHANA BRIDGE
WA HA HA HA HA
TAKE THAT, DARYUN!!!
HA HA HA HA HA HA
...AND ARSLAN!!
YOU WON'T BE ABLE TO REACH PESHAWAR SO EASILY WITH THIS BRIDGE OUT, WILL YOU?!

*ABOUT 2 KM OR 1.25 MI

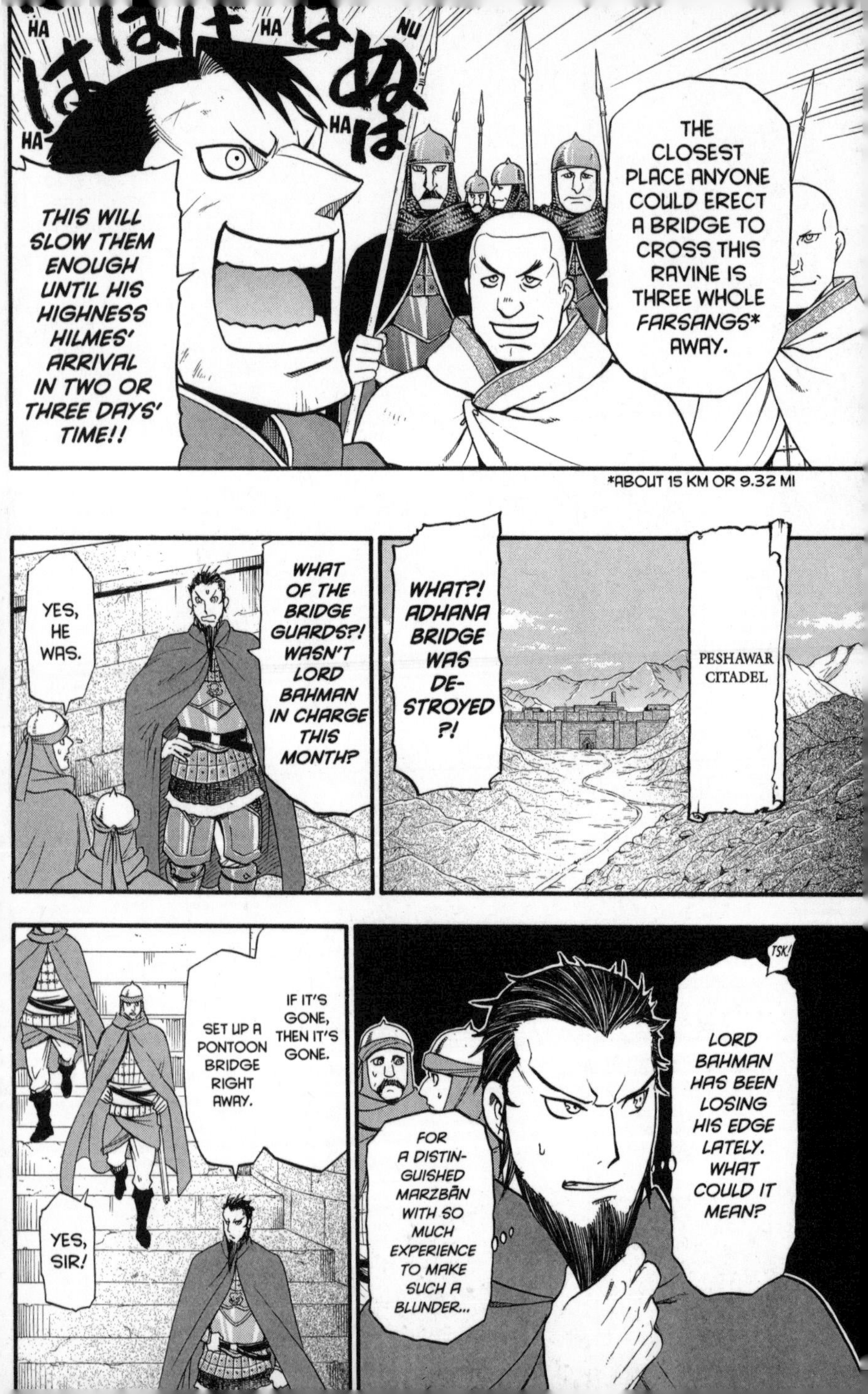
HA HA HA NU HA
THE CLOSEST PLACE ANYONE COULD ERECT A BRIDGE TO CROSS THIS RAVINE IS THREE WHOLE FARSANGS* AWAY.
THIS WILL SLOW THEM ENOUGH UNTIL HIS HIGHNESS HILMES' ARRIVAL IN TWO OR THREE DAYS' TIME!!
*ABOUT 15 KM OR 9.32 MI
PESHAWAR CITADEL
WHAT?! ADHANA BRIDGE WAS DESTROYED?!
WHAT OF THE BRIDGE GUARDS?! WASN'T LORD BAHMAN IN CHARGE THIS MONTH?
YES, HE WAS.
TSK!
LORD BAHMAN HAS BEEN LOSING HIS EDGE LATELY. WHAT COULD IT MEAN?
FOR A DISTINGUISHED MARZBĀN WITH SO MUCH EXPERIENCE TO MAKE SUCH A BLUNDER...
IF IT'S GONE, THEN IT'S GONE.
SET UP A PONTOON BRIDGE RIGHT AWAY.
YES, SIR!

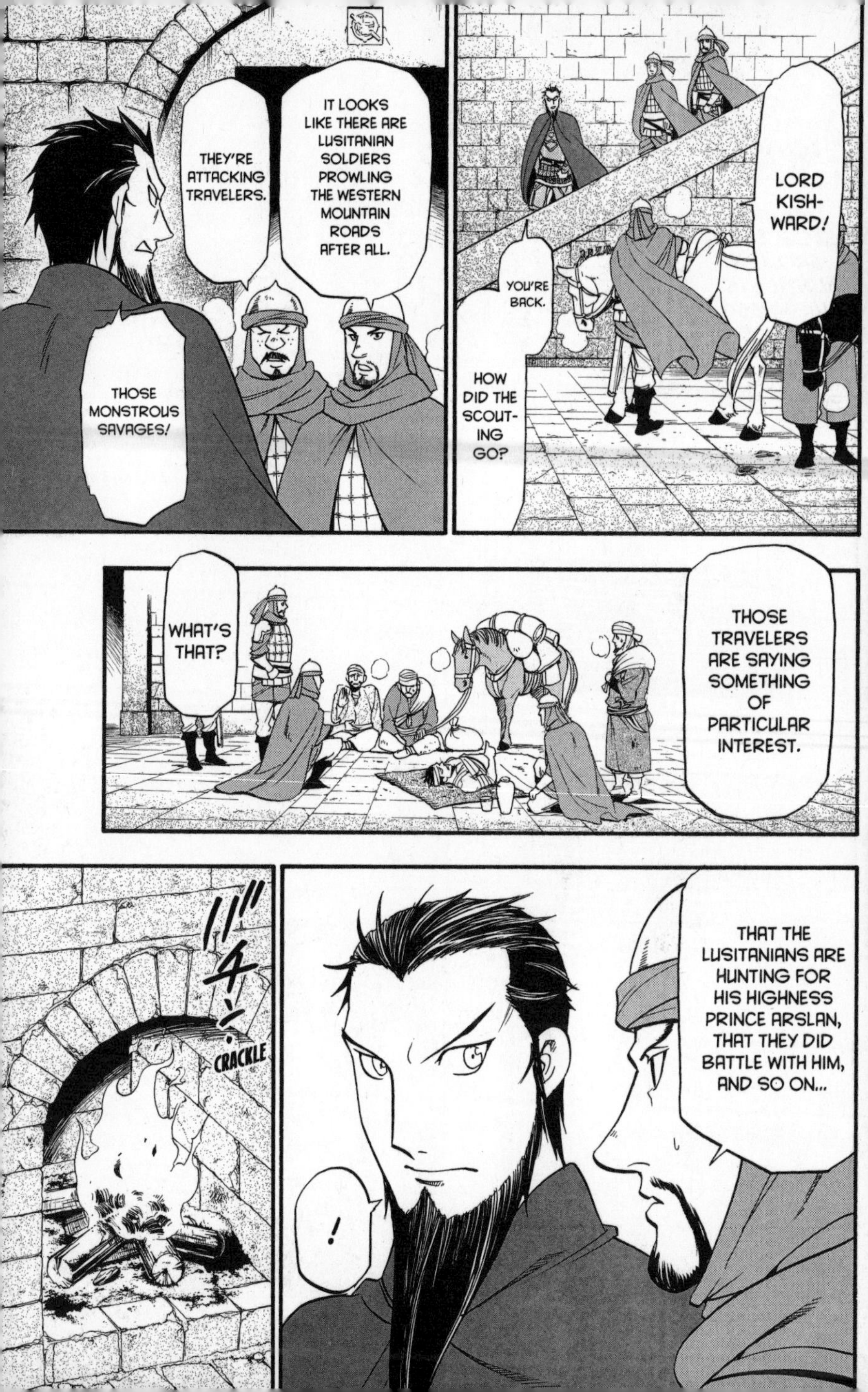
LORD KISHWARD!
YOU'RE BACK.
HOW DID THE SCOUTING GO?
IT LOOKS LIKE THERE ARE LUSITANIAN SOLDIERS PROWLING THE WESTERN MOUNTAIN ROADS AFTER ALL.
THEY'RE ATTACKING TRAVELERS.
THOSE MONSTROUS SAVAGES!
THOSE TRAVELERS ARE SAYING SOMETHING OF PARTICULAR INTEREST.
WHAT'S THAT?
THAT THE LUSITANIANS ARE HUNTING FOR HIS HIGHNESS PRINCE ARSLAN, THAT THEY DID BATTLE WITH HIM, AND SO ON...
!
CRACKLE

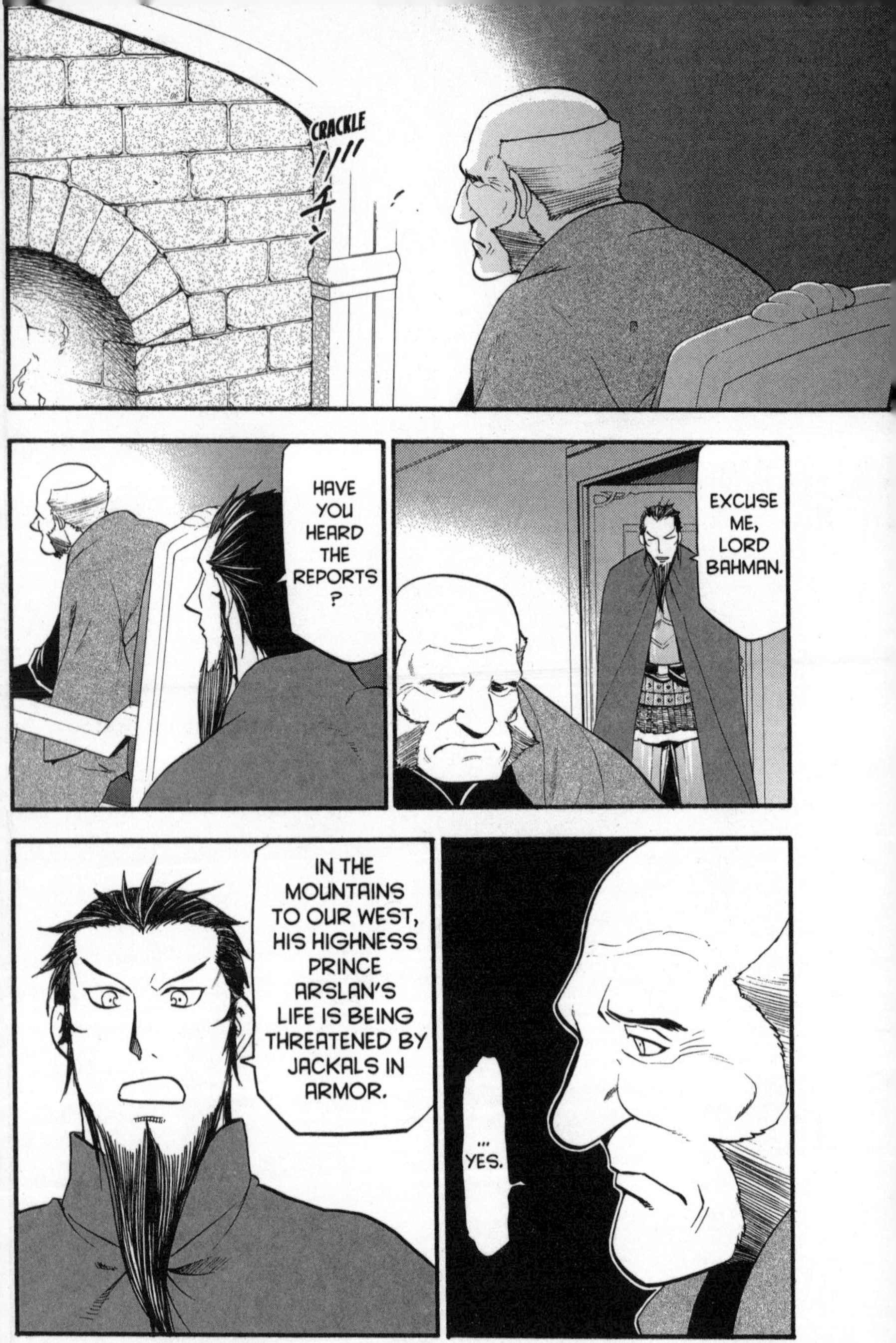
CRACKLE
EXCUSE ME, LORD BAHMAN.
HAVE YOU HEARD THE REPORTS?
...YES.
IN THE MOUNTAINS TO OUR WEST, HIS HIGHNESS PRINCE ARSLAN'S LIFE IS BEING THREATENED BY JACKALS IN ARMOR.

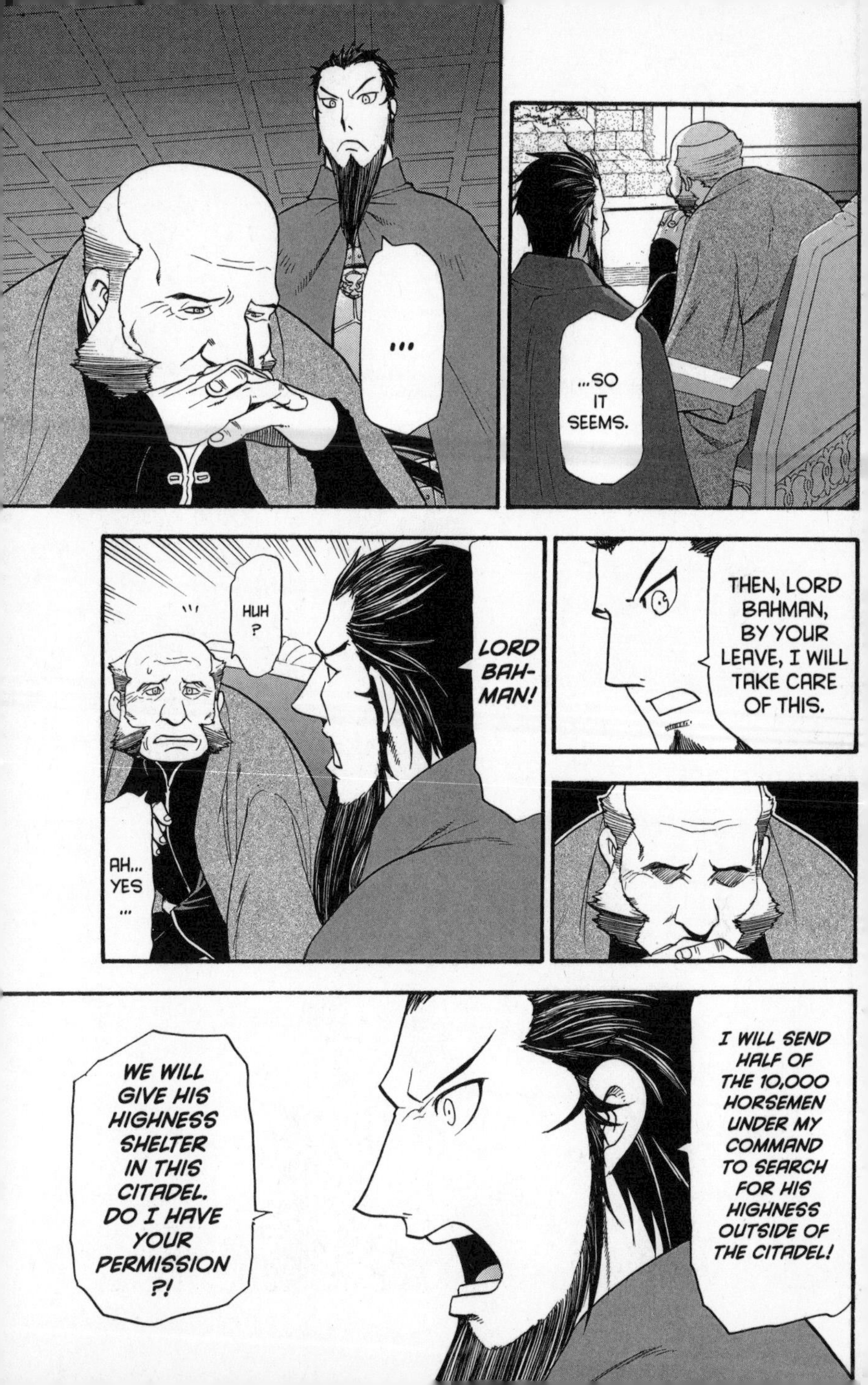
...SO IT SEEMS.
...
THEN, LORD BAHMAN, BY YOUR LEAVE, I WILL TAKE CARE OF THIS.
LORD BAH-MAN!
HUH?
AH... YES ...
I WILL SEND HALF OF THE 10,000 HORSEMEN UNDER MY COMMAND TO SEARCH FOR HIS HIGHNESS OUTSIDE OF THE CITADEL!
WE WILL GIVE HIS HIGHNESS SHELTER IN THIS CITADEL. DO I HAVE YOUR PERMISSION ?!

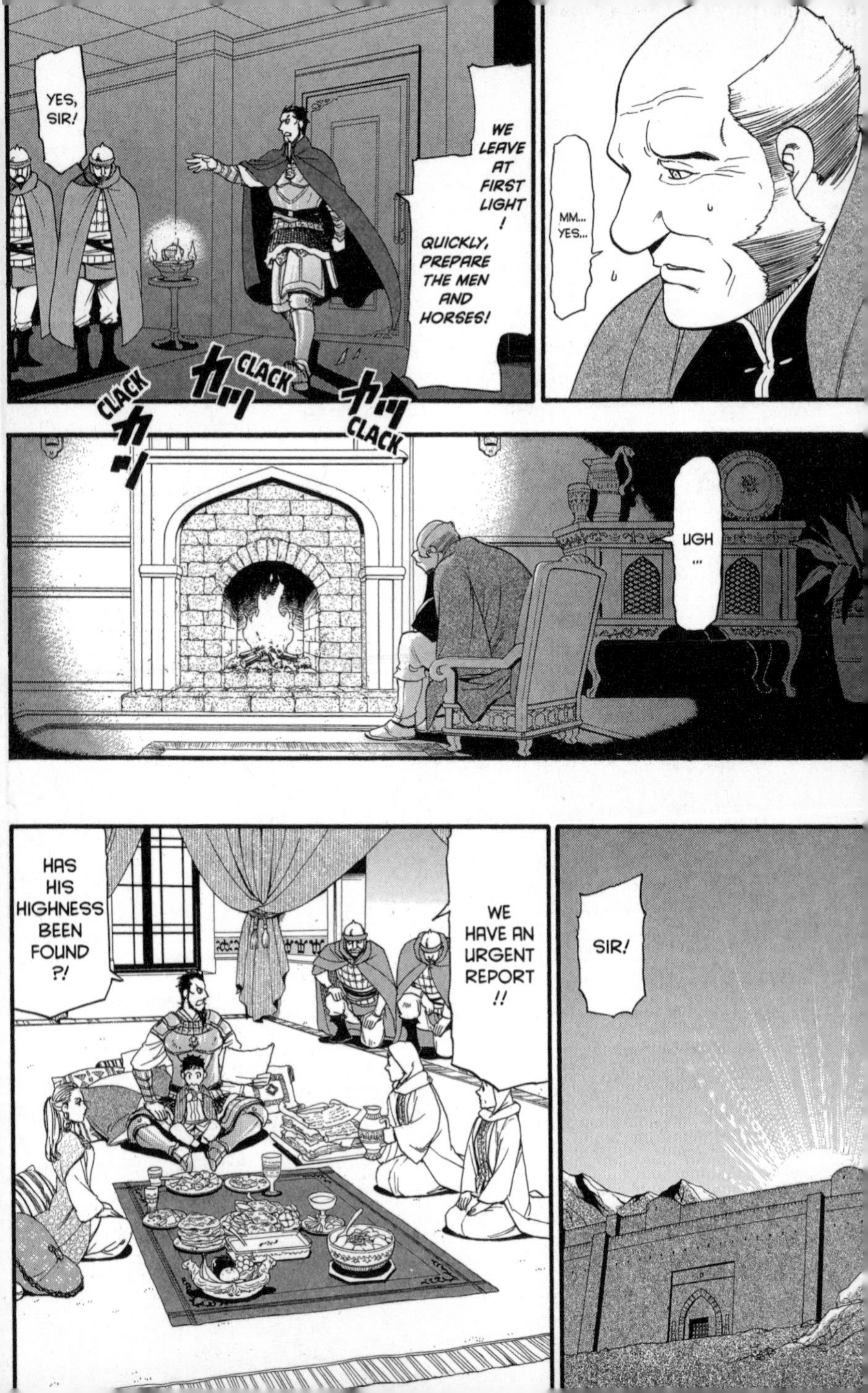
MM... YES...
WE LEAVE AT FIRST LIGHT!
QUICKLY, PREPARE THE MEN AND HORSES!
YES, SIR!
カッ CLACK
カッ CLACK
カッ CLACK
カッ CLACK
UGH ...
SIR!
WE HAVE AN URGENT REPORT!!
HAS HIS HIGHNESS BEEN FOUND?!

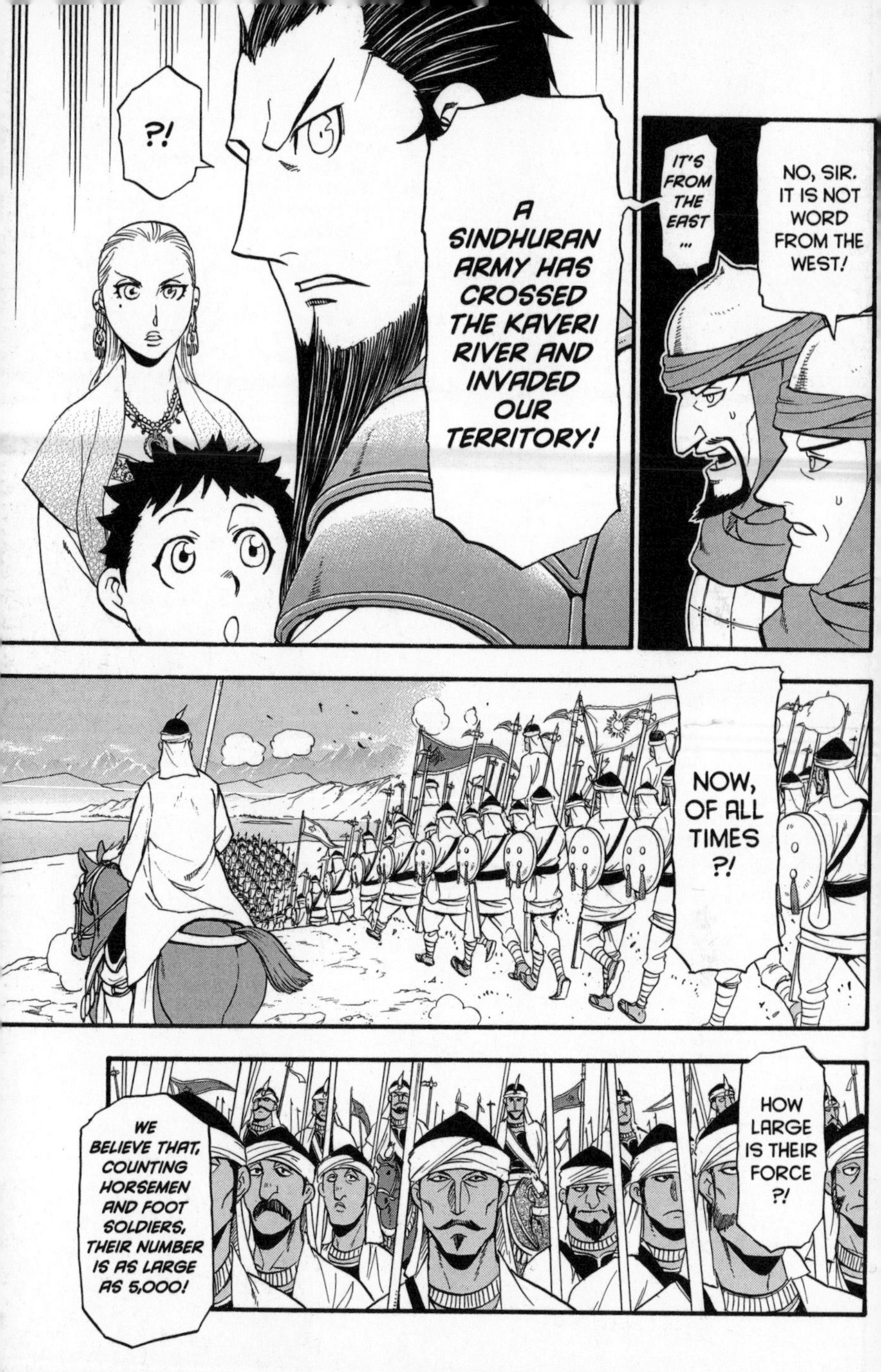
NO, SIR. IT IS NOT WORD FROM THE WEST!
IT'S FROM THE EAST ...
A SINDHURAN ARMY HAS CROSSED THE KAVERI RIVER AND INVADED OUR TERRITORY!
?!
NOW, OF ALL TIMES ?!
HOW LARGE IS THEIR FORCE ?!
WE BELIEVE THAT, COUNTING HORSEMEN AND FOOT SOLDIERS, THEIR NUMBER IS AS LARGE AS 5,000!

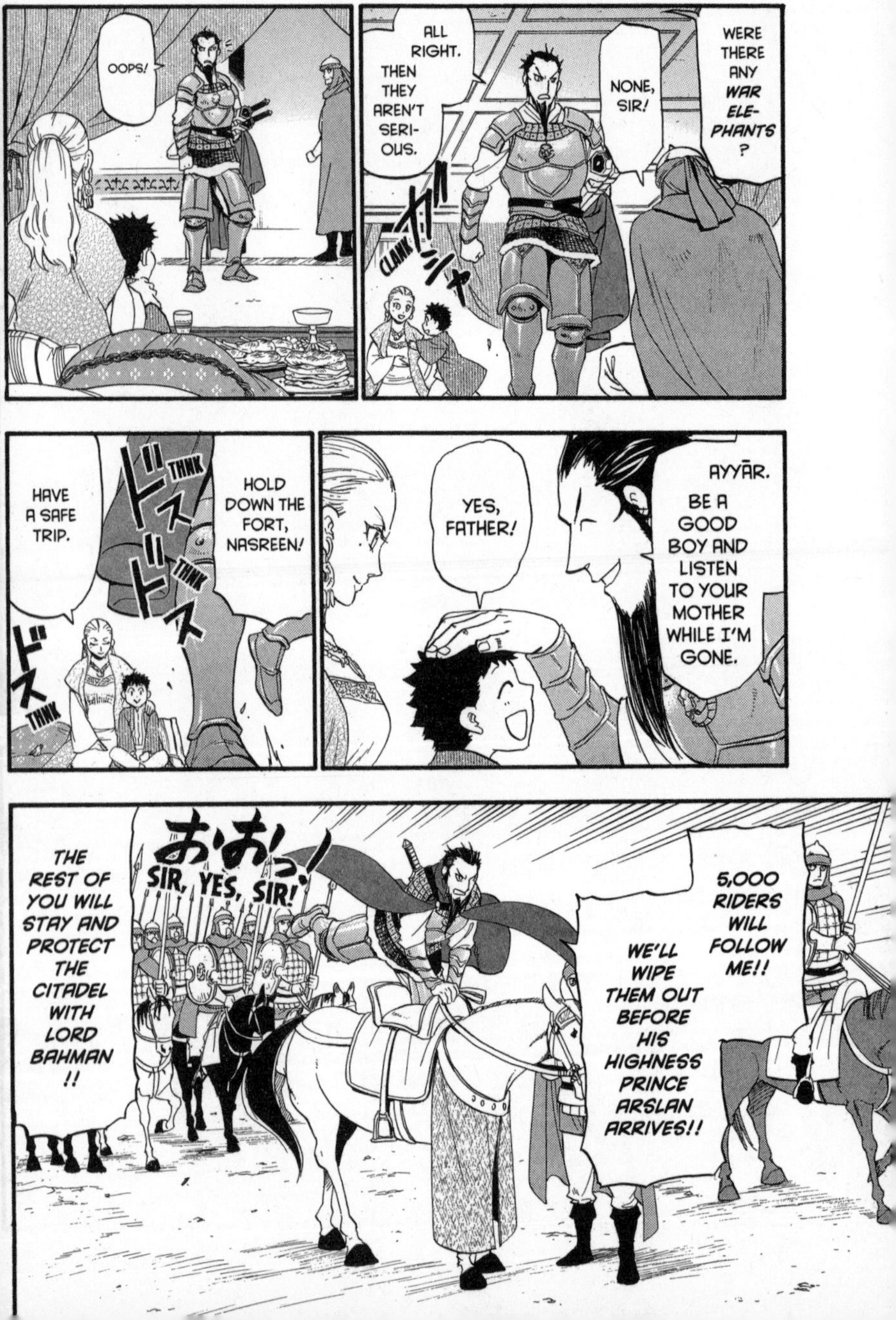
WERE THERE ANY WAR ELEPHANTS?
NONE, SIR!
ALL RIGHT. THEN THEY AREN'T SERIOUS.
ガシャ
CLANK
OOPS!
AYYĀR.
BE A GOOD BOY AND LISTEN TO YOUR MOTHER WHILE I'M GONE.
YES, FATHER!
HOLD DOWN THE FORT, NASREEN!
ドスッ
THNK
ドスッ
THNK
HAVE A SAFE TRIP.
ドス
THNK
5,000 RIDERS WILL FOLLOW ME!!
WE'LL WIPE THEM OUT BEFORE HIS HIGHNESS PRINCE ARSLAN ARRIVES!!
おおっ！
SIR, YES, SIR!
THE REST OF YOU WILL STAY AND PROTECT THE CITADEL WITH LORD BAHMAN!!

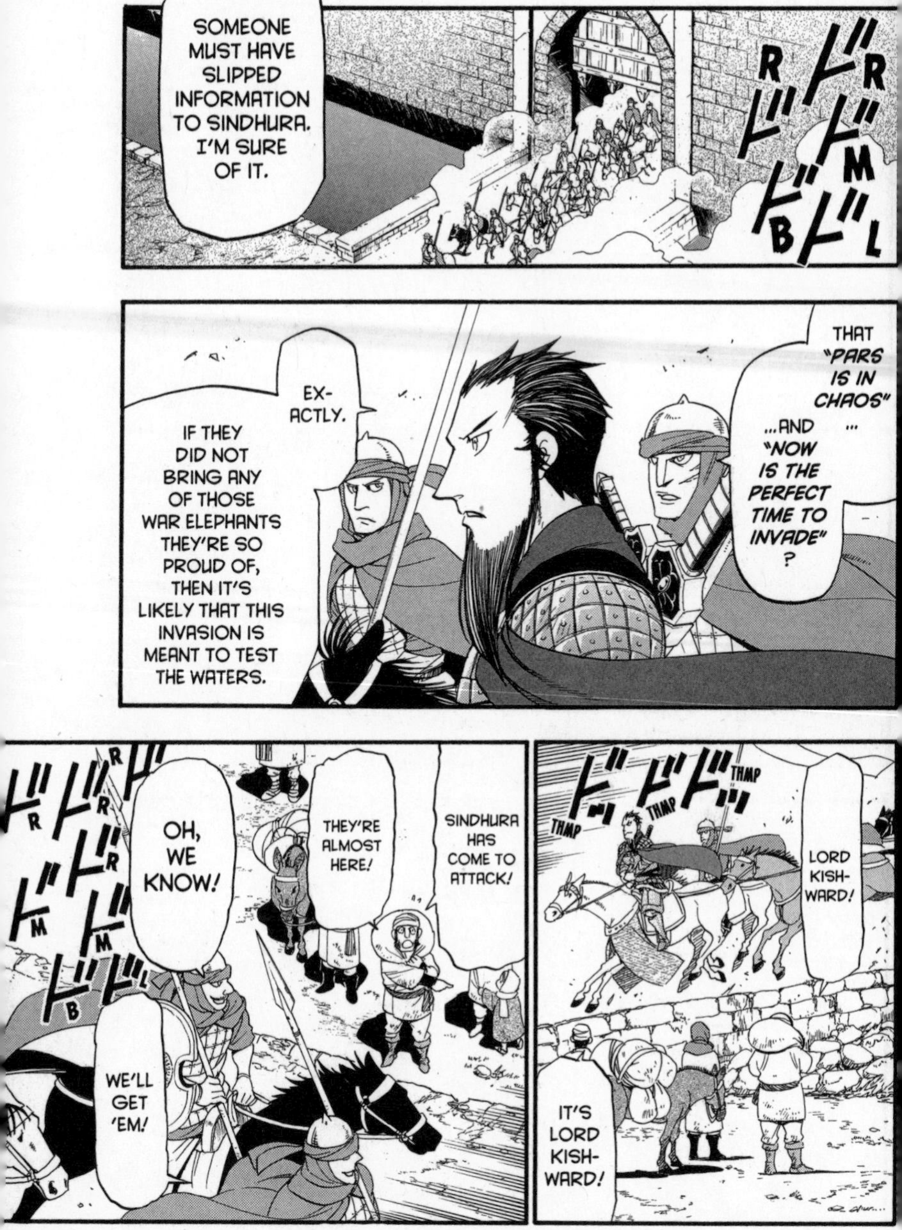
RRMBL
SOMEONE MUST HAVE SLIPPED INFORMATION TO SINDHURA. I'M SURE OF IT.
THAT "PARS IS IN CHAOS"... ...AND "NOW IS THE PERFECT TIME TO INVADE"?
EX-ACTLY.
IF THEY DID NOT BRING ANY OF THOSE WAR ELEPHANTS THEY'RE SO PROUD OF, THEN IT'S LIKELY THAT THIS INVASION IS MEANT TO TEST THE WATERS.
THMP THMP THMP
LORD KISH-WARD!
IT'S LORD KISH-WARD!
SINDHURA HAS COME TO ATTACK!
THEY'RE ALMOST HERE!
OH, WE KNOW!
RRMBL
WE'LL GET 'EM!

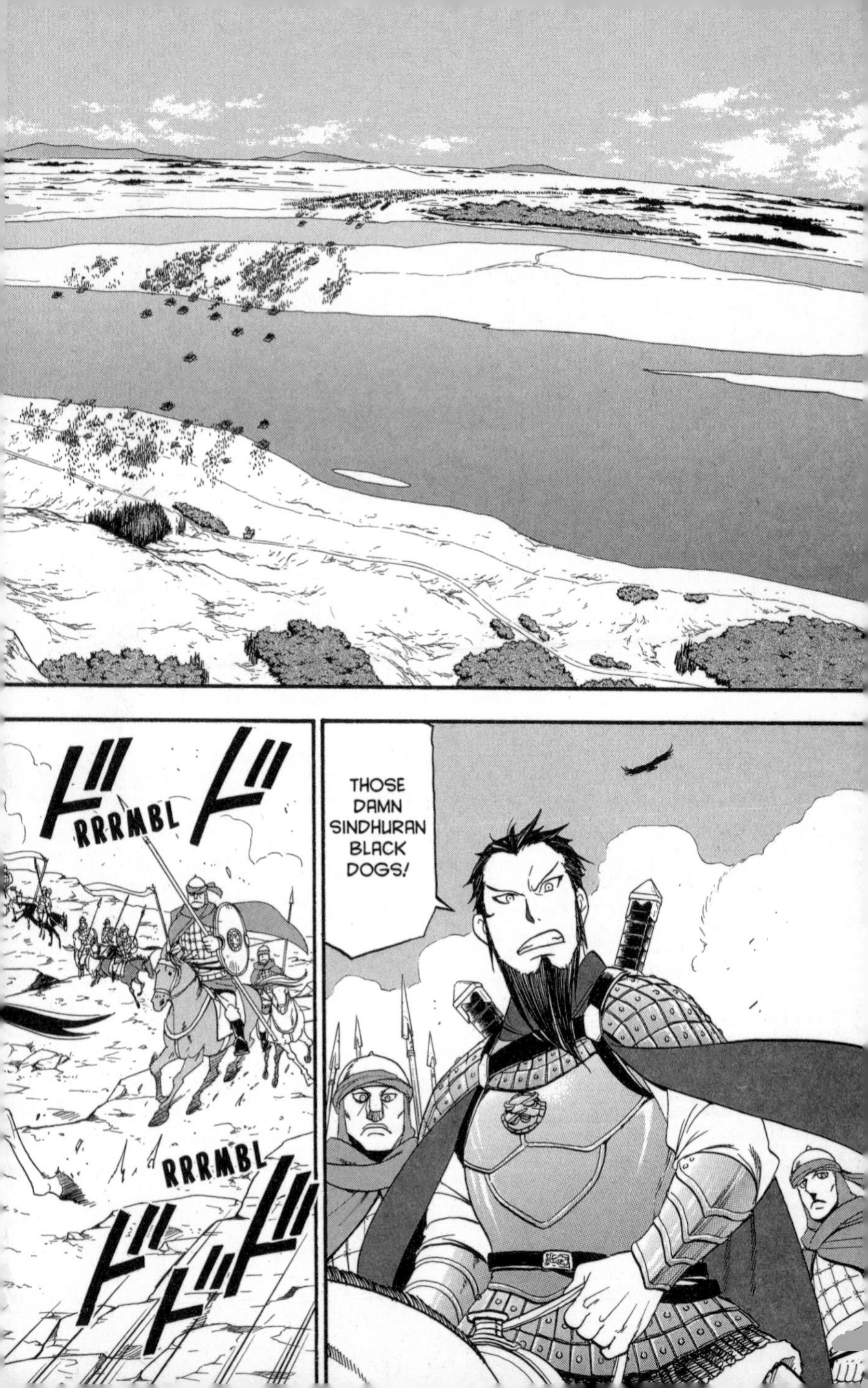
THOSE DAMN SINDHURAN BLACK DOGS!
ドド
RRRMBL
RRRMBL
ドドドド

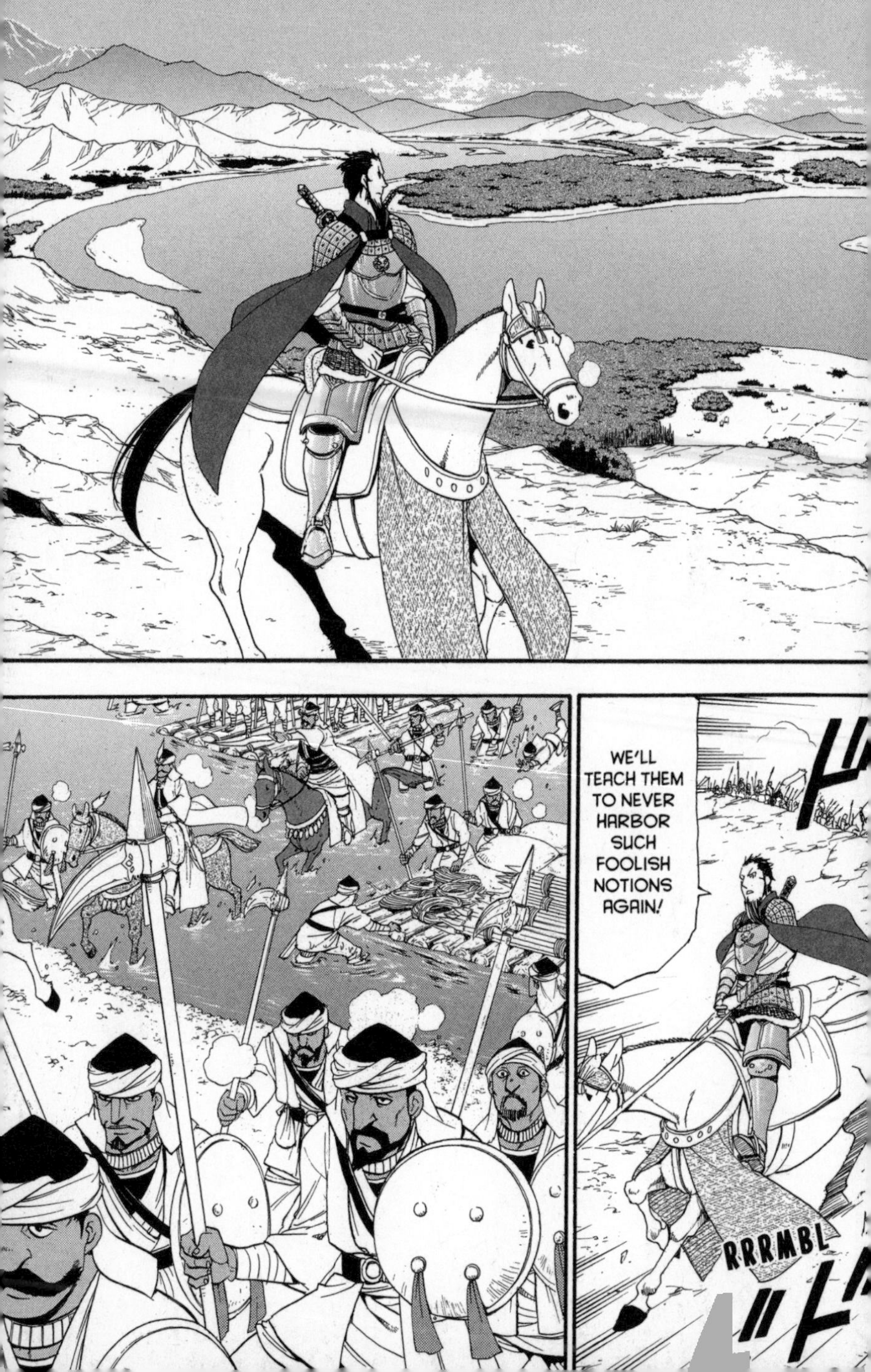
WE'LL TEACH THEM TO NEVER HARBOR SUCH FOOLISH NOTIONS AGAIN!
RRRMBL

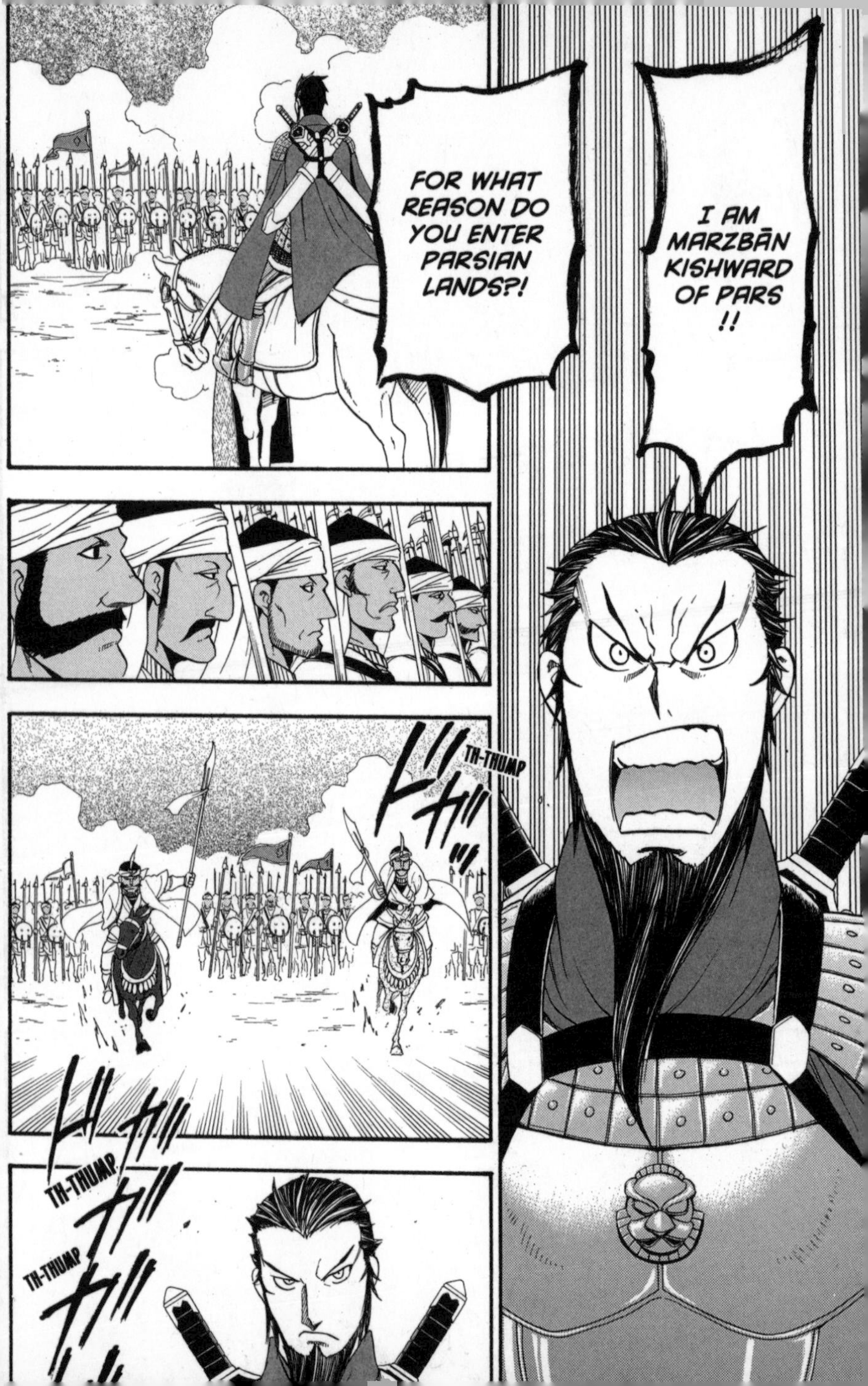
I AM MARZBĀN KISHWARD OF PARS !!
FOR WHAT REASON DO YOU ENTER PARSIAN LANDS?!
TH-THUMP
TH-THUMP
TH-THUMP

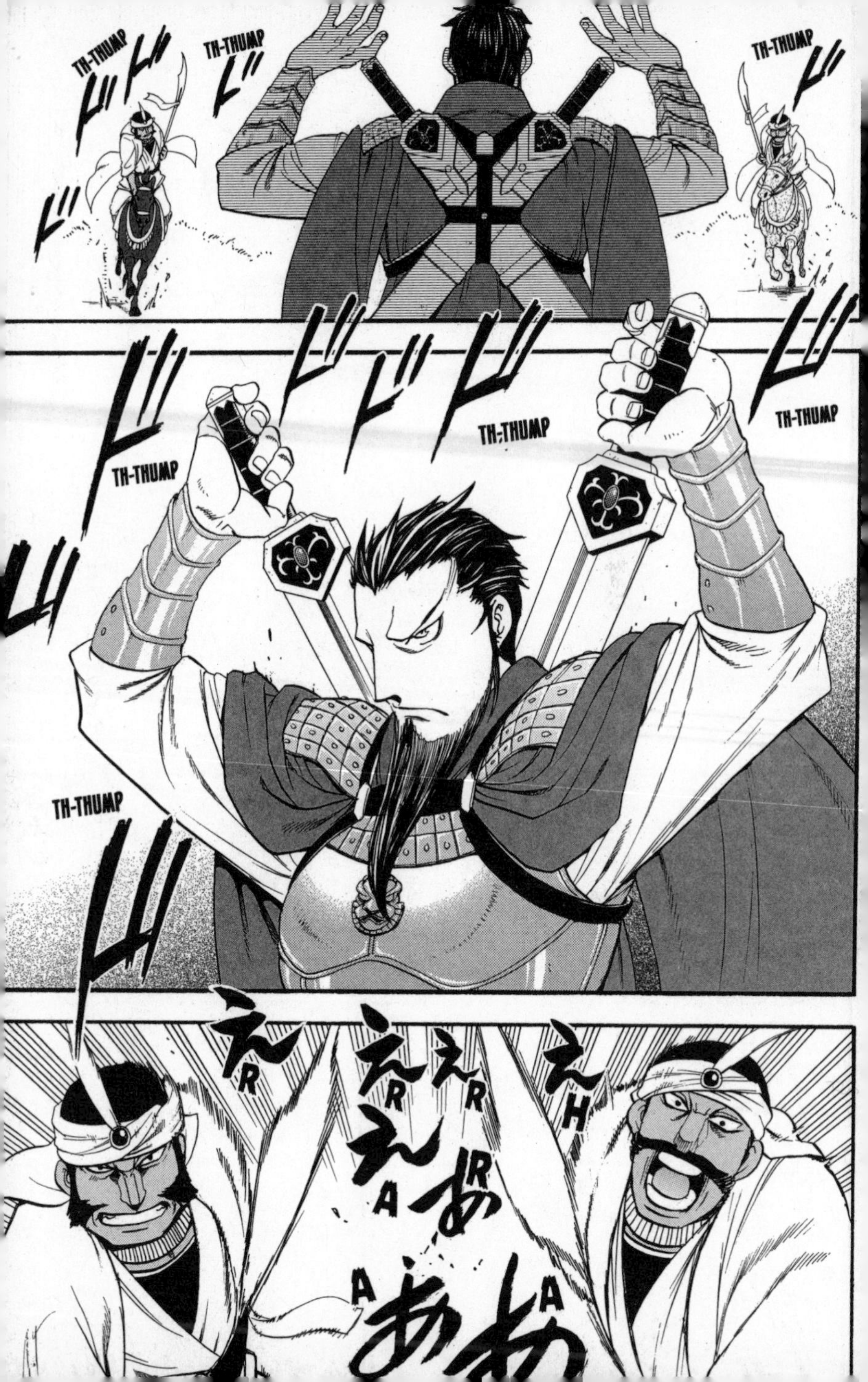
TH-THUMP
TH-THUMP
TH-THUMP
TH-THUMP
TH-THUMP
TH-THUMP
TH-THUMP

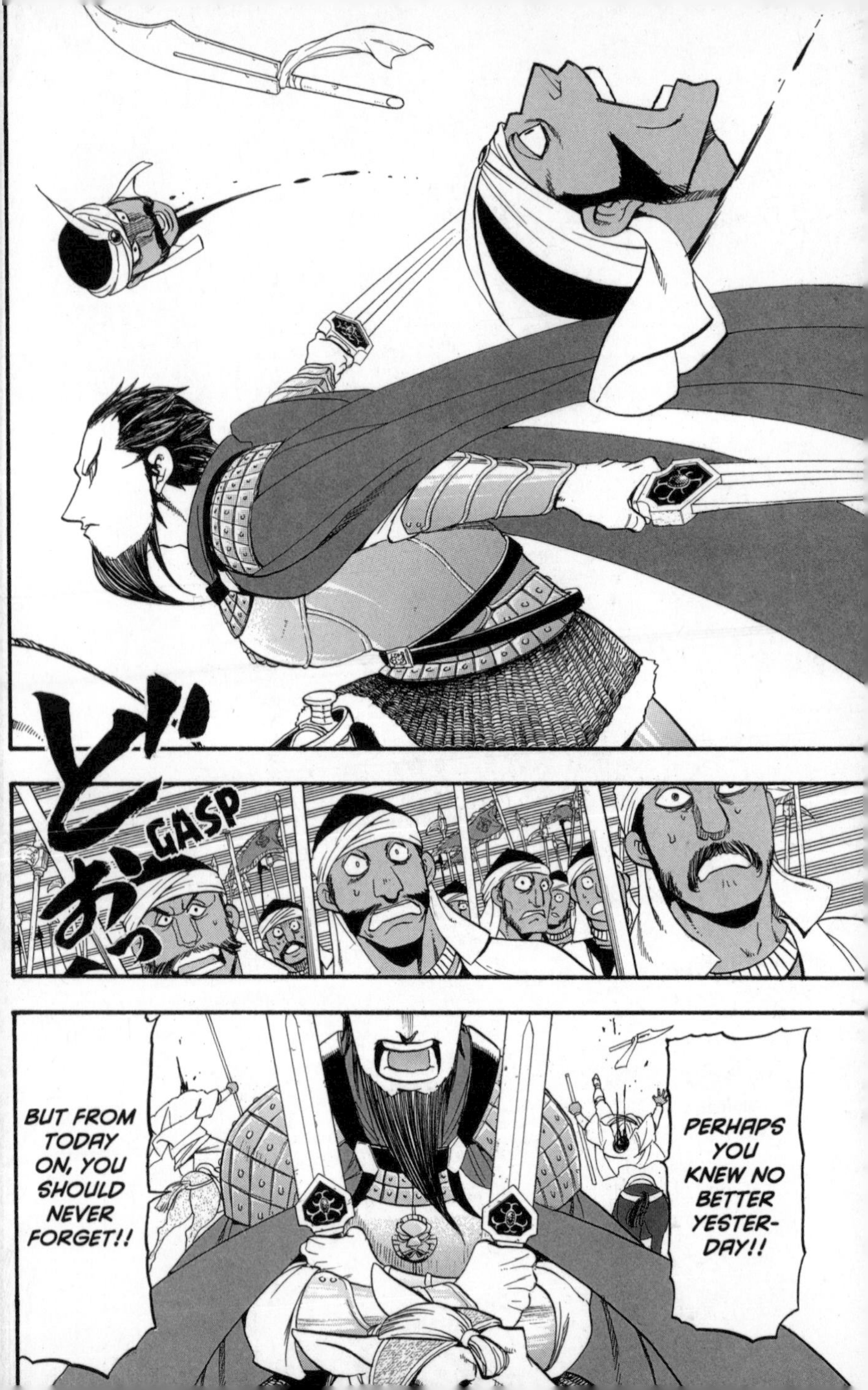
GASP
どどおっ
PERHAPS YOU KNEW NO BETTER YESTER-DAY!!
BUT FROM TODAY ON, YOU SHOULD NEVER FORGET!!

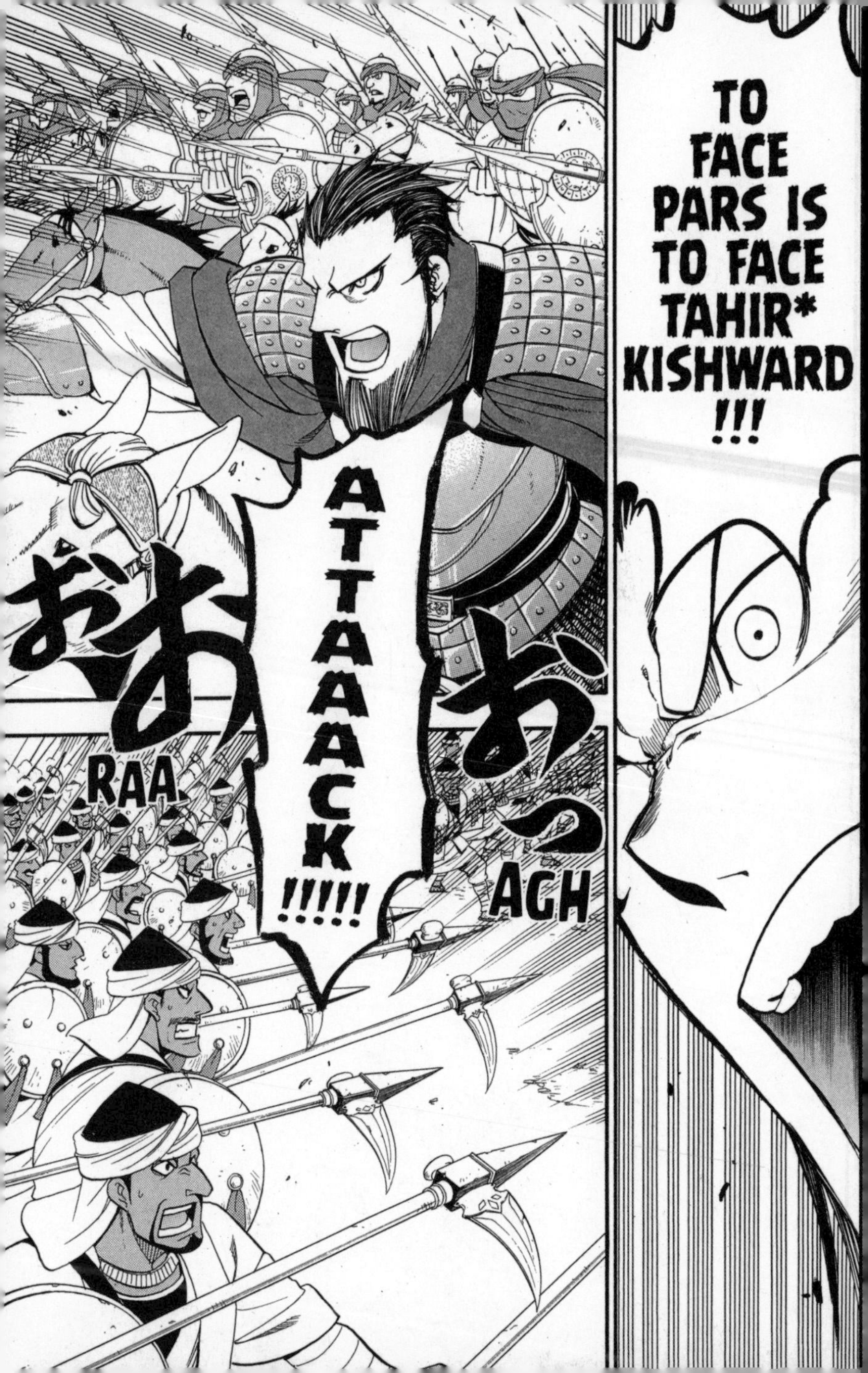
TO FACE PARS IS TO FACE TAHIR* KISHWARD!!!
ATTAAACK!!!!!
RAA
AGH

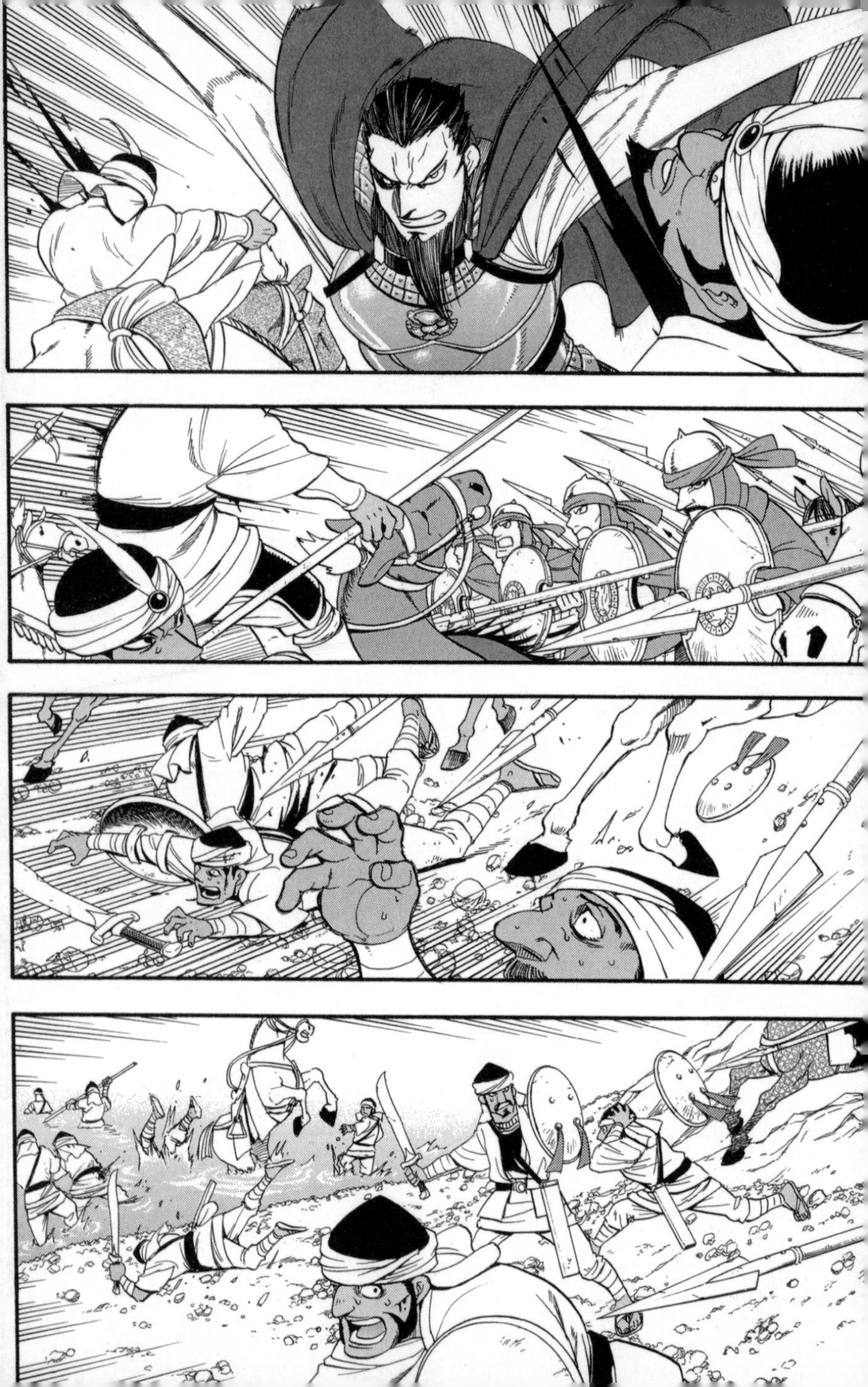

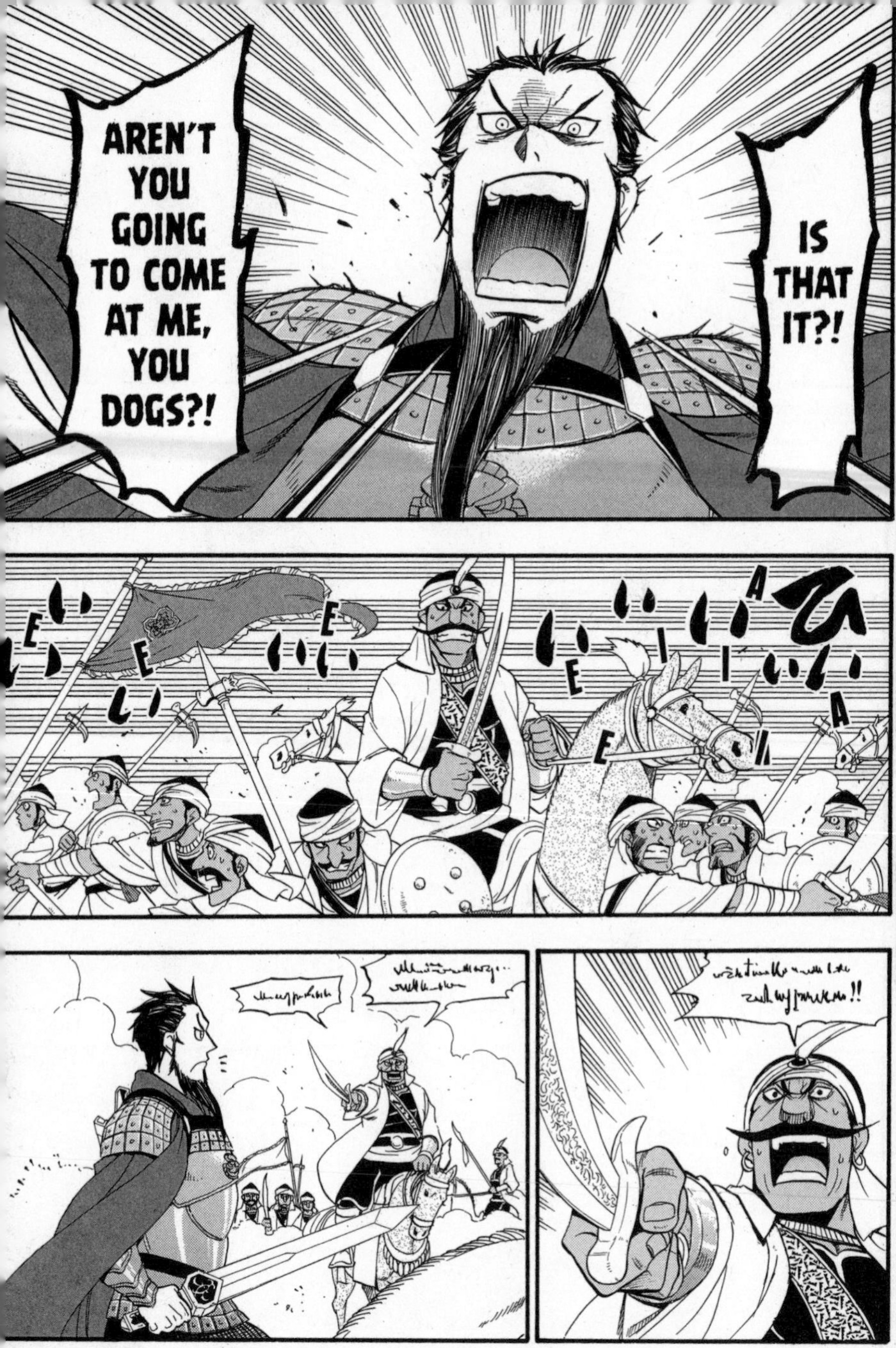
IS THAT IT?!
AREN'T YOU GOING TO COME AT ME, YOU DOGS?!

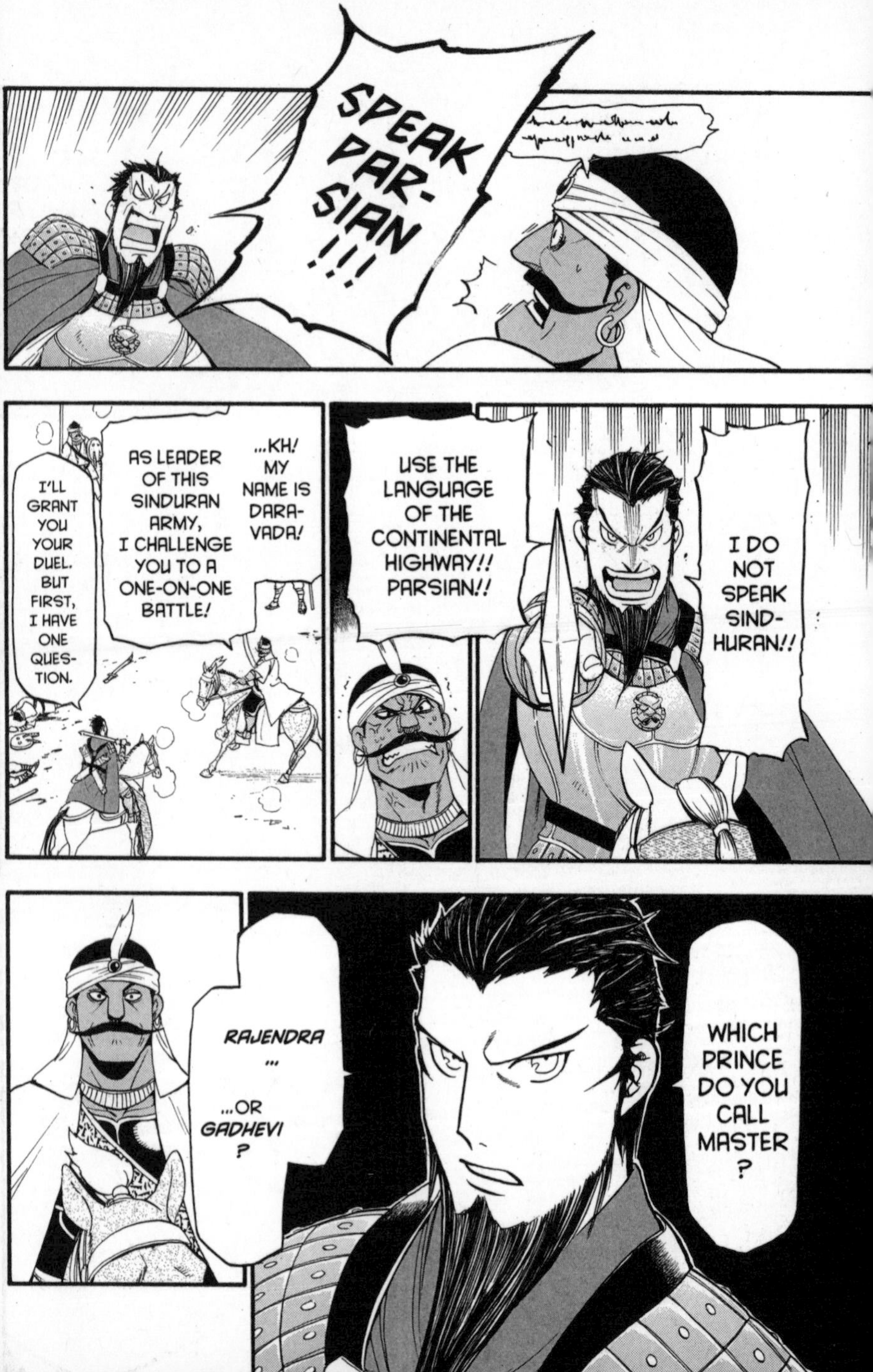
SPEAK PAR-SIAN!!!
I DO NOT SPEAK SIND-HURAN!!
USE THE LANGUAGE OF THE CONTINENTAL HIGHWAY!! PARSIAN!!
...KH! MY NAME IS DARA-VADA!
AS LEADER OF THIS SINDURAN ARMY, I CHALLENGE YOU TO A ONE-ON-ONE BATTLE!
I'LL GRANT YOU YOUR DUEL. BUT FIRST, I HAVE ONE QUES-TION.
WHICH PRINCE DO YOU CALL MASTER?
RAJENDRA...
...OR *GADHEVI*?

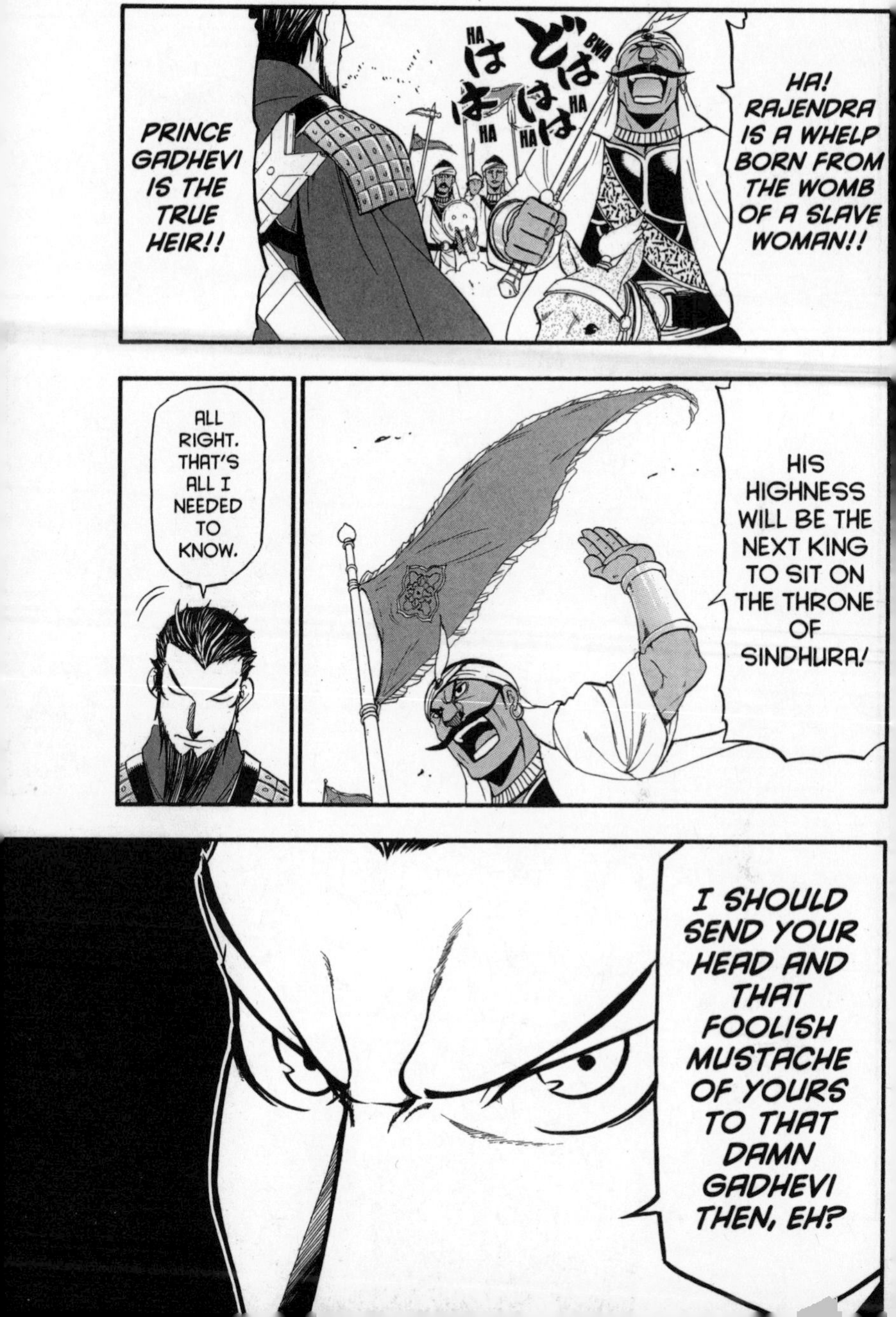
HA! RAJENDRA IS A WHELP BORN FROM THE WOMB OF A SLAVE WOMAN!!
どははははは
BWA HA HA HA HA
PRINCE GADHEVI IS THE TRUE HEIR!!
HIS HIGHNESS WILL BE THE NEXT KING TO SIT ON THE THRONE OF SINDHURA!
ALL RIGHT. THAT'S ALL I NEEDED TO KNOW.
I SHOULD SEND YOUR HEAD AND THAT FOOLISH MUSTACHE OF YOURS TO THAT DAMN GADHEVI THEN, EH?

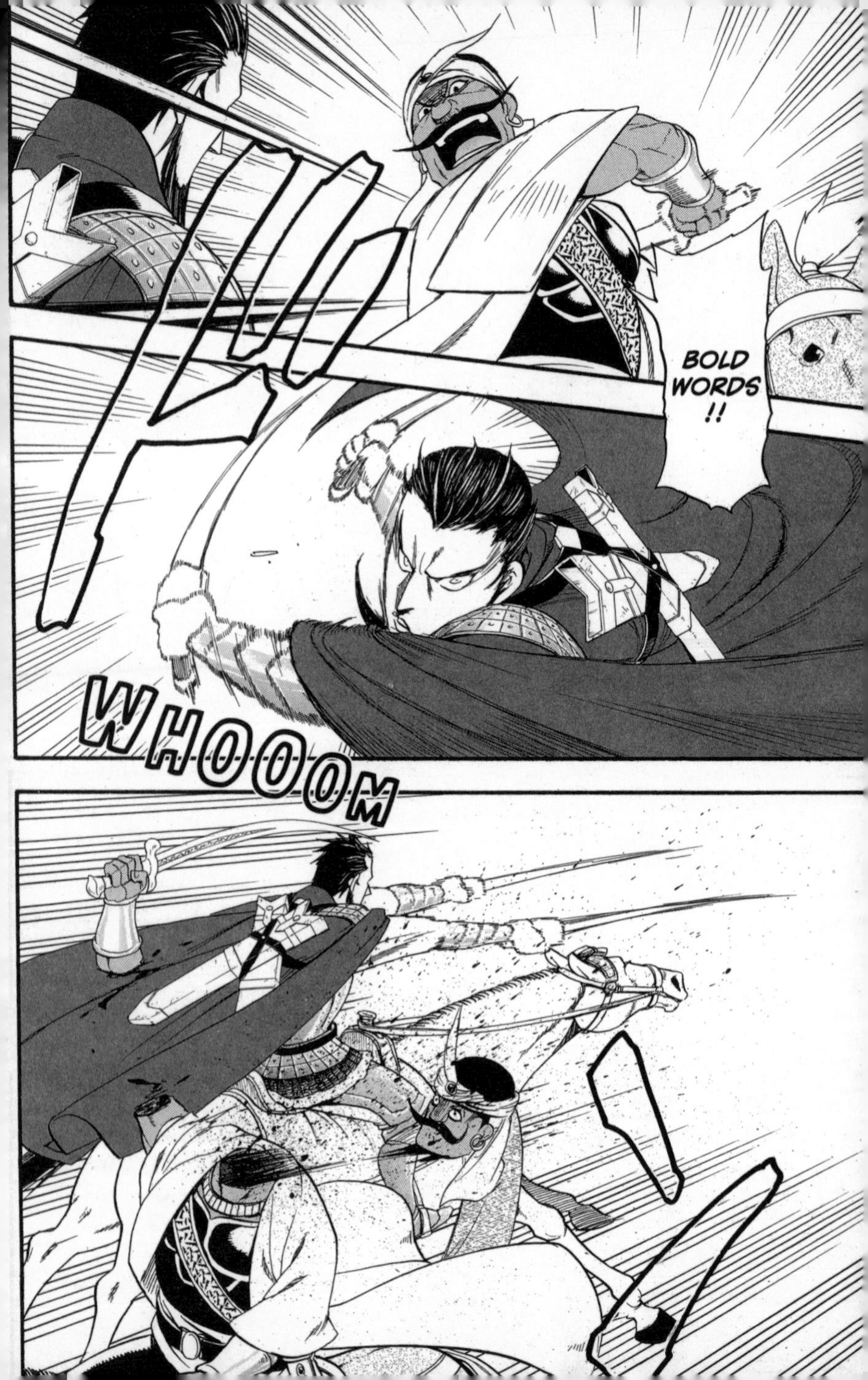
BOLD WORDS !!
WHOOOOM

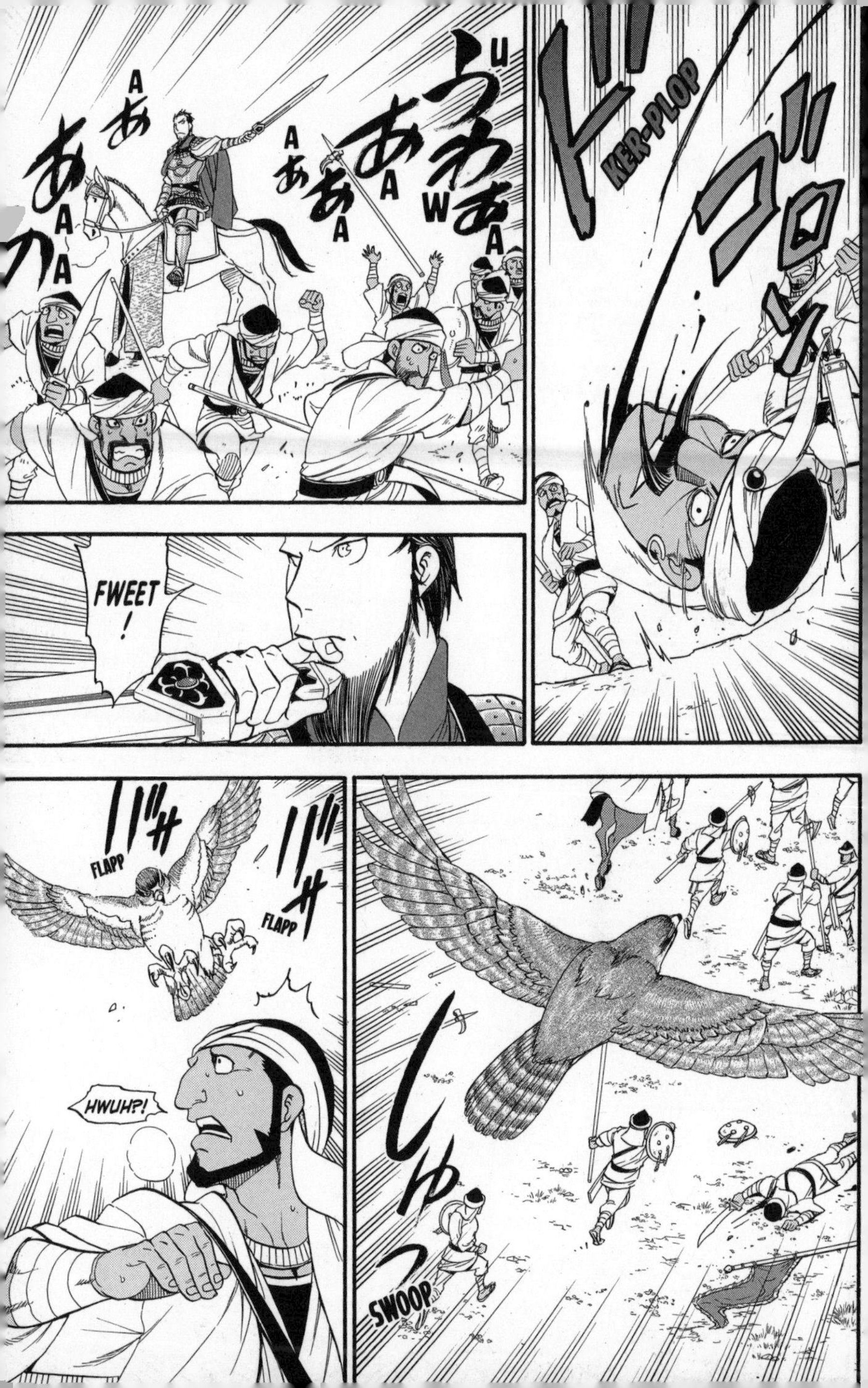

KER-PLOP
A
A
A
A
A
A
A
W
A
U
FWEET!
SWOOP
FLAPP
FLAPP
HWUH?!

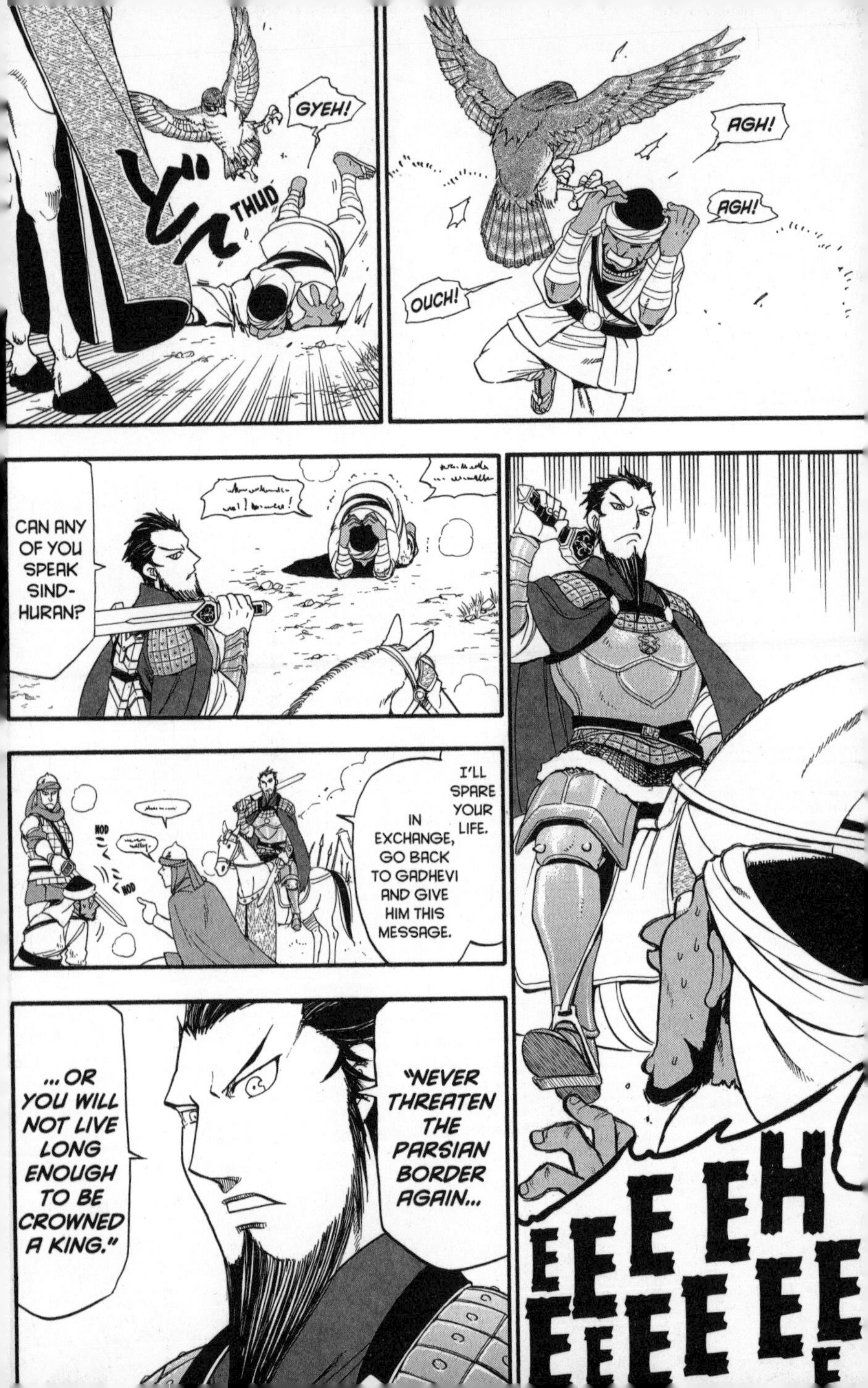
AGH!
AGH!
OUCH!
GYEH!
THUD
EEEEEEEEH
CAN ANY OF YOU SPEAK SIND-HURAN?
I'LL SPARE YOUR LIFE.
IN EXCHANGE, GO BACK TO GADHEVI AND GIVE HIM THIS MESSAGE.
NOD
NOD
"NEVER THREATEN THE PARSIAN BORDER AGAIN...
...OR YOU WILL NOT LIVE LONG ENOUGH TO BE CROWNED A KING."

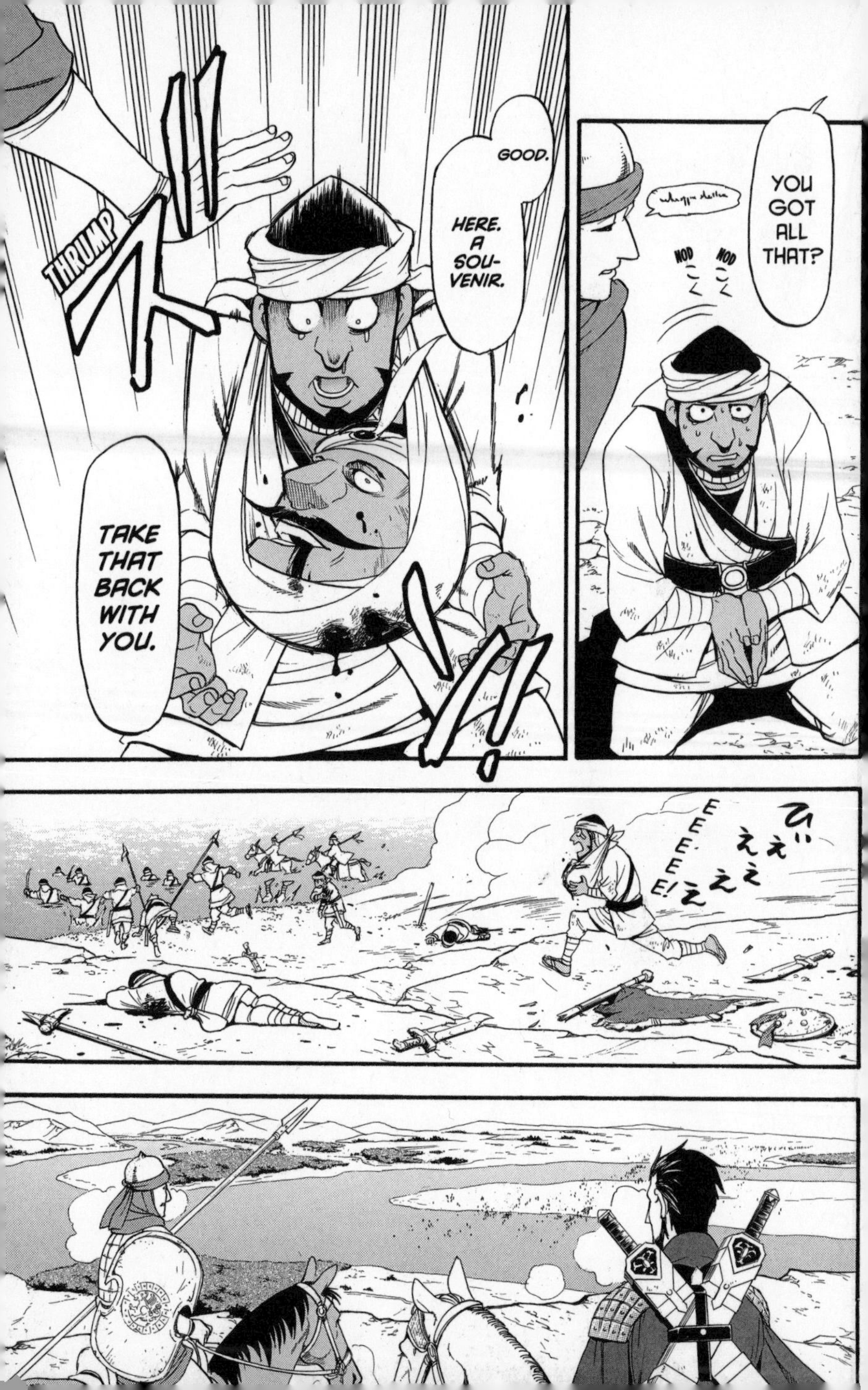
YOU GOT ALL THAT?
NOD NOD
GOOD.
HERE. A SOU-VENIR.
TAKE THAT BACK WITH YOU.
THRUMP
EEEEEE!

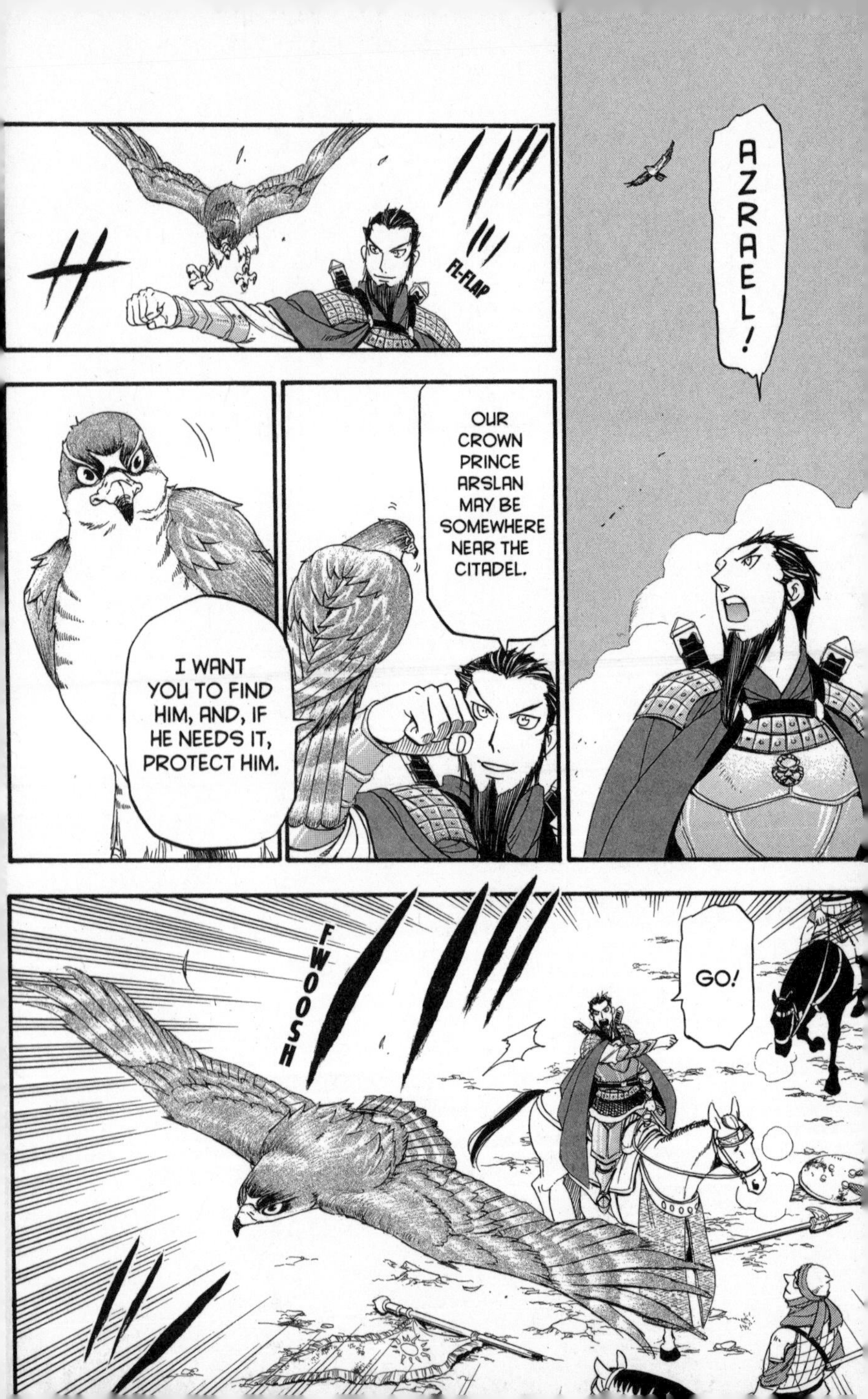
AZRAEL!
FL-FLAP
OUR CROWN PRINCE ARSLAN MAY BE SOMEWHERE NEAR THE CITADEL.
I WANT YOU TO FIND HIM, AND, IF HE NEEDS IT, PROTECT HIM.
GO!
FWOOSH

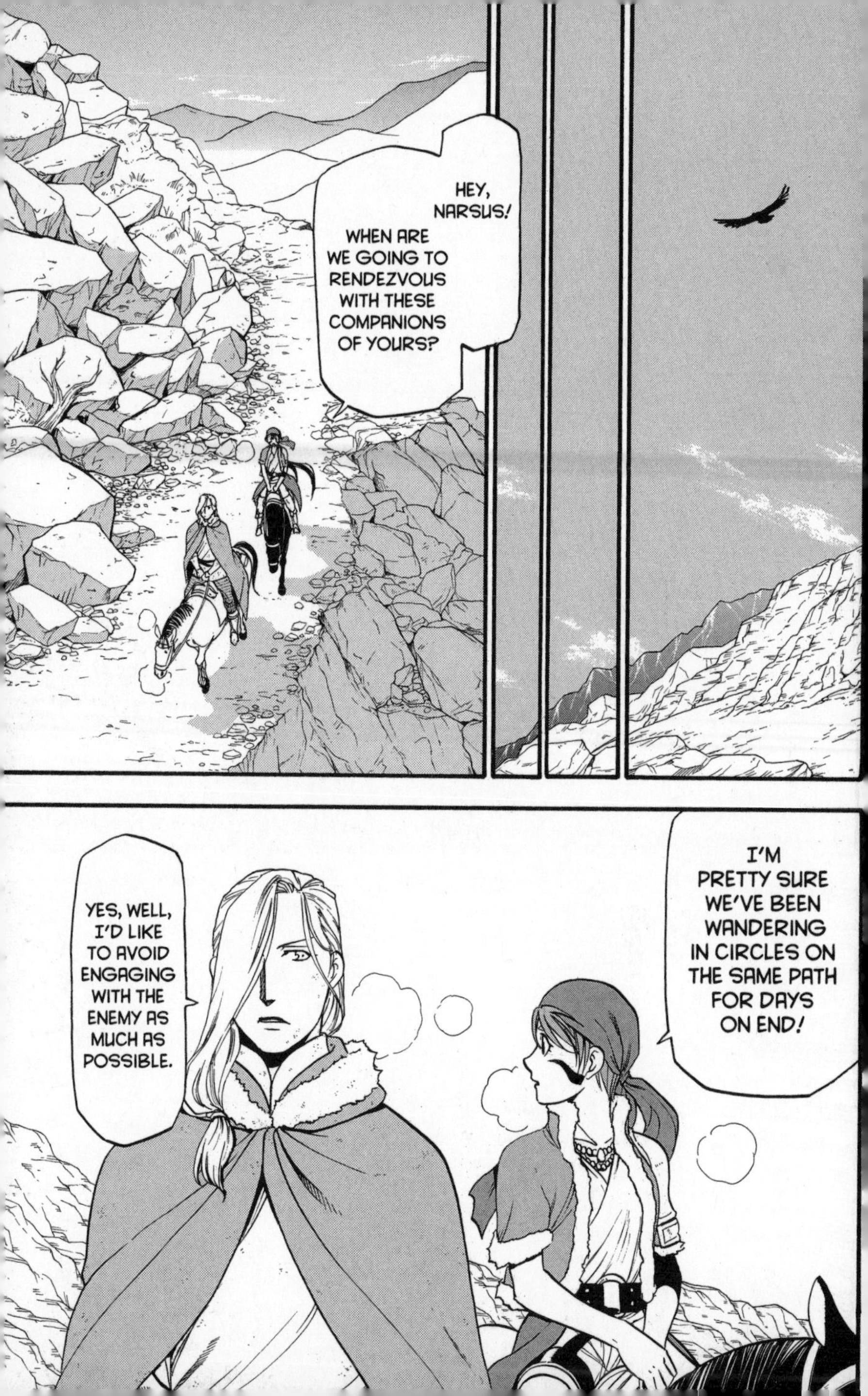
HEY, NARSUS! WHEN ARE WE GOING TO RENDEZVOUS WITH THESE COMPANIONS OF YOURS?
I'M PRETTY SURE WE'VE BEEN WANDERING IN CIRCLES ON THE SAME PATH FOR DAYS ON END!
YES, WELL, I'D LIKE TO AVOID ENGAGING WITH THE ENEMY AS MUCH AS POSSIBLE.

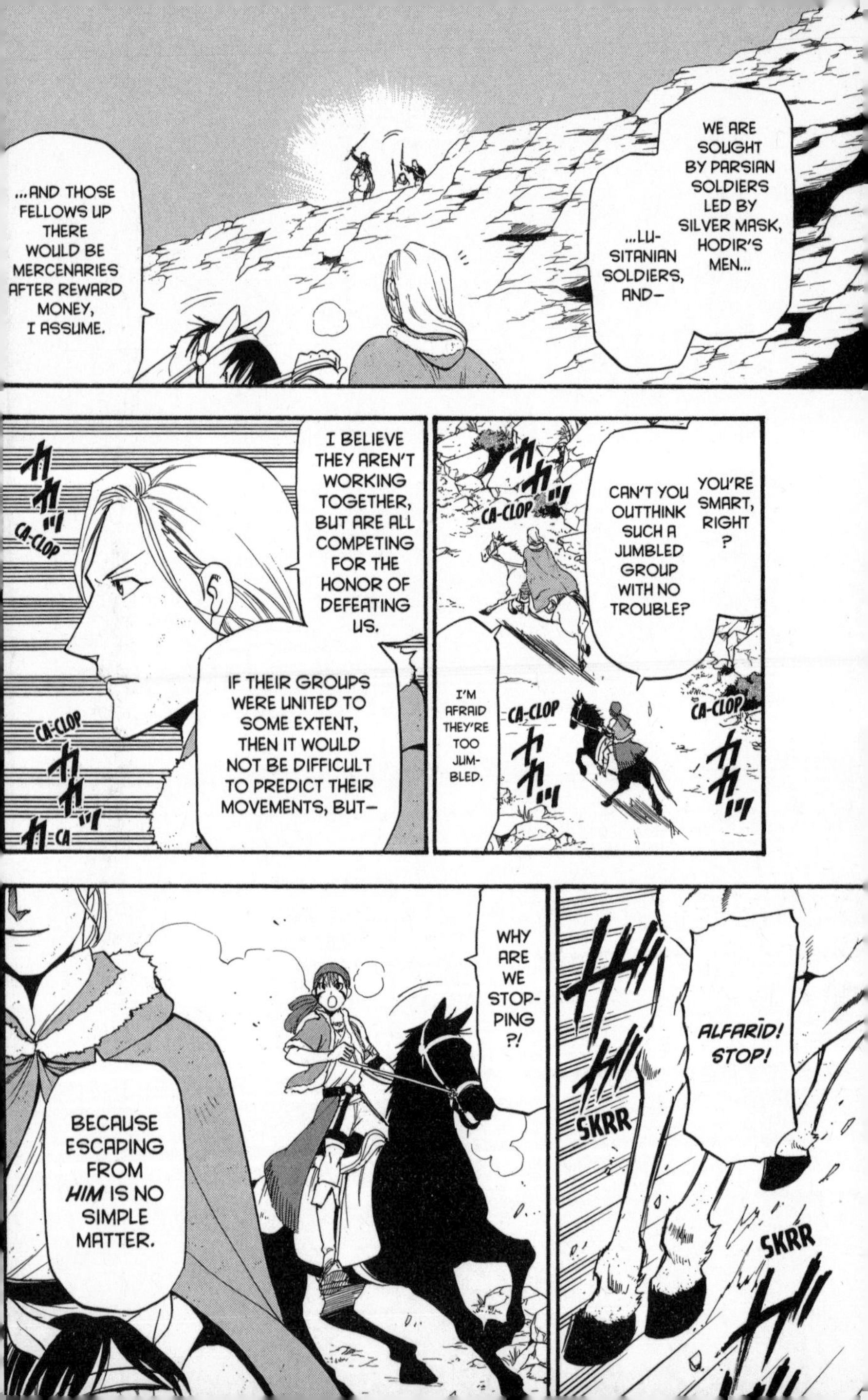
WE ARE SOUGHT BY PARSIAN SOLDIERS LED BY SILVER MASK, HODIR'S MEN...
...LU-SITANIAN SOLDIERS, AND—
...AND THOSE FELLOWS UP THERE WOULD BE MERCENARIES AFTER REWARD MONEY, I ASSUME.
YOU'RE SMART, RIGHT?
CAN'T YOU OUTTHINK SUCH A JUMBLED GROUP WITH NO TROUBLE?
CA-CLOP
I'M AFRAID THEY'RE TOO JUM-BLED.
CA-CLOP
CA-CLOP
I BELIEVE THEY AREN'T WORKING TOGETHER, BUT ARE ALL COMPETING FOR THE HONOR OF DEFEATING US.
CA-CLOP
IF THEIR GROUPS WERE UNITED TO SOME EXTENT, THEN IT WOULD NOT BE DIFFICULT TO PREDICT THEIR MOVEMENTS, BUT—
CA-CLOP
CA
ALFARID! STOP!
SKRR
SKRR
WHY ARE WE STOP-PING?!
BECAUSE ESCAPING FROM *HIM* IS NO SIMPLE MATTER.

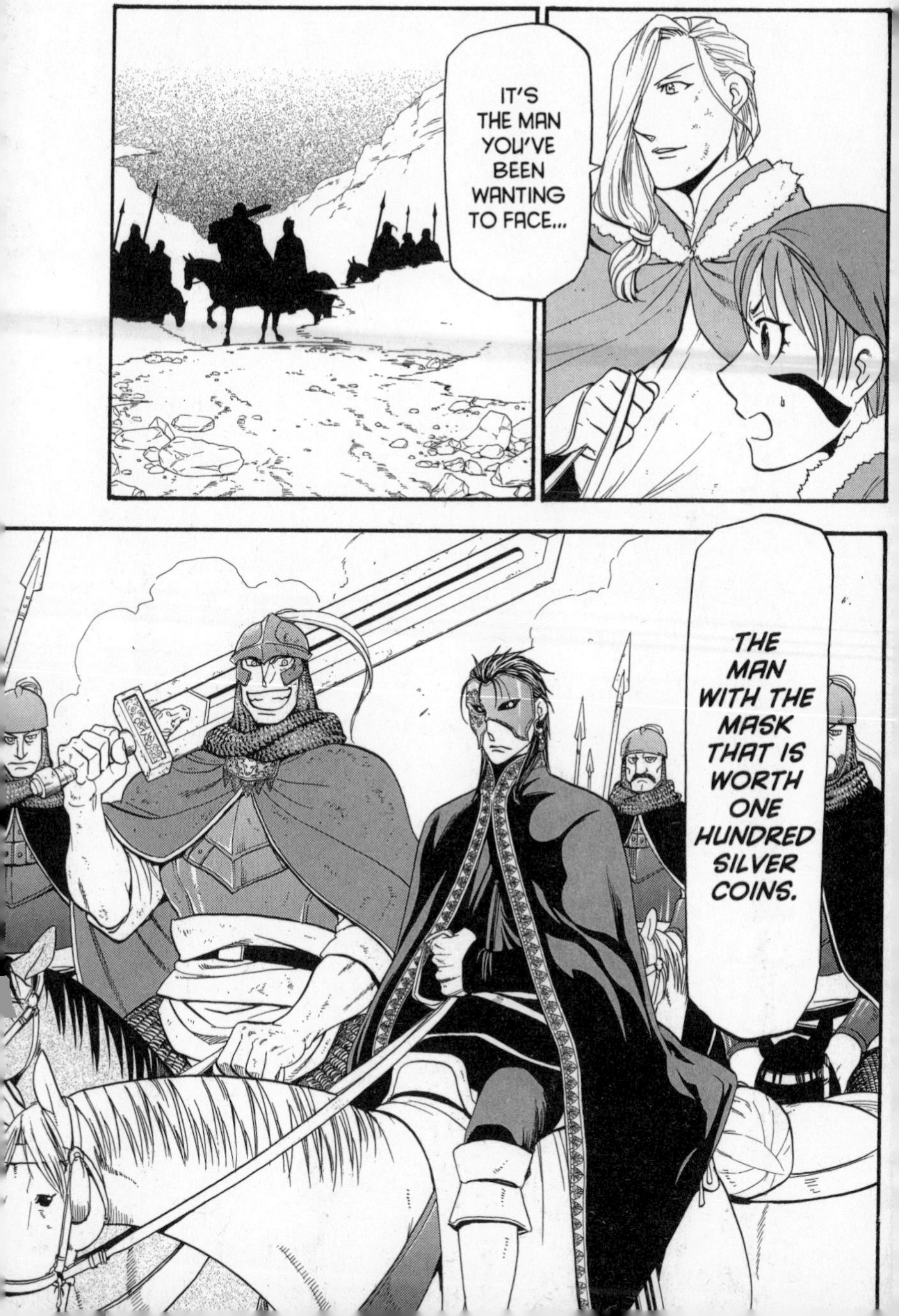
IT'S THE MAN YOU'VE BEEN WANTING TO FACE...
THE MAN WITH THE MASK THAT IS WORTH ONE HUNDRED SILVER COINS.

THE HEROIC LEGEND OF
ARSLAN

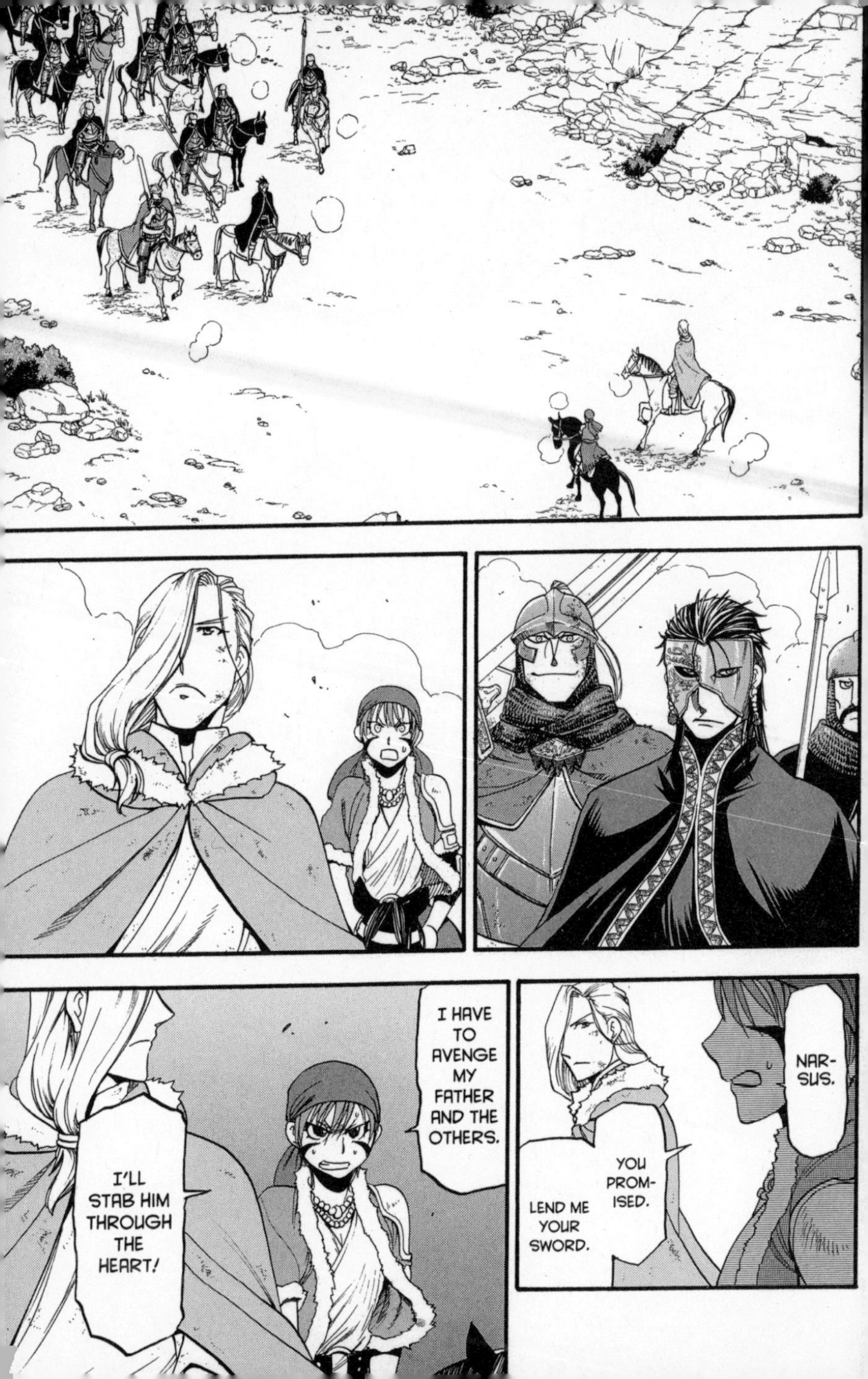
NARSUS.
YOU PROMISED.
LEND ME YOUR SWORD.
I HAVE TO AVENGE MY FATHER AND THE OTHERS.
I'LL STAB HIM THROUGH THE HEART!

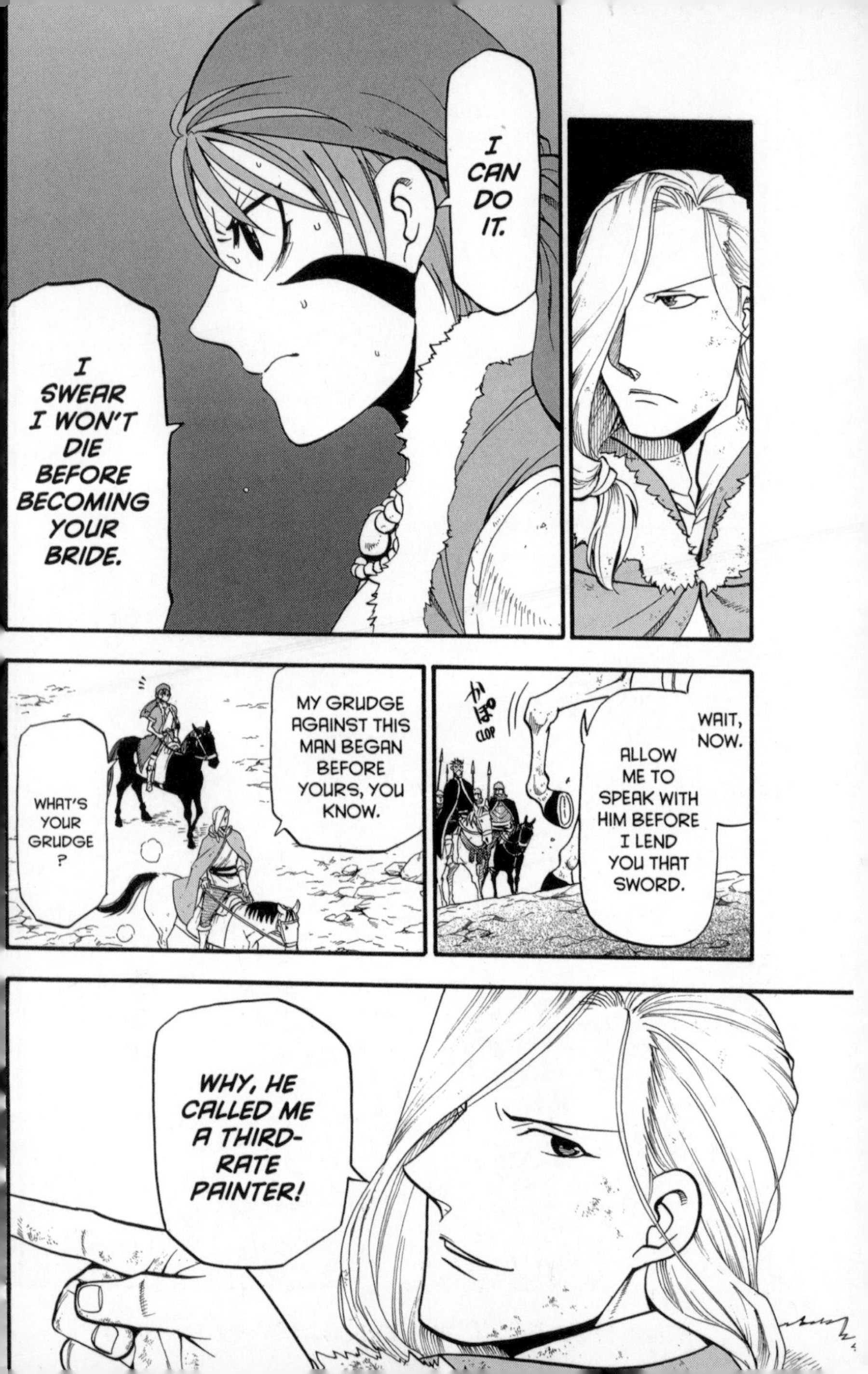
I CAN DO IT.
I SWEAR I WON'T DIE BEFORE BECOMING YOUR BRIDE.
かぽ
CLOP
WAIT, NOW.
ALLOW ME TO SPEAK WITH HIM BEFORE I LEND YOU THAT SWORD.
MY GRUDGE AGAINST THIS MAN BEGAN BEFORE YOURS, YOU KNOW.
WHAT'S YOUR GRUDGE?
WHY, HE CALLED ME A THIRD-RATE PAINTER!

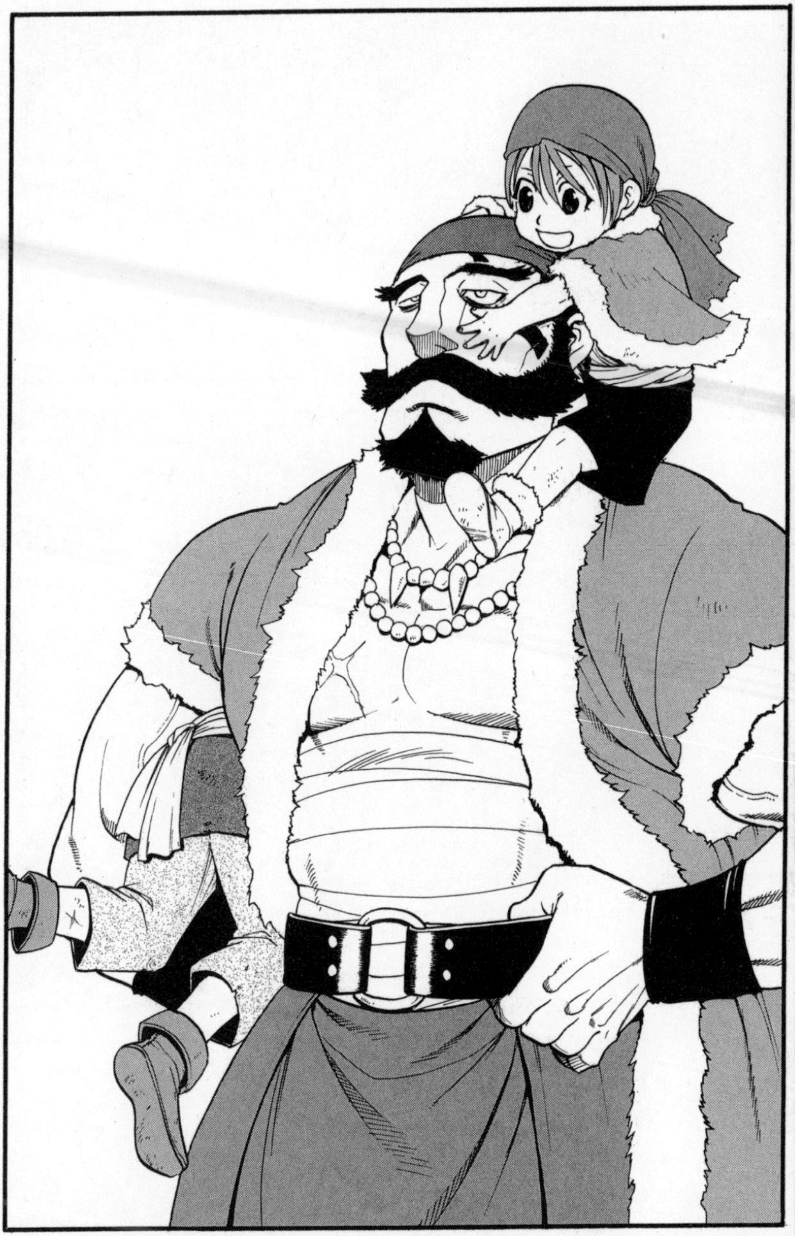

Chapter 36: The Character of a King

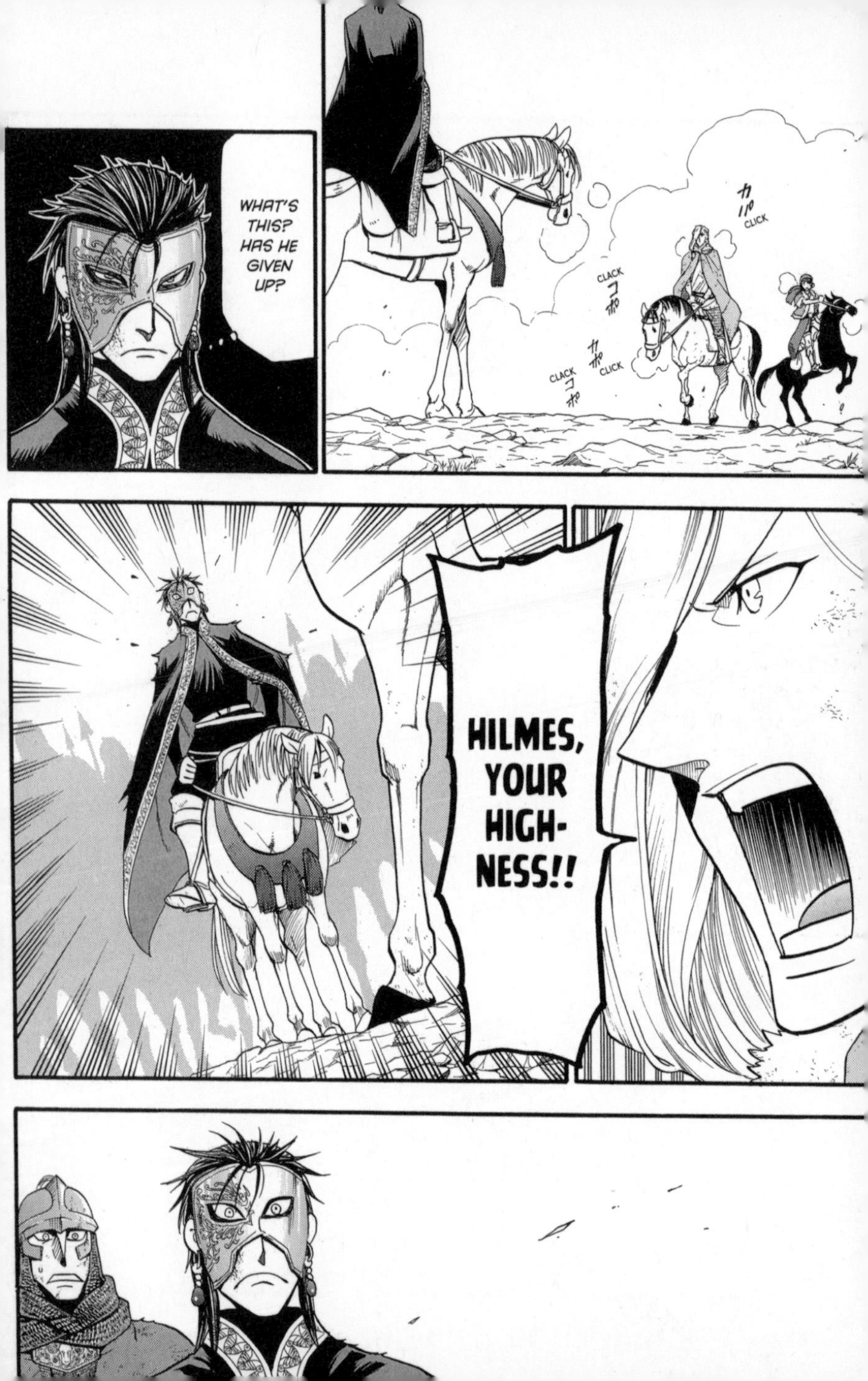
CLICK
CLACK
CLICK
CLACK
WHAT'S THIS? HAS HE GIVEN UP?
HILMES, YOUR HIGH-NESS!!

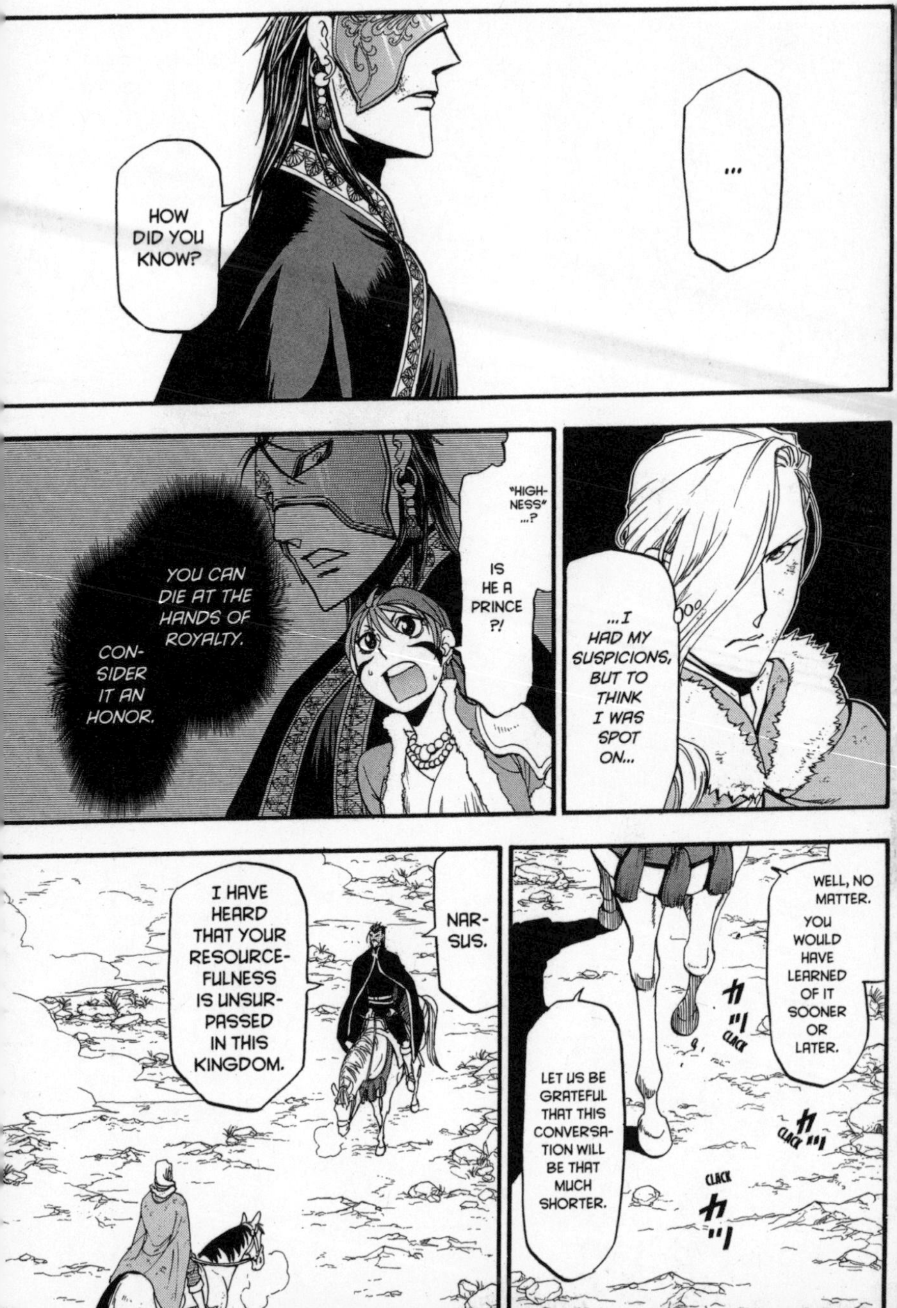
...
HOW DID YOU KNOW?
...I HAD MY SUSPICIONS, BUT TO THINK I WAS SPOT ON...
"HIGHNESS" ...?
IS HE A PRINCE ?!
YOU CAN DIE AT THE HANDS OF ROYALTY.
CONSIDER IT AN HONOR.
WELL, NO MATTER.
YOU WOULD HAVE LEARNED OF IT SOONER OR LATER.
CLACK
CLACK
CLACK
LET US BE GRATEFUL THAT THIS CONVERSATION WILL BE THAT MUCH SHORTER.
NARSUS.
I HAVE HEARD THAT YOUR RESOURCEFULNESS IS UNSURPASSED IN THIS KINGDOM.

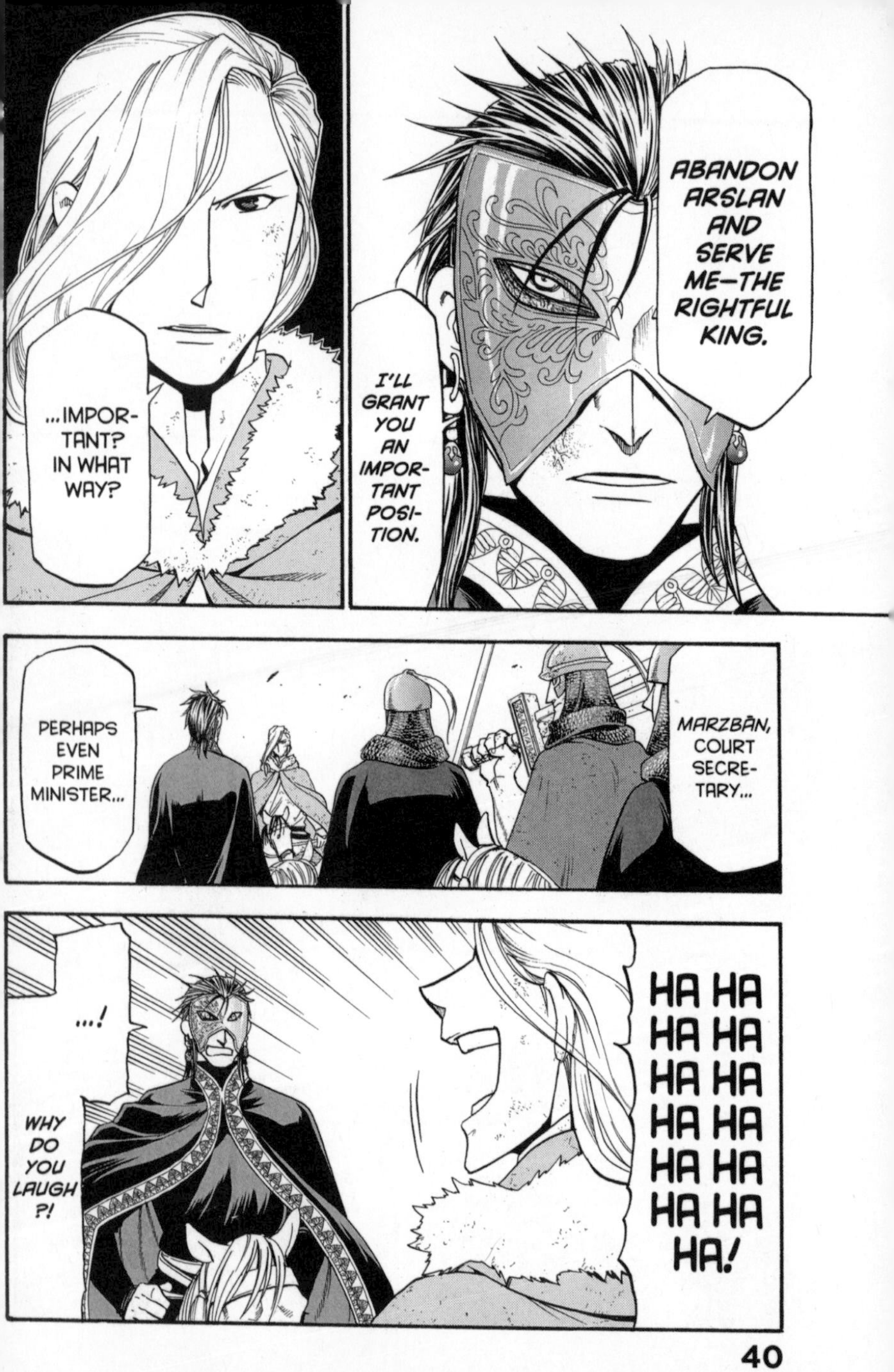
ABANDON ARSLAN AND SERVE ME—THE RIGHTFUL KING.
I'LL GRANT YOU AN IMPORTANT POSITION.
...IMPORTANT? IN WHAT WAY?
MARZBĀN, COURT SECRETARY...
PERHAPS EVEN PRIME MINISTER...
HA HA HA HA HA HA HA HA HA HA HA HA HA!
...!
WHY DO YOU LAUGH?!

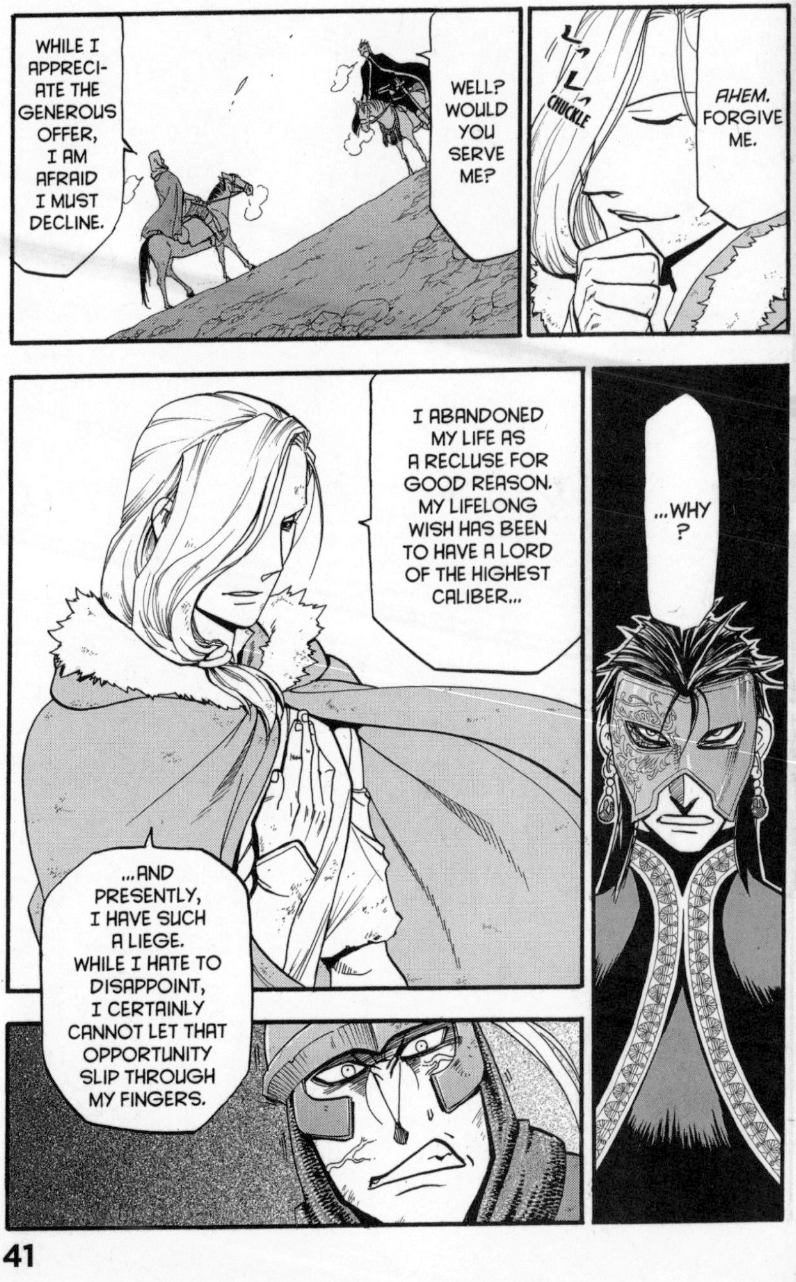
CHUCKLE
AHEM. FORGIVE ME.
WELL? WOULD YOU SERVE ME?
WHILE I APPRECIATE THE GENEROUS OFFER, I AM AFRAID I MUST DECLINE.
...WHY?
I ABANDONED MY LIFE AS A RECLUSE FOR GOOD REASON. MY LIFELONG WISH HAS BEEN TO HAVE A LORD OF THE HIGHEST CALIBER...
...AND PRESENTLY, I HAVE SUCH A LIEGE. WHILE I HATE TO DISAPPOINT, I CERTAINLY CANNOT LET THAT OPPORTUNITY SLIP THROUGH MY FINGERS.

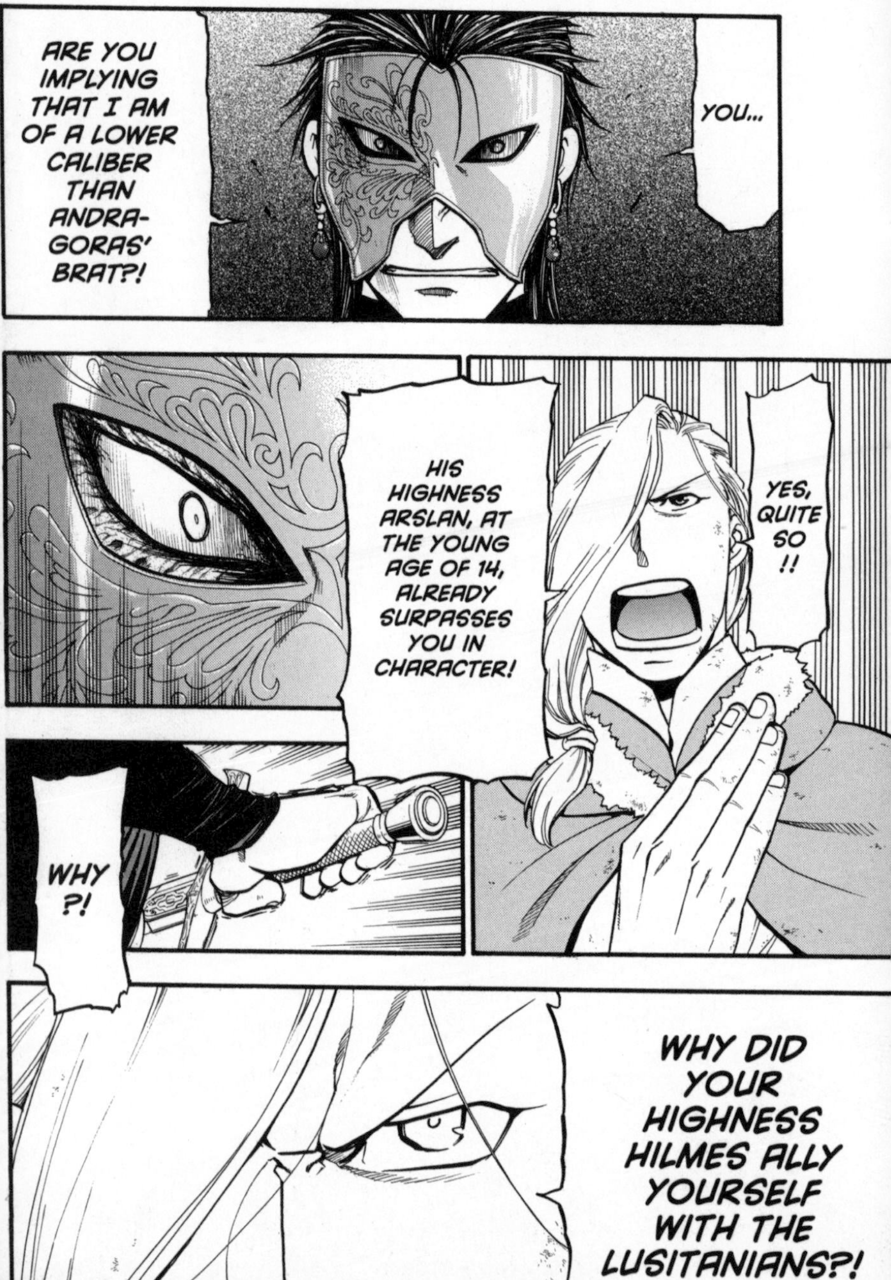
YOU...
ARE YOU IMPLYING THAT I AM OF A LOWER CALIBER THAN ANDRA-GORAS' BRAT?!
YES, QUITE SO !!
HIS HIGHNESS ARSLAN, AT THE YOUNG AGE OF 14, ALREADY SURPASSES YOU IN CHARACTER!
WHY ?!
WHY DID YOUR HIGHNESS HILMES ALLY YOURSELF WITH THE LUSITANIANS?!

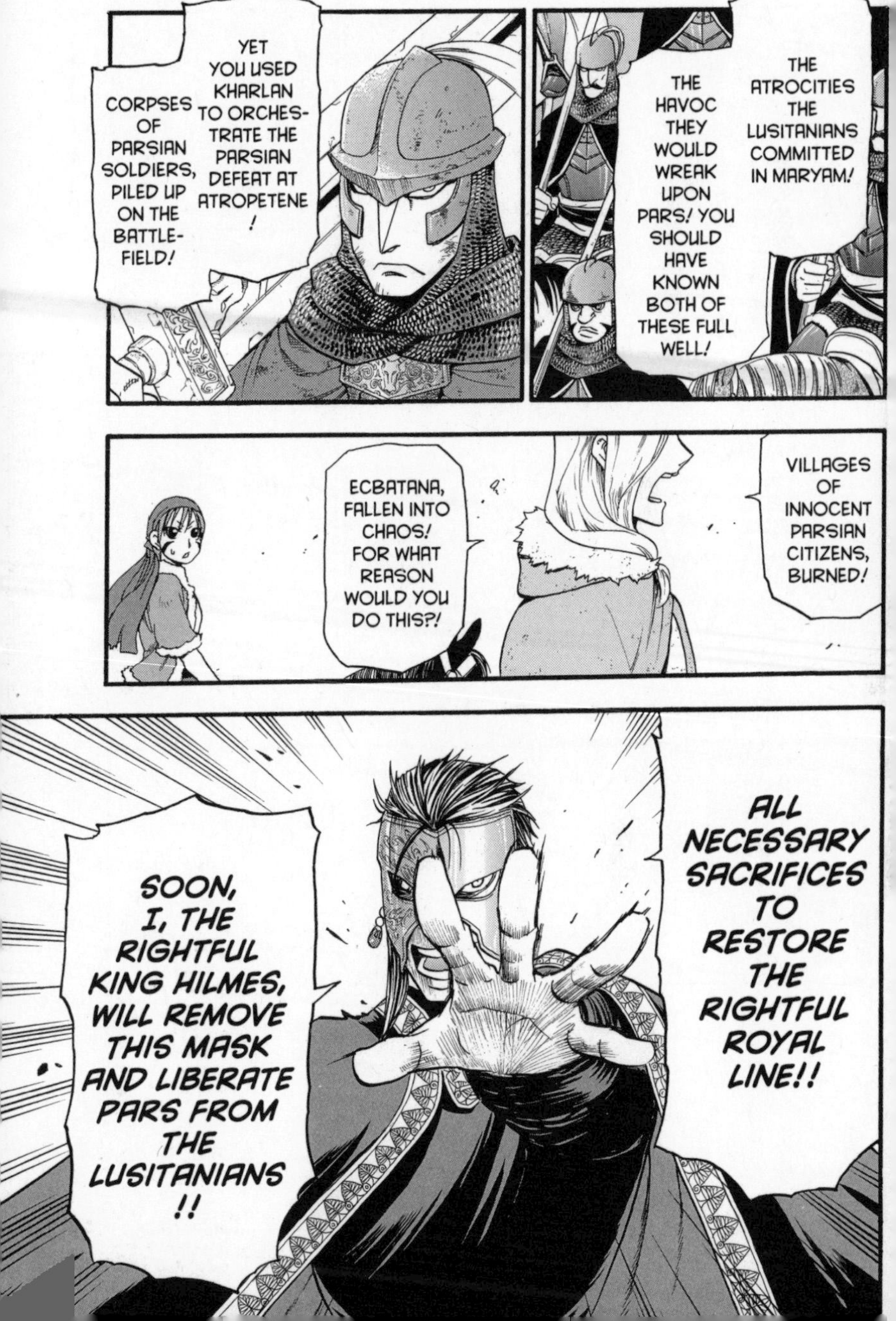
THE ATROCITIES THE LUSITANIANS COMMITTED IN MARYAM!
THE HAVOC THEY WOULD WREAK UPON PARS! YOU SHOULD HAVE KNOWN BOTH OF THESE FULL WELL!
YET YOU USED KHARLAN TO ORCHES-TRATE THE PARSIAN DEFEAT AT ATROPETENE!
CORPSES OF PARSIAN SOLDIERS, PILED UP ON THE BATTLE-FIELD!
VILLAGES OF INNOCENT PARSIAN CITIZENS, BURNED!
ECBATANA, FALLEN INTO CHAOS! FOR WHAT REASON WOULD YOU DO THIS?!
ALL NECESSARY SACRIFICES TO RESTORE THE RIGHTFUL ROYAL LINE!!
SOON, I, THE RIGHTFUL KING HILMES, WILL REMOVE THIS MASK AND LIBERATE PARS FROM THE LUSITANIANS!!

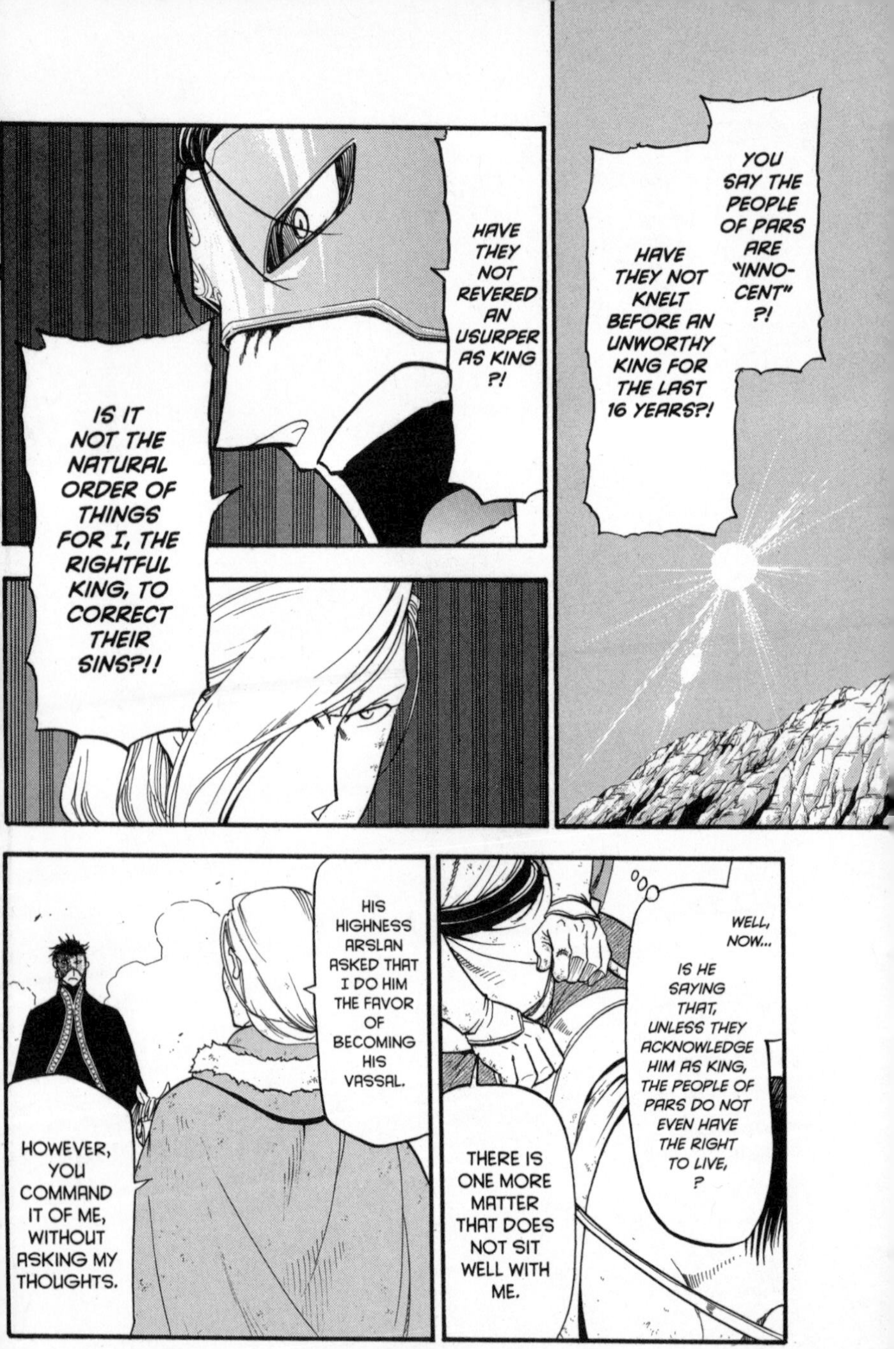
YOU SAY THE PEOPLE OF PARS ARE "INNO-CENT"?!
HAVE THEY NOT KNELT BEFORE AN UNWORTHY KING FOR THE LAST 16 YEARS?!
HAVE THEY NOT REVERED AN USURPER AS KING?!
IS IT NOT THE NATURAL ORDER OF THINGS FOR I, THE RIGHTFUL KING, TO CORRECT THEIR SINS?!!
WELL, NOW...
IS HE SAYING THAT, UNLESS THEY ACKNOWLEDGE HIM AS KING, THE PEOPLE OF PARS DO NOT EVEN HAVE THE RIGHT TO LIVE, ?
THERE IS ONE MORE MATTER THAT DOES NOT SIT WELL WITH ME.
HIS HIGHNESS ARSLAN ASKED THAT I DO HIM THE FAVOR OF BECOMING HIS VASSAL.
HOWEVER, YOU COMMAND IT OF ME, WITHOUT ASKING MY THOUGHTS.

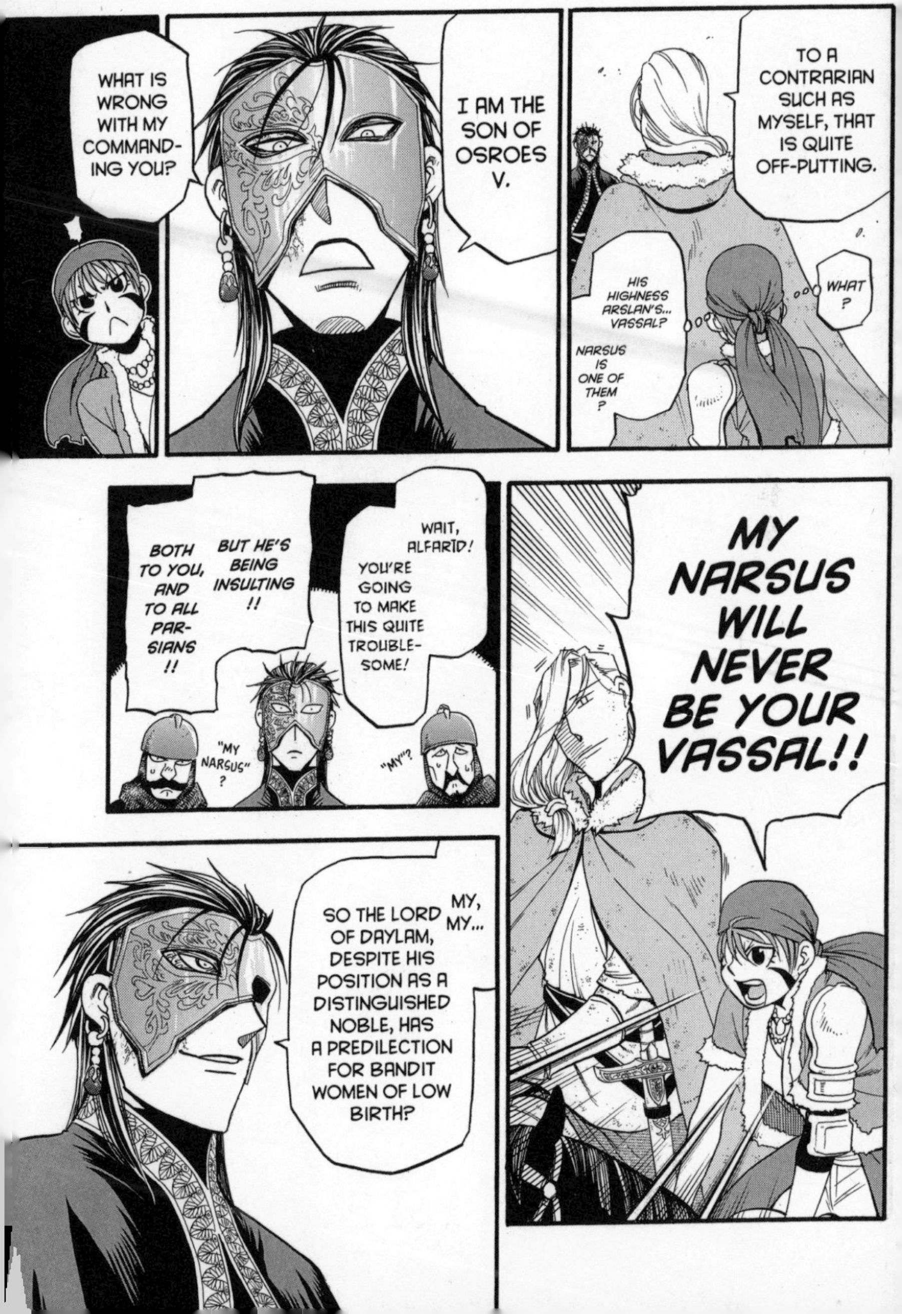
TO A CONTRARIAN SUCH AS MYSELF, THAT IS QUITE OFF-PUTTING.
WHAT ?
HIS HIGHNESS ARSLAN'S... VASSAL?
NARSUS IS ONE OF THEM ?
I AM THE SON OF OSROES V.
WHAT IS WRONG WITH MY COMMAND-ING YOU?
MY NARSUS WILL NEVER BE YOUR VASSAL!!
WAIT, ALFARID! YOU'RE GOING TO MAKE THIS QUITE TROUBLE-SOME!
BUT HE'S BEING INSULTING !!
BOTH TO YOU, AND TO ALL PAR-SIANS !!
"MY"?
"MY NARSUS" ?
MY, MY...
SO THE LORD OF DAYLAM, DESPITE HIS POSITION AS A DISTINGUISHED NOBLE, HAS A PREDILECTION FOR BANDIT WOMEN OF LOW BIRTH?

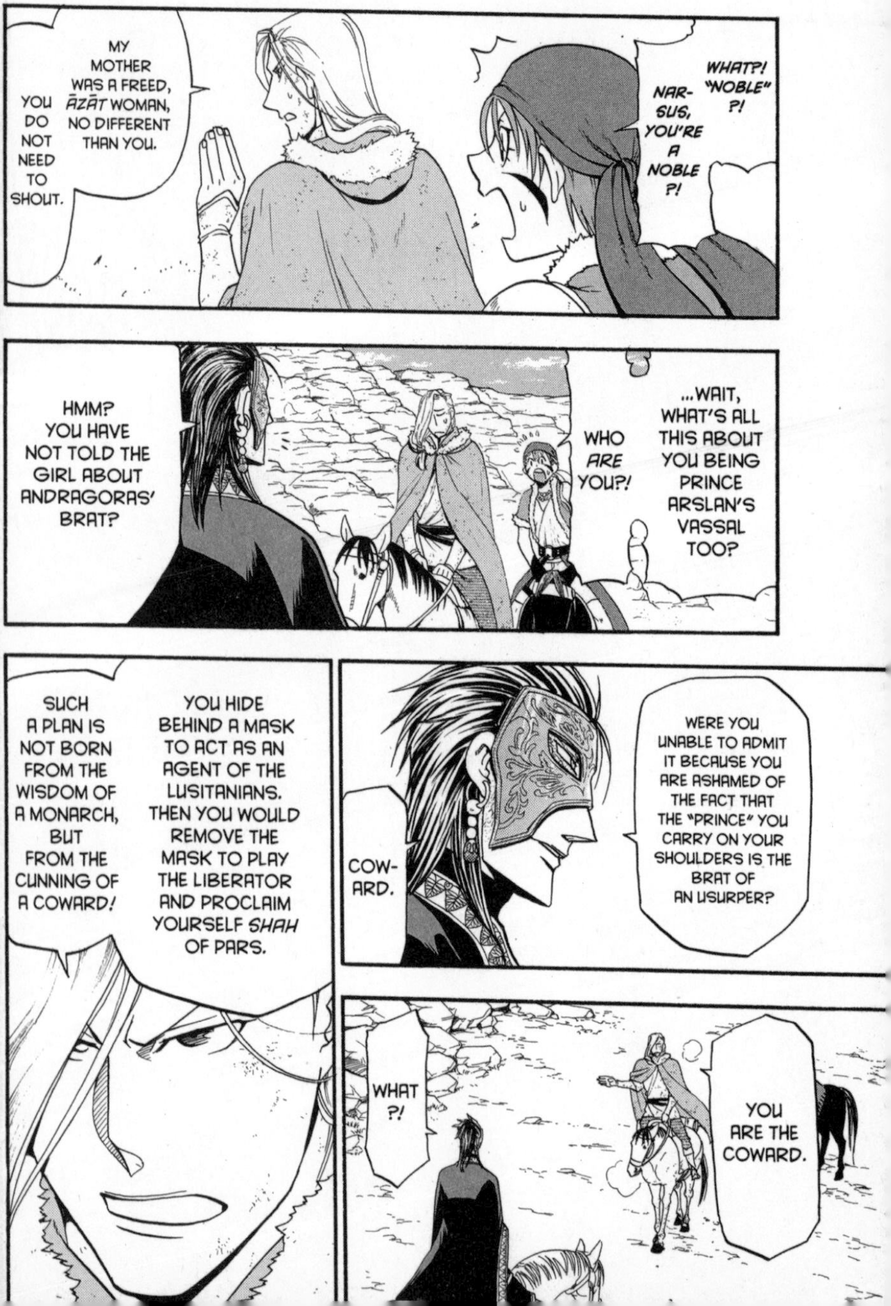
WHAT?! "NOBLE"?!
NARSUS, YOU'RE A NOBLE?!
MY MOTHER WAS A FREED, ĀZĀT WOMAN, NO DIFFERENT THAN YOU.
YOU DO NOT NEED TO SHOUT.
...WAIT, WHAT'S ALL THIS ABOUT YOU BEING PRINCE ARSLAN'S VASSAL TOO?
WHO ARE YOU?!
HMM? YOU HAVE NOT TOLD THE GIRL ABOUT ANDRAGORAS' BRAT?
WERE YOU UNABLE TO ADMIT IT BECAUSE YOU ARE ASHAMED OF THE FACT THAT THE "PRINCE" YOU CARRY ON YOUR SHOULDERS IS THE BRAT OF AN USURPER?
COWARD.
YOU ARE THE COWARD.
WHAT?!
YOU HIDE BEHIND A MASK TO ACT AS AN AGENT OF THE LUSITANIANS. THEN YOU WOULD REMOVE THE MASK TO PLAY THE LIBERATOR AND PROCLAIM YOURSELF SHAH OF PARS.
SUCH A PLAN IS NOT BORN FROM THE WISDOM OF A MONARCH, BUT FROM THE CUNNING OF A COWARD!

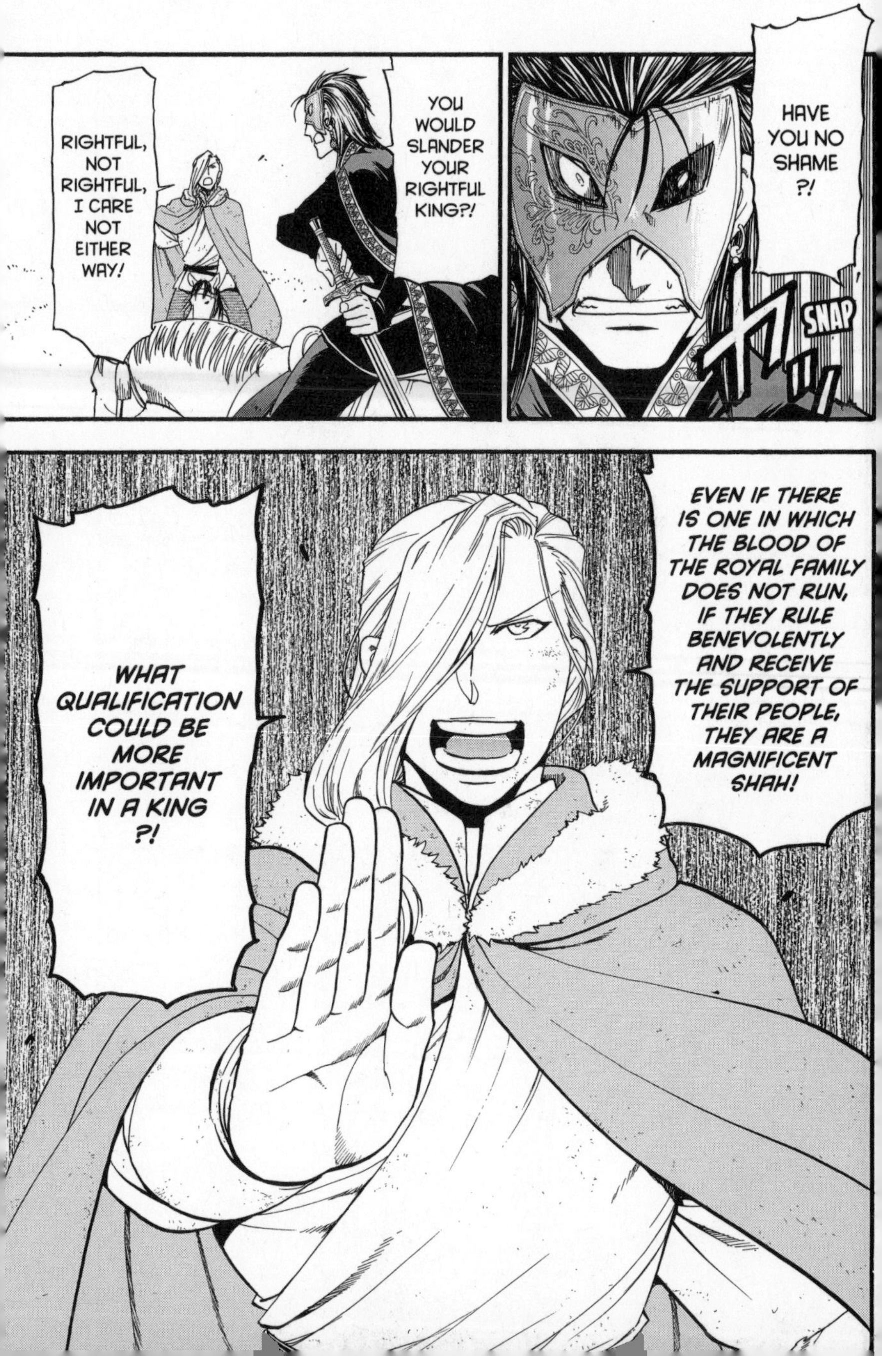
HAVE YOU NO SHAME ?!
SNAP
YOU WOULD SLANDER YOUR RIGHTFUL KING?!
RIGHTFUL, NOT RIGHTFUL, I CARE NOT EITHER WAY!
EVEN IF THERE IS ONE IN WHICH THE BLOOD OF THE ROYAL FAMILY DOES NOT RUN, IF THEY RULE BENEVOLENTLY AND RECEIVE THE SUPPORT OF THEIR PEOPLE, THEY ARE A MAGNIFICENT SHAH!
WHAT QUALIFICATION COULD BE MORE IMPORTANT IN A KING ?!

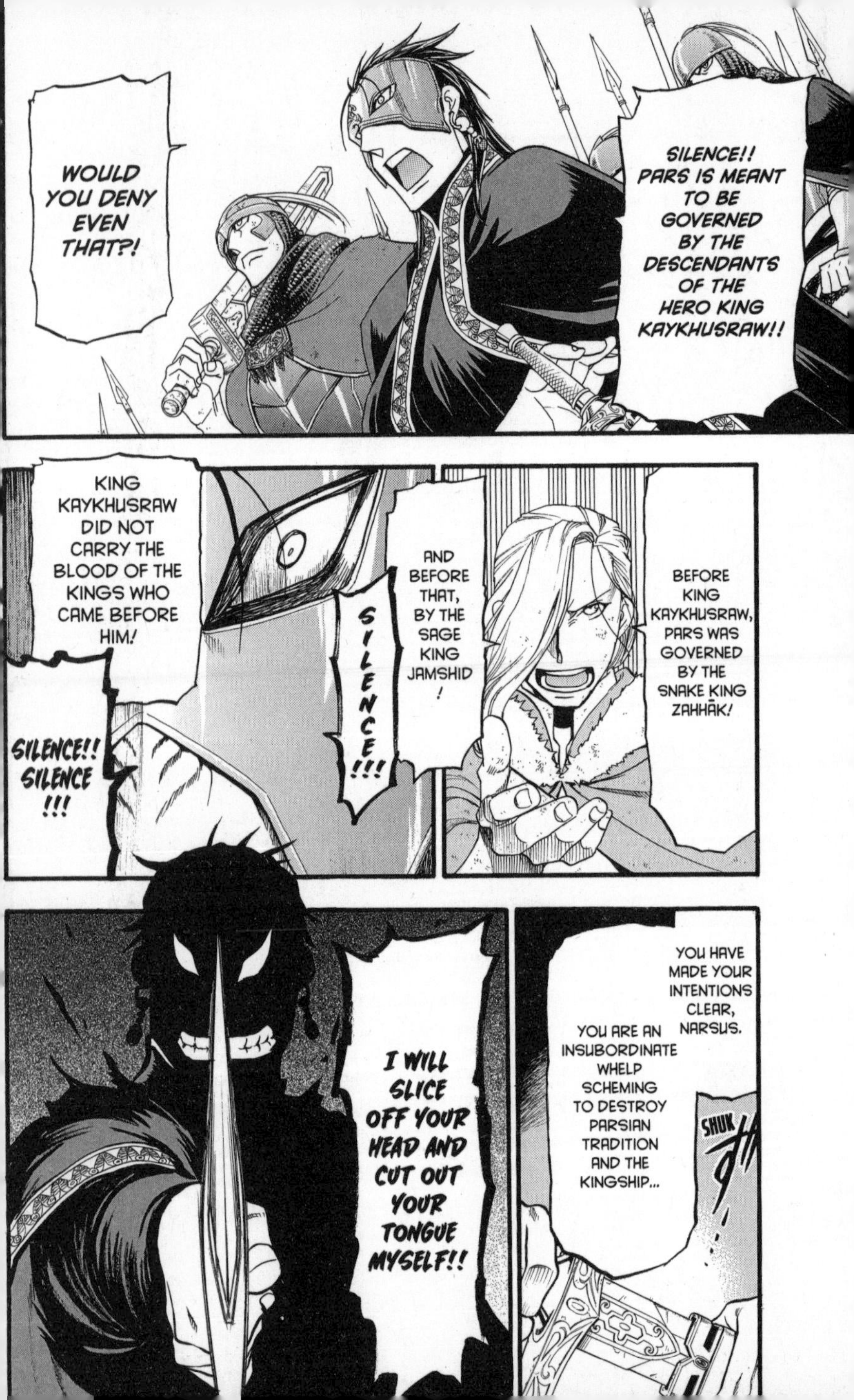
SILENCE!! PARS IS MEANT TO BE GOVERNED BY THE DESCENDANTS OF THE HERO KING KAYKHUSRAW!!
WOULD YOU DENY EVEN THAT?!
BEFORE KING KAYKHUSRAW, PARS WAS GOVERNED BY THE SNAKE KING ZAHHĀK!
AND BEFORE THAT, BY THE SAGE KING JAMSHID!
SILENCE!!!
KING KAYKHUSRAW DID NOT CARRY THE BLOOD OF THE KINGS WHO CAME BEFORE HIM!
SILENCE!! SILENCE!!!
YOU HAVE MADE YOUR INTENTIONS CLEAR, NARSUS.
YOU ARE AN INSUBORDINATE WHELP SCHEMING TO DESTROY PARSIAN TRADITION AND THE KINGSHIP...
SHUK
I WILL SLICE OFF YOUR HEAD AND CUT OUT YOUR TONGUE MYSELF!!

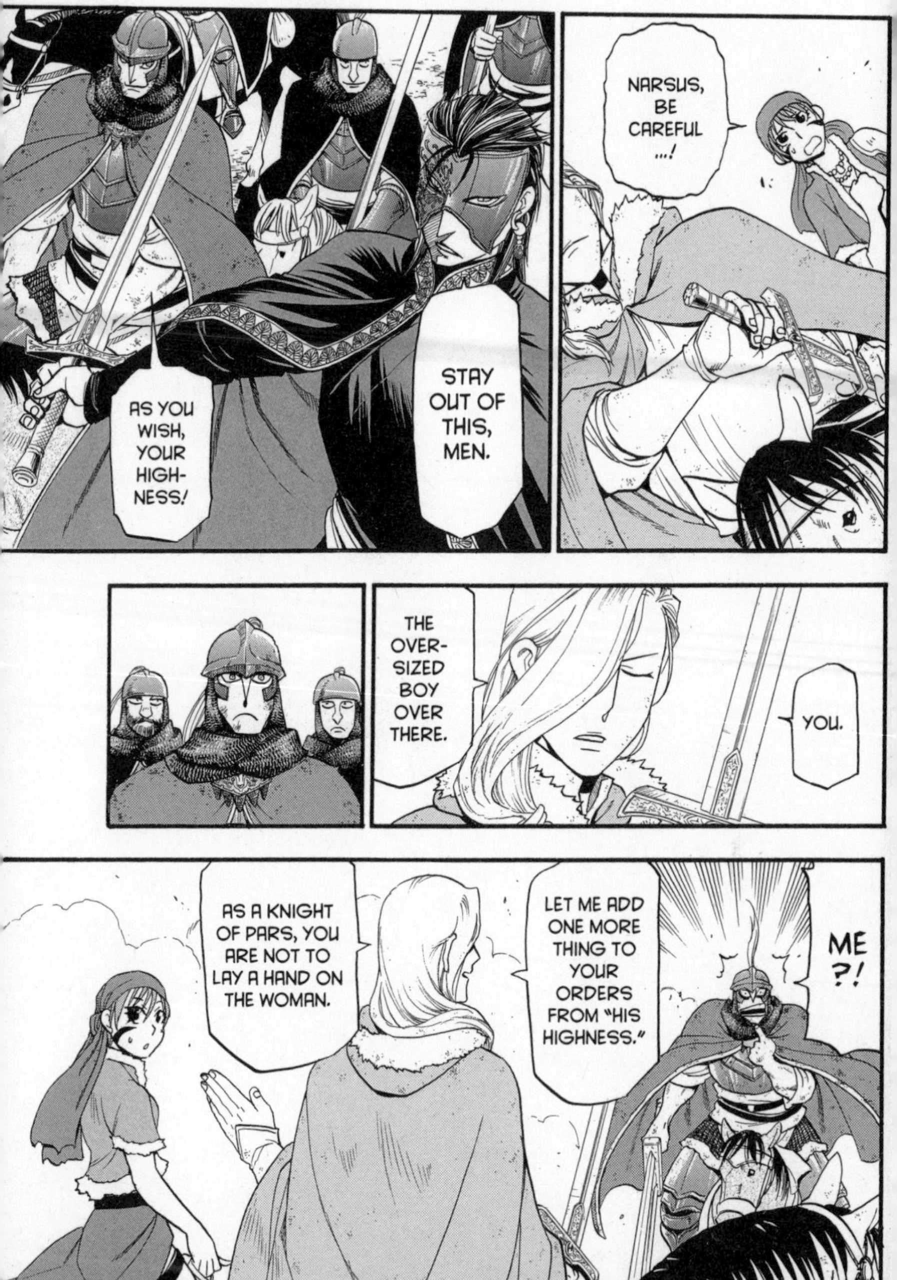
NARSUS, BE CAREFUL ...!
STAY OUT OF THIS, MEN.
AS YOU WISH, YOUR HIGH-NESS!
YOU.
THE OVER-SIZED BOY OVER THERE.
ME ?!
LET ME ADD ONE MORE THING TO YOUR ORDERS FROM "HIS HIGHNESS."
AS A KNIGHT OF PARS, YOU ARE NOT TO LAY A HAND ON THE WOMAN.

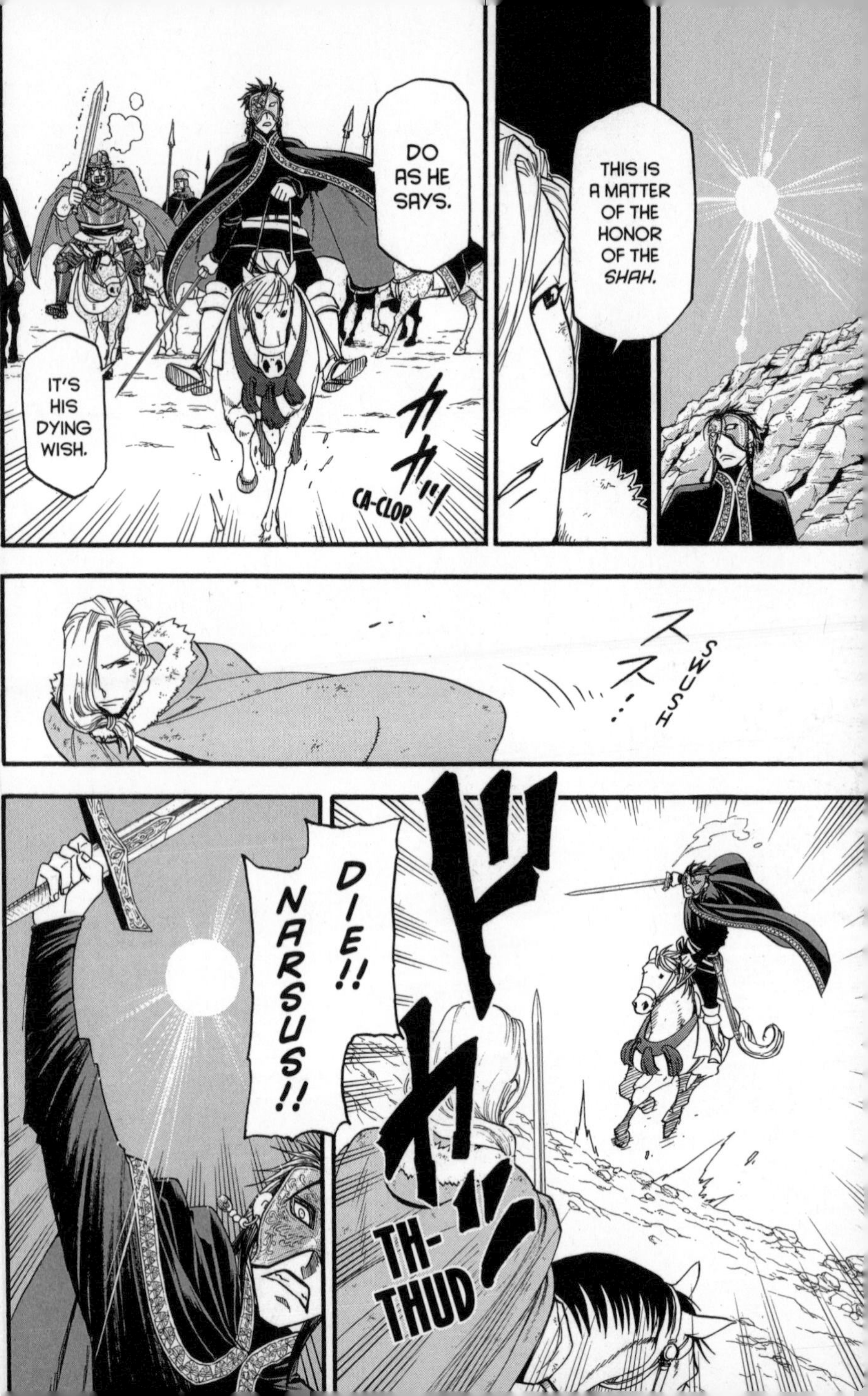
THIS IS A MATTER OF THE HONOR OF THE *SHAH.*
DO AS HE SAYS.
IT'S HIS DYING WISH.
カカッ
CA-CLOP
スス…
SWUSH
ドカッ
TH-THUD
DIE!! NARSUS!!

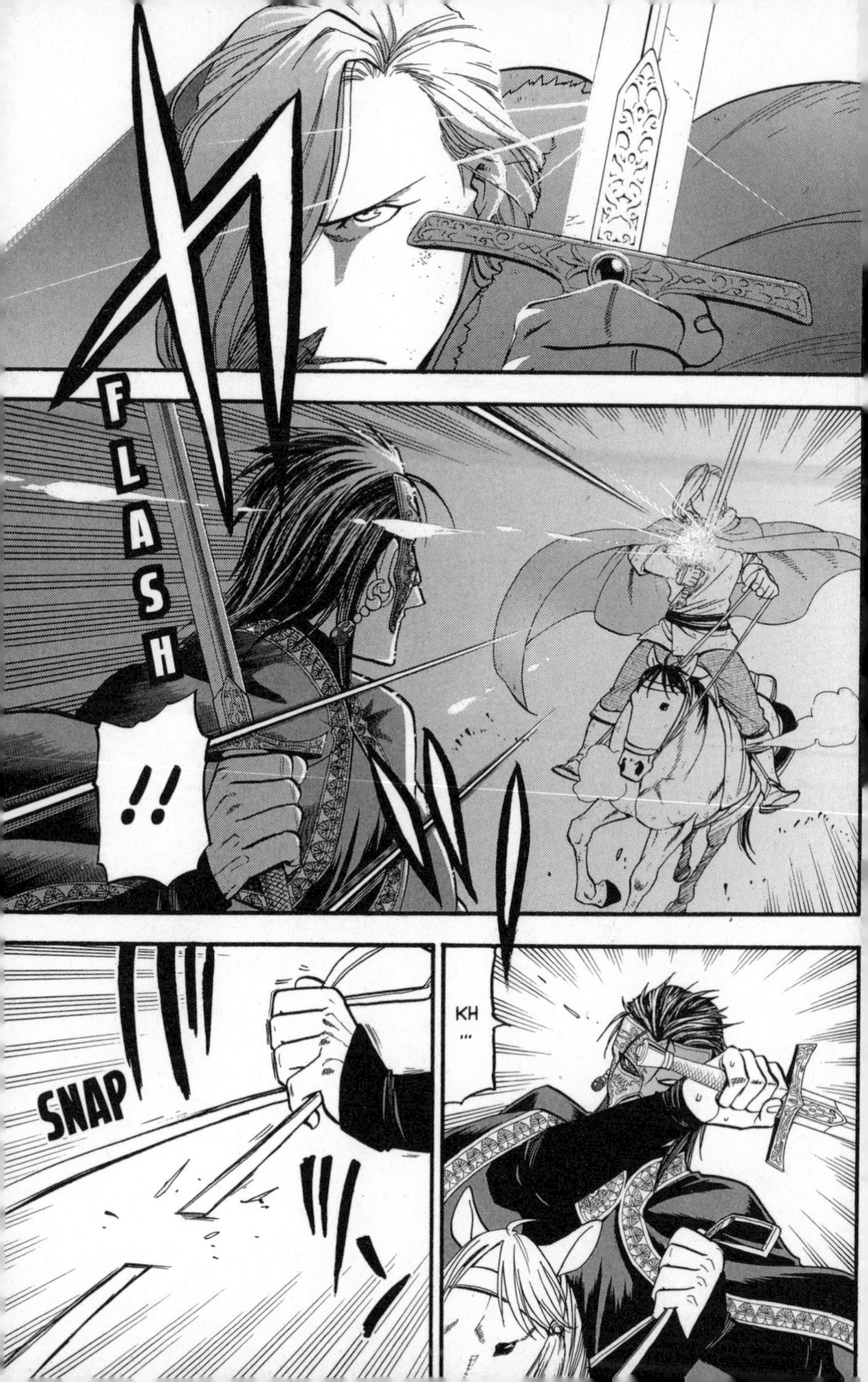
FLASH
!!
KH ...
SNAP

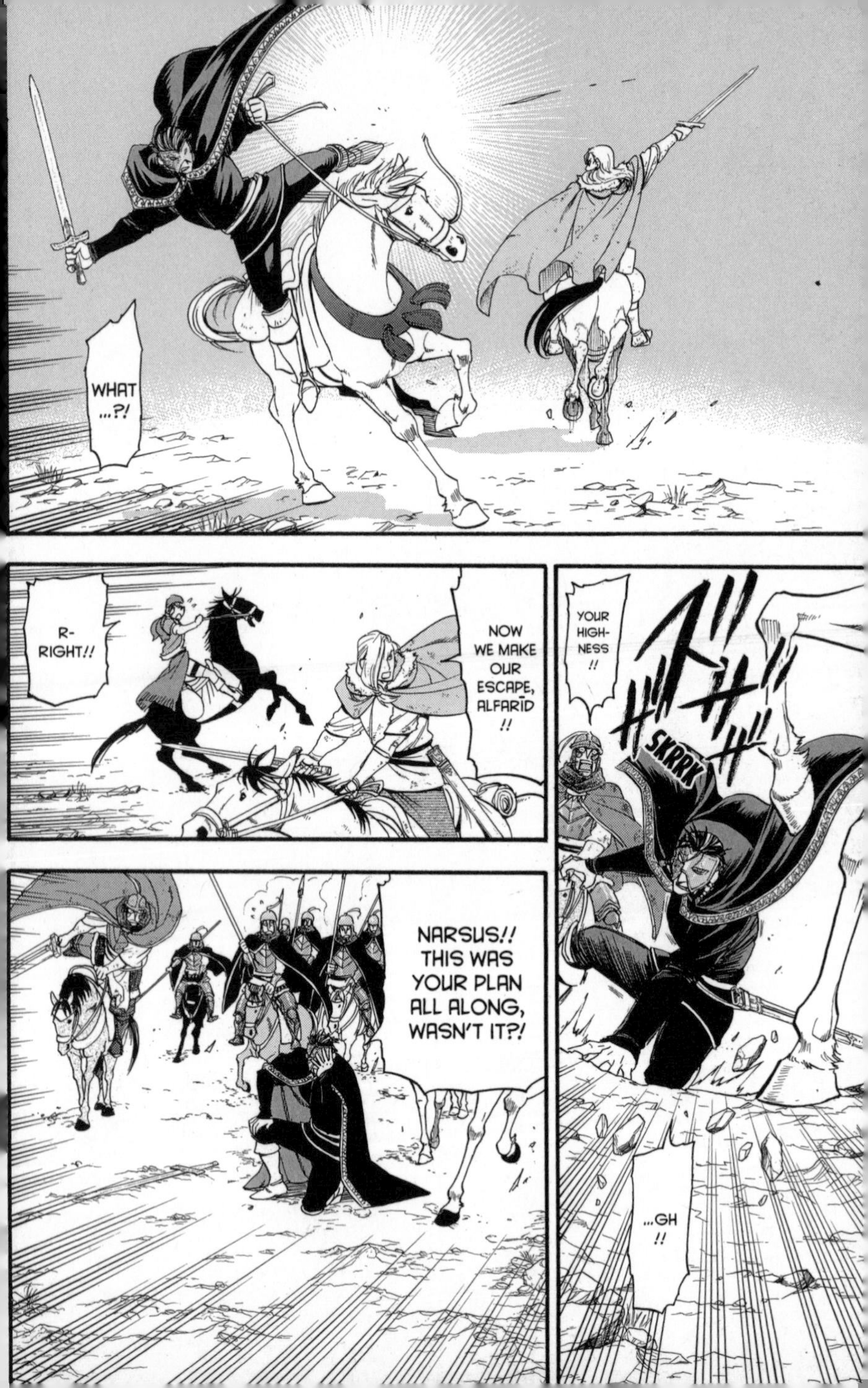
WHAT ...?!
YOUR HIGHNESS!!
SKRRK
...GH!!
NOW WE MAKE OUR ESCAPE, ALFARĪD!!
R-RIGHT!!
NARSUS!! THIS WAS YOUR PLAN ALL ALONG, WASN'T IT?!

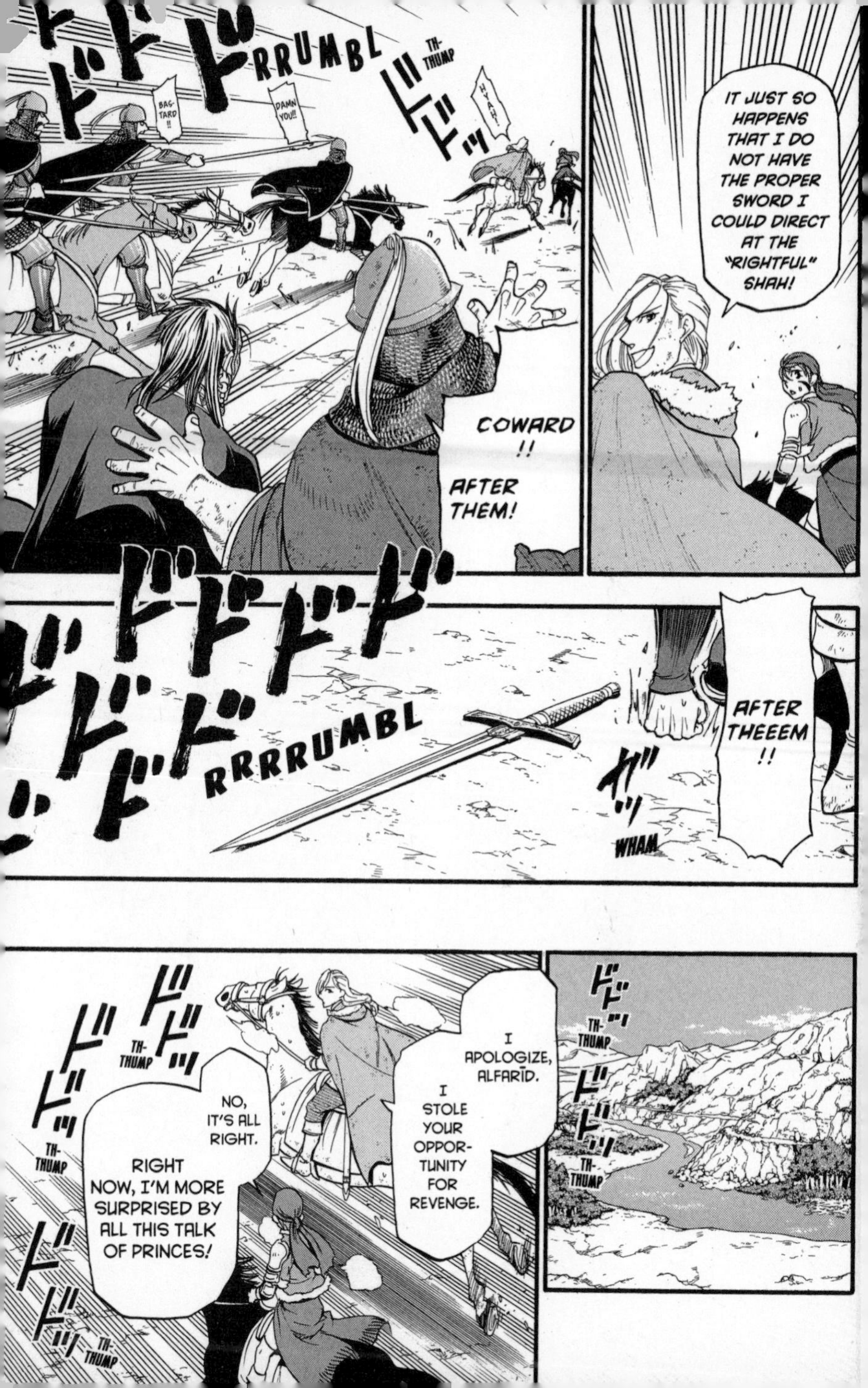
IT JUST SO HAPPENS THAT I DO NOT HAVE THE PROPER SWORD I COULD DIRECT AT THE "RIGHTFUL" SHAH!
RRUMBL
TH-THUMP
HYAH!
DAMN YOU!!
BAS-TARD!!
COWARD!!
AFTER THEM!
AFTER THEEEM!!
WHAM
RRRRUMBL
TH-THUMP
TH-THUMP
I APOLOGIZE, ALFARĪD.
I STOLE YOUR OPPOR-TUNITY FOR REVENGE.
NO, IT'S ALL RIGHT.
RIGHT NOW, I'M MORE SURPRISED BY ALL THIS TALK OF PRINCES!
TH-THUMP
TH-THUMP
TH-THUMP

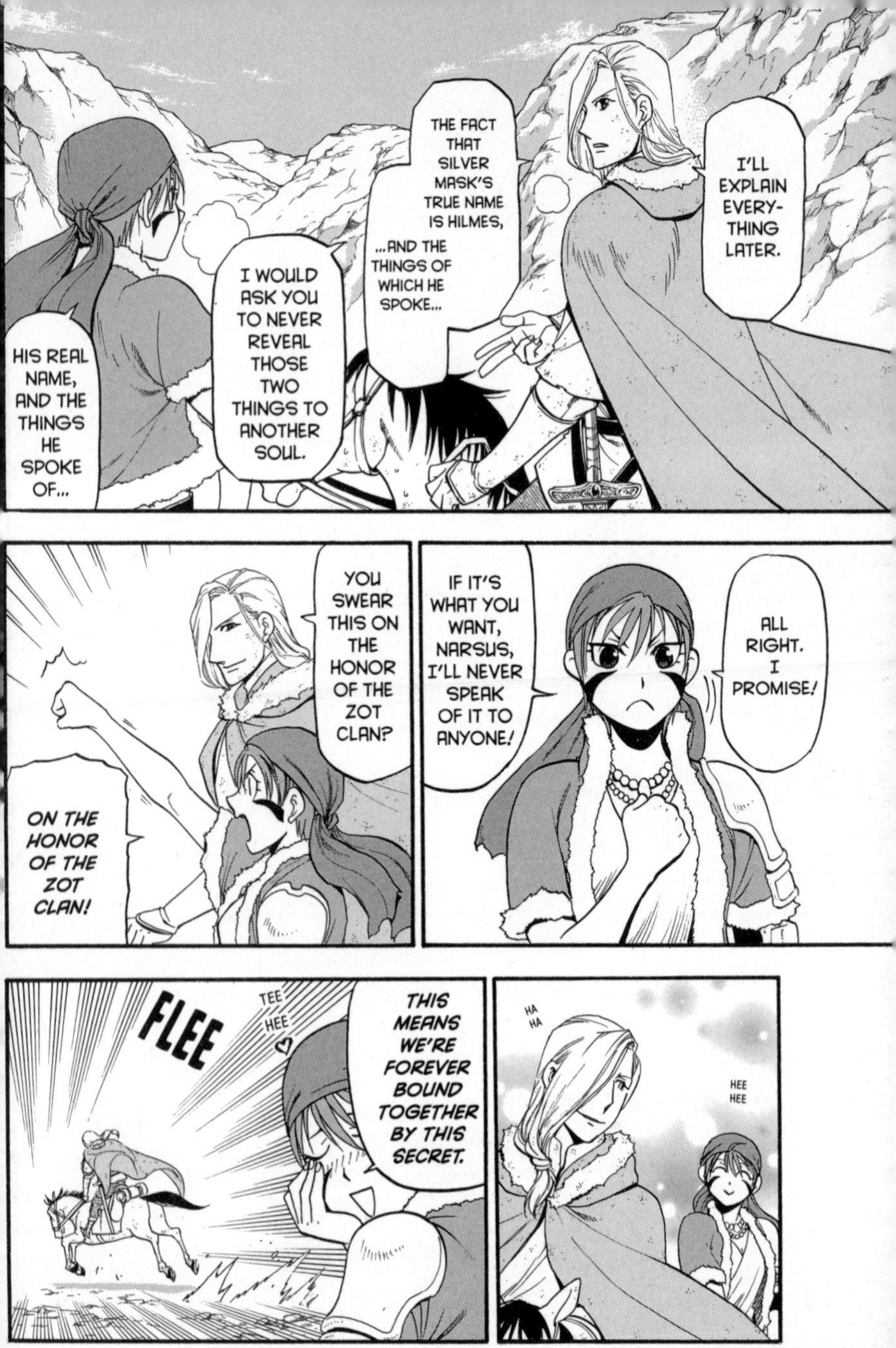
I'LL EXPLAIN EVERY-THING LATER.
THE FACT THAT SILVER MASK'S TRUE NAME IS HILMES,
...AND THE THINGS OF WHICH HE SPOKE...
I WOULD ASK YOU TO NEVER REVEAL THOSE TWO THINGS TO ANOTHER SOUL.
HIS REAL NAME, AND THE THINGS HE SPOKE OF...
ALL RIGHT. I PROMISE!
IF IT'S WHAT YOU WANT, NARSUS, I'LL NEVER SPEAK OF IT TO ANYONE!
YOU SWEAR THIS ON THE HONOR OF THE ZOT CLAN?
ON THE HONOR OF THE ZOT CLAN!
HA HA
HEE HEE
THIS MEANS WE'RE FOREVER BOUND TOGETHER BY THIS SECRET.
TEE HEE ♡
FLEE

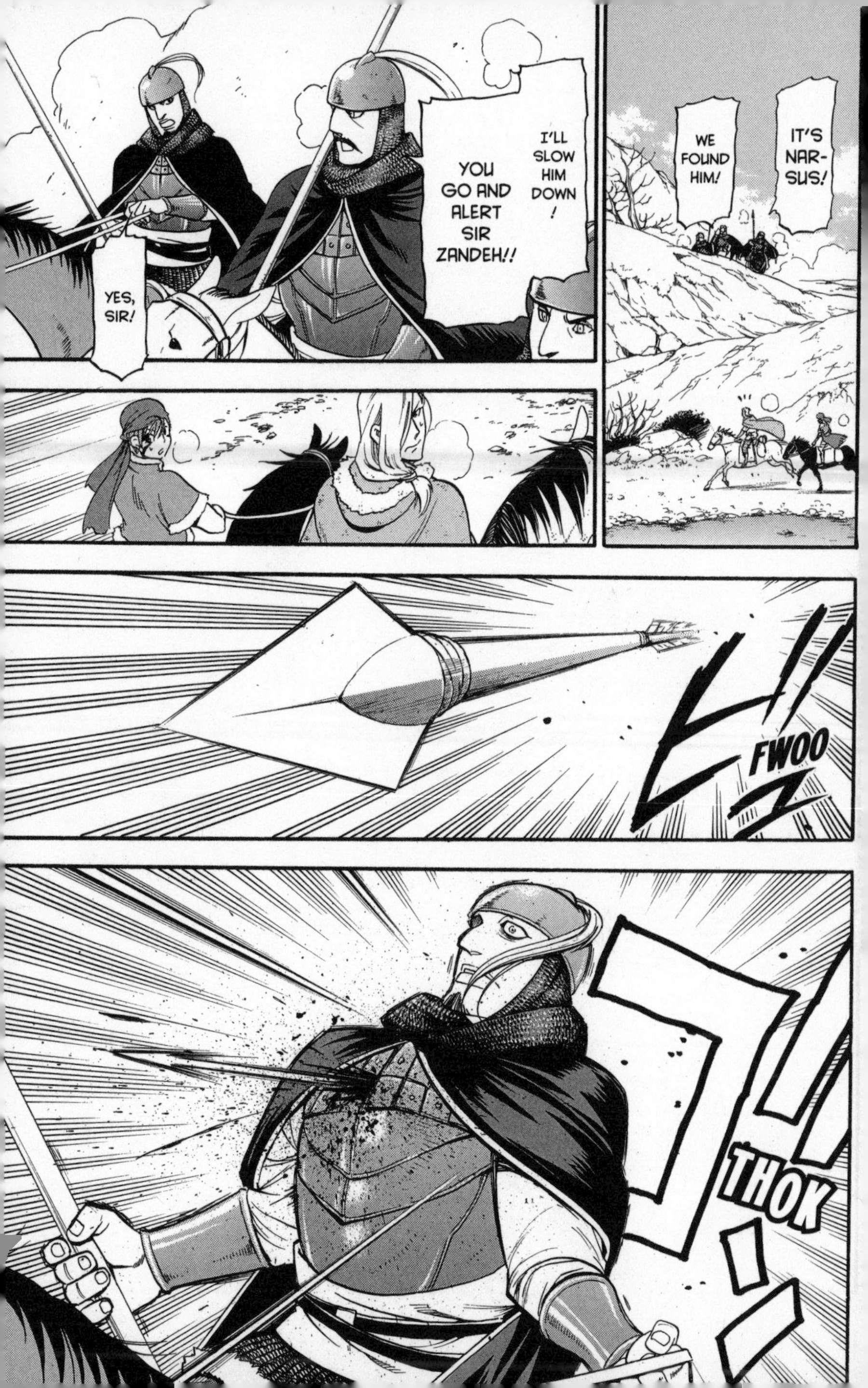
IT'S NAR-SUS!
WE FOUND HIM!
I'LL SLOW HIM DOWN!
YOU GO AND ALERT SIR ZANDEH!!
YES, SIR!
FWOO
THOK

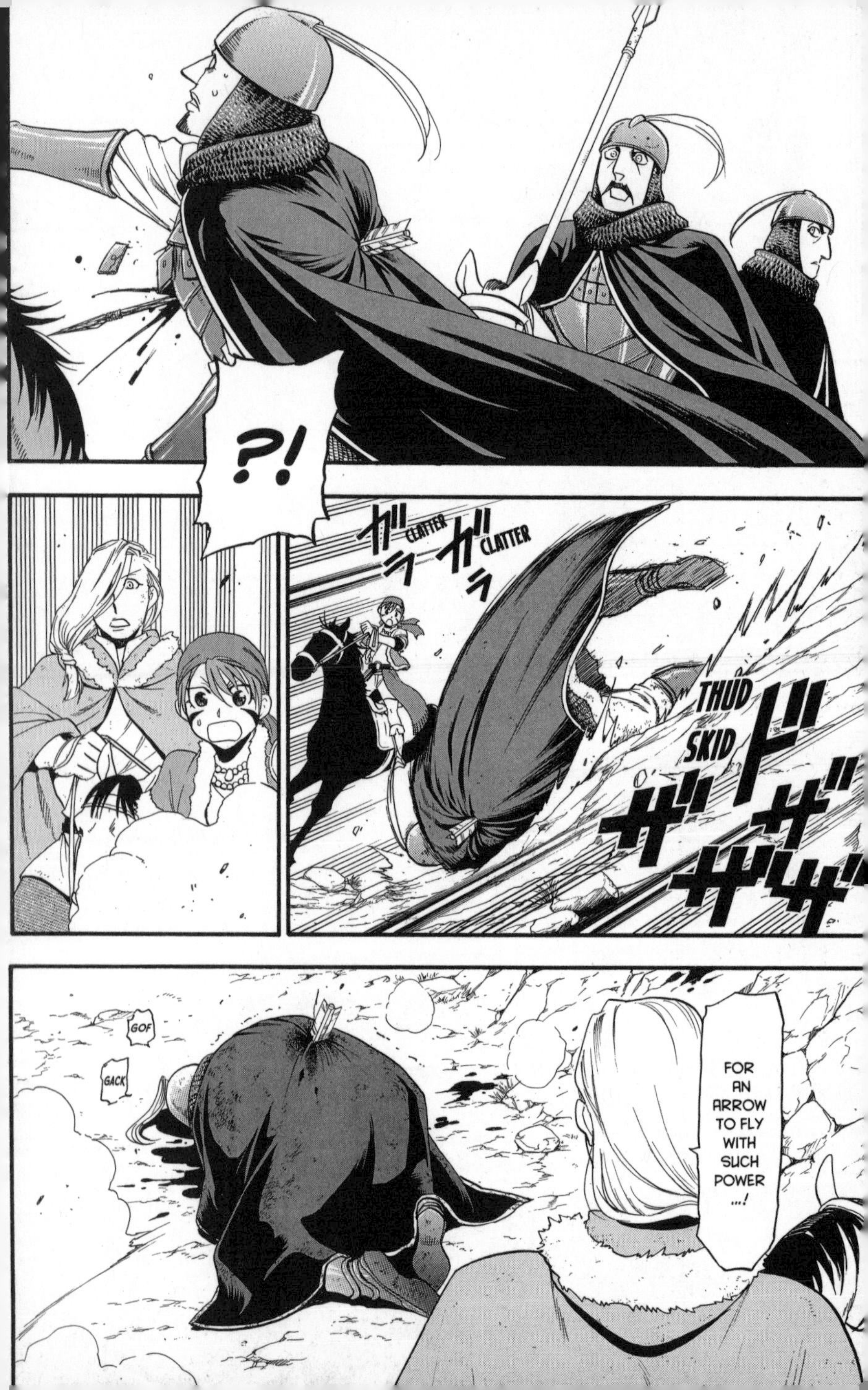
?!
CLATTER CLATTER
THUD SKID
FOR AN ARROW TO FLY WITH SUCH POWER ...!
GOF
GACK

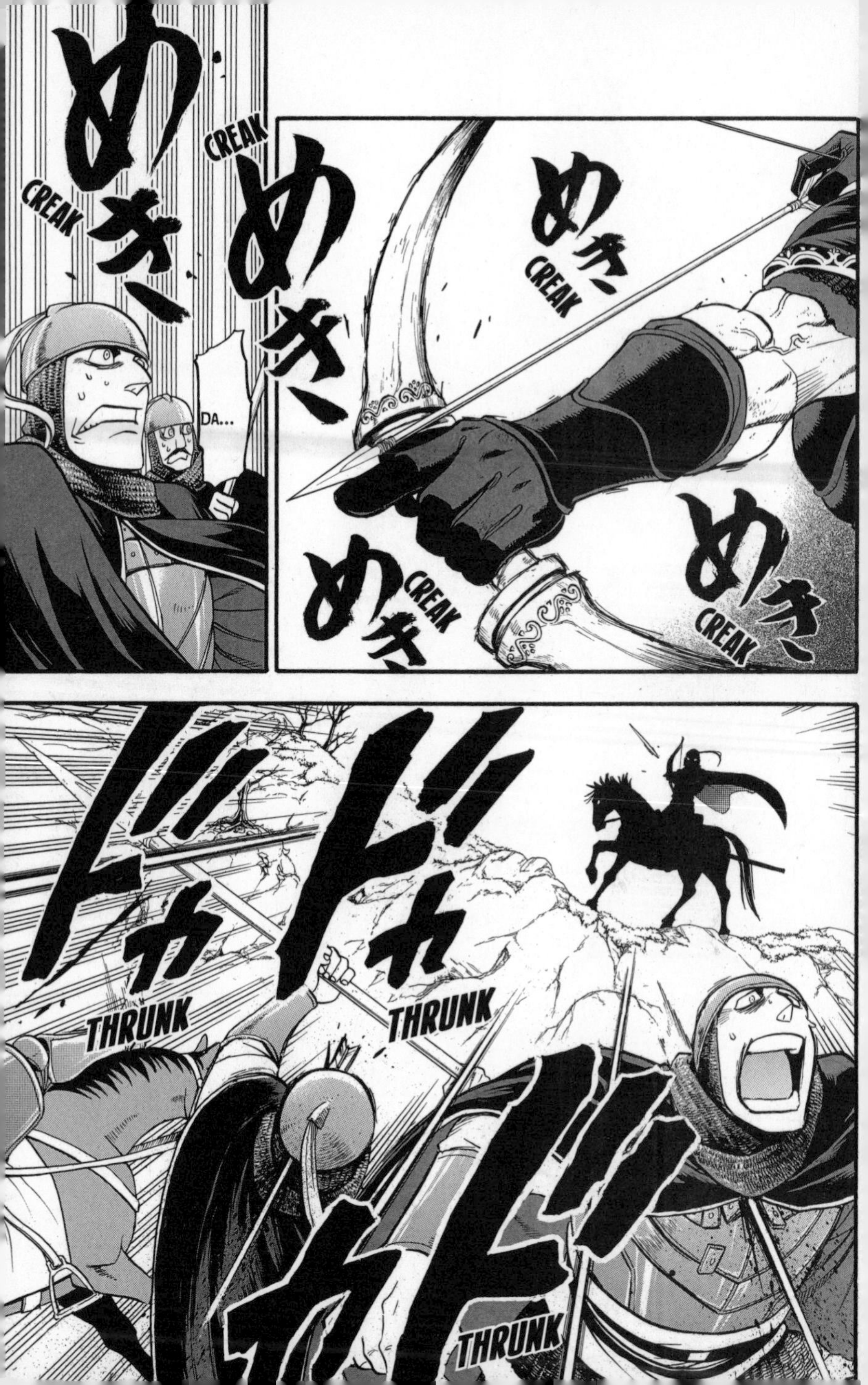
めき
CREAK
めき
CREAK
めき
CREAK
めき
CREAK
めき
CREAK
DA...
THRUNK
THRUNK
THRUNK

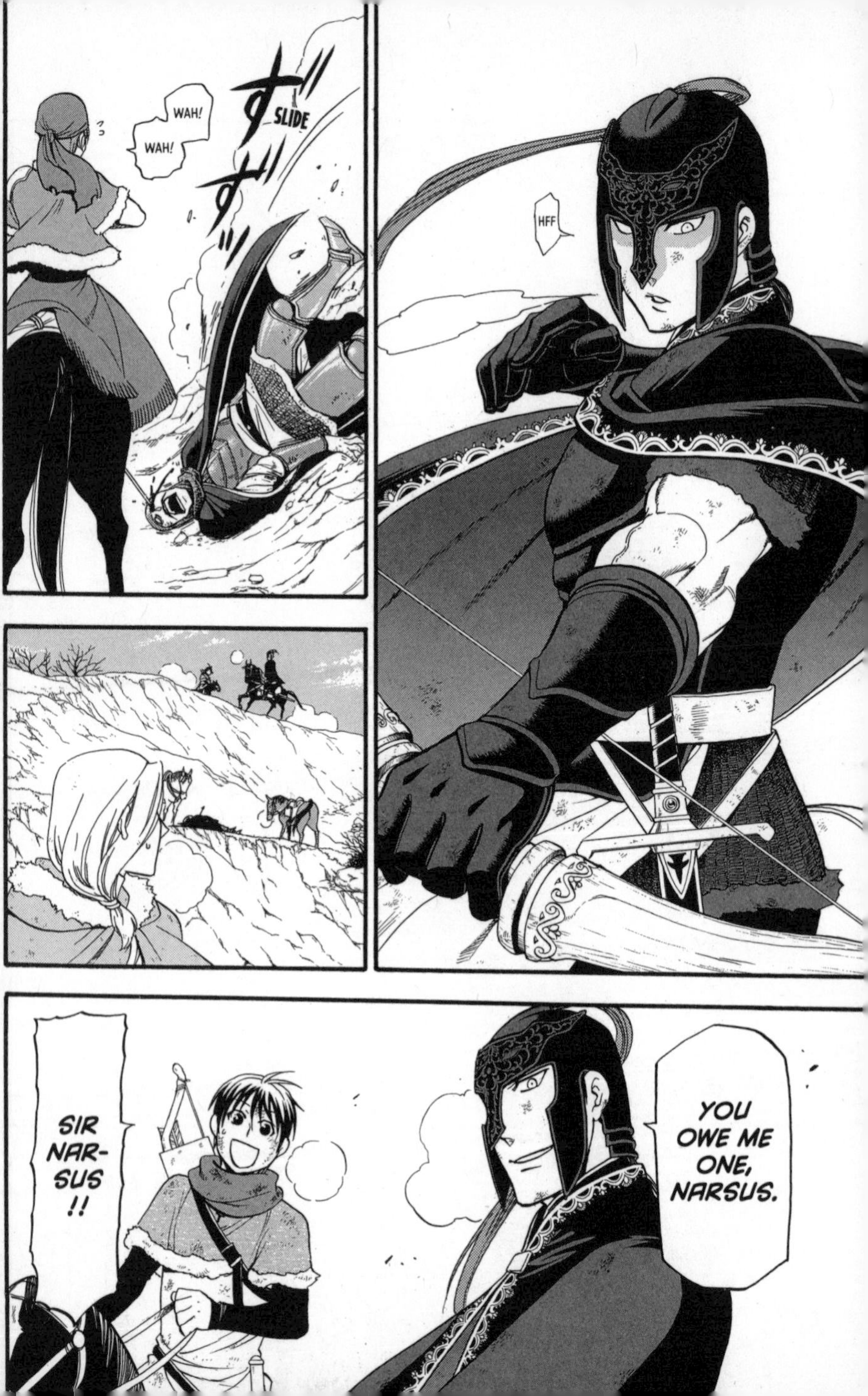
HFF
WAH!
WAH!
SLIDE
YOU OWE ME ONE, NARSUS.
SIR NARSUS!!

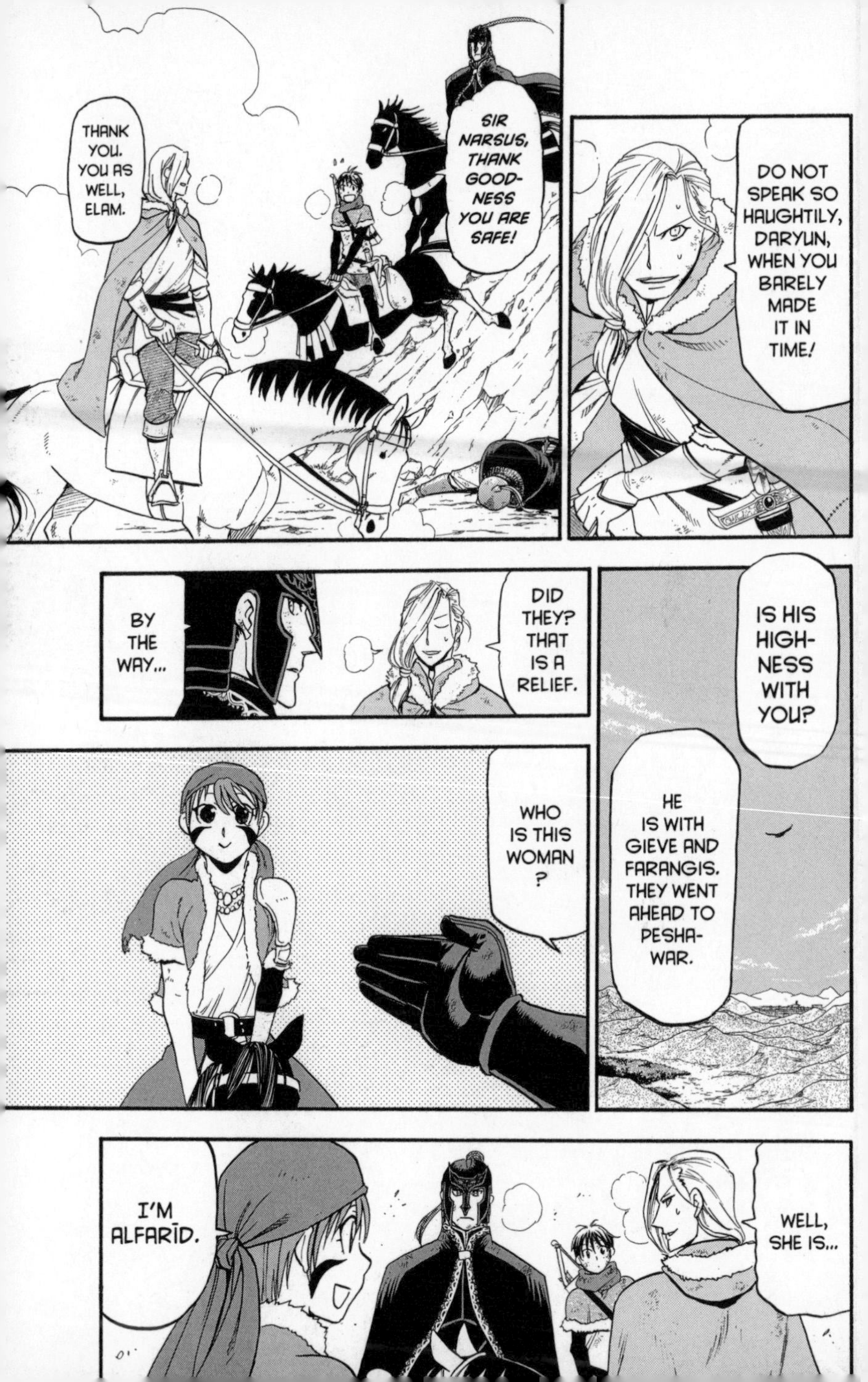
DO NOT SPEAK SO HAUGHTILY, DARYUN, WHEN YOU BARELY MADE IT IN TIME!
SIR NARSUS, THANK GOODNESS YOU ARE SAFE!
THANK YOU. YOU AS WELL, ELAM.
IS HIS HIGHNESS WITH YOU?
HE IS WITH GIEVE AND FARANGIS. THEY WENT AHEAD TO PESHAWAR.
DID THEY? THAT IS A RELIEF.
BY THE WAY...
WHO IS THIS WOMAN?
WELL, SHE IS...
I'M ALFARĪD.

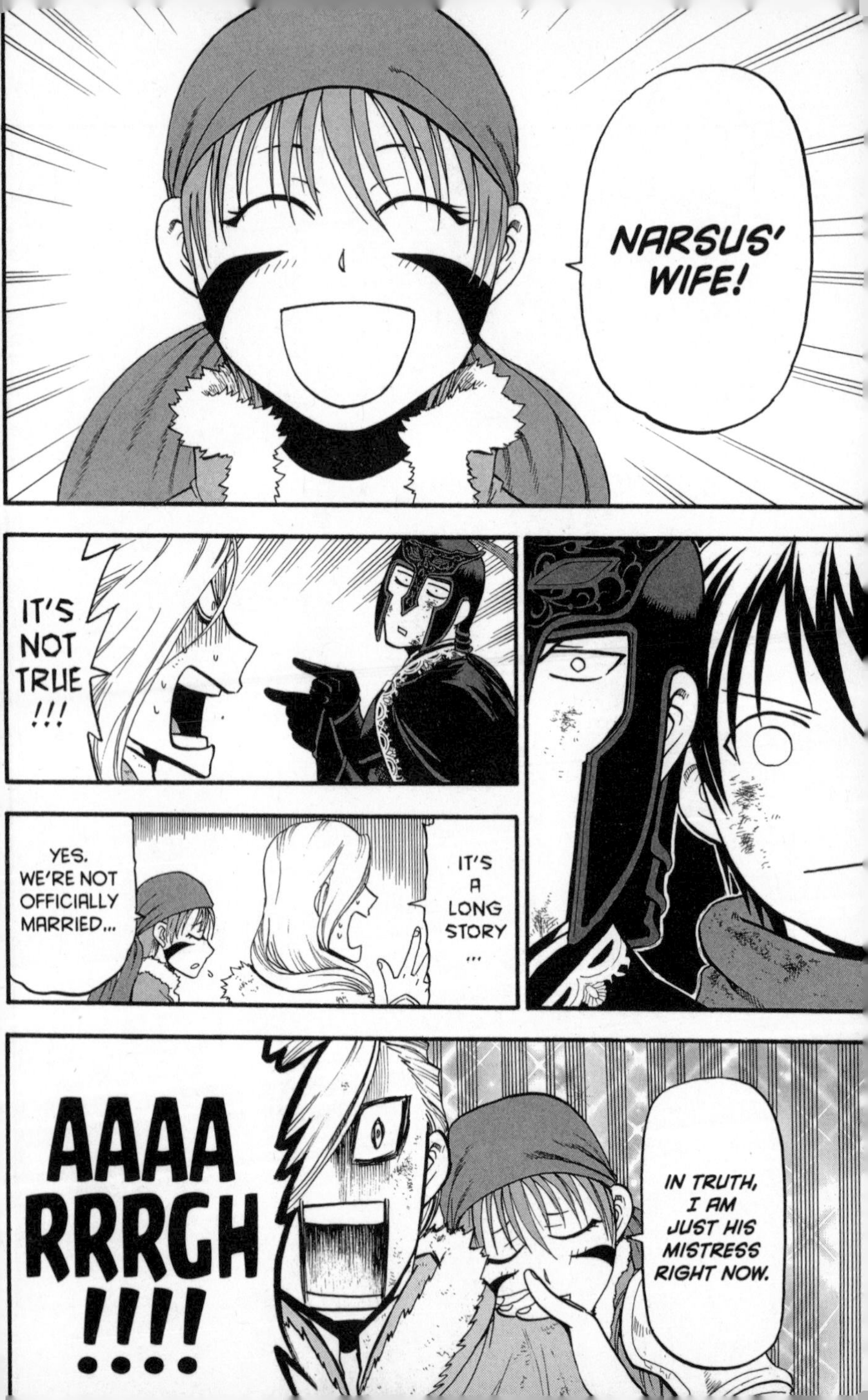
NARSUS' WIFE!
IT'S NOT TRUE!!!
IT'S A LONG STORY...
YES. WE'RE NOT OFFICIALLY MARRIED...
IN TRUTH, I AM JUST HIS MISTRESS RIGHT NOW.
AAAARRRGH!!!!

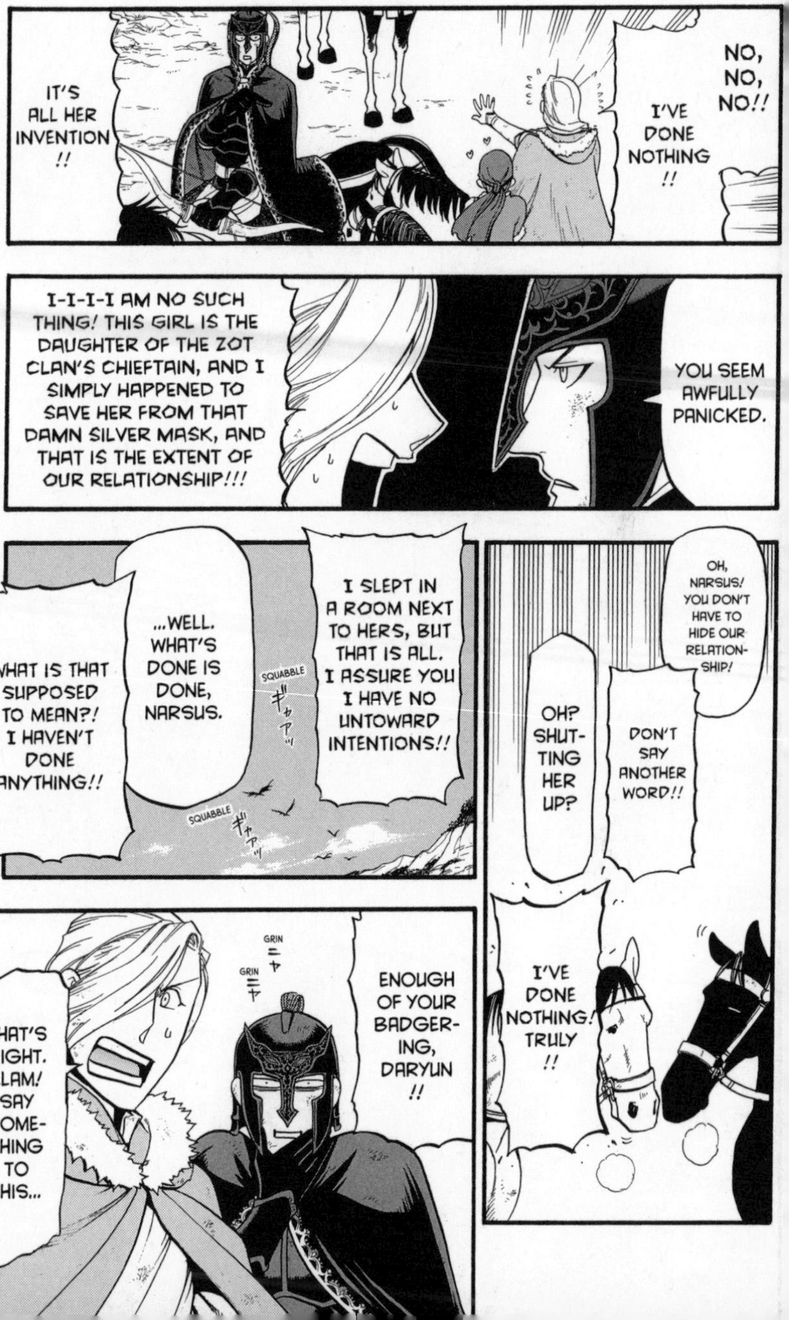
NO, NO, NO!!
I'VE DONE NOTHING!!
IT'S ALL HER INVENTION!!
YOU SEEM AWFULLY PANICKED.
I-I-I-I AM NO SUCH THING! THIS GIRL IS THE DAUGHTER OF THE ZOT CLAN'S CHIEFTAIN, AND I SIMPLY HAPPENED TO SAVE HER FROM THAT DAMN SILVER MASK, AND THAT IS THE EXTENT OF OUR RELATIONSHIP!!!
OH, NARSUS! YOU DON'T HAVE TO HIDE OUR RELATIONSHIP!
DON'T SAY ANOTHER WORD!!
OH? SHUTTING HER UP?
I SLEPT IN A ROOM NEXT TO HERS, BUT THAT IS ALL. I ASSURE YOU I HAVE NO UNTOWARD INTENTIONS!!
SQUABBLE
...WELL. WHAT'S DONE IS DONE, NARSUS.
WHAT IS THAT SUPPOSED TO MEAN?! I HAVEN'T DONE ANYTHING!!
SQUABBLE
I'VE DONE NOTHING! TRULY!!
ENOUGH OF YOUR BADGERING, DARYUN!!
GRIN
GRIN
THAT'S RIGHT. ELAM! SAY SOMETHING TO THIS...

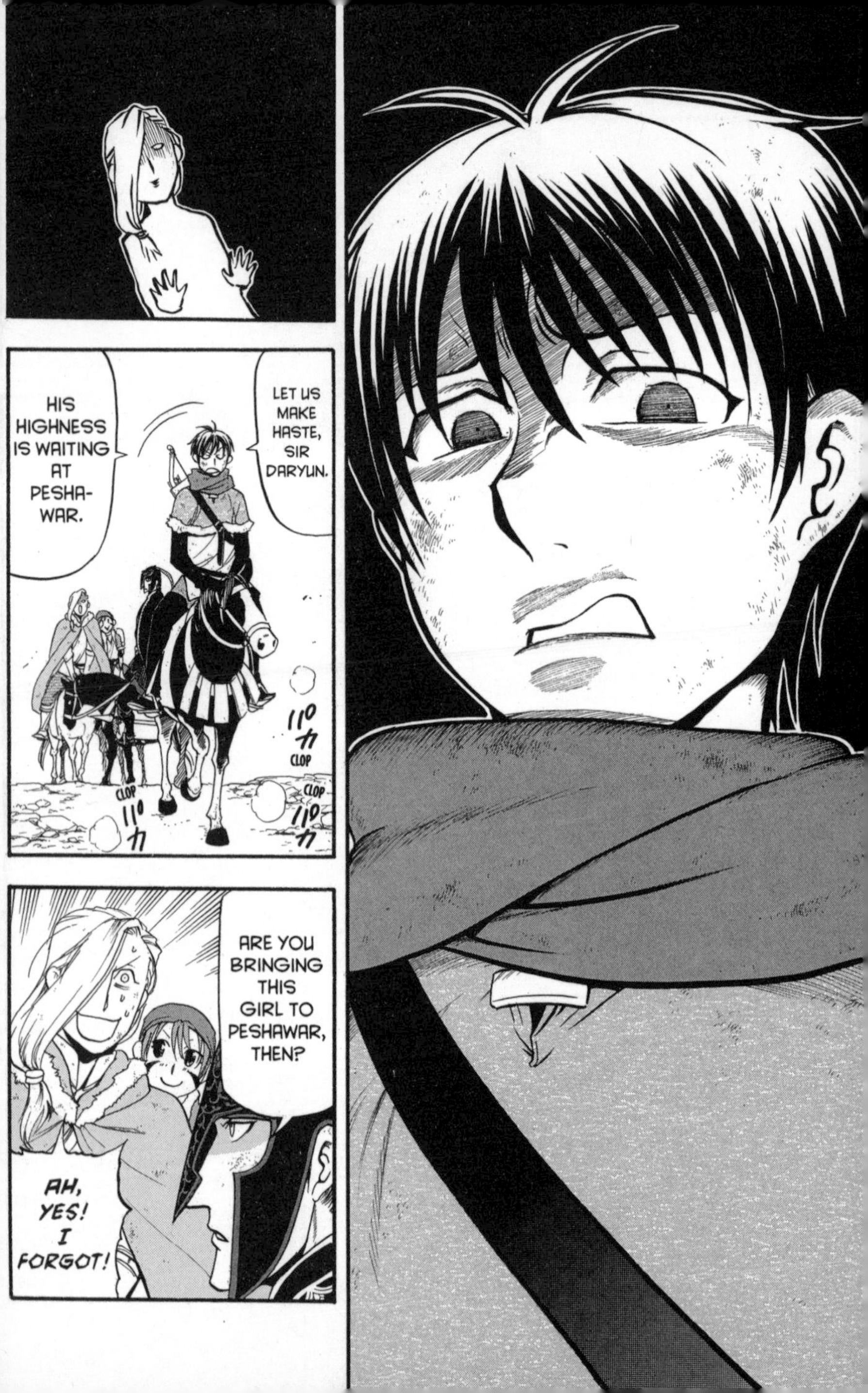
LET US MAKE HASTE, SIR DARYUN.
HIS HIGHNESS IS WAITING AT PESHAWAR.
CLOP
CLOP
CLOP
ARE YOU BRINGING THIS GIRL TO PESHAWAR, THEN?
AH, YES! I FORGOT!

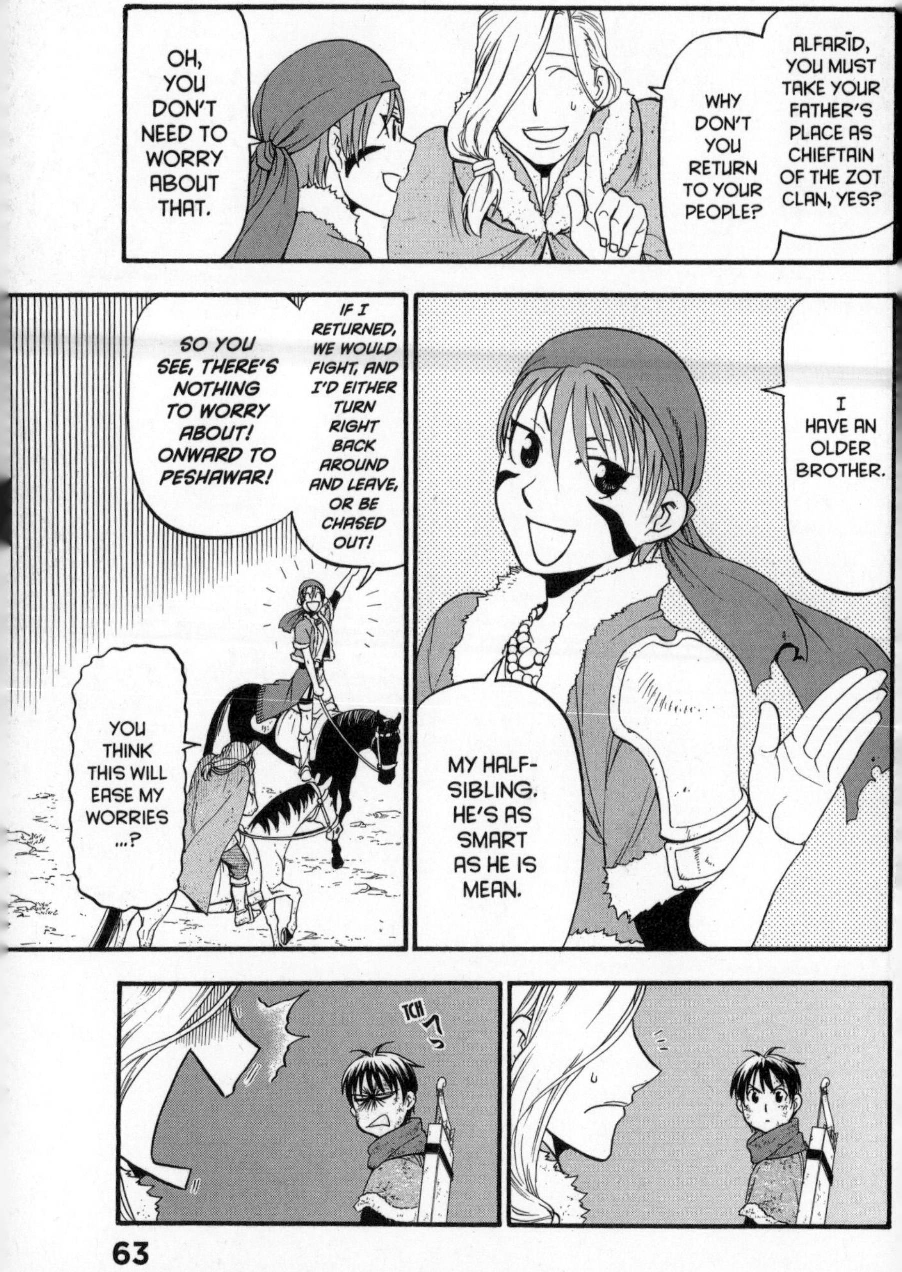
ALFARĪD, YOU MUST TAKE YOUR FATHER'S PLACE AS CHIEFTAIN OF THE ZOT CLAN, YES?
WHY DON'T YOU RETURN TO YOUR PEOPLE?
OH, YOU DON'T NEED TO WORRY ABOUT THAT.
I HAVE AN OLDER BROTHER.
MY HALF-SIBLING. HE'S AS SMART AS HE IS MEAN.
IF I RETURNED, WE WOULD FIGHT, AND I'D EITHER TURN RIGHT BACK AROUND AND LEAVE, OR BE CHASED OUT!
SO YOU SEE, THERE'S NOTHING TO WORRY ABOUT! ONWARD TO PESHAWAR!
YOU THINK THIS WILL EASE MY WORRIES ...?
TCH

THE HEROIC LEGEND OF
ARSLAN

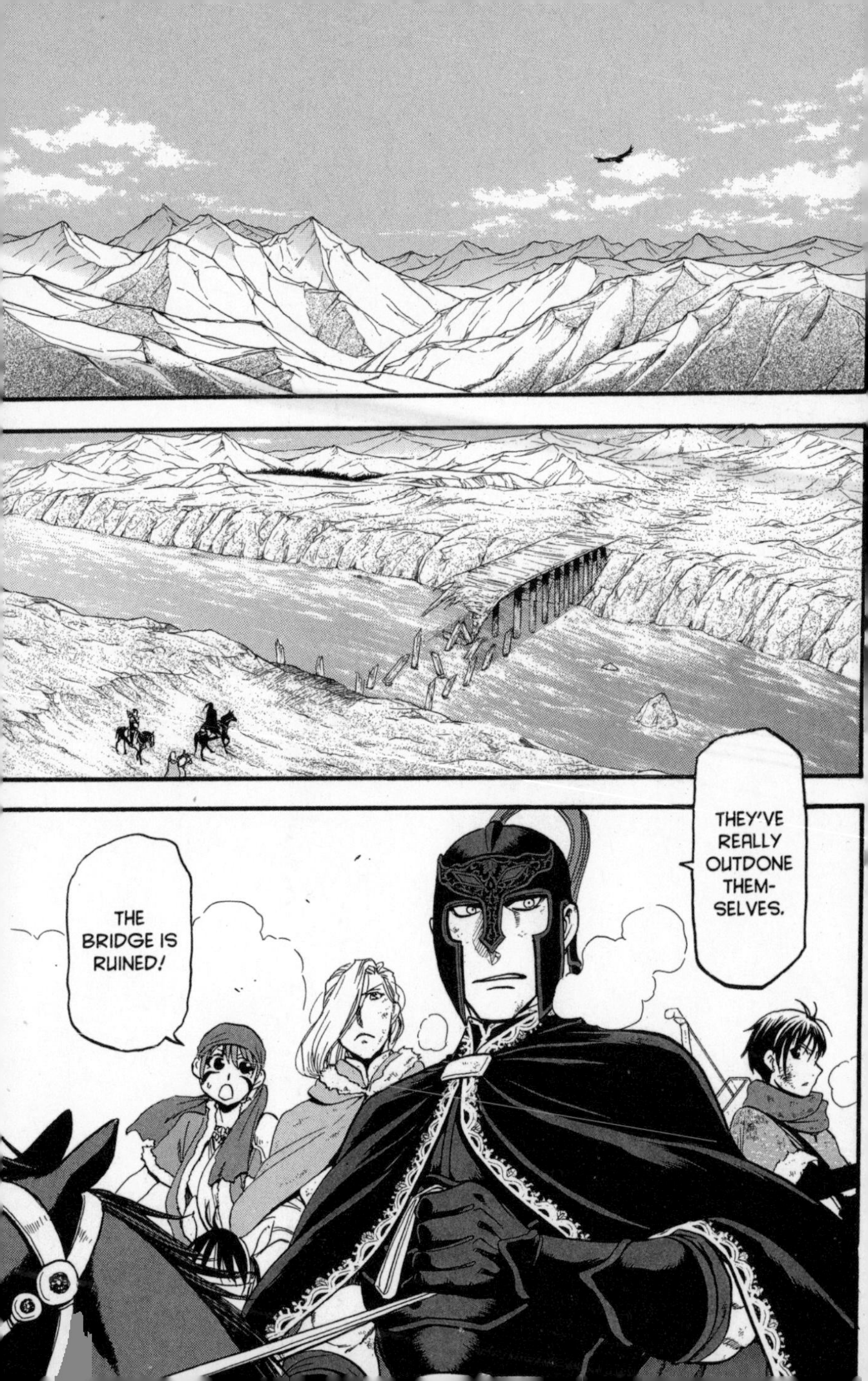
THEY'VE REALLY OUTDONE THEM-SELVES.
THE BRIDGE IS RUINED!

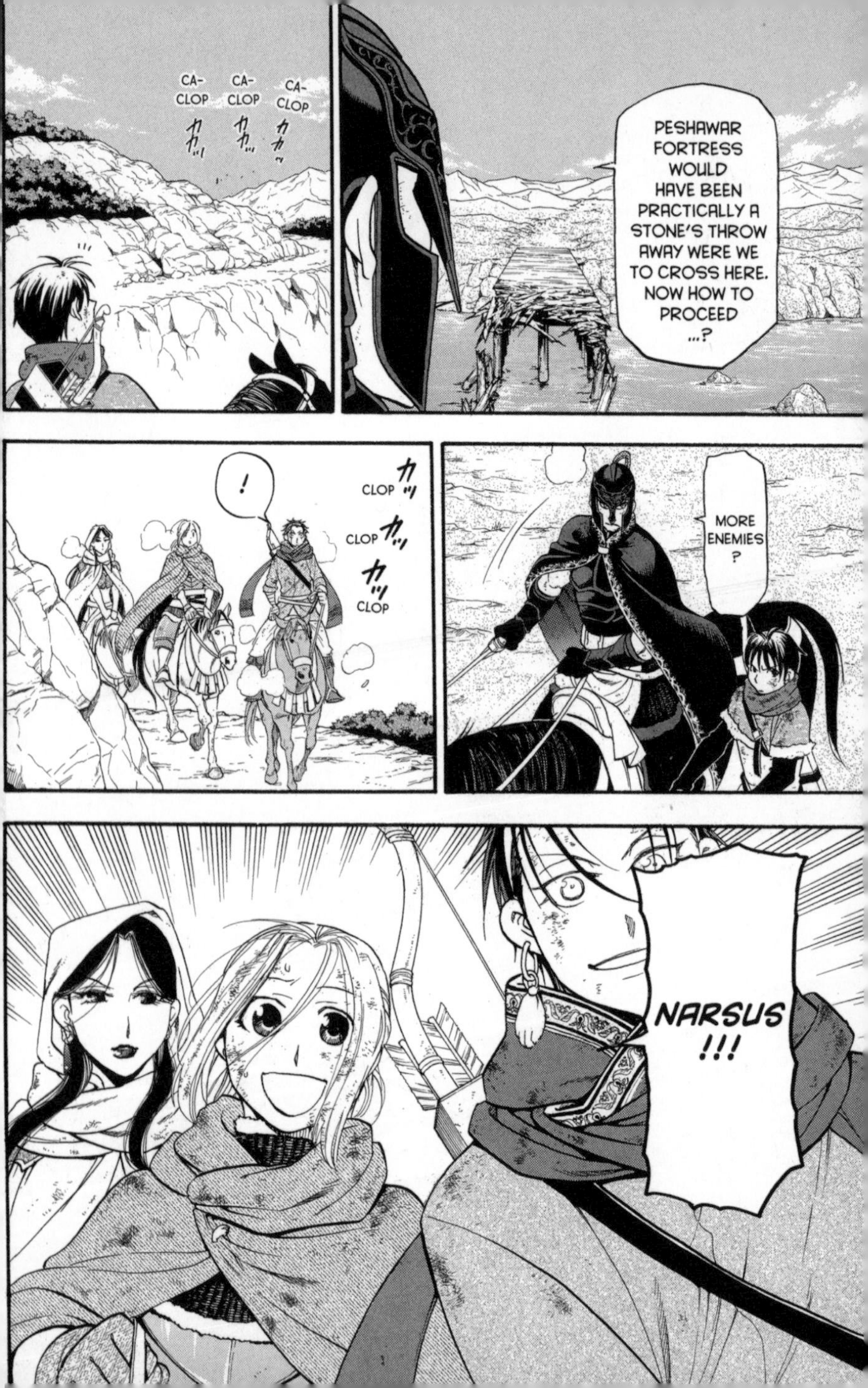
PESHAWAR FORTRESS WOULD HAVE BEEN PRACTICALLY A STONE'S THROW AWAY WERE WE TO CROSS HERE. NOW HOW TO PROCEED ...?
CA-CLOP
CA-CLOP
CA-CLOP
MORE ENEMIES ?
CLOP
CLOP
CLOP
!
NARSUS !!!

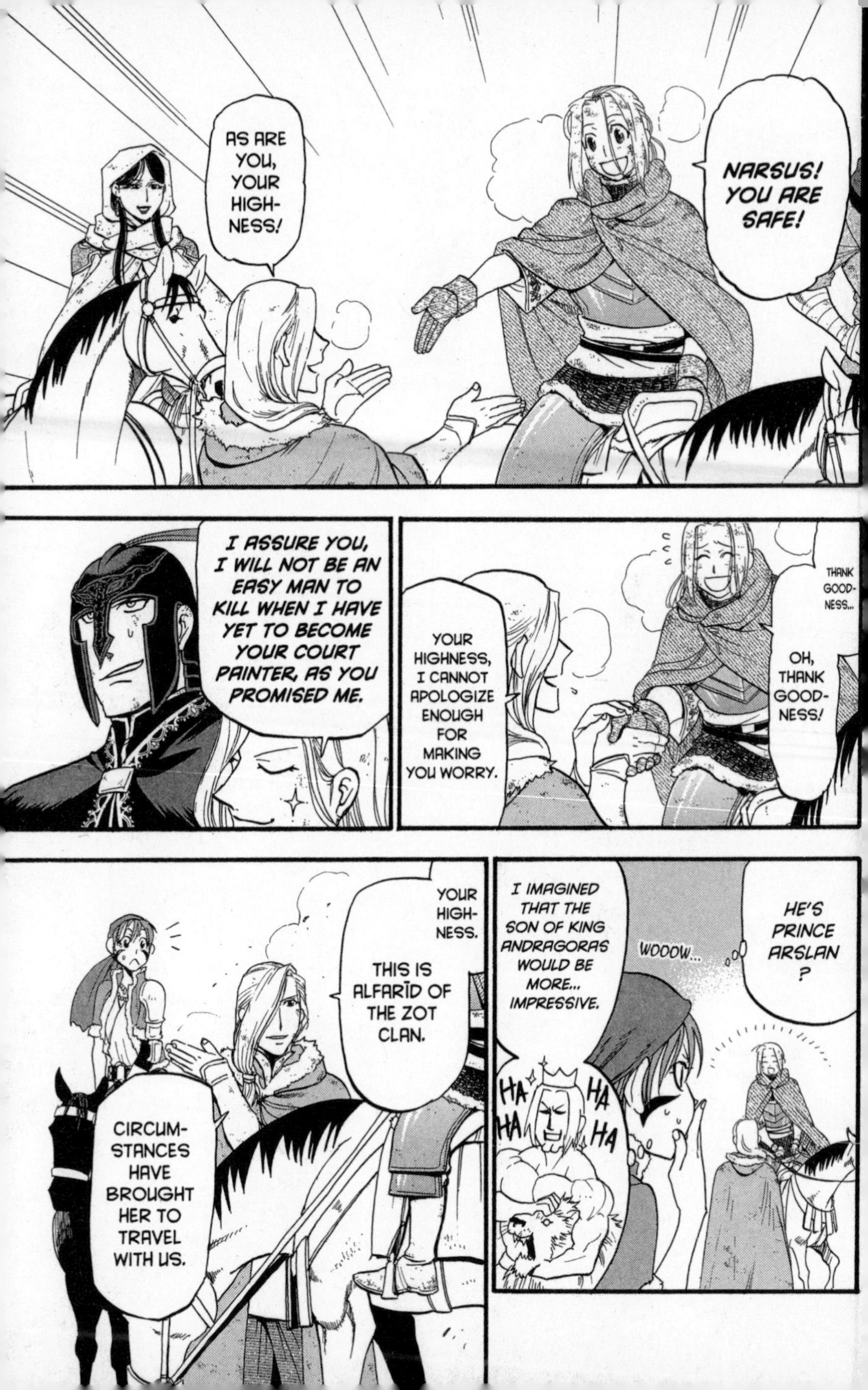
NARSUS! YOU ARE SAFE!
AS ARE YOU, YOUR HIGHNESS!
THANK GOODNESS...
OH, THANK GOODNESS!
YOUR HIGHNESS, I CANNOT APOLOGIZE ENOUGH FOR MAKING YOU WORRY.
I ASSURE YOU, I WILL NOT BE AN EASY MAN TO KILL WHEN I HAVE YET TO BECOME YOUR COURT PAINTER, AS YOU PROMISED ME.
HE'S PRINCE ARSLAN?
WOOOW...
I IMAGINED THAT THE SON OF KING ANDRAGORAS WOULD BE MORE... IMPRESSIVE.
HA HA HA HA
YOUR HIGHNESS.
THIS IS ALFARĪD OF THE ZOT CLAN.
CIRCUM-STANCES HAVE BROUGHT HER TO TRAVEL WITH US.

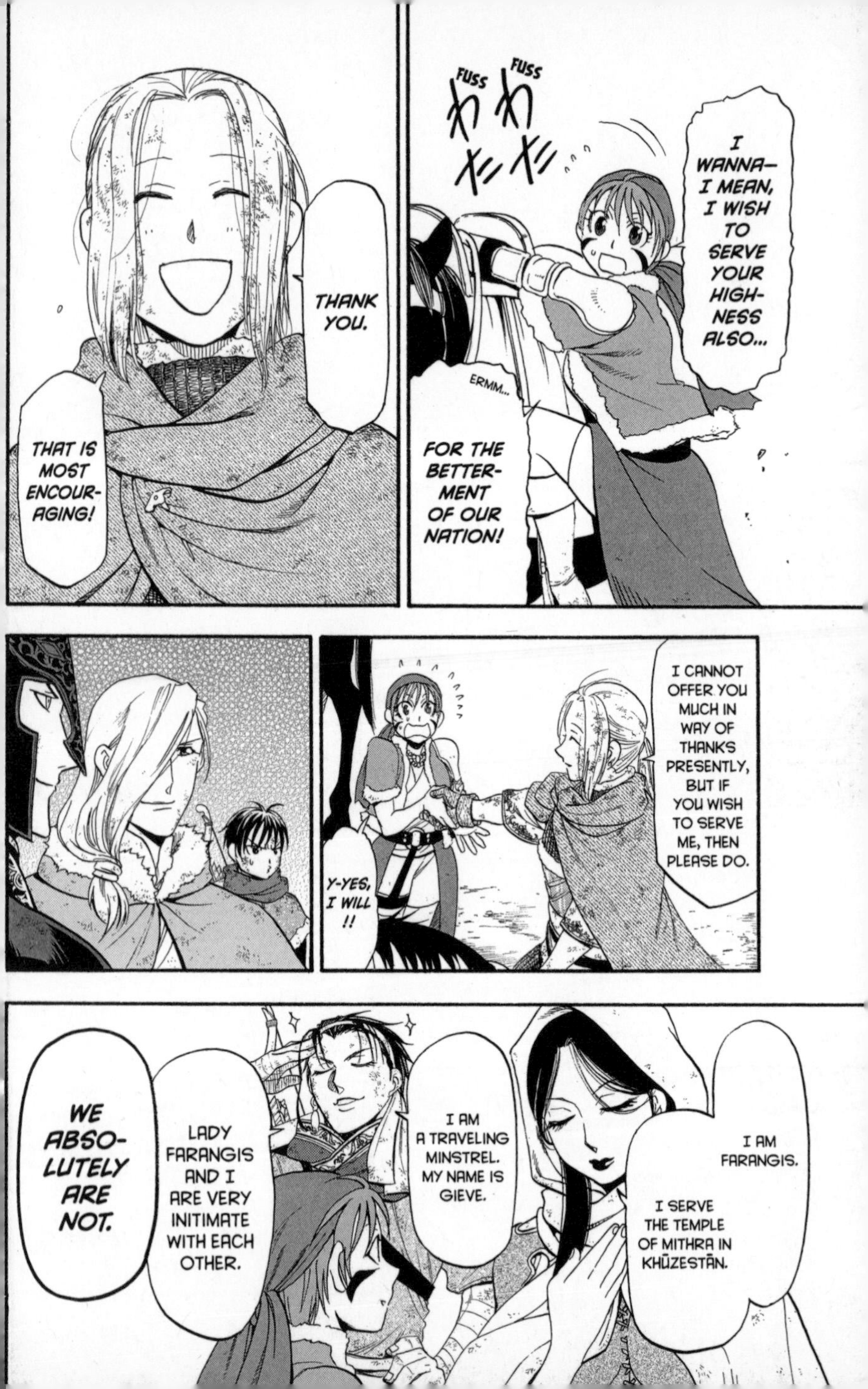
FUSS FUSS
わたわた
I WANNA— I MEAN, I WISH TO SERVE YOUR HIGHNESS ALSO...
ERMM...
FOR THE BETTERMENT OF OUR NATION!
THANK YOU.
THAT IS MOST ENCOURAGING!
I CANNOT OFFER YOU MUCH IN WAY OF THANKS PRESENTLY, BUT IF YOU WISH TO SERVE ME, THEN PLEASE DO.
Y-YES, I WILL!!
I AM FARANGIS.
I SERVE THE TEMPLE OF MITHRA IN KHŪZESTĀN.
I AM A TRAVELING MINSTREL. MY NAME IS GIEVE.
LADY FARANGIS AND I ARE VERY INITIMATE WITH EACH OTHER.
WE ABSOLUTELY ARE NOT.

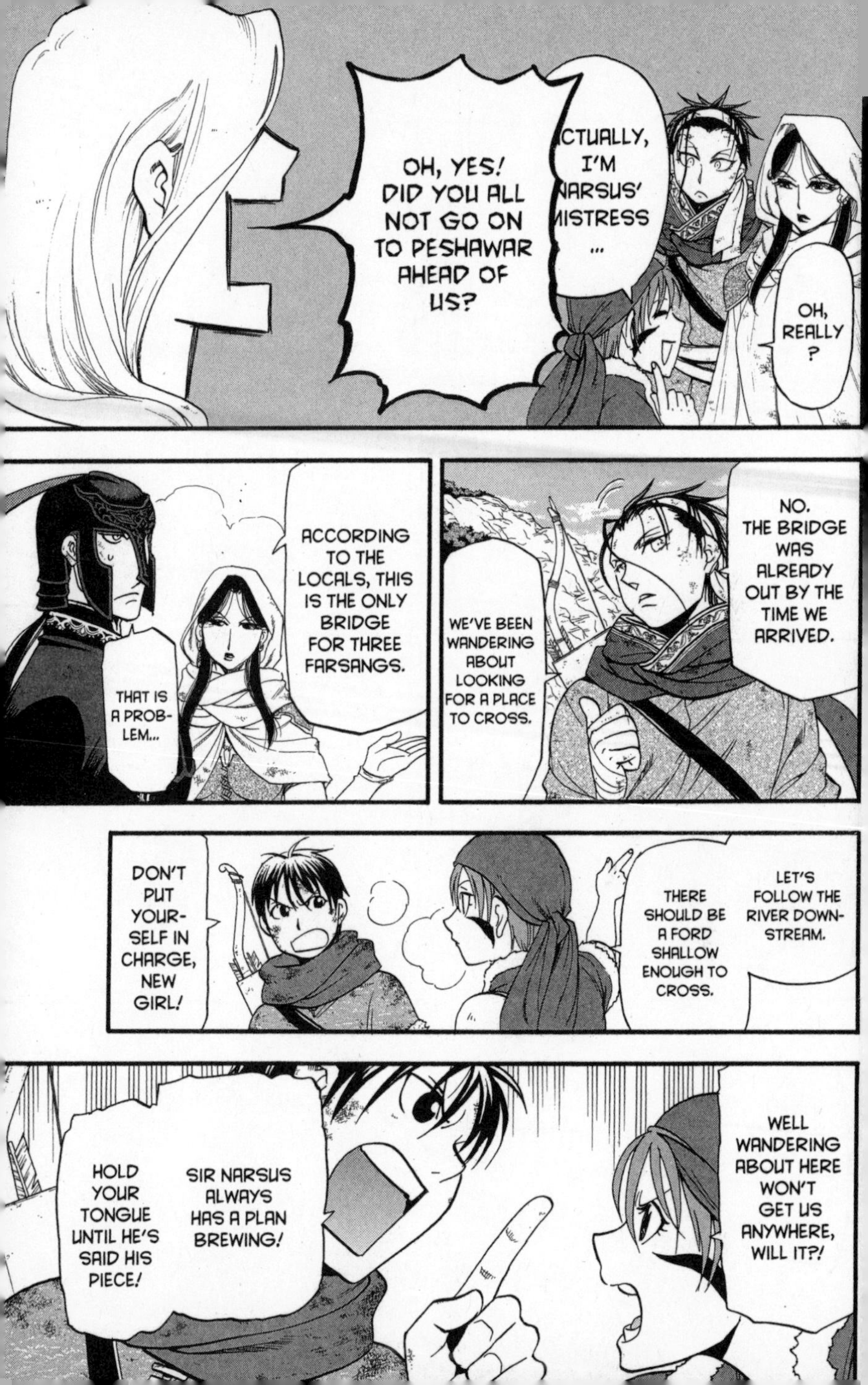
CTUALLY, I'M NARSUS' ISTRESS ...
OH, REALLY?
OH, YES! DID YOU ALL NOT GO ON TO PESHAWAR AHEAD OF US?
NO. THE BRIDGE WAS ALREADY OUT BY THE TIME WE ARRIVED.
WE'VE BEEN WANDERING ABOUT LOOKING FOR A PLACE TO CROSS.
ACCORDING TO THE LOCALS, THIS IS THE ONLY BRIDGE FOR THREE FARSANGS.
THAT IS A PROB-LEM...
LET'S FOLLOW THE RIVER DOWN-STREAM.
THERE SHOULD BE A FORD SHALLOW ENOUGH TO CROSS.
DON'T PUT YOUR-SELF IN CHARGE, NEW GIRL!
WELL WANDERING ABOUT HERE WON'T GET US ANYWHERE, WILL IT?!
SIR NARSUS ALWAYS HAS A PLAN BREWING!
HOLD YOUR TONGUE UNTIL HE'S SAID HIS PIECE!

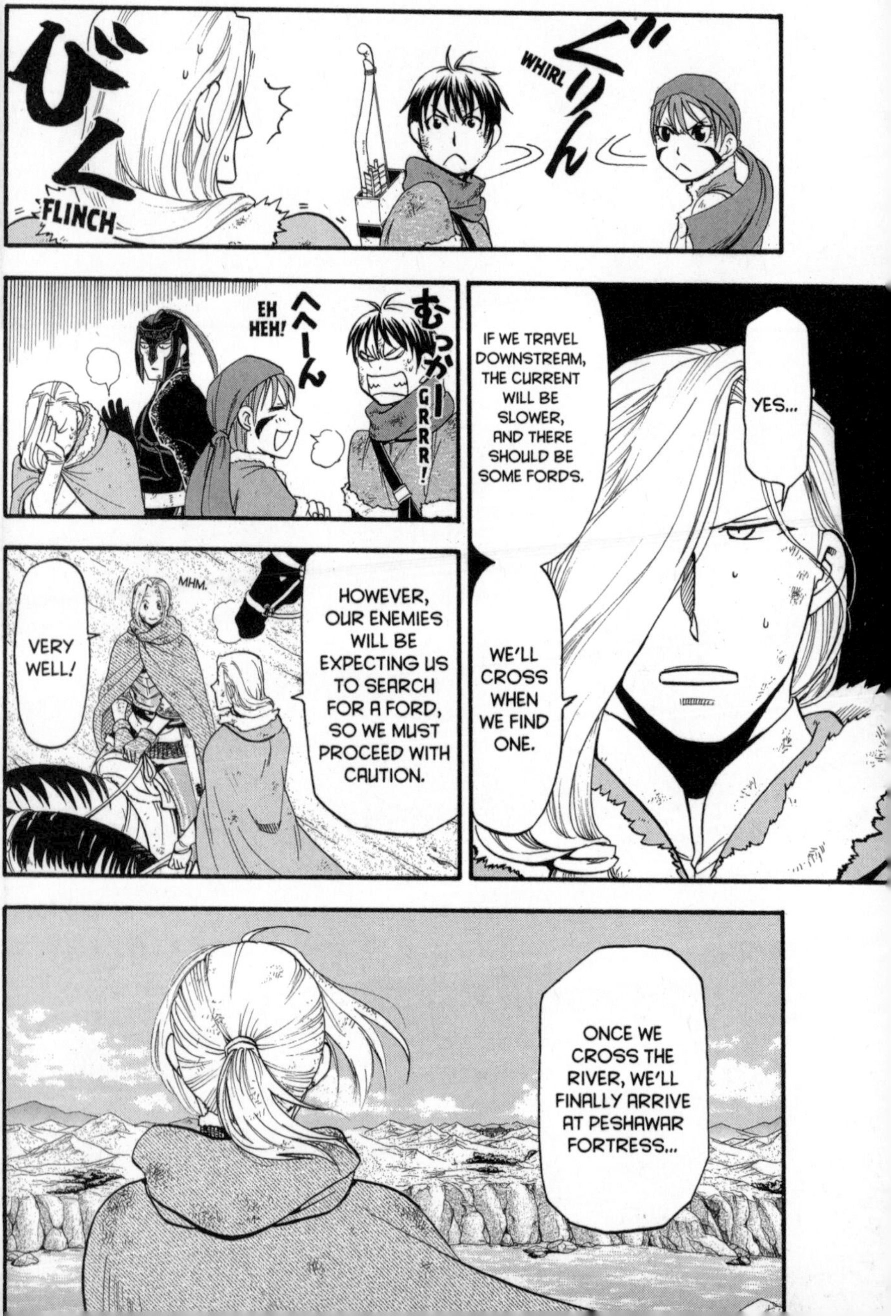
ぐりん
WHIRL
びく
FLINCH
IF WE TRAVEL DOWNSTREAM, THE CURRENT WILL BE SLOWER, AND THERE SHOULD BE SOME FORDS.
YES...
WE'LL CROSS WHEN WE FIND ONE.
むっかー
GRRR!
へへーん
EH HEH!
HOWEVER, OUR ENEMIES WILL BE EXPECTING US TO SEARCH FOR A FORD, SO WE MUST PROCEED WITH CAUTION.
MHM.
VERY WELL!
ONCE WE CROSS THE RIVER, WE'LL FINALLY ARRIVE AT PESHAWAR FORTRESS...

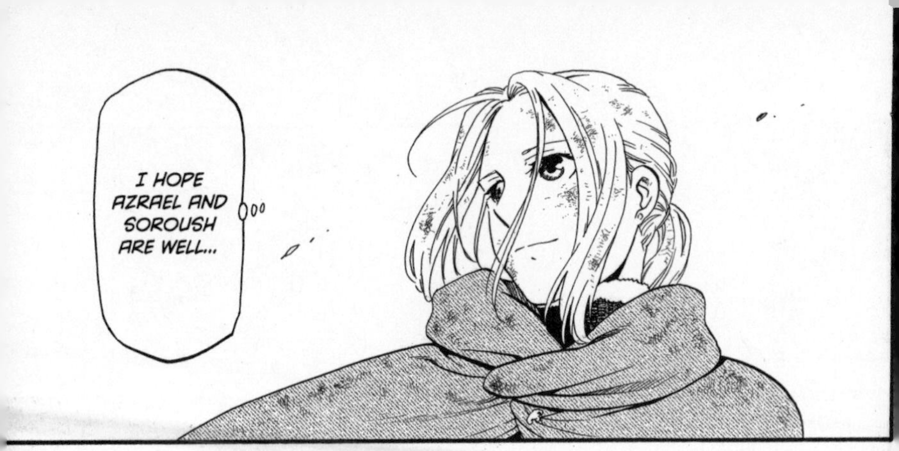
I HOPE AZRAEL AND SOROUSH ARE WELL...

Chapter 37: Fortress of Sandstone

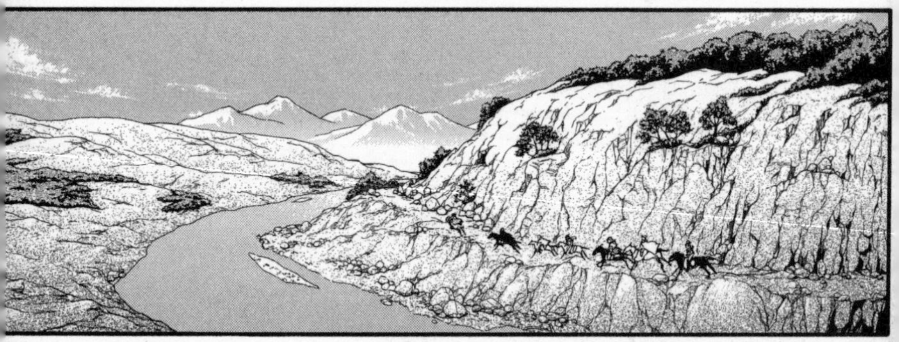

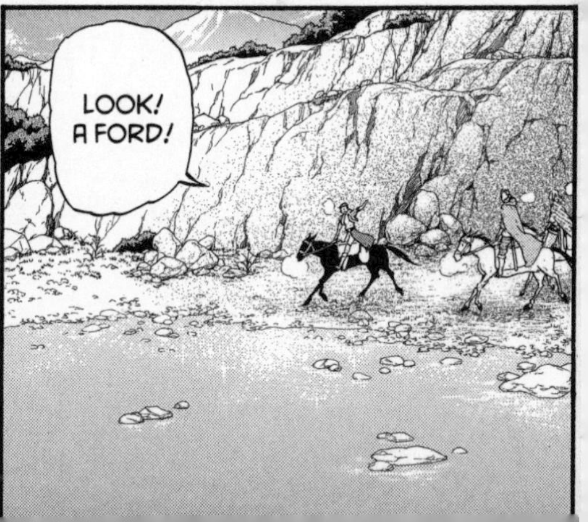
LOOK! A FORD!

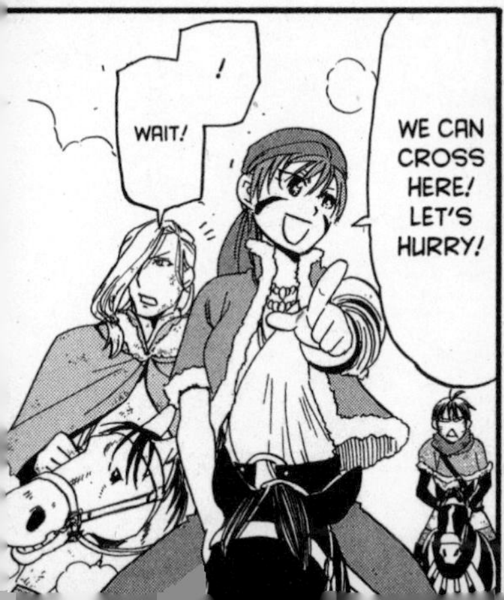
WE CAN CROSS HERE! LET'S HURRY!
!
WAIT!

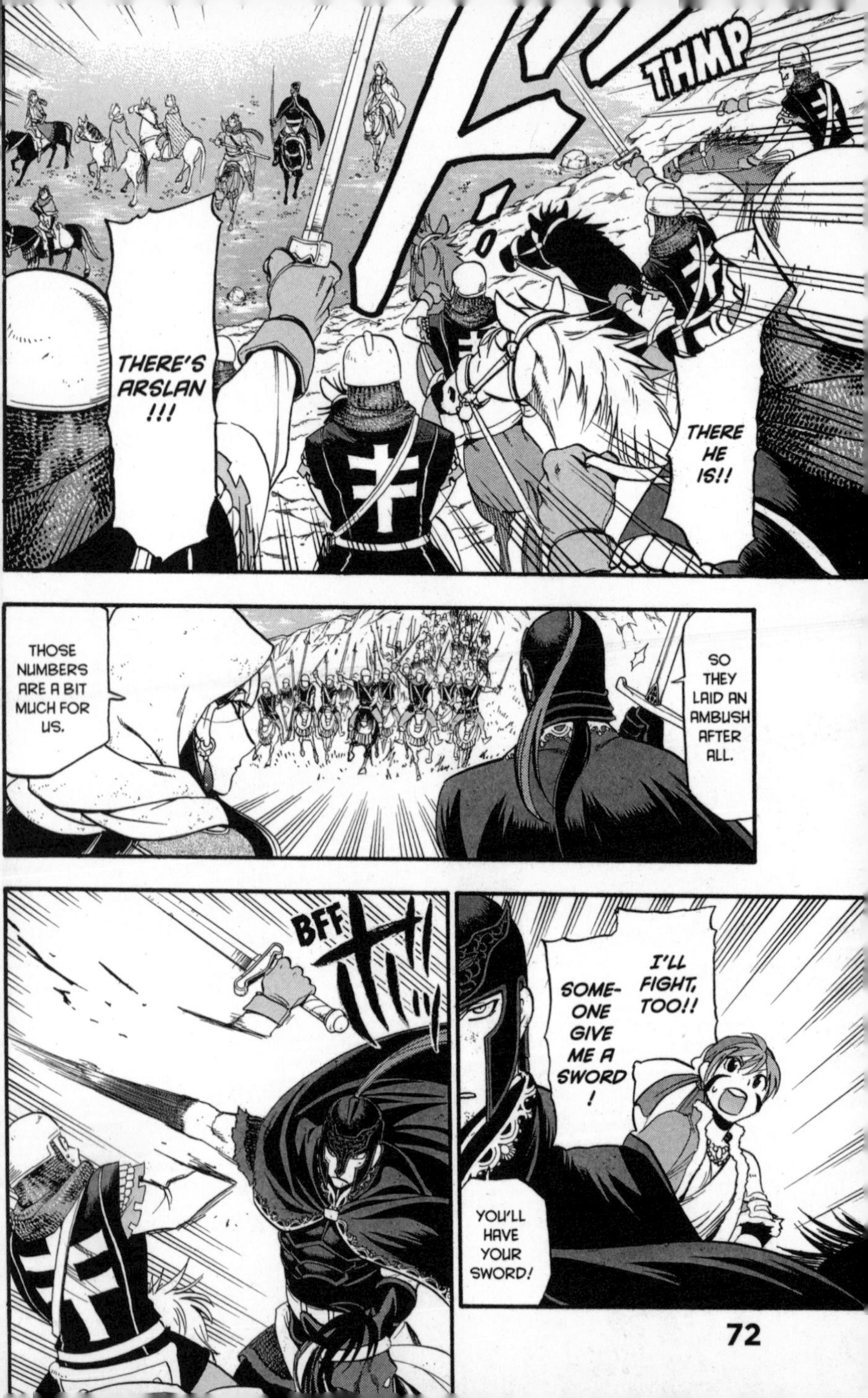
THMP
THERE HE IS!!
THERE'S ARSLAN!!!
SO THEY LAID AN AMBUSH AFTER ALL.
THOSE NUMBERS ARE A BIT MUCH FOR US.
I'LL FIGHT, TOO!!
SOME-ONE GIVE ME A SWORD!
YOU'LL HAVE YOUR SWORD!
BFF

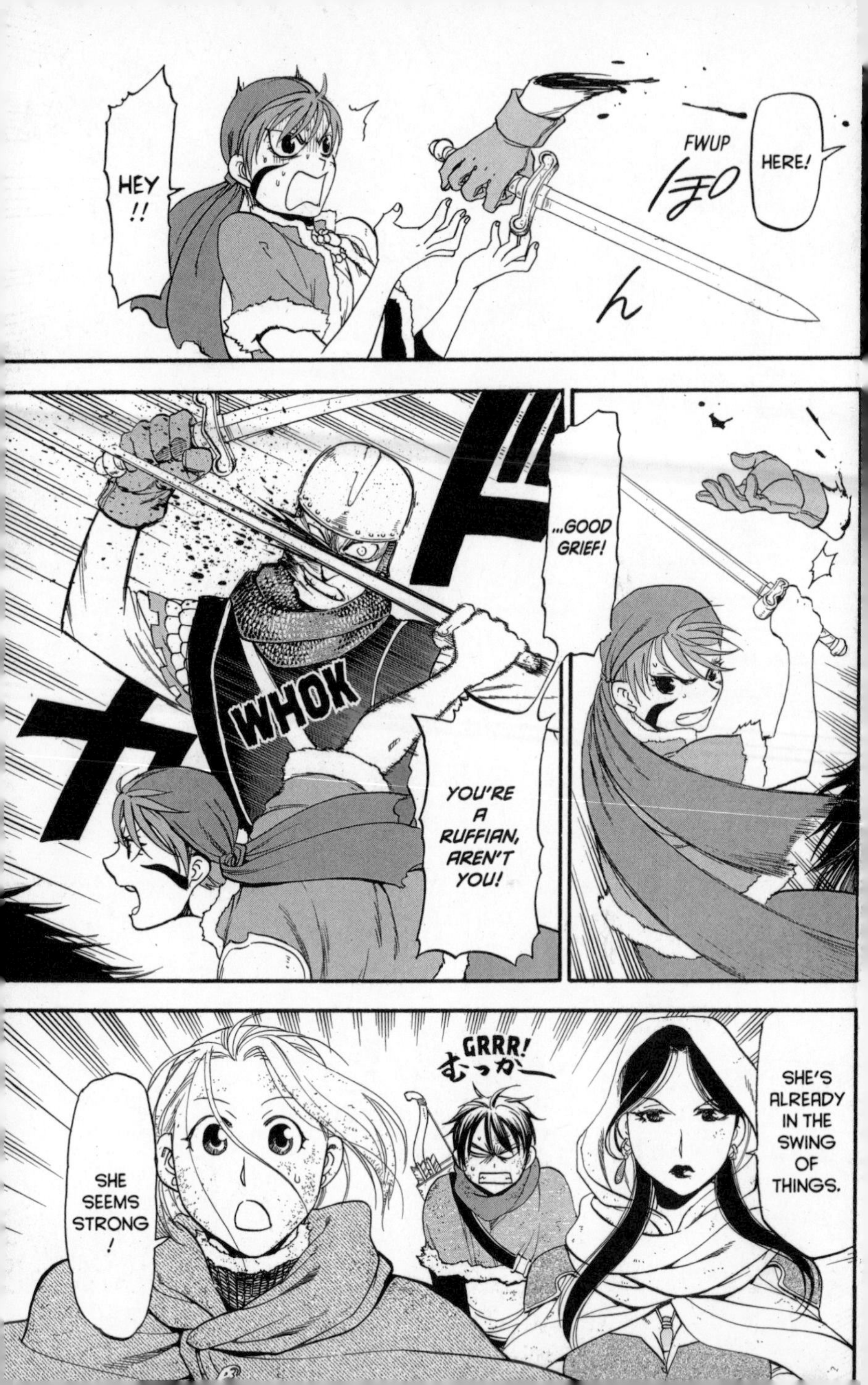
HERE!
FWUP
HEY!!
...GOOD GRIEF!
YOU'RE A RUFFIAN, AREN'T YOU!
WHOK
SHE'S ALREADY IN THE SWING OF THINGS.
GRRR!
むっかー
SHE SEEMS STRONG!

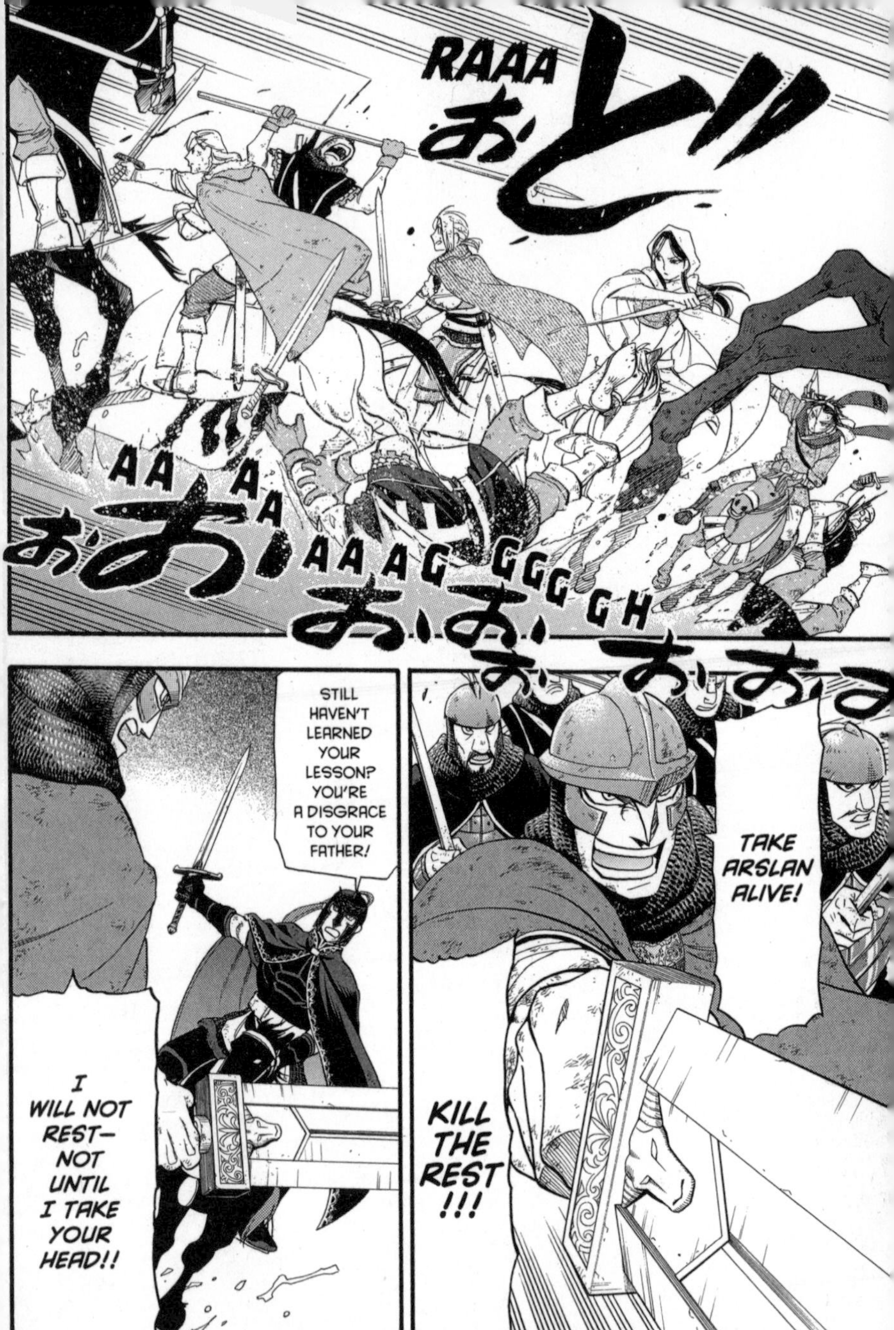
RAAA
AA A A AAAG GGGG GH
TAKE ARSLAN ALIVE!
KILL THE REST!!!
STILL HAVEN'T LEARNED YOUR LESSON? YOU'RE A DISGRACE TO YOUR FATHER!
I WILL NOT REST— NOT UNTIL I TAKE YOUR HEAD!!

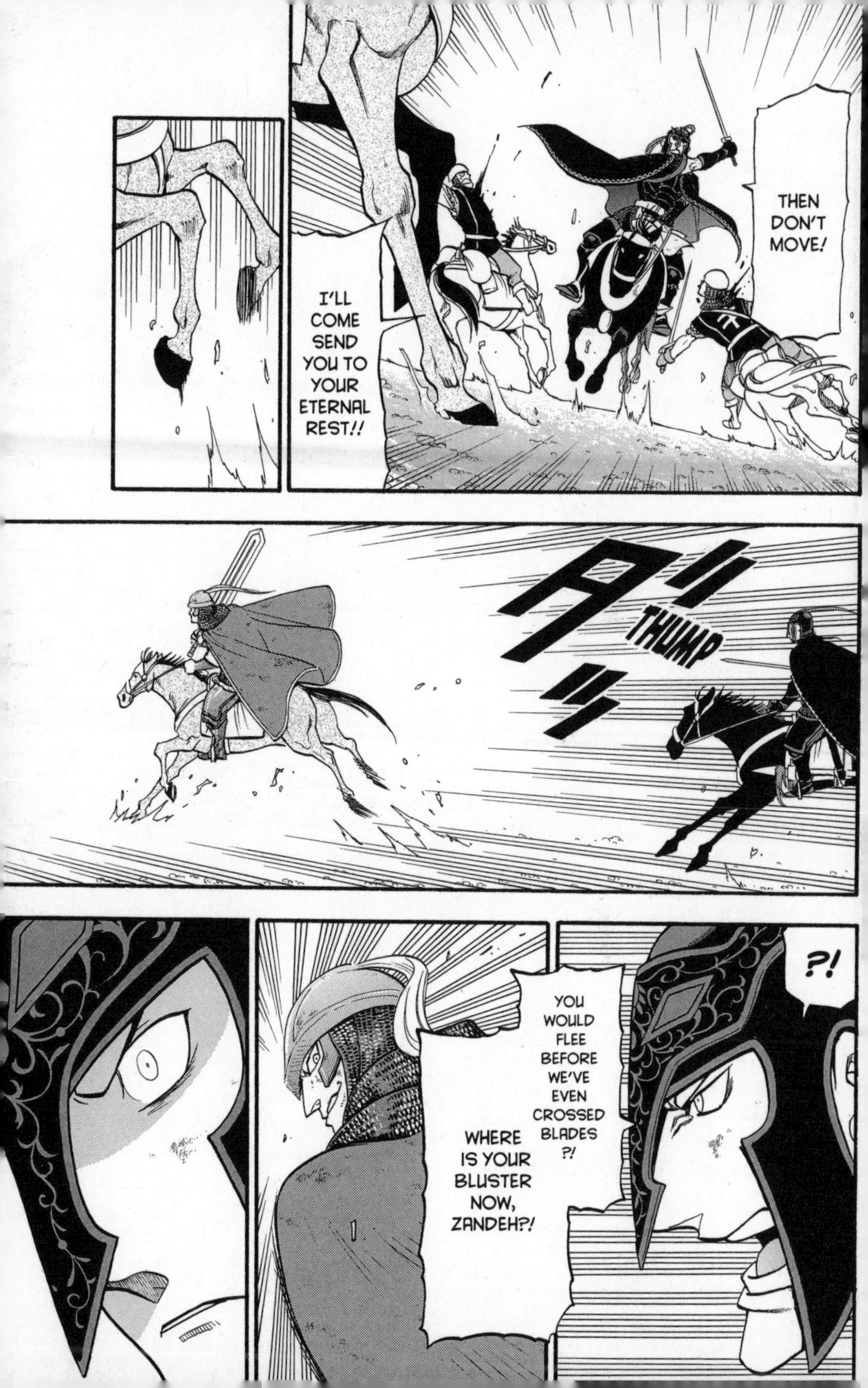
THEN DON'T MOVE!
I'LL COME SEND YOU TO YOUR ETERNAL REST!!
THUMP
?!
YOU WOULD FLEE BEFORE WE'VE EVEN CROSSED BLADES?!
WHERE IS YOUR BLUSTER NOW, ZANDEH?!

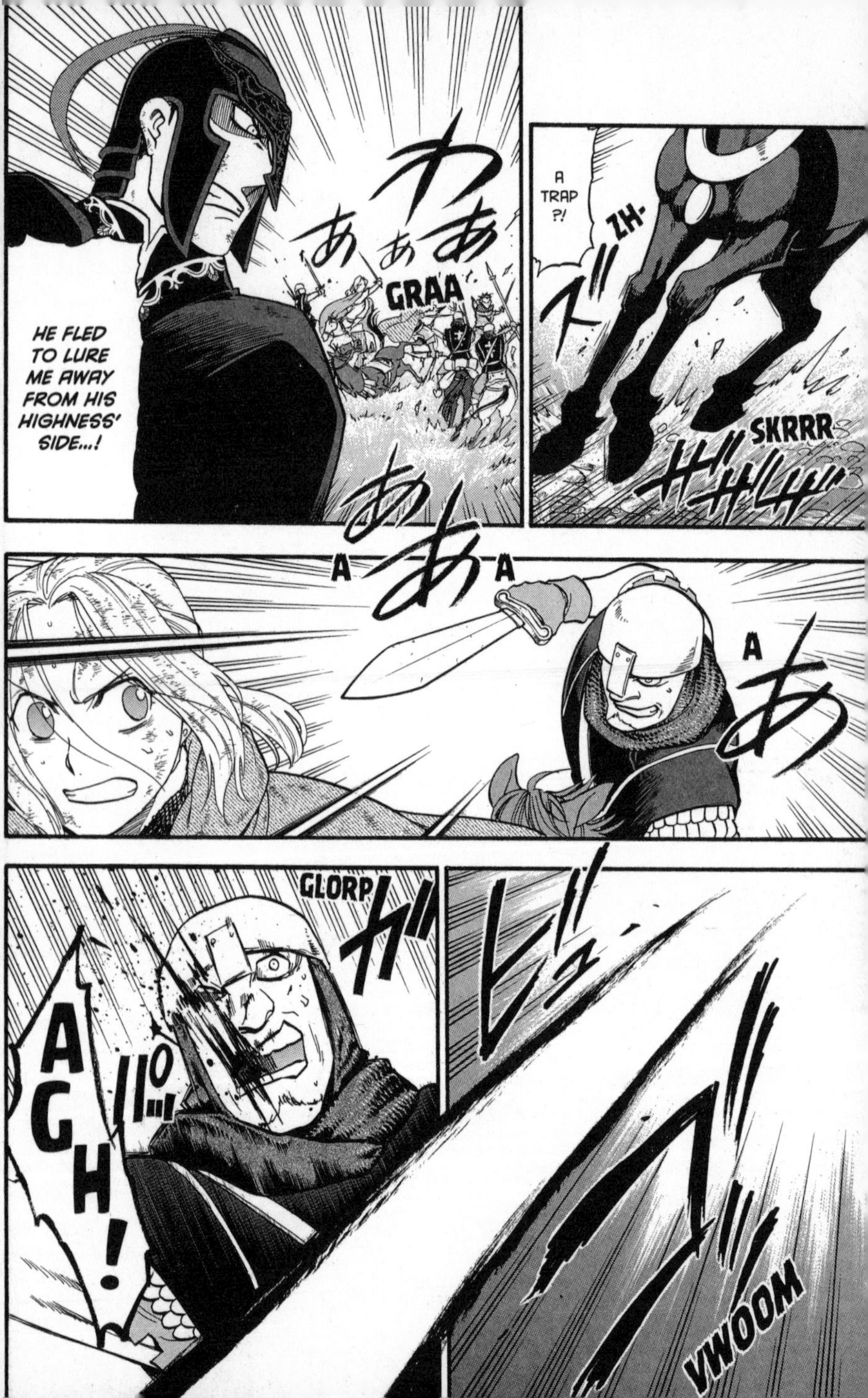
A TRAP ?!
ZH-
SKRRR
GRAA
HE FLED TO LURE ME AWAY FROM HIS HIGHNESS' SIDE...!
A
A
A
VWOOM
GLORP
AGH!

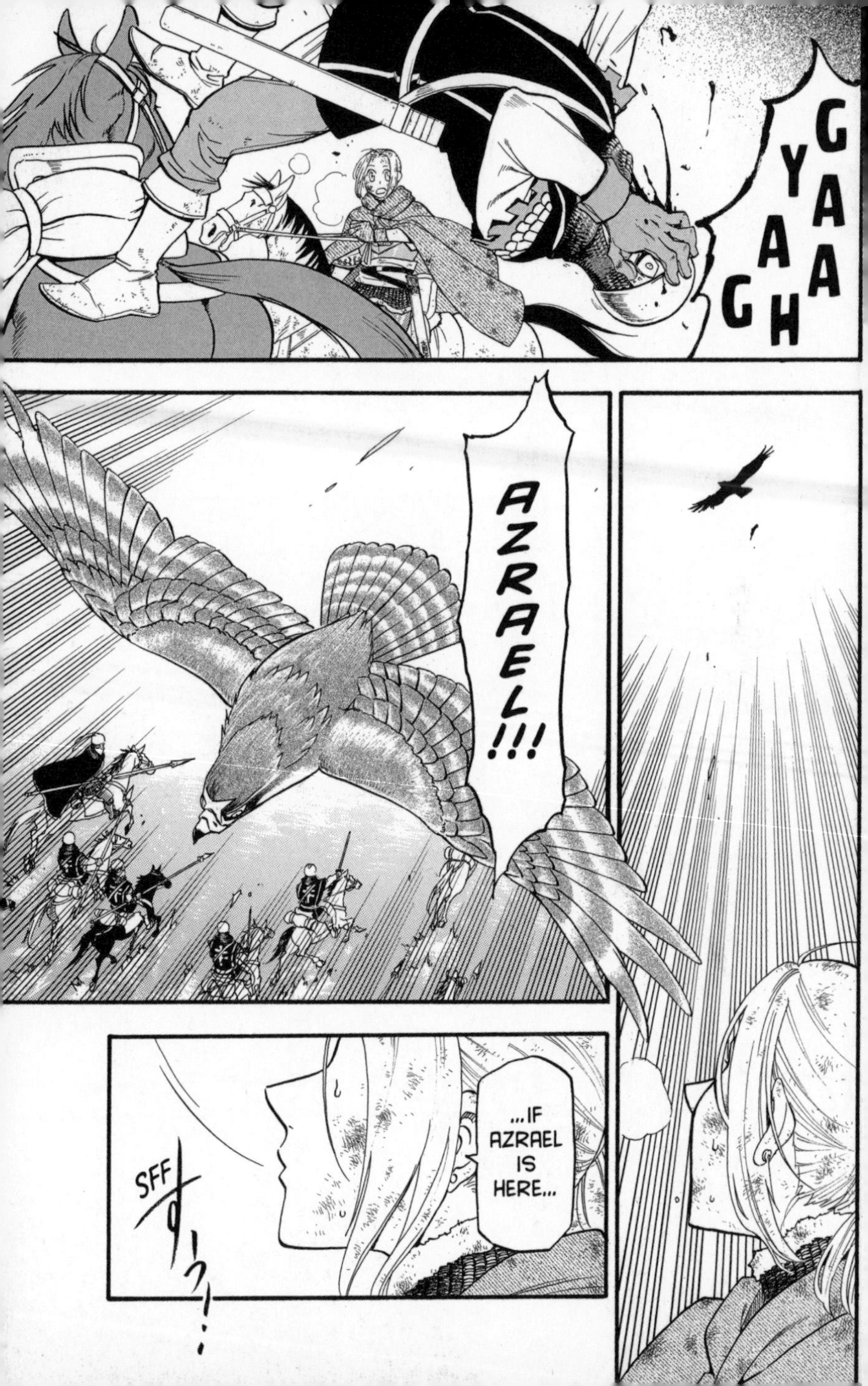
GYAAAGH
AZRAEL!!!
...IF AZRAEL IS HERE...
SFF

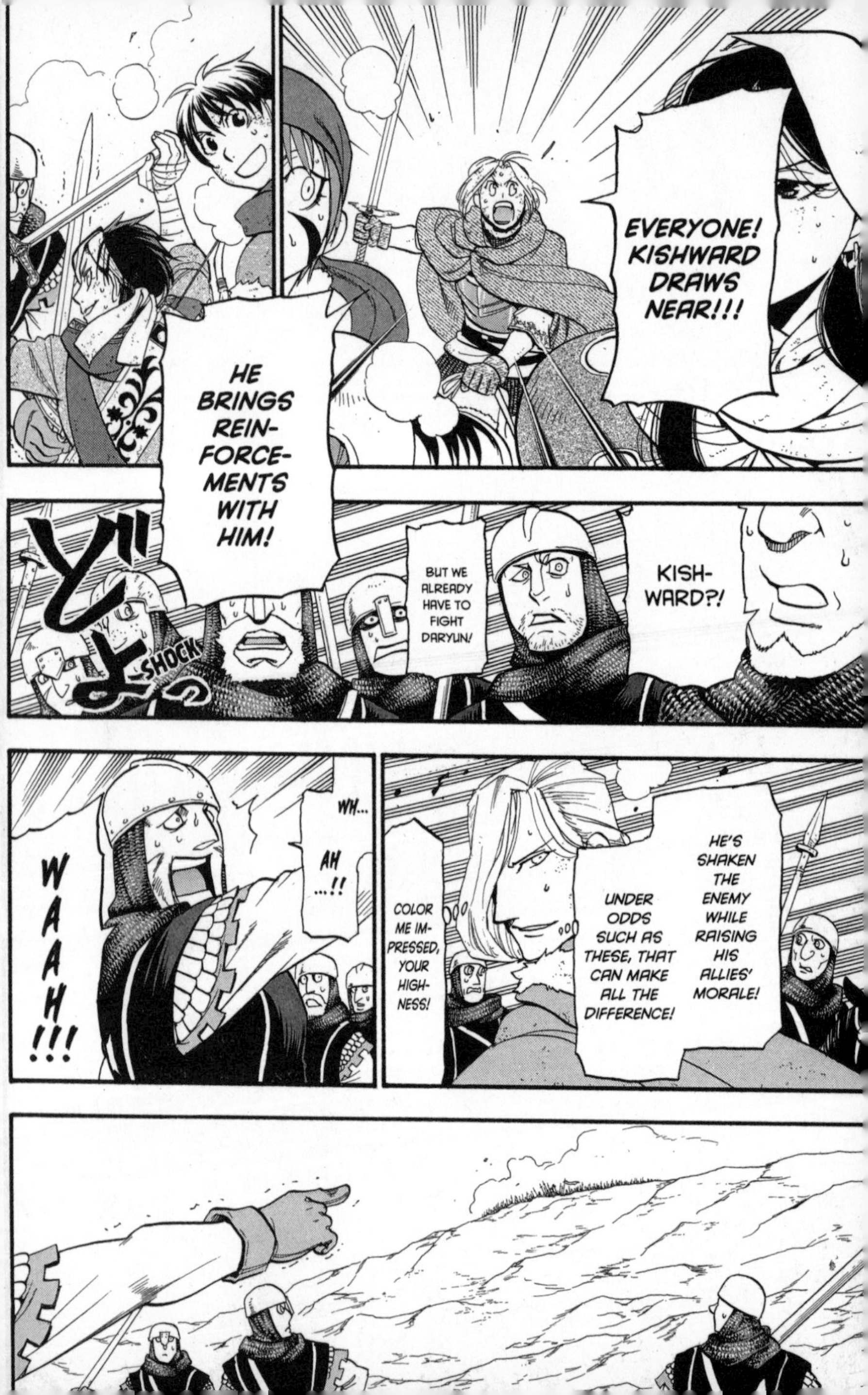
EVERYONE! KISHWARD DRAWS NEAR!!!
HE BRINGS REIN-FORCE-MENTS WITH HIM!
KISH-WARD?!
BUT WE ALREADY HAVE TO FIGHT DARYUN!
SHOCK
HE'S SHAKEN THE ENEMY WHILE RAISING HIS ALLIES' MORALE!
UNDER ODDS SUCH AS THESE, THAT CAN MAKE ALL THE DIFFERENCE!
COLOR ME IM-PRESSED, YOUR HIGH-NESS!
WH...
AH ...!!
WAAAH!!!

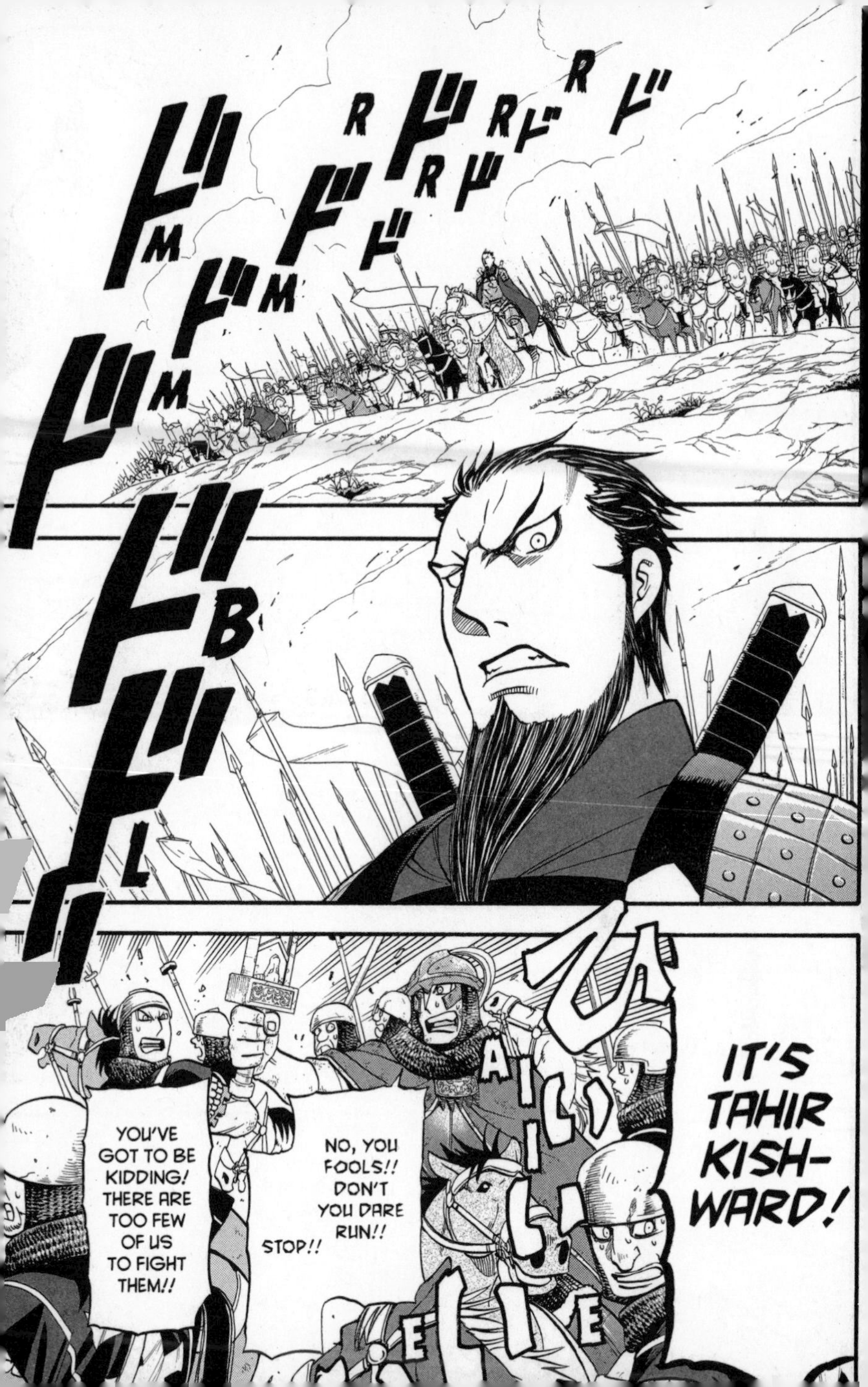
R
R
R
R
M
M
M
B
L
IT'S TAHIR KISH-WARD!
AIIIEE
NO, YOU FOOLS!! DON'T YOU DARE RUN!!
STOP!!
YOU'VE GOT TO BE KIDDING! THERE ARE TOO FEW OF US TO FIGHT THEM!!

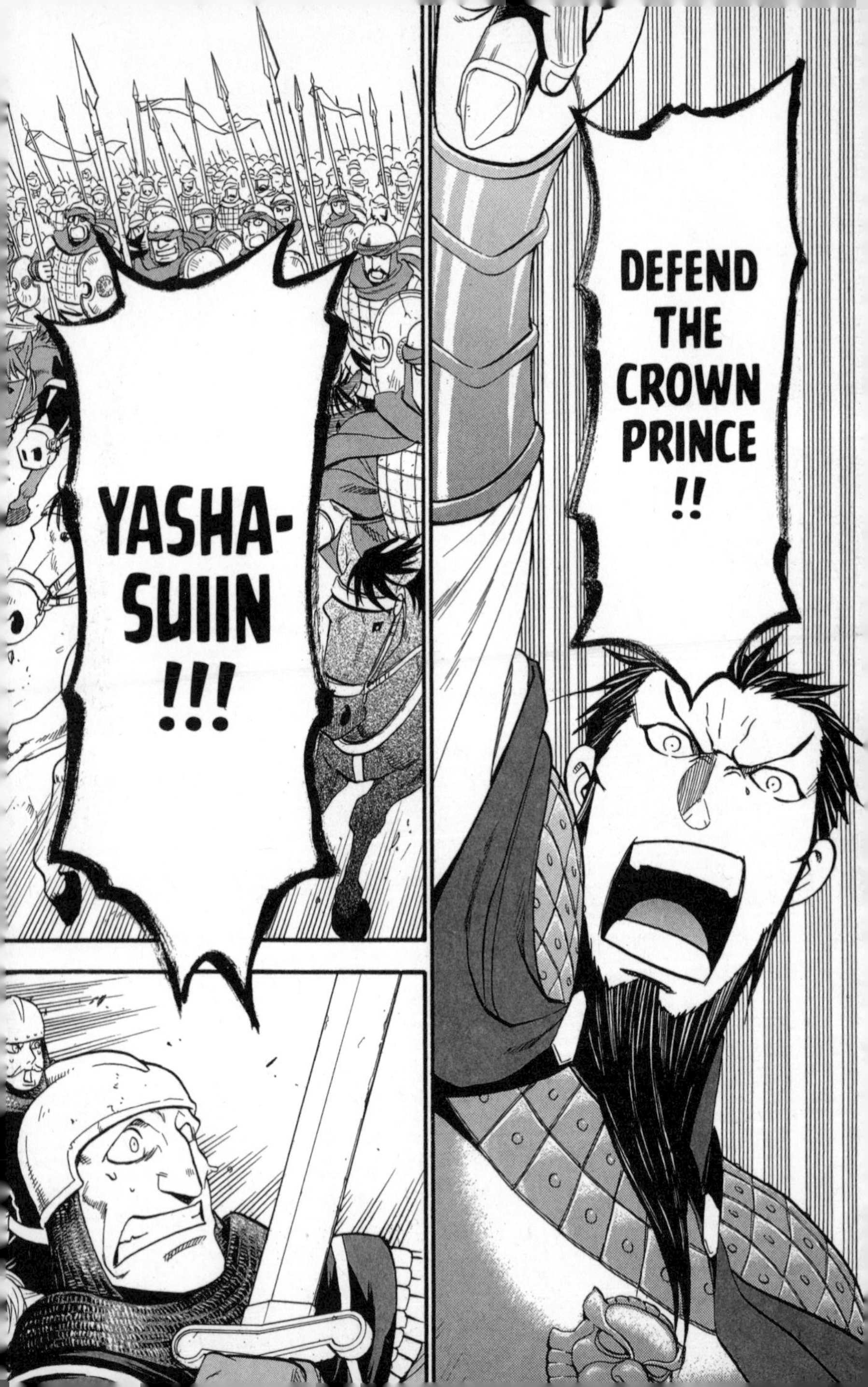
DEFEND THE CROWN PRINCE !!
YASHA-SUIIN !!!

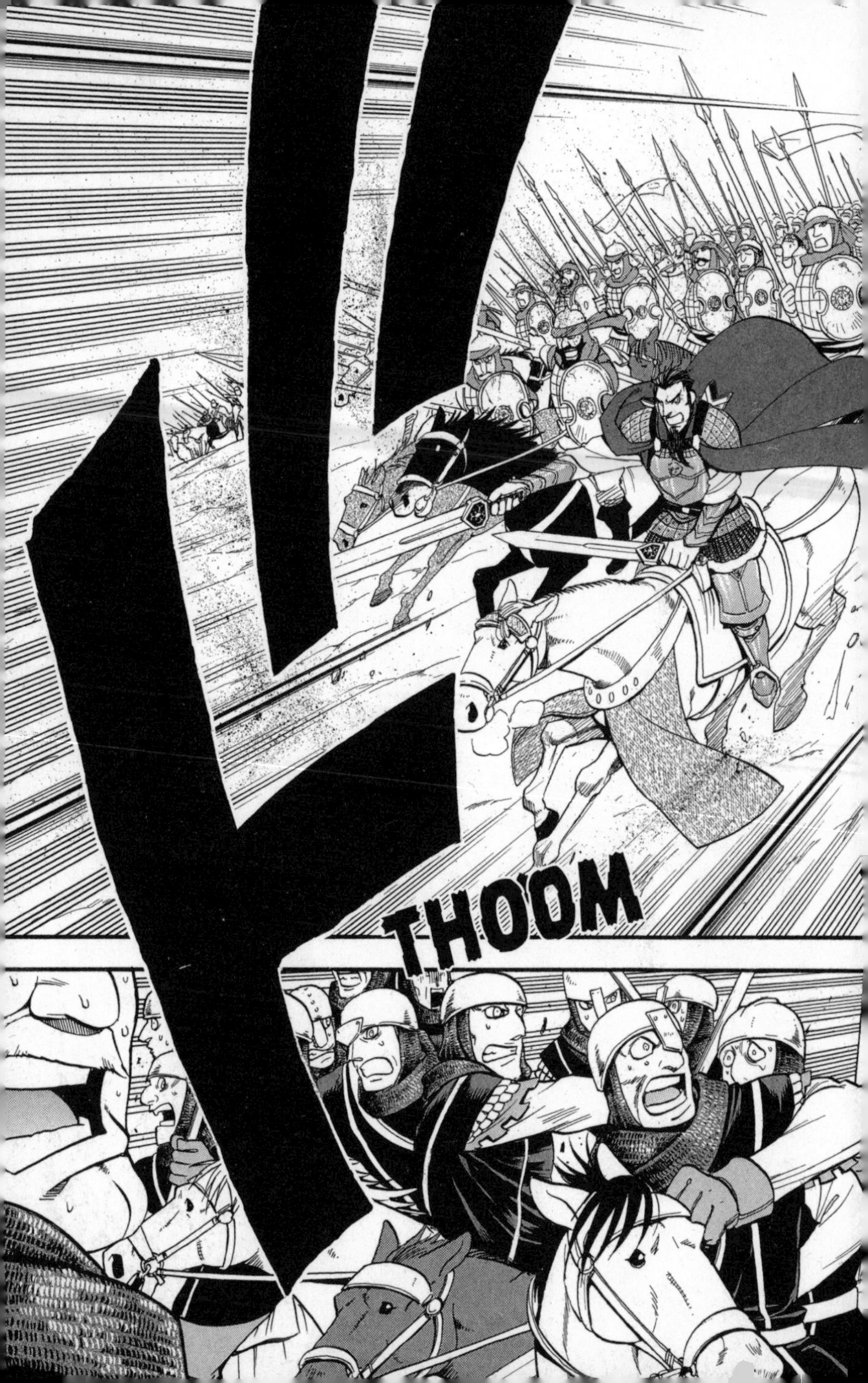
THOOM

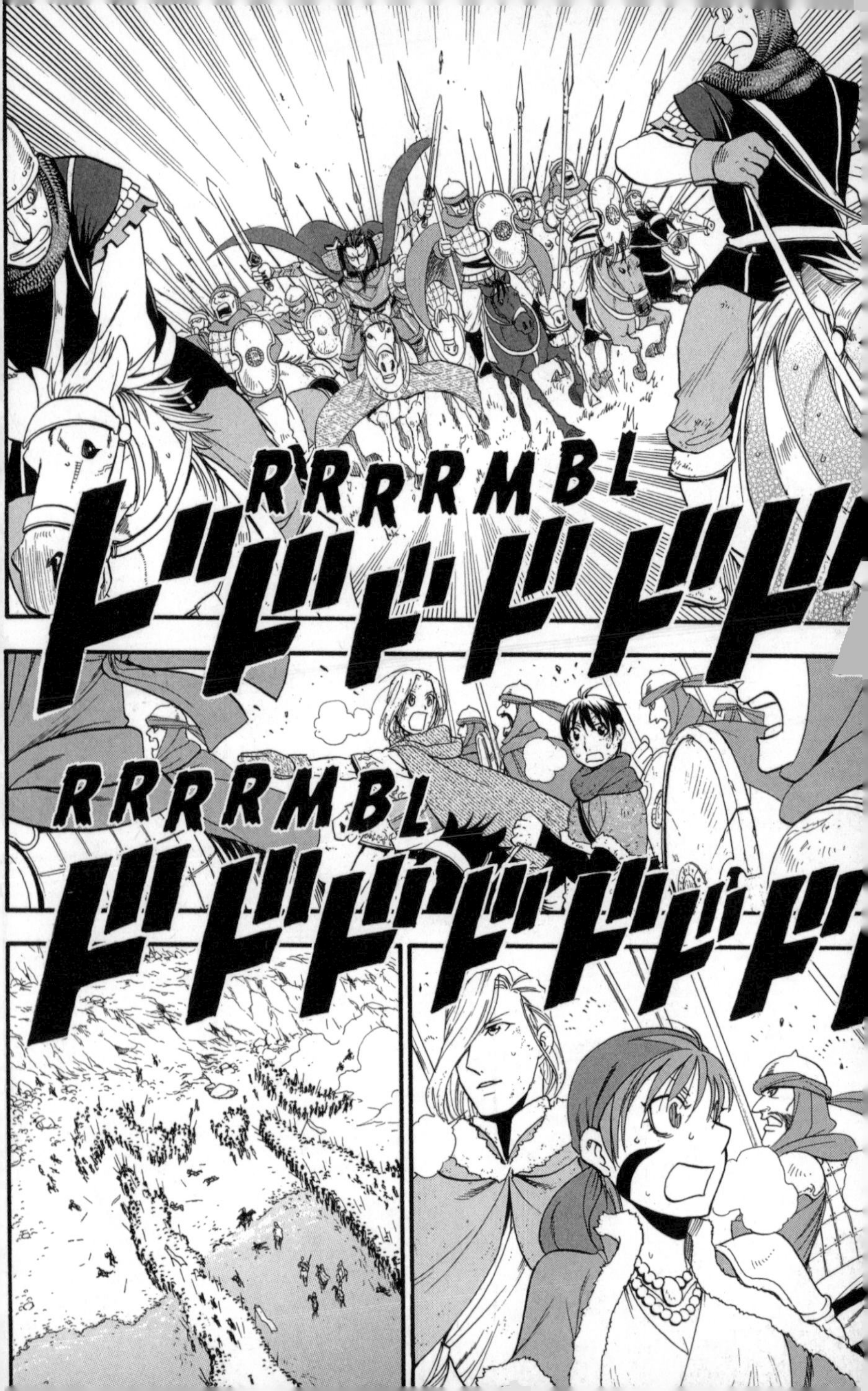
RRRRRMBL
トドドドドドドド
RRRRRMBL
ドドドドドドドドド

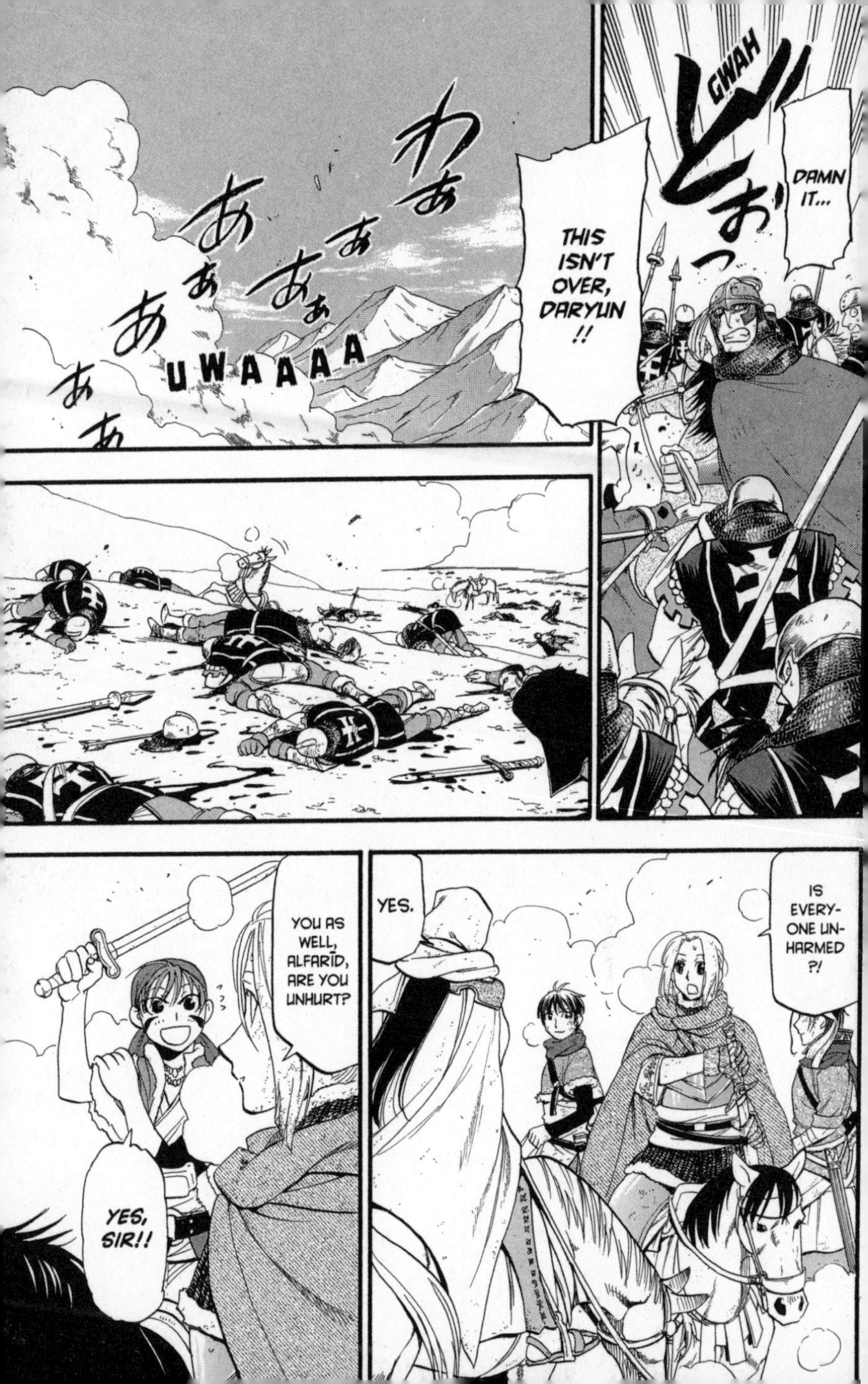
GWAH
DAMN IT...
THIS ISN'T OVER, DARYUN!!
UWAAAA
IS EVERY-ONE UN-HARMED?!
YES.
YOU AS WELL, ALFARID, ARE YOU UNHURT?
YES, SIR!!

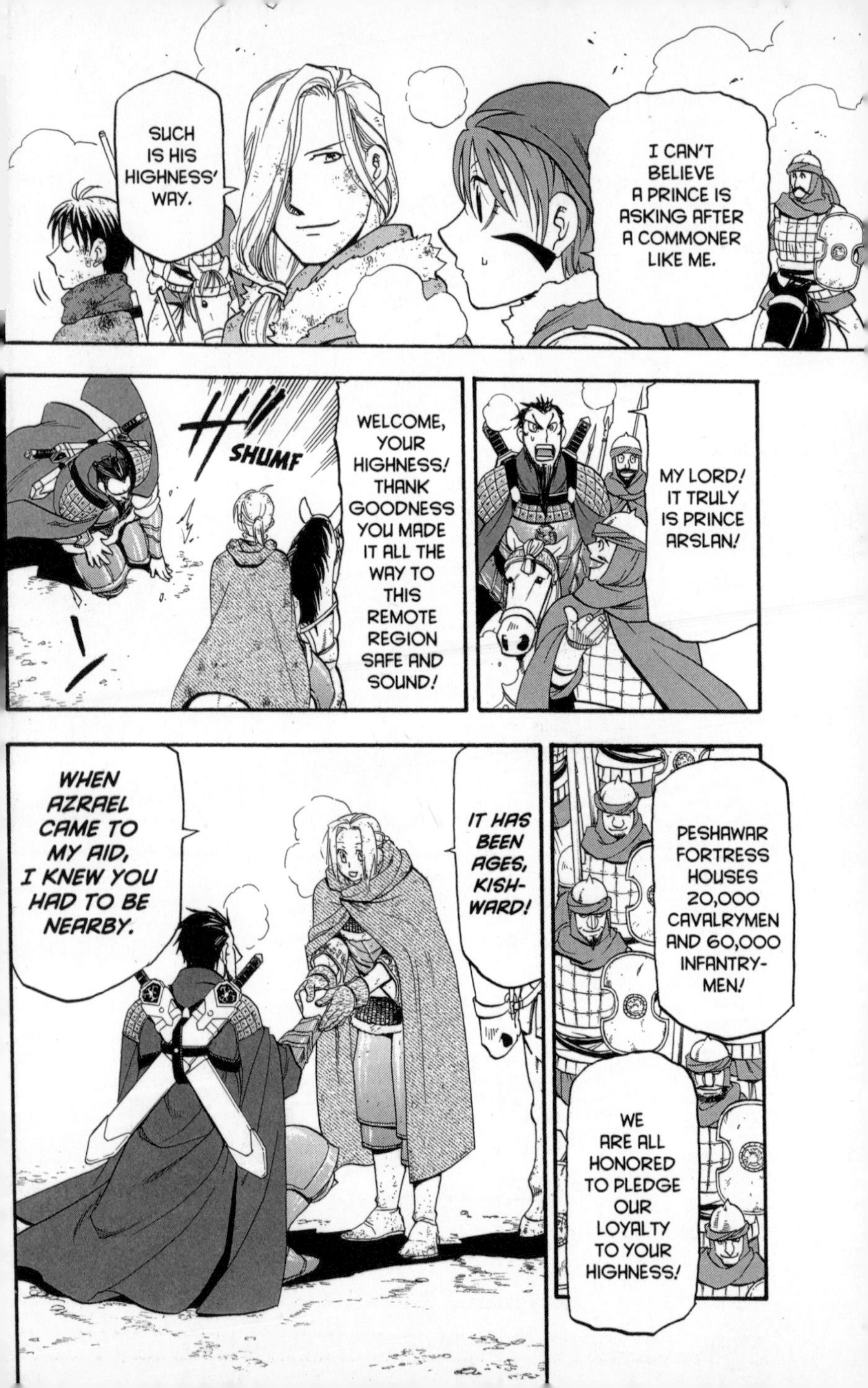
I CAN'T BELIEVE A PRINCE IS ASKING AFTER A COMMONER LIKE ME.
SUCH IS HIS HIGHNESS' WAY.
MY LORD! IT TRULY IS PRINCE ARSLAN!
WELCOME, YOUR HIGHNESS! THANK GOODNESS YOU MADE IT ALL THE WAY TO THIS REMOTE REGION SAFE AND SOUND!
SHUMF
PESHAWAR FORTRESS HOUSES 20,000 CAVALRYMEN AND 60,000 INFANTRYMEN!
WE ARE ALL HONORED TO PLEDGE OUR LOYALTY TO YOUR HIGHNESS!
IT HAS BEEN AGES, KISHWARD!
WHEN AZRAEL CAME TO MY AID, I KNEW YOU HAD TO BE NEARBY.

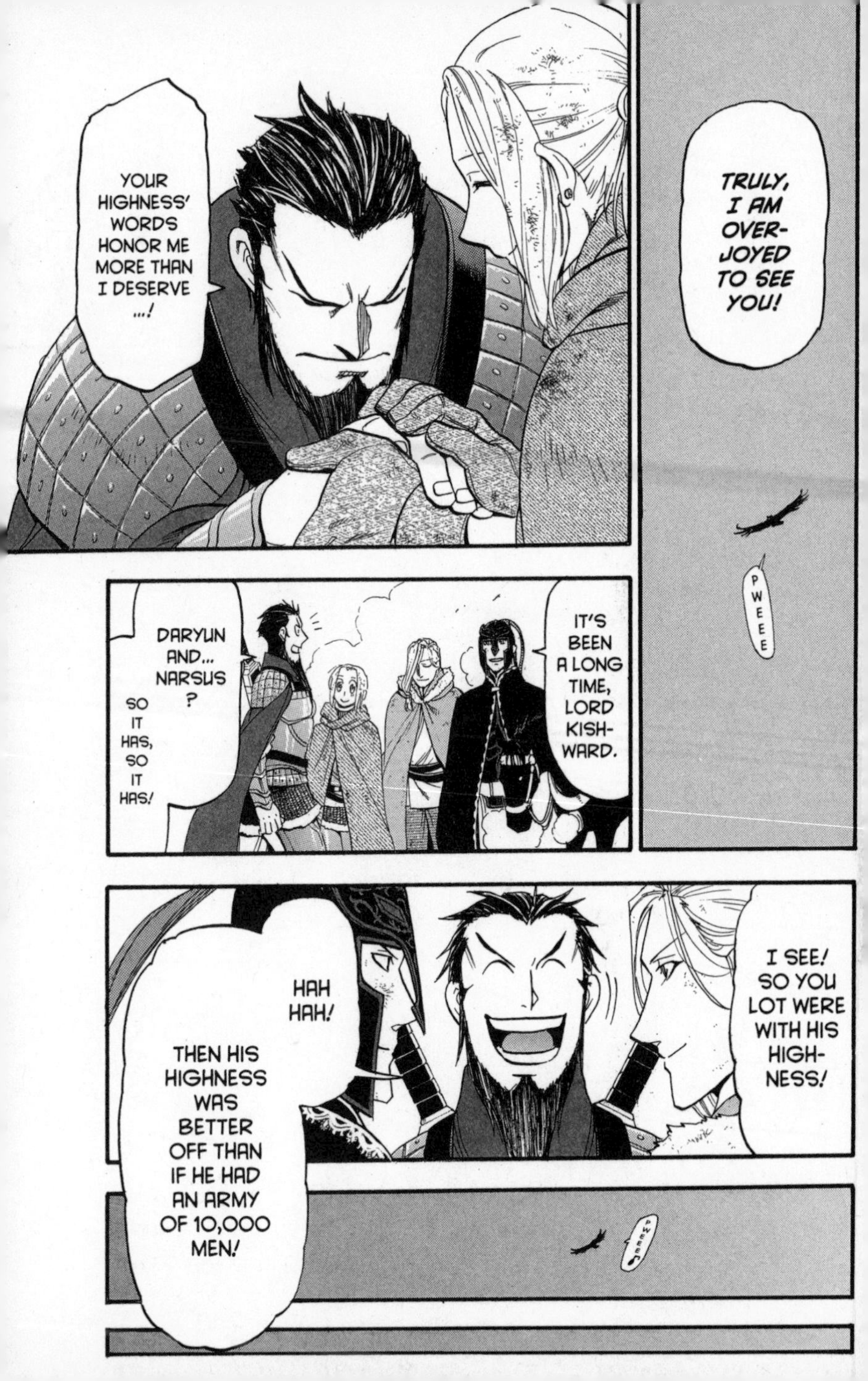
TRULY, I AM OVER-JOYED TO SEE YOU!
PWEEE
YOUR HIGHNESS' WORDS HONOR ME MORE THAN I DESERVE ...!
IT'S BEEN A LONG TIME, LORD KISH-WARD.
DARYUN AND... NARSUS?
SO IT HAS, SO IT HAS!
I SEE! SO YOU LOT WERE WITH HIS HIGH-NESS!
HAH HAH!
THEN HIS HIGHNESS WAS BETTER OFF THAN IF HE HAD AN ARMY OF 10,000 MEN!
PWEEE

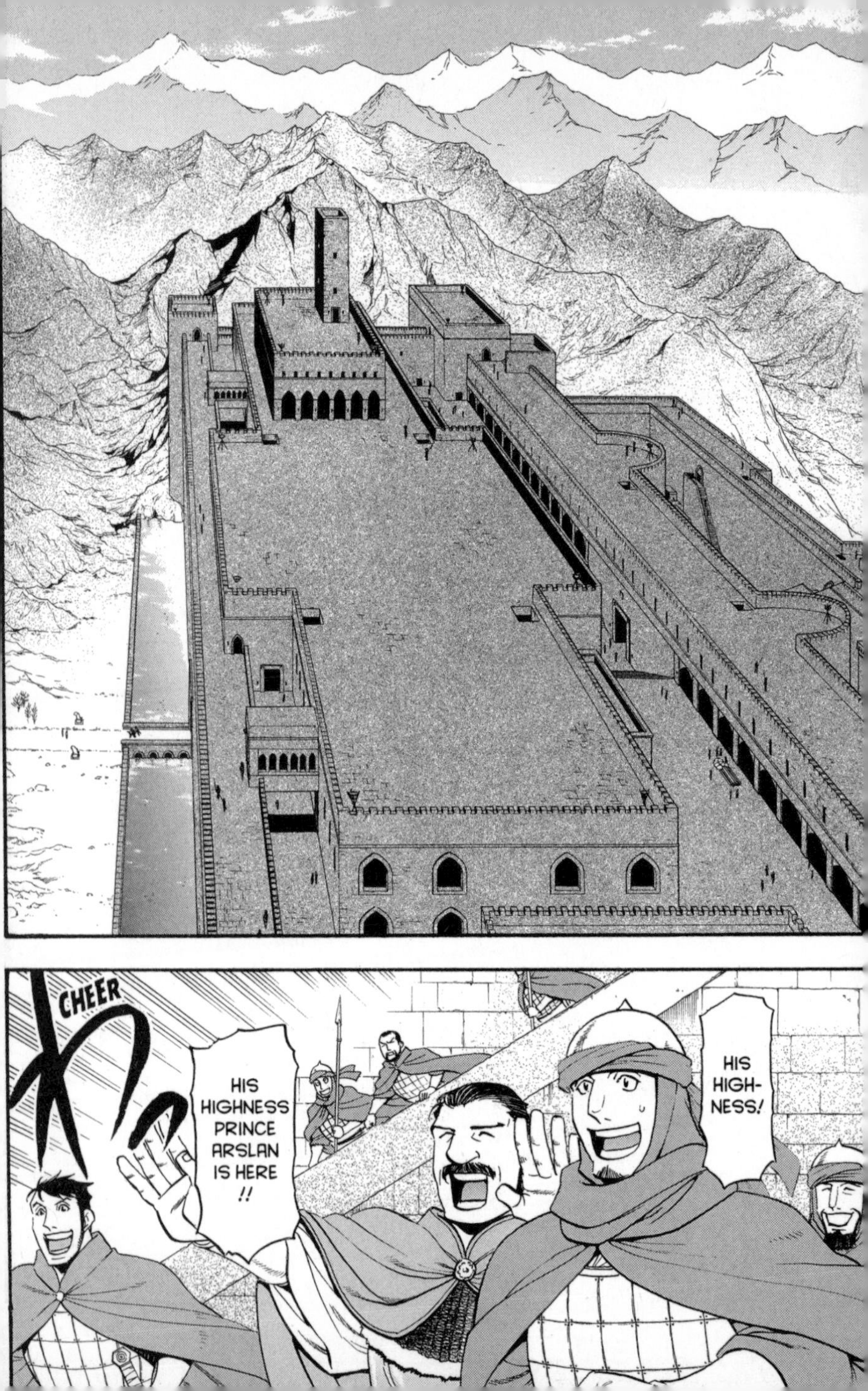
HIS HIGH-NESS!
HIS HIGHNESS PRINCE ARSLAN IS HERE !!
CHEER

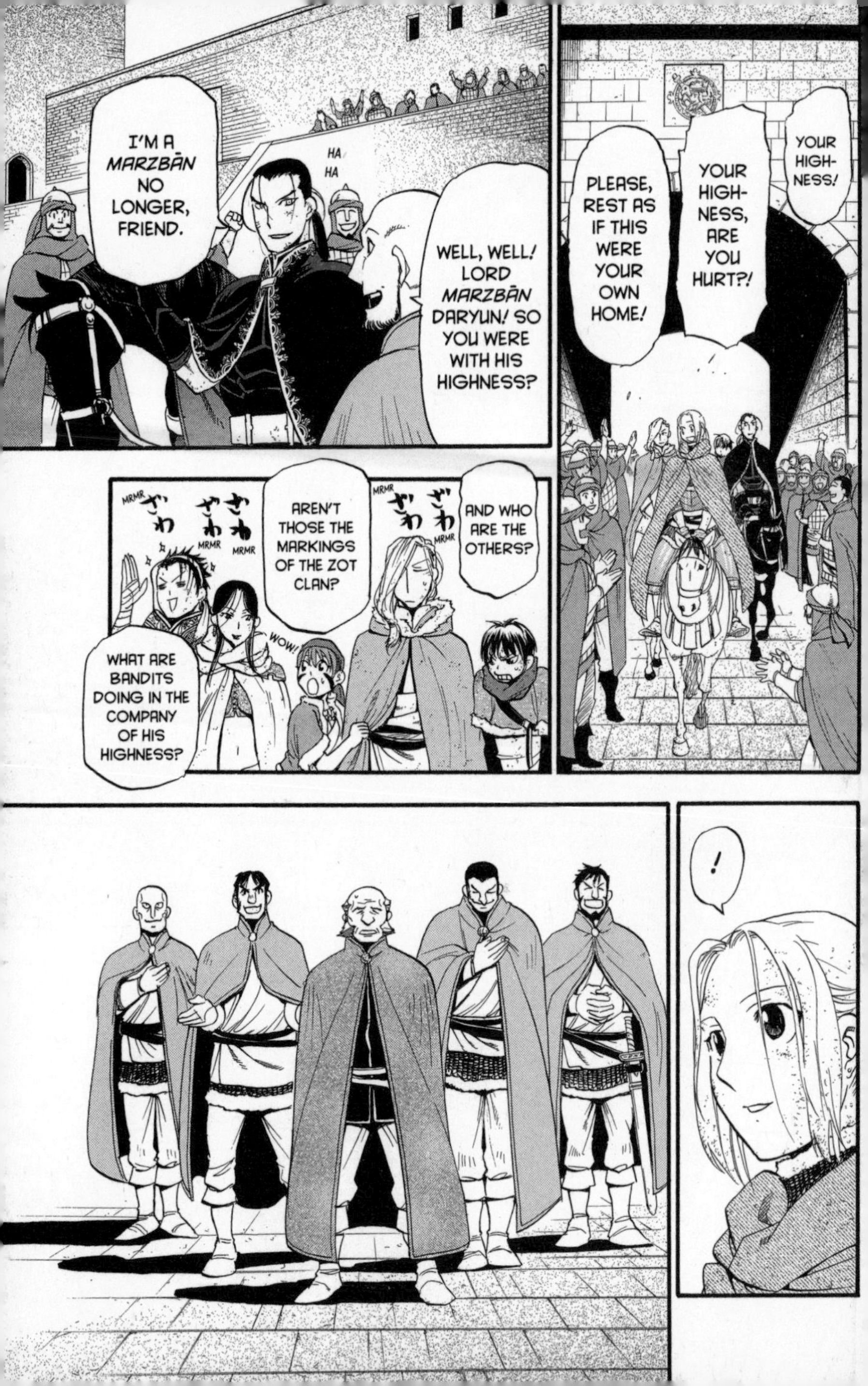
YOUR HIGHNESS!
YOUR HIGHNESS, ARE YOU HURT?!
PLEASE, REST AS IF THIS WERE YOUR OWN HOME!
WELL, WELL! LORD MARZBĀN DARYUN! SO YOU WERE WITH HIS HIGHNESS?
HA HA
I'M A MARZBĀN NO LONGER, FRIEND.
AND WHO ARE THE OTHERS?
ざわ ざわ MRMR
AREN'T THOSE THE MARKINGS OF THE ZOT CLAN?
ざわ ざわ MRMR MRMR
ざわ MRMR
WOW!
WHAT ARE BANDITS DOING IN THE COMPANY OF HIS HIGHNESS?
!

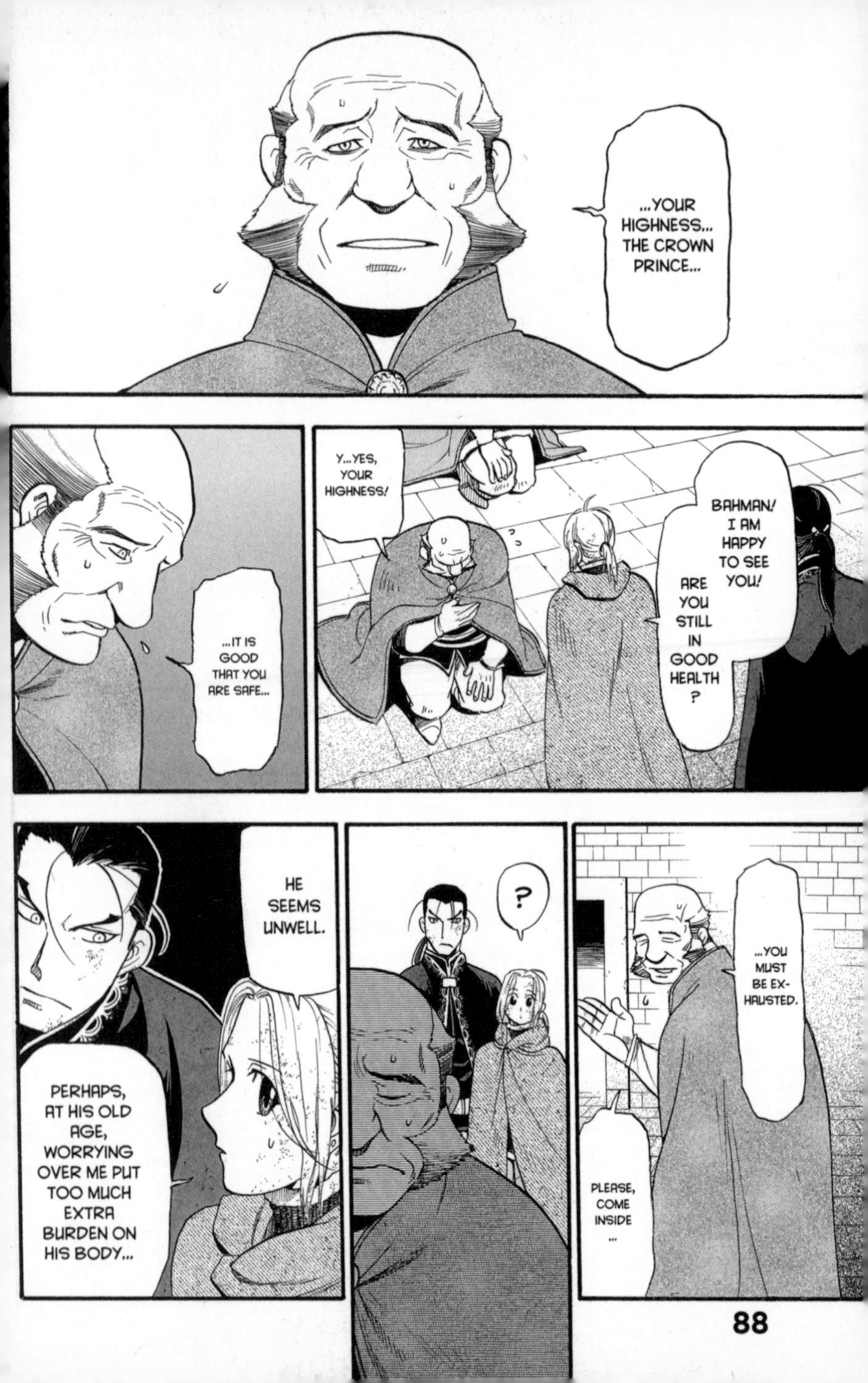
...YOUR HIGHNESS... THE CROWN PRINCE...
BAHMAN! I AM HAPPY TO SEE YOU!
ARE YOU STILL IN GOOD HEALTH?
Y...YES, YOUR HIGHNESS!
...IT IS GOOD THAT YOU ARE SAFE...
...YOU MUST BE EX-HAUSTED.
PLEASE, COME INSIDE ...
?
HE SEEMS UNWELL.
PERHAPS, AT HIS OLD AGE, WORRYING OVER ME PUT TOO MUCH EXTRA BURDEN ON HIS BODY...

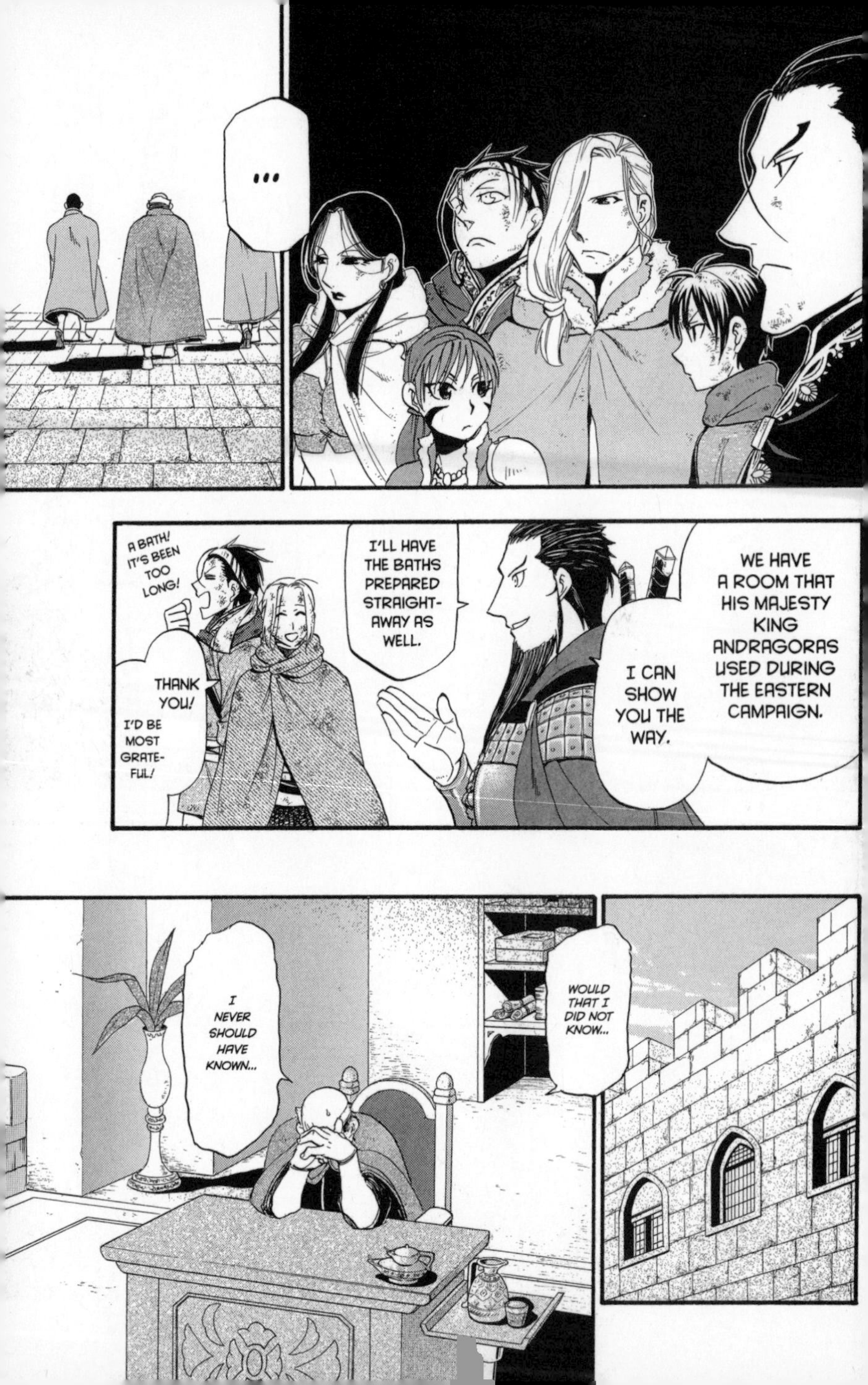
...
WE HAVE A ROOM THAT HIS MAJESTY KING ANDRAGORAS USED DURING THE EASTERN CAMPAIGN.
I CAN SHOW YOU THE WAY.
I'LL HAVE THE BATHS PREPARED STRAIGHT-AWAY AS WELL.
A BATH! IT'S BEEN TOO LONG!
THANK YOU!
I'D BE MOST GRATE-FUL!
WOULD THAT I DID NOT KNOW...
I NEVER SHOULD HAVE KNOWN...

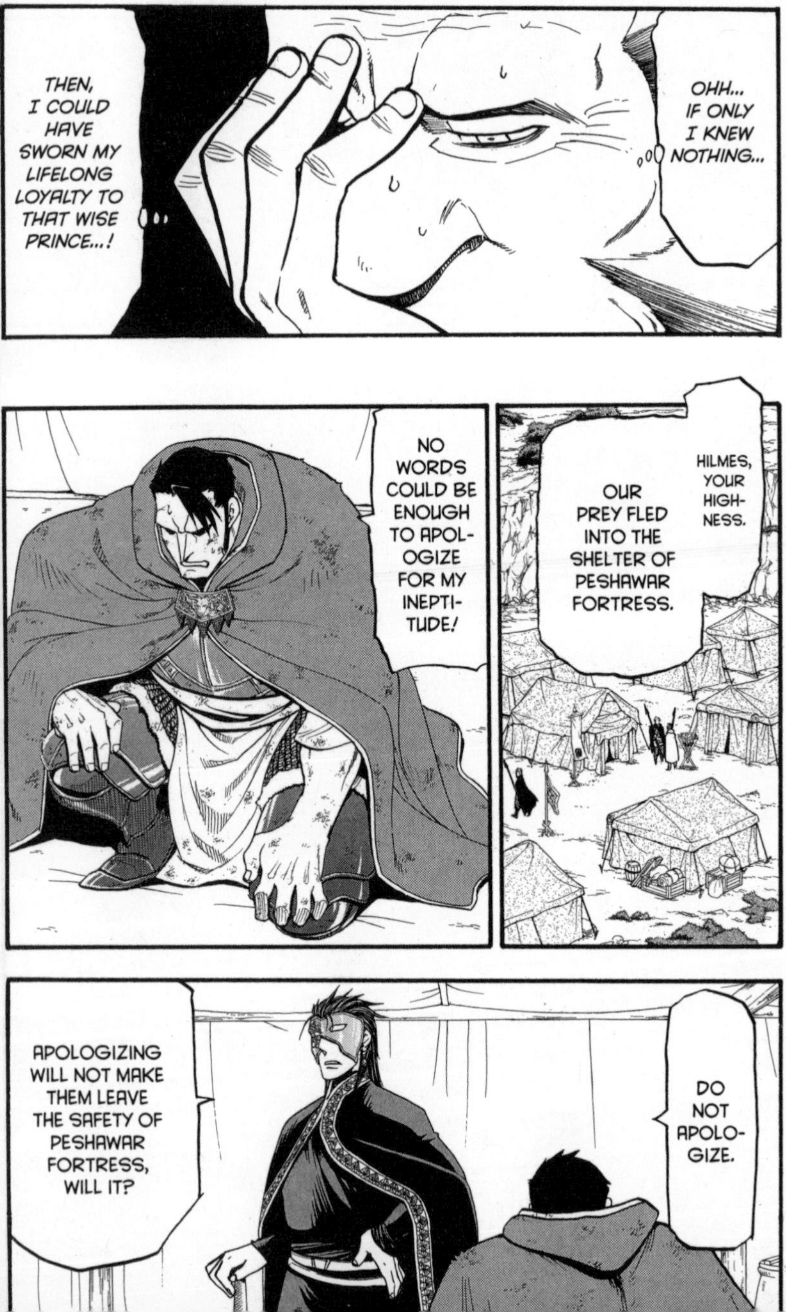
OHH... IF ONLY I KNEW NOTHING...
THEN, I COULD HAVE SWORN MY LIFELONG LOYALTY TO THAT WISE PRINCE...!
HILMES, YOUR HIGHNESS.
OUR PREY FLED INTO THE SHELTER OF PESHAWAR FORTRESS.
NO WORDS COULD BE ENOUGH TO APOLOGIZE FOR MY INEPTITUDE!
DO NOT APOLOGIZE.
APOLOGIZING WILL NOT MAKE THEM LEAVE THE SAFETY OF PESHAWAR FORTRESS, WILL IT?

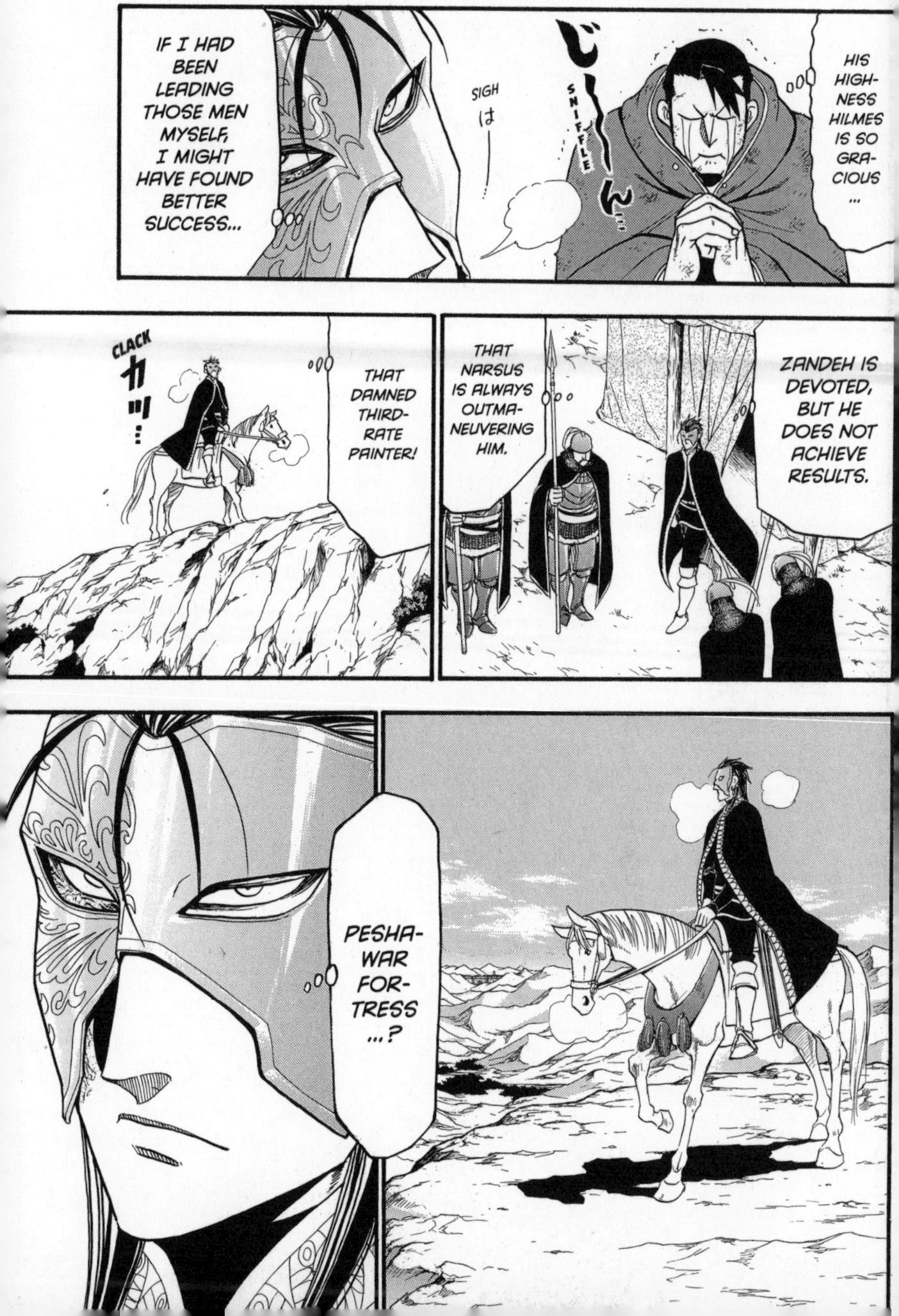

HIS HIGHNESS HILMES IS SO GRACIOUS...
SNIFFLE
じ〜〜ん…
SIGH
は—…
IF I HAD BEEN LEADING THOSE MEN MYSELF, I MIGHT HAVE FOUND BETTER SUCCESS...
ZANDEH IS DEVOTED, BUT HE DOES NOT ACHIEVE RESULTS.
THAT NARSUS IS ALWAYS OUTMANEUVERING HIM.
THAT DAMNED THIRD-RATE PAINTER!
CLACK
カッ…
PESHAWAR FORTRESS...?

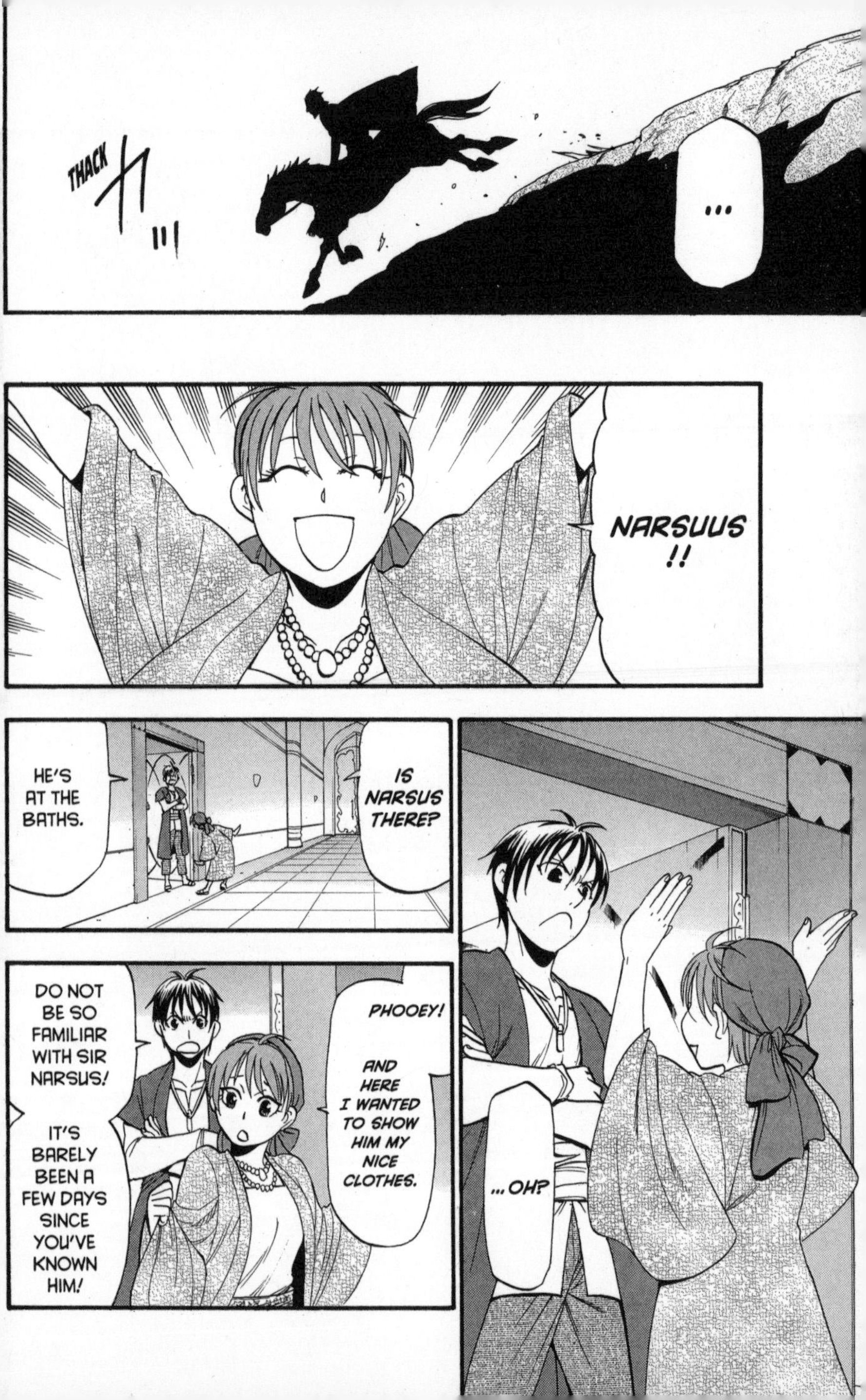
...
THACK
NARSUUS !!
...OH?
IS NARSUS THERE?
HE'S AT THE BATHS.
PHOOEY!
AND HERE I WANTED TO SHOW HIM MY NICE CLOTHES.
DO NOT BE SO FAMILIAR WITH SIR NARSUS!
IT'S BARELY BEEN A FEW DAYS SINCE YOU'VE KNOWN HIM!

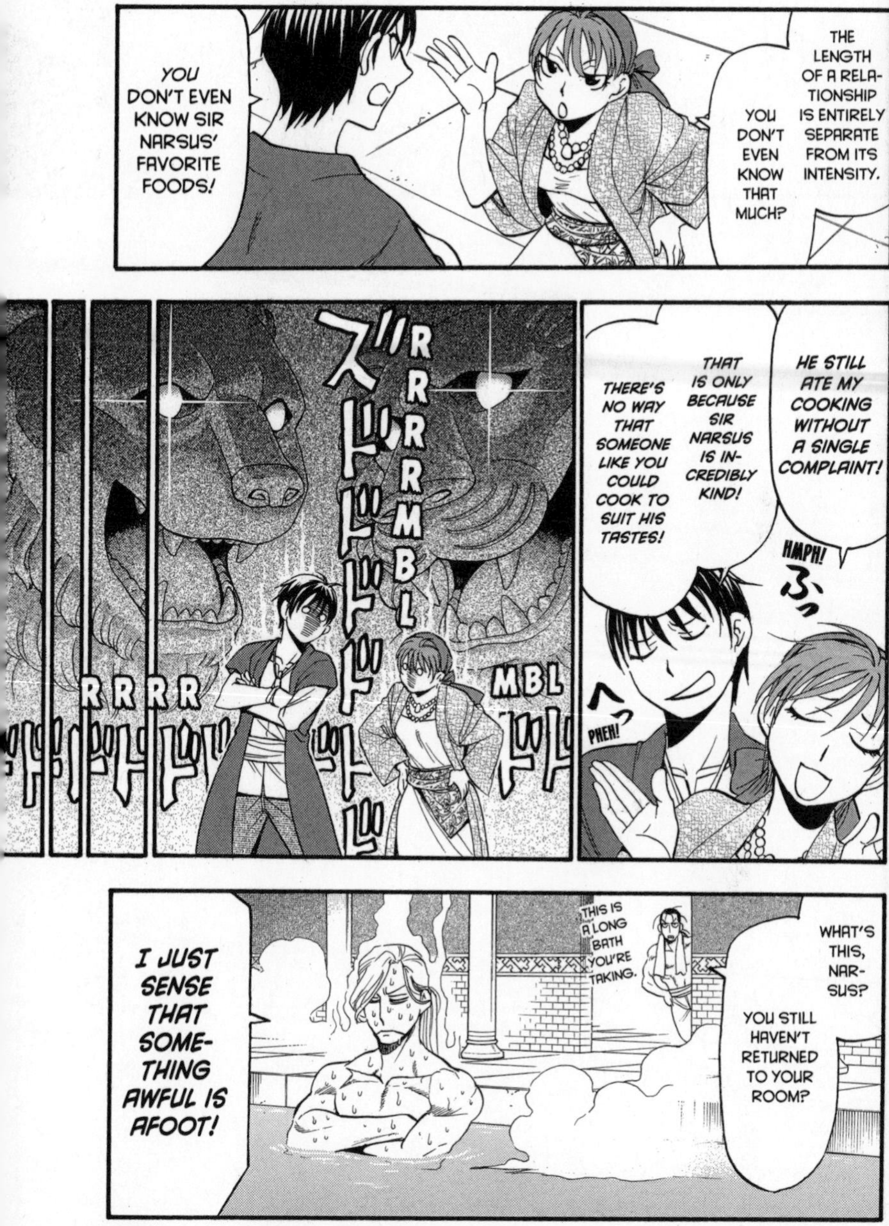
THE LENGTH OF A RELATIONSHIP IS ENTIRELY SEPARATE FROM ITS INTENSITY.
YOU DON'T EVEN KNOW THAT MUCH?
YOU DON'T EVEN KNOW SIR NARSUS' FAVORITE FOODS!
HE STILL ATE MY COOKING WITHOUT A SINGLE COMPLAINT!
HMPH! ふっ
THAT IS ONLY BECAUSE SIR NARSUS IS INCREDIBLY KIND!
THERE'S NO WAY THAT SOMEONE LIKE YOU COULD COOK TO SUIT HIS TASTES!
PHEH! へっ
RRRRMBL
ズドドドド
MBL
ドド
RRRR
ドドドド
WHAT'S THIS, NARSUS?
YOU STILL HAVEN'T RETURNED TO YOUR ROOM?
THIS IS A LONG BATH YOU'RE TAKING.
I JUST SENSE THAT SOMETHING AWFUL IS AFOOT!

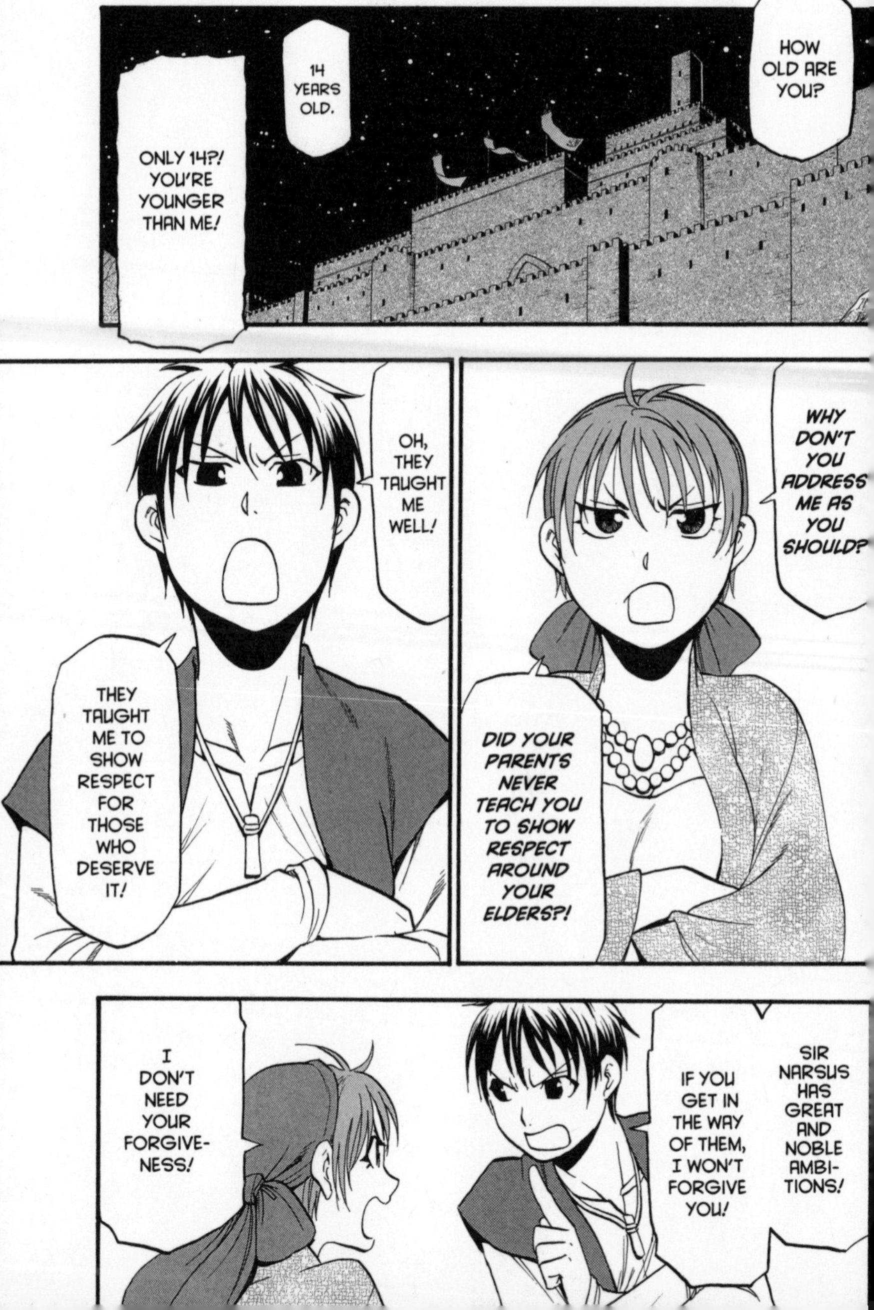
HOW OLD ARE YOU?
14 YEARS OLD.
ONLY 14?! YOU'RE YOUNGER THAN ME!
WHY DON'T YOU ADDRESS ME AS YOU SHOULD?
DID YOUR PARENTS NEVER TEACH YOU TO SHOW RESPECT AROUND YOUR ELDERS?!
OH, THEY TAUGHT ME WELL!
THEY TAUGHT ME TO SHOW RESPECT FOR THOSE WHO DESERVE IT!
SIR NARSUS HAS GREAT AND NOBLE AMBITIONS!
IF YOU GET IN THE WAY OF THEM, I WON'T FORGIVE YOU!
I DON'T NEED YOUR FORGIVENESS!

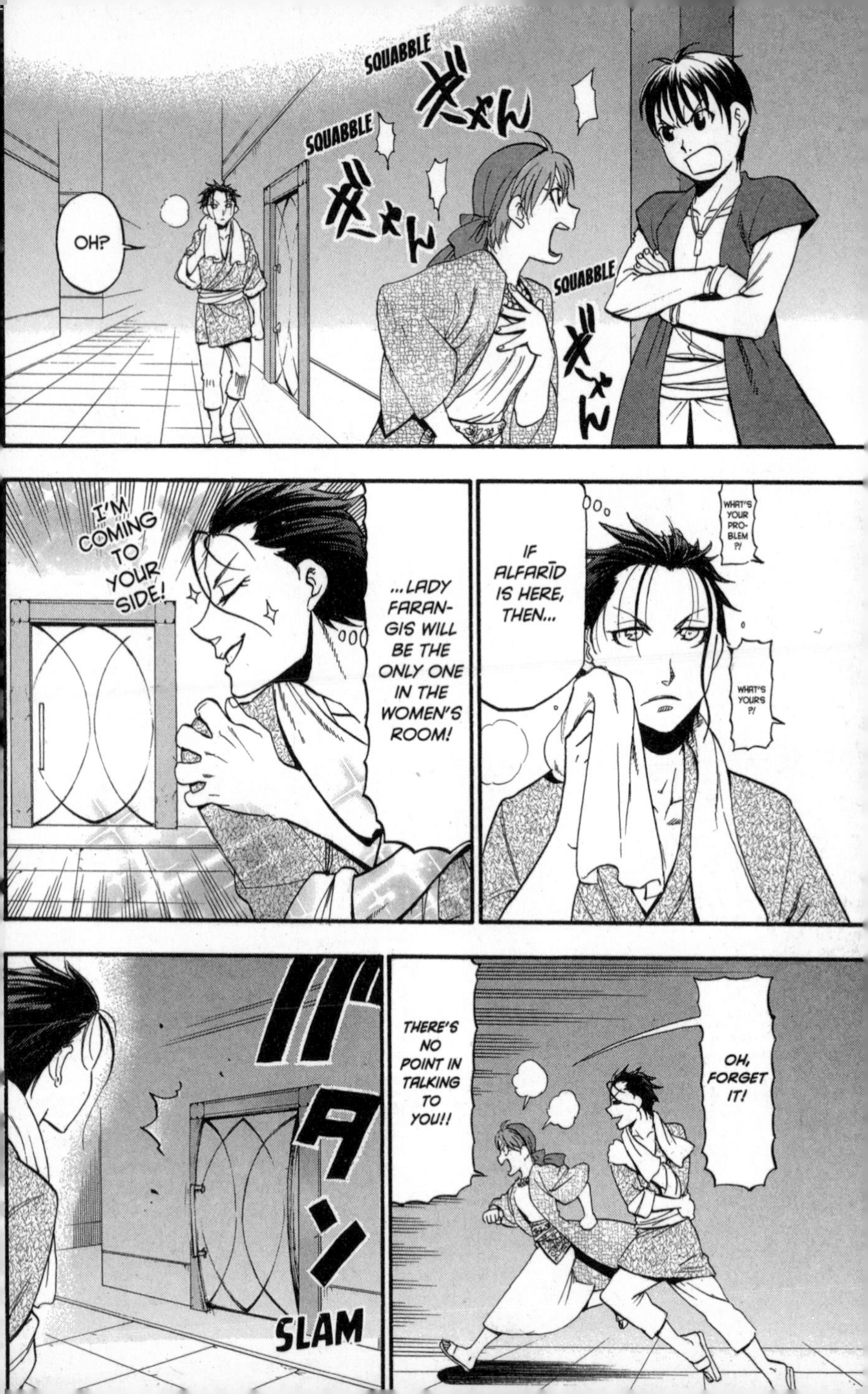
SQUABBLE
SQUABBLE
SQUABBLE
OH?
WHAT'S YOUR PRO-BLEM ?!
IF ALFARĪD IS HERE, THEN...
WHAT'S YOURS ?!
...LADY FARAN-GIS WILL BE THE ONLY ONE IN THE WOMEN'S ROOM!
I'M COMING TO YOUR SIDE!
OH, FORGET IT!
THERE'S NO POINT IN TALKING TO YOU!!
SLAM

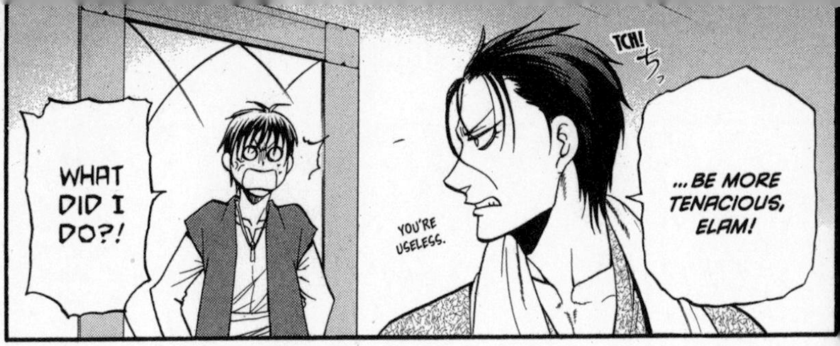
TCH!
...BE MORE TENACIOUS, ELAM!
YOU'RE USELESS.
WHAT DID I DO?!

Chapter 38: Two Princes

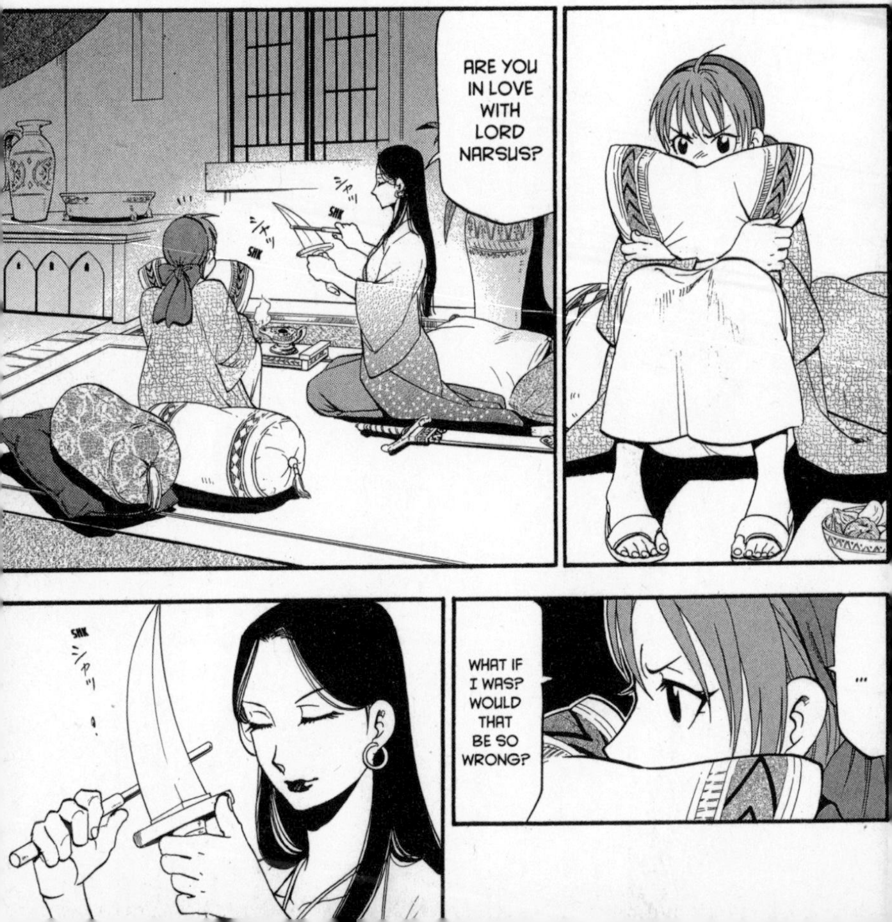
ARE YOU IN LOVE WITH LORD NARSUS?
SHK
SHK
...
WHAT IF I WAS? WOULD THAT BE SO WRONG?
SHK

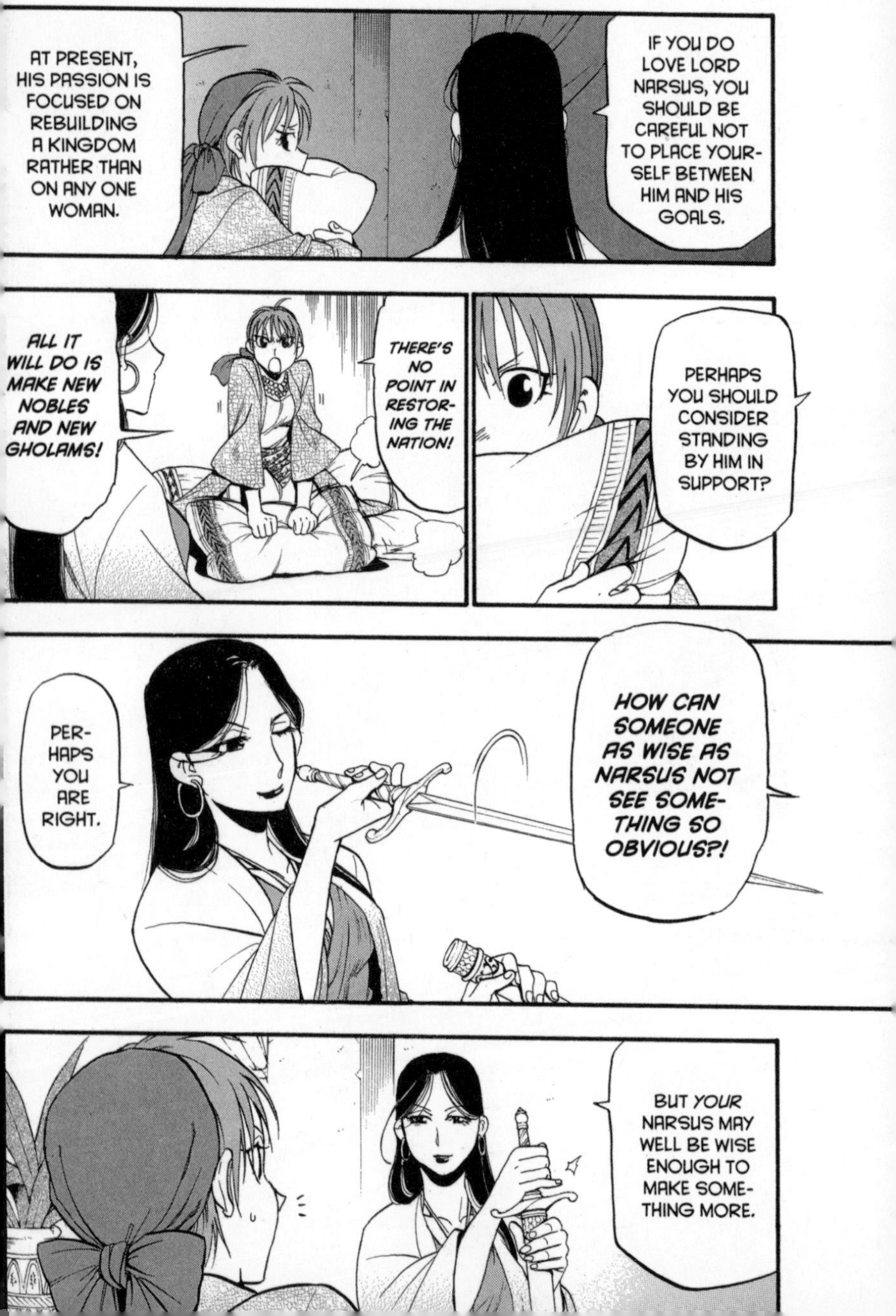
IF YOU DO LOVE LORD NARSUS, YOU SHOULD BE CAREFUL NOT TO PLACE YOURSELF BETWEEN HIM AND HIS GOALS.
AT PRESENT, HIS PASSION IS FOCUSED ON REBUILDING A KINGDOM RATHER THAN ON ANY ONE WOMAN.
PERHAPS YOU SHOULD CONSIDER STANDING BY HIM IN SUPPORT?
THERE'S NO POINT IN RESTORING THE NATION!
ALL IT WILL DO IS MAKE NEW NOBLES AND NEW GHOLAMS!
HOW CAN SOMEONE AS WISE AS NARSUS NOT SEE SOMETHING SO OBVIOUS?!
PERHAPS YOU ARE RIGHT.
BUT *YOUR* NARSUS MAY WELL BE WISE ENOUGH TO MAKE SOMETHING MORE.

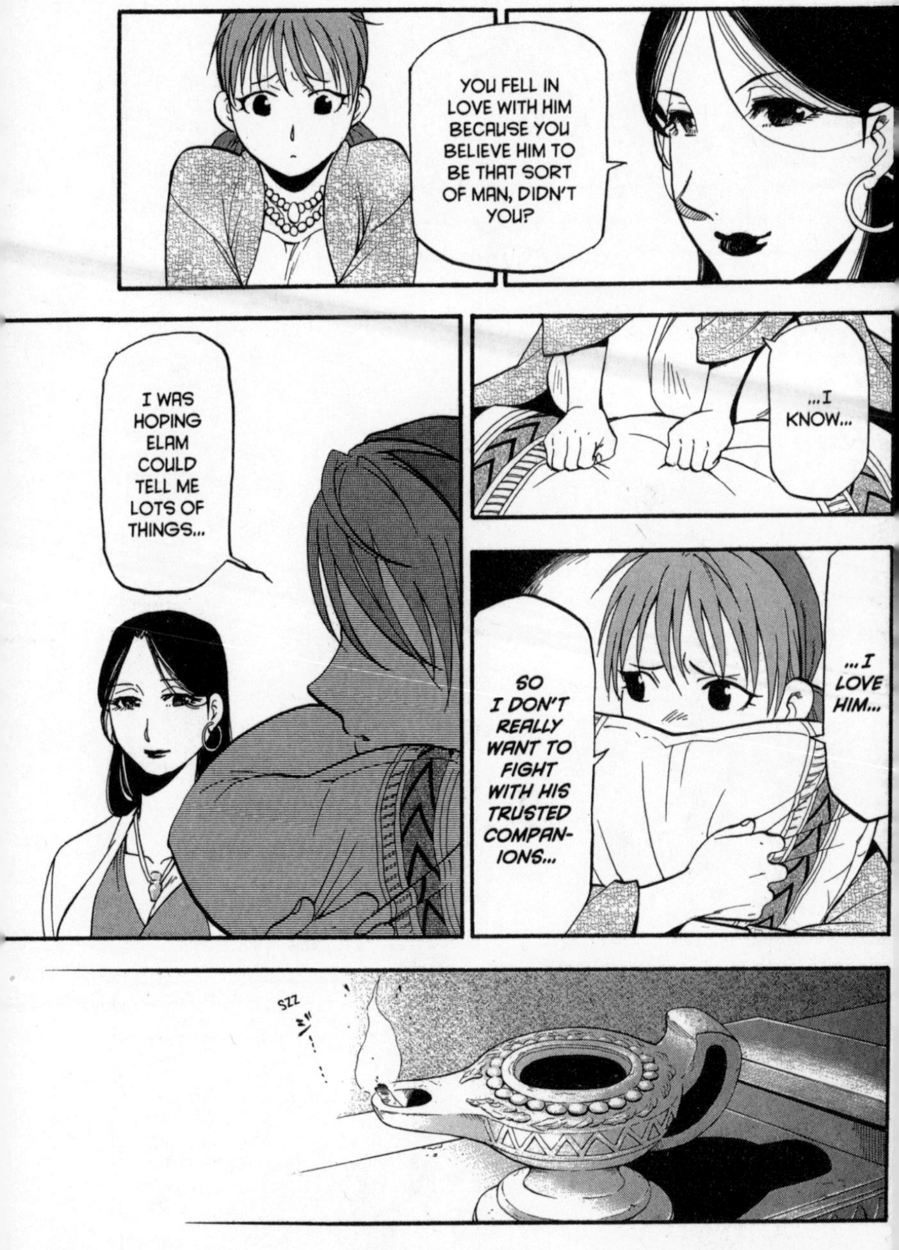
YOU FELL IN LOVE WITH HIM BECAUSE YOU BELIEVE HIM TO BE THAT SORT OF MAN, DIDN'T YOU?
...I KNOW...
...I LOVE HIM...
SO I DON'T REALLY WANT TO FIGHT WITH HIS TRUSTED COMPAN-IONS...
I WAS HOPING ELAM COULD TELL ME LOTS OF THINGS...
SZZ

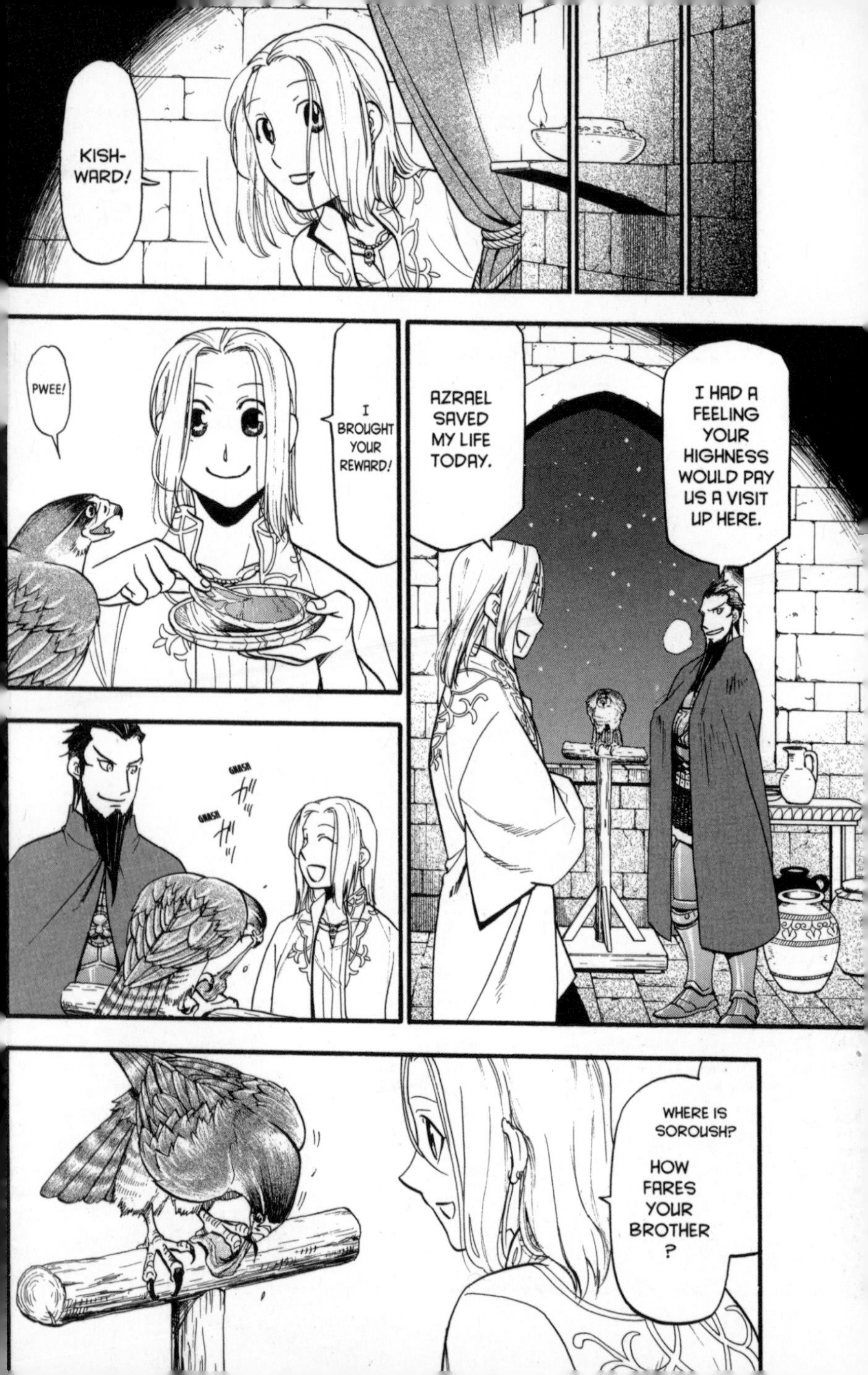
KISH-WARD!
I HAD A FEELING YOUR HIGHNESS WOULD PAY US A VISIT UP HERE.
AZRAEL SAVED MY LIFE TODAY.
I BROUGHT YOUR REWARD!
PWEE!
GNASH
GNASH
WHERE IS SOROUSH?
HOW FARES YOUR BROTHER?

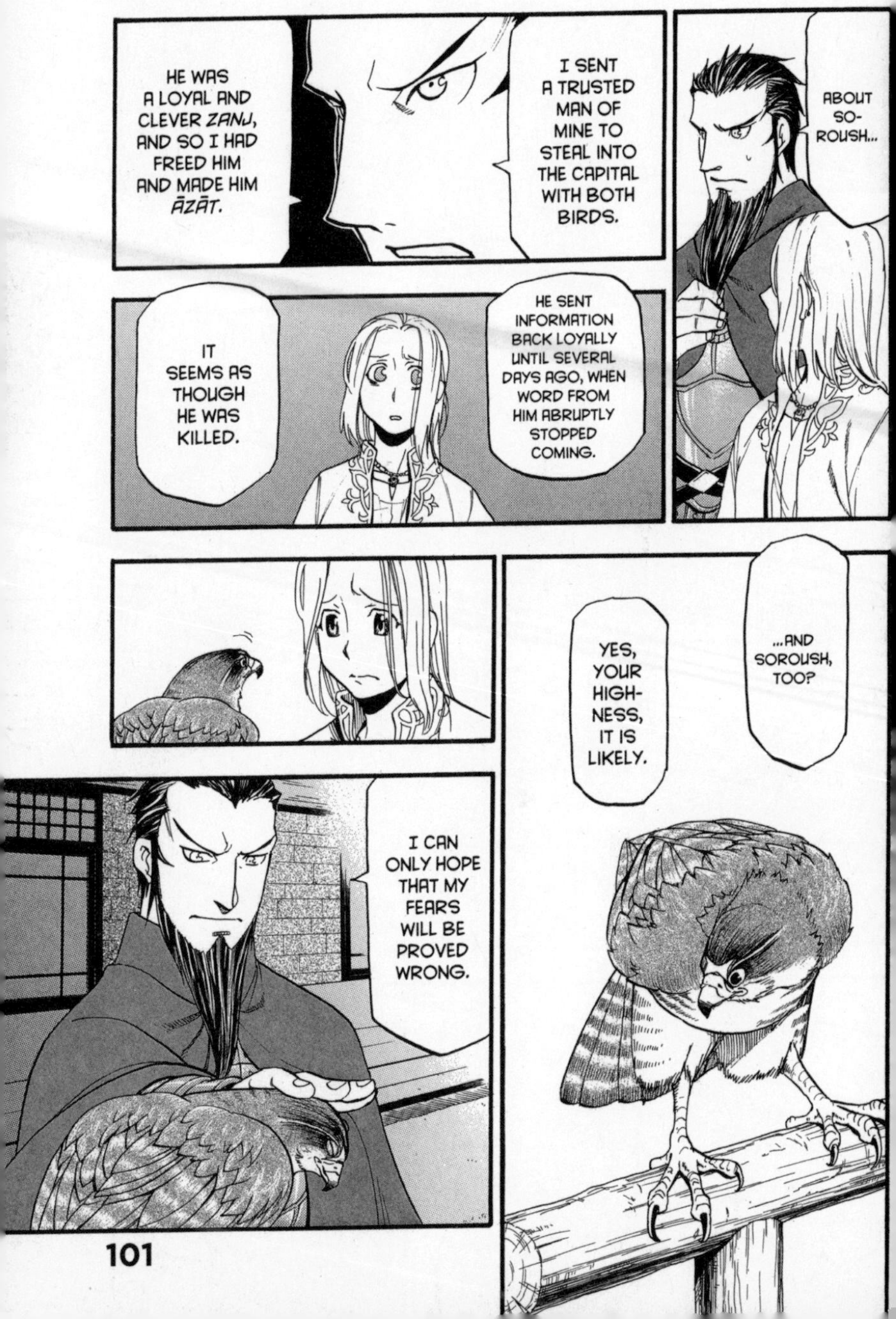
ABOUT SO-ROUSH...
I SENT A TRUSTED MAN OF MINE TO STEAL INTO THE CAPITAL WITH BOTH BIRDS.
HE WAS A LOYAL AND CLEVER *ZANJ*, AND SO I HAD FREED HIM AND MADE HIM *ĀZĀT*.
HE SENT INFORMATION BACK LOYALLY UNTIL SEVERAL DAYS AGO, WHEN WORD FROM HIM ABRUPTLY STOPPED COMING.
IT SEEMS AS THOUGH HE WAS KILLED.
...AND SOROUSH, TOO?
YES, YOUR HIGH-NESS, IT IS LIKELY.
I CAN ONLY HOPE THAT MY FEARS WILL BE PROVED WRONG.

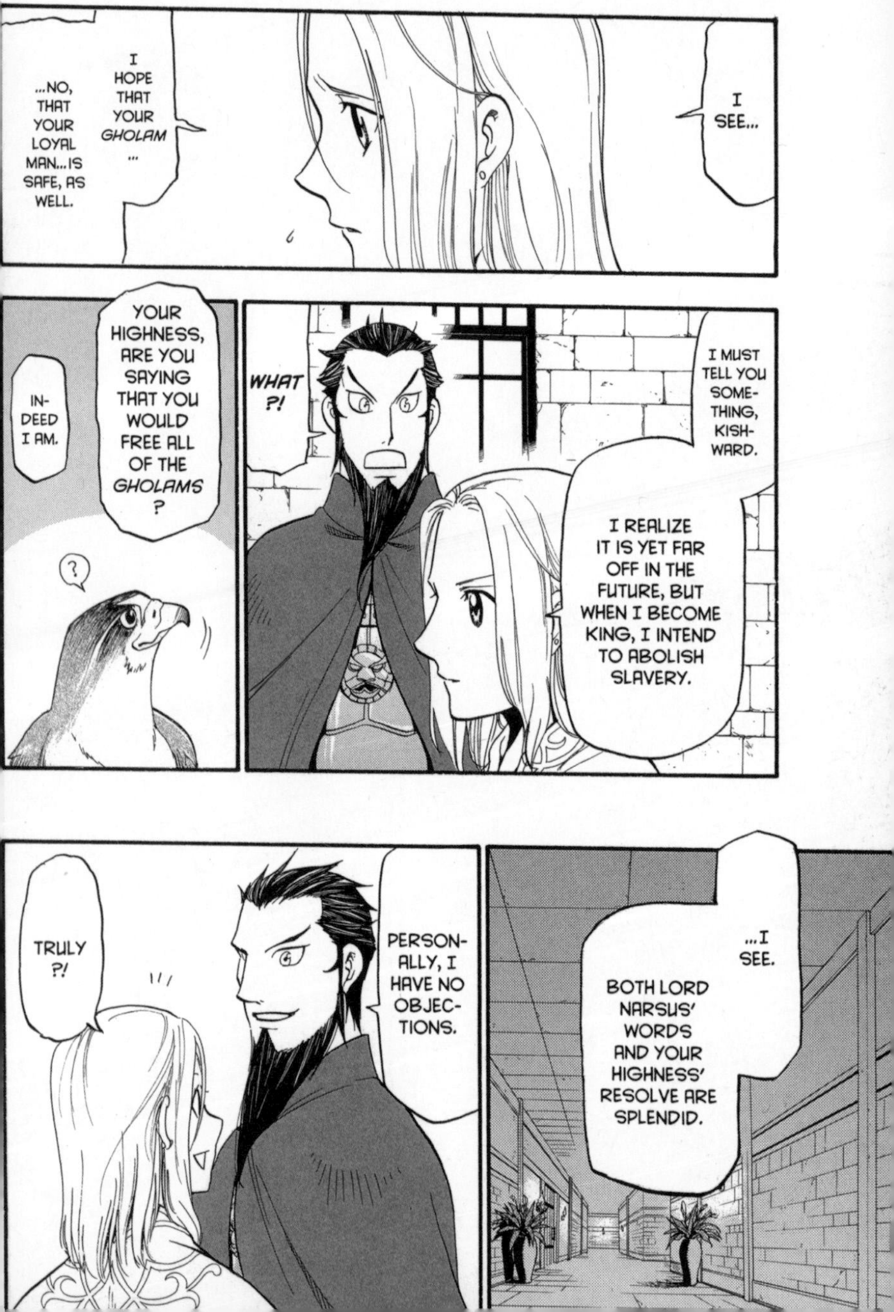
I SEE...
I HOPE THAT YOUR GHOLAM ...
...NO, THAT YOUR LOYAL MAN...IS SAFE, AS WELL.
I MUST TELL YOU SOMETHING, KISHWARD.
I REALIZE IT IS YET FAR OFF IN THE FUTURE, BUT WHEN I BECOME KING, I INTEND TO ABOLISH SLAVERY.
WHAT?!
YOUR HIGHNESS, ARE YOU SAYING THAT YOU WOULD FREE ALL OF THE GHOLAMS?
INDEED I AM.
?
...I SEE.
BOTH LORD NARSUS' WORDS AND YOUR HIGHNESS' RESOLVE ARE SPLENDID.
PERSONALLY, I HAVE NO OBJECTIONS.
TRULY?!

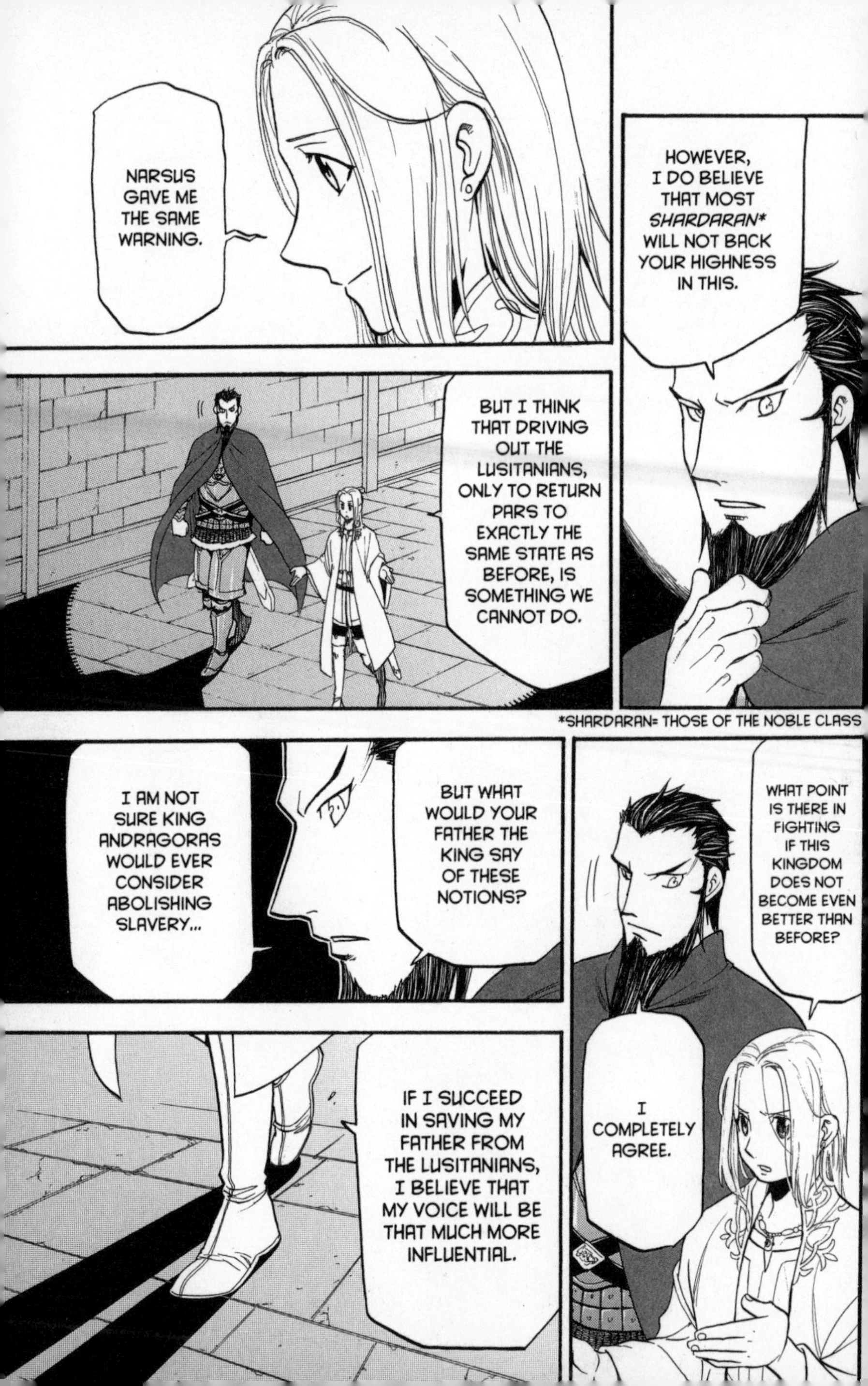
HOWEVER, I DO BELIEVE THAT MOST *SHARDARAN** WILL NOT BACK YOUR HIGHNESS IN THIS.
NARSUS GAVE ME THE SAME WARNING.
BUT I THINK THAT DRIVING OUT THE LUSITANIANS, ONLY TO RETURN PARS TO EXACTLY THE SAME STATE AS BEFORE, IS SOMETHING WE CANNOT DO.
WHAT POINT IS THERE IN FIGHTING IF THIS KINGDOM DOES NOT BECOME EVEN BETTER THAN BEFORE?
I COMPLETELY AGREE.
BUT WHAT WOULD YOUR FATHER THE KING SAY OF THESE NOTIONS?
I AM NOT SURE KING ANDRAGORAS WOULD EVER CONSIDER ABOLISHING SLAVERY...
IF I SUCCEED IN SAVING MY FATHER FROM THE LUSITANIANS, I BELIEVE THAT MY VOICE WILL BE THAT MUCH MORE INFLUENTIAL.

*SHARDARAN= THOSE OF THE NOBLE CLASS

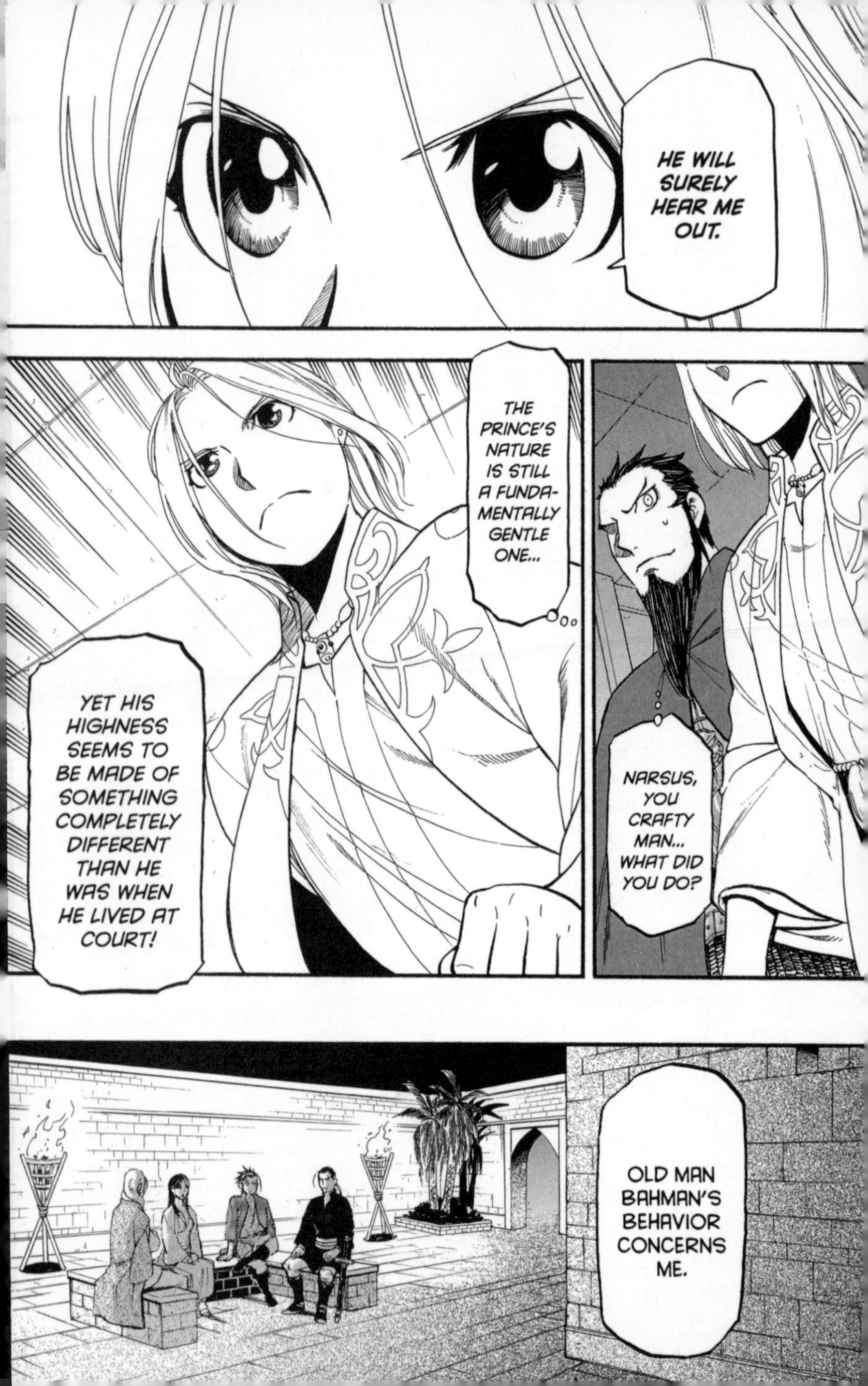
HE WILL SURELY HEAR ME OUT.
NARSUS, YOU CRAFTY MAN... WHAT DID YOU DO?
THE PRINCE'S NATURE IS STILL A FUNDA-MENTALLY GENTLE ONE...
YET HIS HIGHNESS SEEMS TO BE MADE OF SOMETHING COMPLETELY DIFFERENT THAN HE WAS WHEN HE LIVED AT COURT!
OLD MAN BAHMAN'S BEHAVIOR CONCERNS ME.

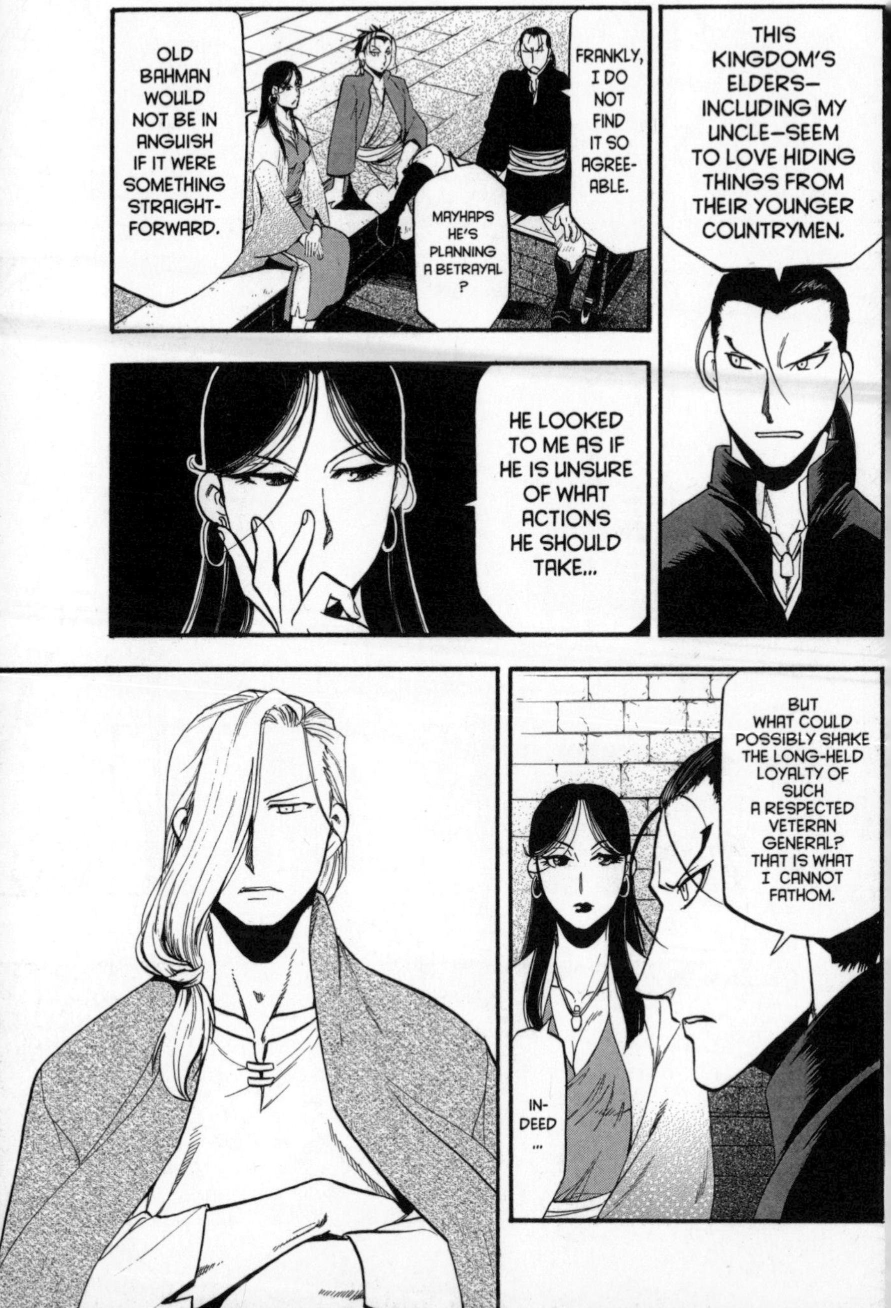
THIS KINGDOM'S ELDERS—INCLUDING MY UNCLE—SEEM TO LOVE HIDING THINGS FROM THEIR YOUNGER COUNTRYMEN.
FRANKLY, I DO NOT FIND IT SO AGREEABLE.
MAYHAPS HE'S PLANNING A BETRAYAL?
OLD BAHMAN WOULD NOT BE IN ANGUISH IF IT WERE SOMETHING STRAIGHTFORWARD.
HE LOOKED TO ME AS IF HE IS UNSURE OF WHAT ACTIONS HE SHOULD TAKE...
BUT WHAT COULD POSSIBLY SHAKE THE LONG-HELD LOYALTY OF SUCH A RESPECTED VETERAN GENERAL? THAT IS WHAT I CANNOT FATHOM.
INDEED...

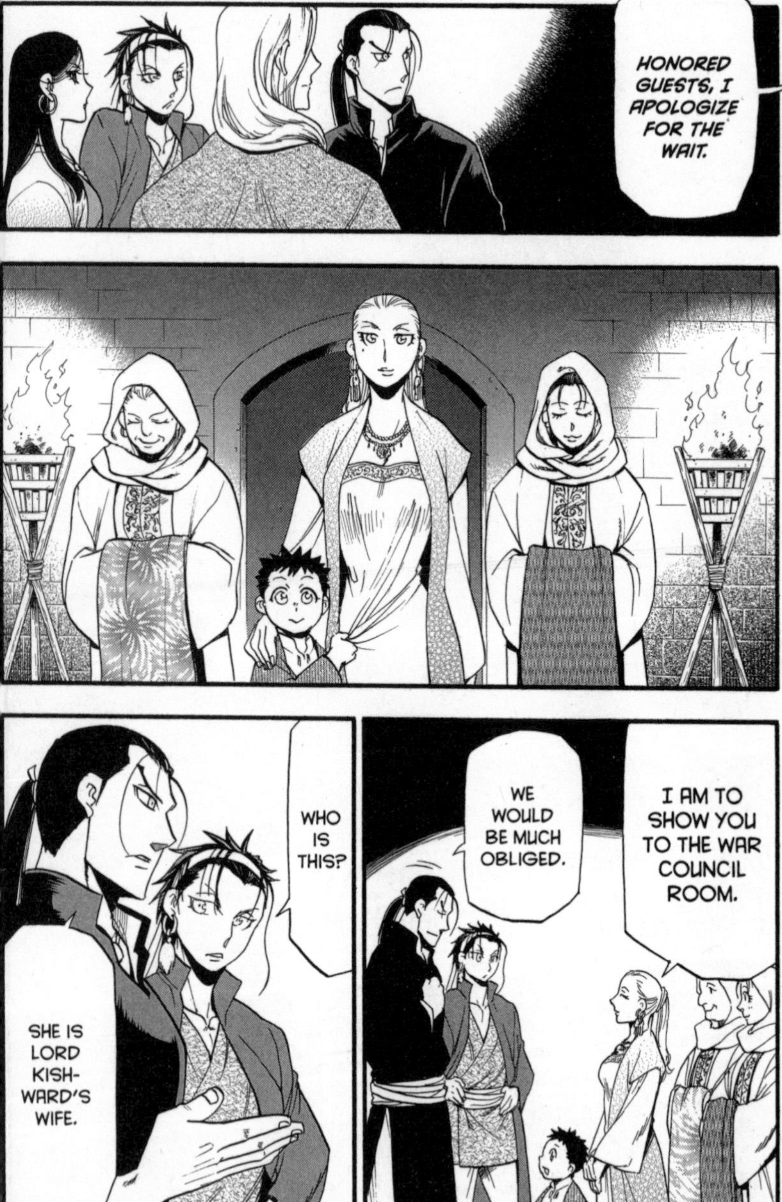
HONORED GUESTS, I APOLOGIZE FOR THE WAIT.
I AM TO SHOW YOU TO THE WAR COUNCIL ROOM.
WE WOULD BE MUCH OBLIGED.
WHO IS THIS?
SHE IS LORD KISH-WARD'S WIFE.

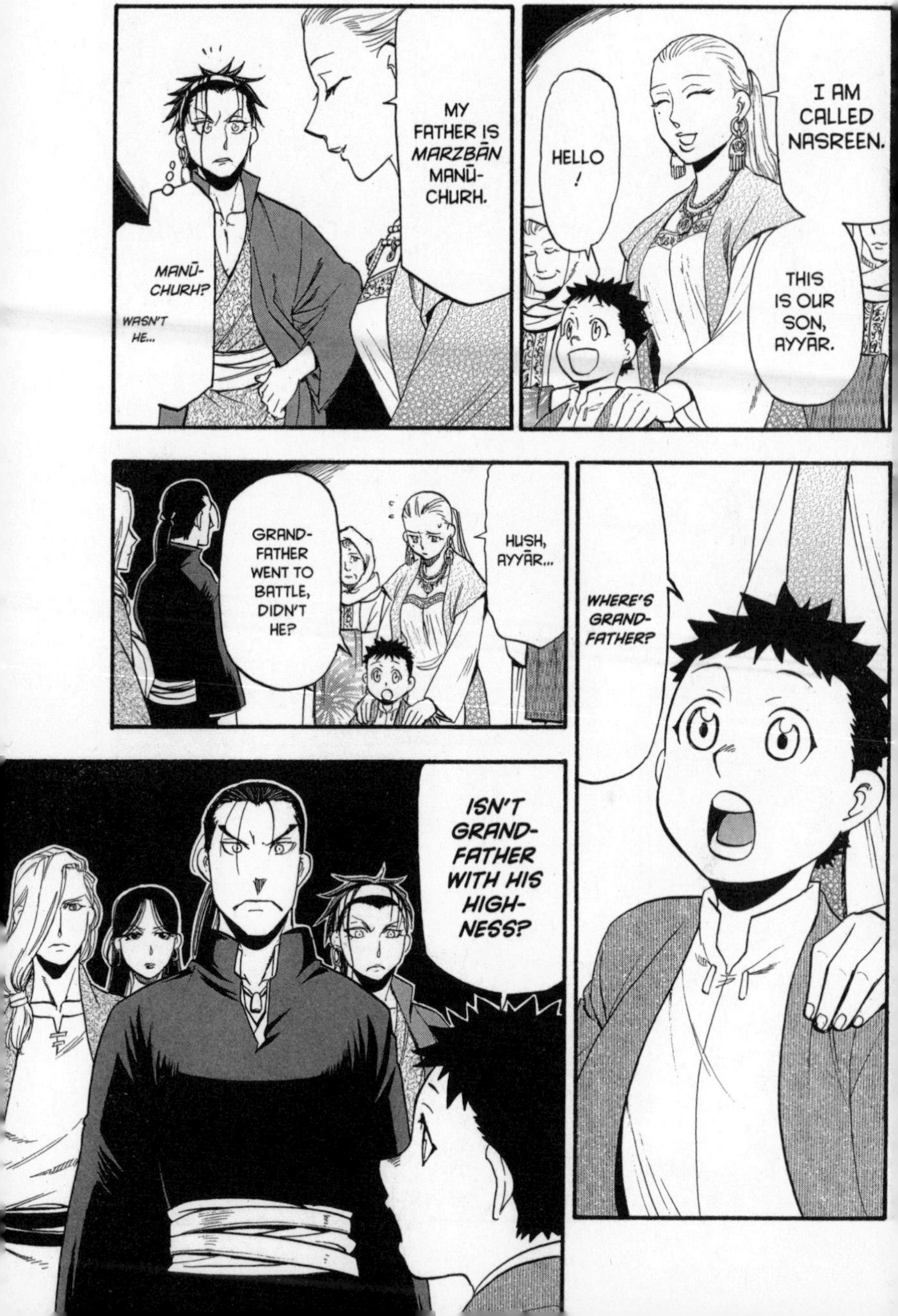
I AM CALLED NASREEN.
HELLO!
THIS IS OUR SON, AYYĀR.
MY FATHER IS MARZBĀN MANŪ-CHURH.
MANŪ-CHURH?
WASN'T HE...
WHERE'S GRAND-FATHER?
HUSH, AYYĀR...
GRAND-FATHER WENT TO BATTLE, DIDN'T HE?
ISN'T GRAND-FATHER WITH HIS HIGH-NESS?

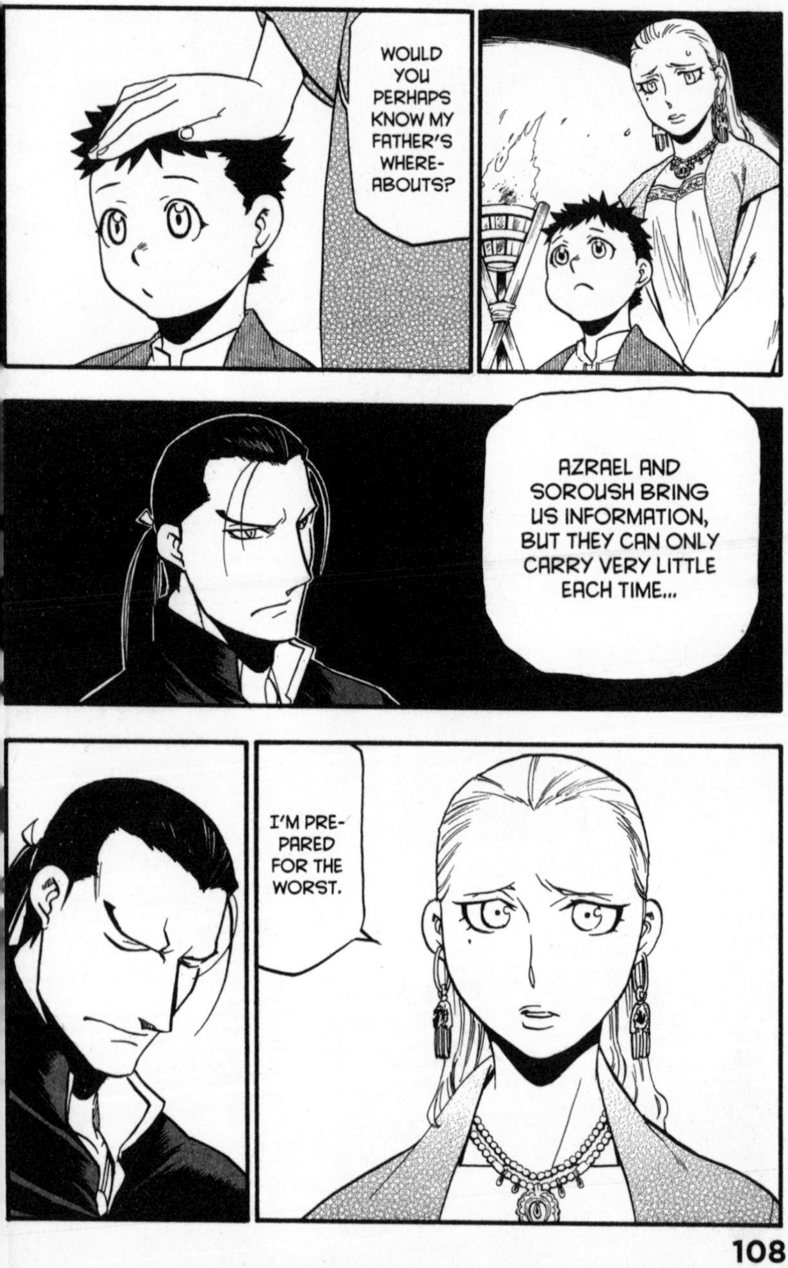
WOULD YOU PERHAPS KNOW MY FATHER'S WHERE-ABOUTS?
AZRAEL AND SOROUSH BRING US INFORMATION, BUT THEY CAN ONLY CARRY VERY LITTLE EACH TIME...
I'M PRE-PARED FOR THE WORST.

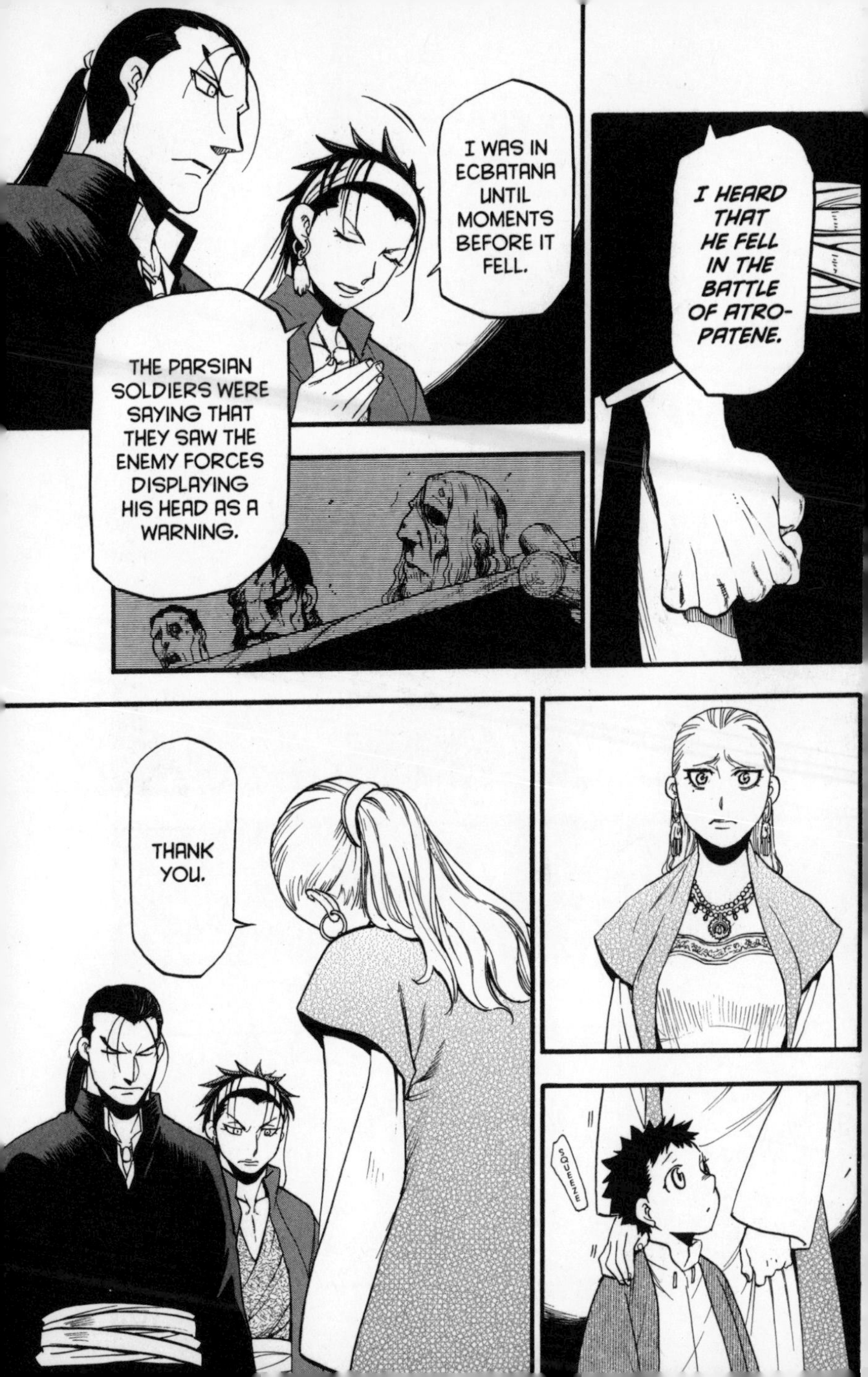
I HEARD THAT HE FELL IN THE BATTLE OF ATRO-PATENE.
I WAS IN ECBATANA UNTIL MOMENTS BEFORE IT FELL.
THE PARSIAN SOLDIERS WERE SAYING THAT THEY SAW THE ENEMY FORCES DISPLAYING HIS HEAD AS A WARNING.
SQUEEZE
THANK YOU.

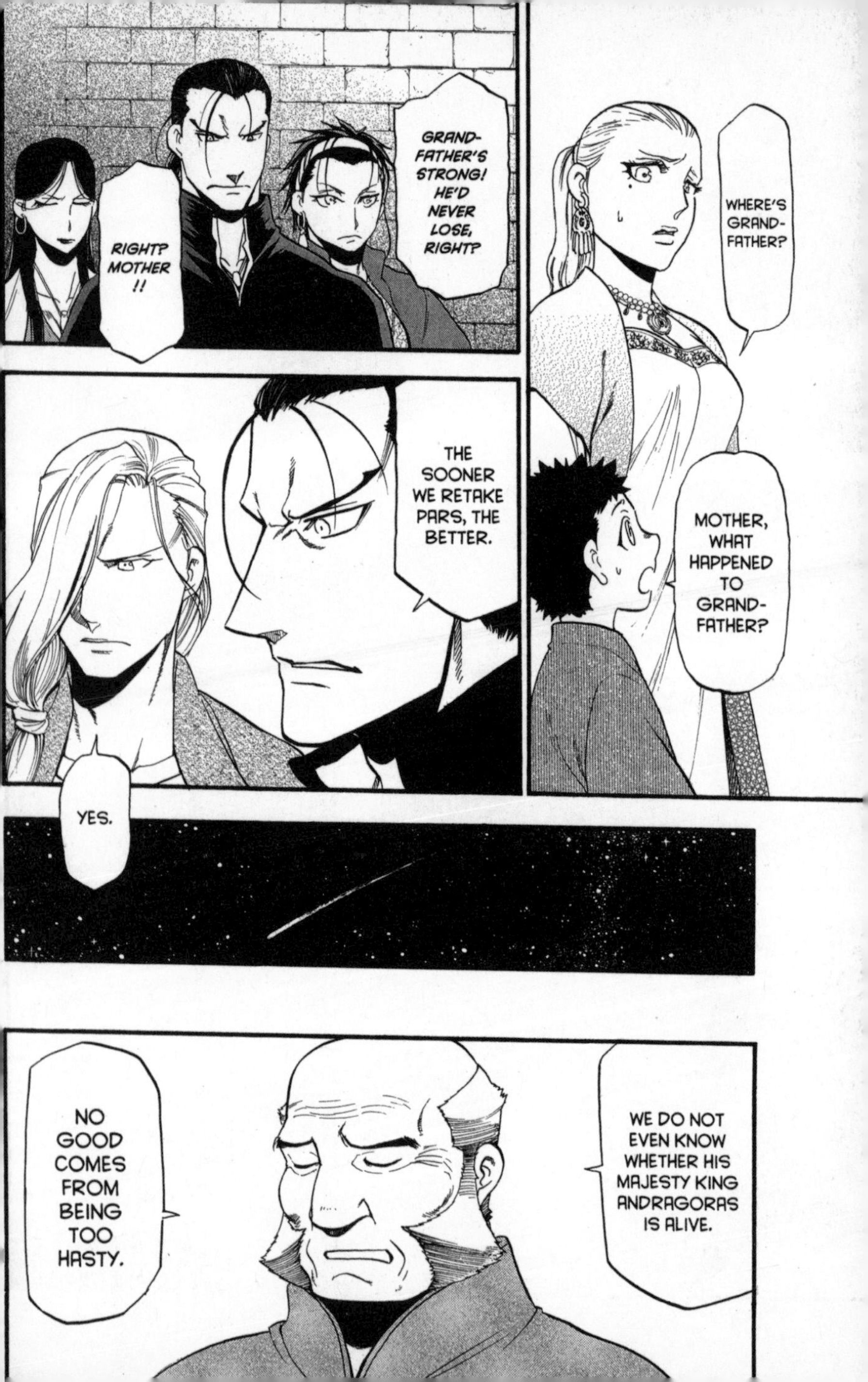
WHERE'S GRAND-FATHER?
MOTHER, WHAT HAPPENED TO GRAND-FATHER?
GRAND-FATHER'S STRONG! HE'D NEVER LOSE, RIGHT?
RIGHT? MOTHER !!
THE SOONER WE RETAKE PARS, THE BETTER.
YES.
WE DO NOT EVEN KNOW WHETHER HIS MAJESTY KING ANDRAGORAS IS ALIVE.
NO GOOD COMES FROM BEING TOO HASTY.

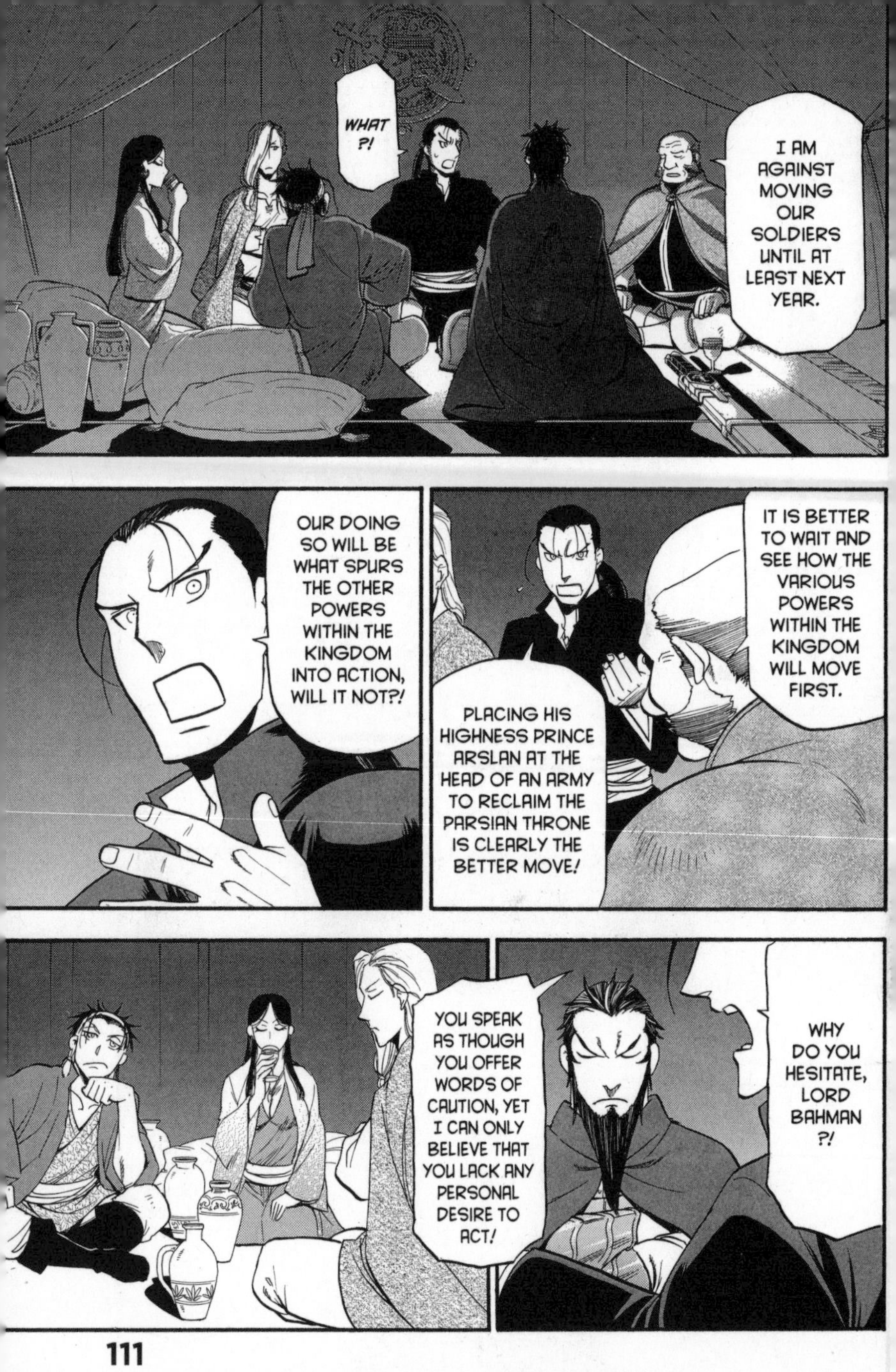
I AM AGAINST MOVING OUR SOLDIERS UNTIL AT LEAST NEXT YEAR.
WHAT?!
IT IS BETTER TO WAIT AND SEE HOW THE VARIOUS POWERS WITHIN THE KINGDOM WILL MOVE FIRST.
PLACING HIS HIGHNESS PRINCE ARSLAN AT THE HEAD OF AN ARMY TO RECLAIM THE PARSIAN THRONE IS CLEARLY THE BETTER MOVE!
OUR DOING SO WILL BE WHAT SPURS THE OTHER POWERS WITHIN THE KINGDOM INTO ACTION, WILL IT NOT?!
WHY DO YOU HESITATE, LORD BAHMAN?!
YOU SPEAK AS THOUGH YOU OFFER WORDS OF CAUTION, YET I CAN ONLY BELIEVE THAT YOU LACK ANY PERSONAL DESIRE TO ACT!

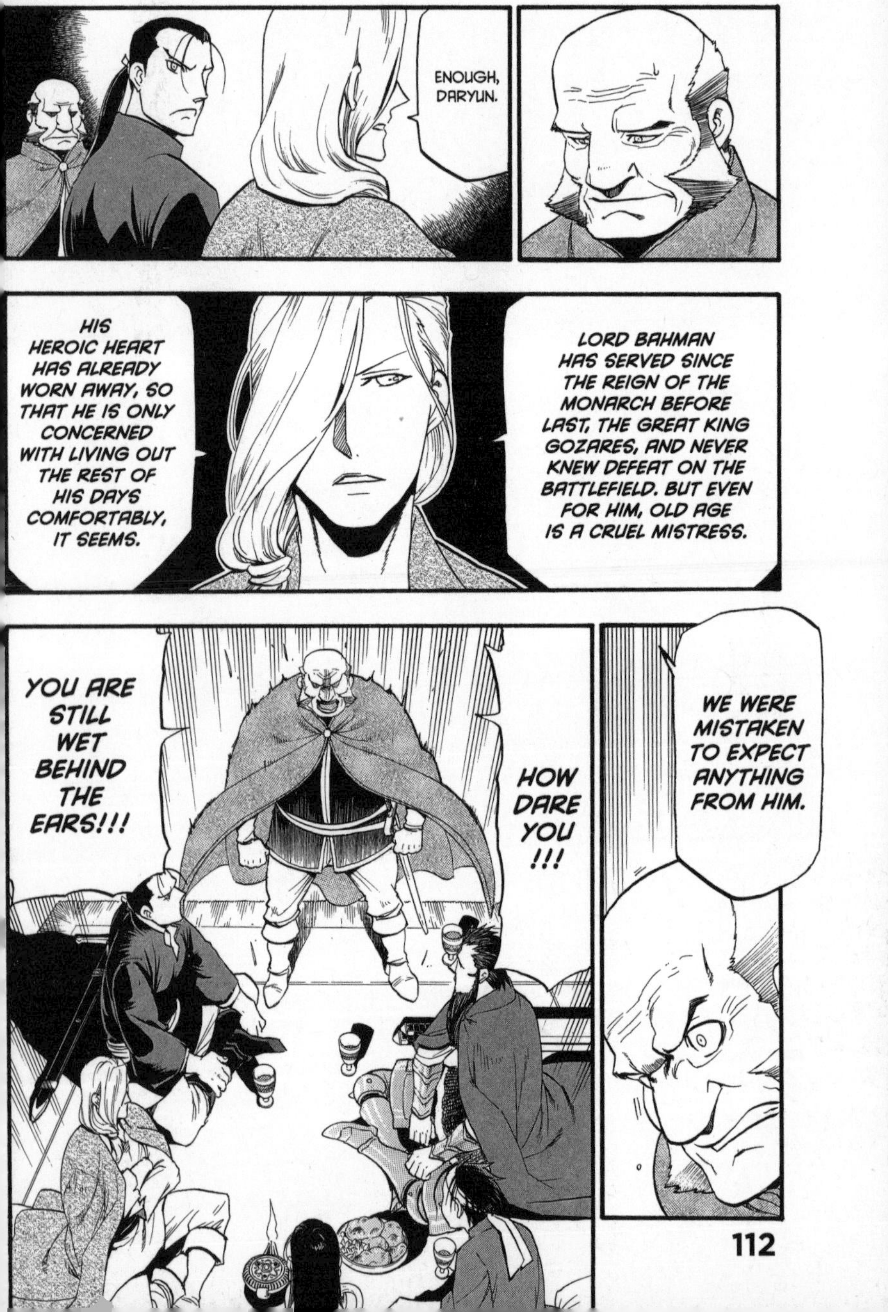
ENOUGH, DARYUN.
LORD BAHMAN HAS SERVED SINCE THE REIGN OF THE MONARCH BEFORE LAST, THE GREAT KING GOZARES, AND NEVER KNEW DEFEAT ON THE BATTLEFIELD. BUT EVEN FOR HIM, OLD AGE IS A CRUEL MISTRESS.
HIS HEROIC HEART HAS ALREADY WORN AWAY, SO THAT HE IS ONLY CONCERNED WITH LIVING OUT THE REST OF HIS DAYS COMFORTABLY, IT SEEMS.
WE WERE MISTAKEN TO EXPECT ANYTHING FROM HIM.
HOW DARE YOU!!!
YOU ARE STILL WET BEHIND THE EARS!!!

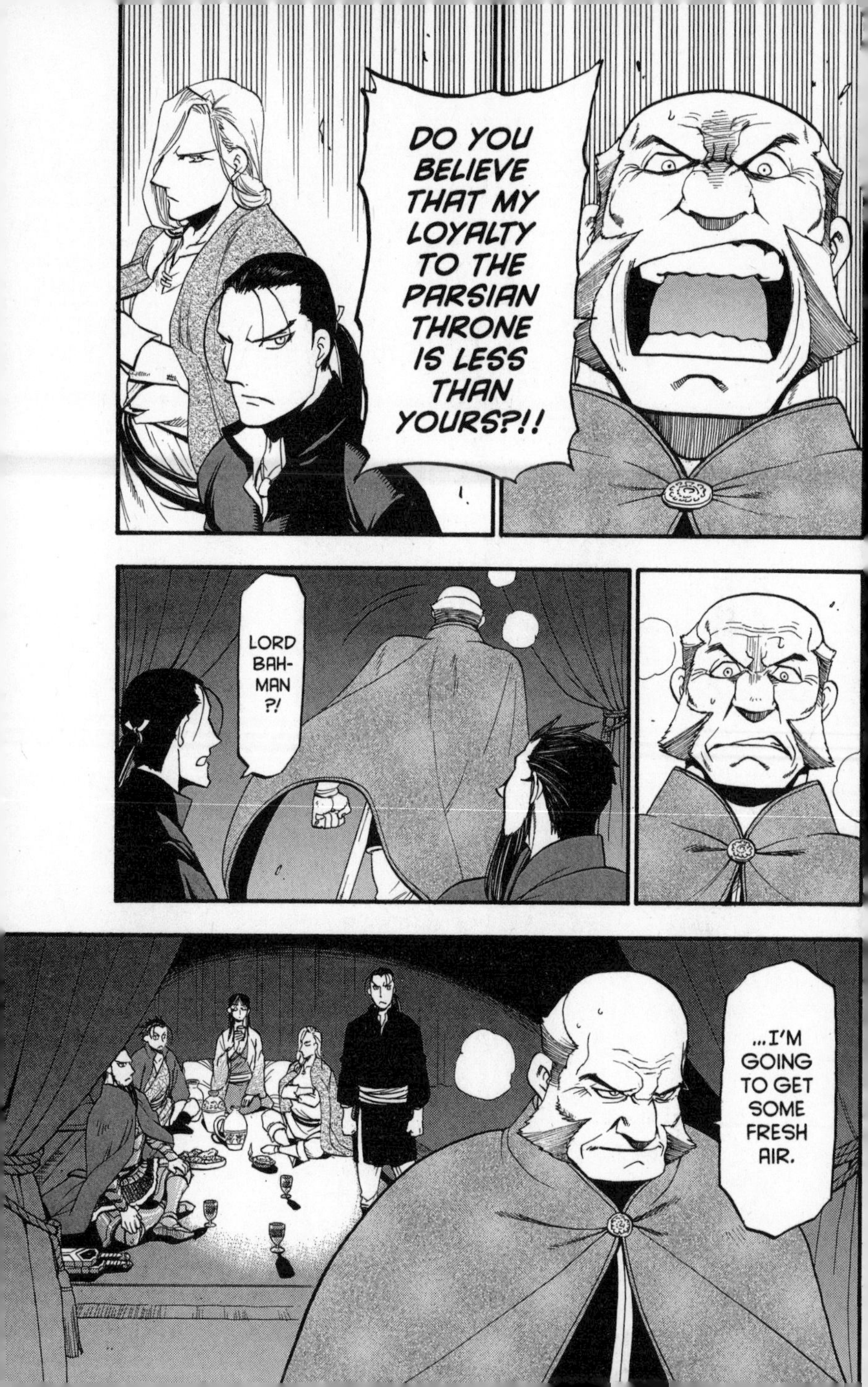
DO YOU BELIEVE THAT MY LOYALTY TO THE PARSIAN THRONE IS LESS THAN YOURS?!!
LORD BAH-MAN ?!
...I'M GOING TO GET SOME FRESH AIR.

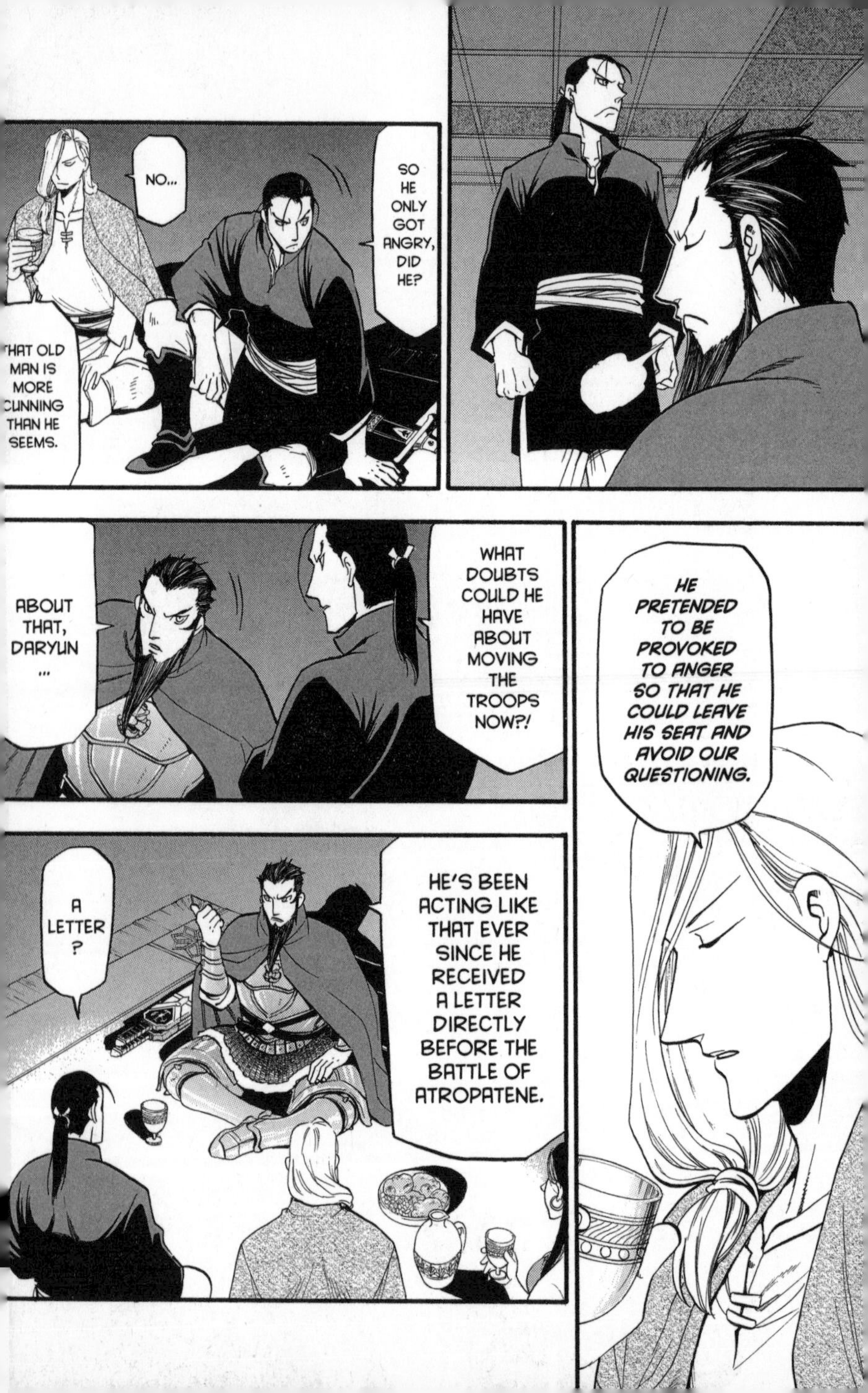
SO HE ONLY GOT ANGRY, DID HE?
NO...
THAT OLD MAN IS MORE CUNNING THAN HE SEEMS.
HE PRETENDED TO BE PROVOKED TO ANGER SO THAT HE COULD LEAVE HIS SEAT AND AVOID OUR QUESTIONING.
WHAT DOUBTS COULD HE HAVE ABOUT MOVING THE TROOPS NOW?!
ABOUT THAT, DARYUN ...
HE'S BEEN ACTING LIKE THAT EVER SINCE HE RECEIVED A LETTER DIRECTLY BEFORE THE BATTLE OF ATROPATENE.
A LETTER ?

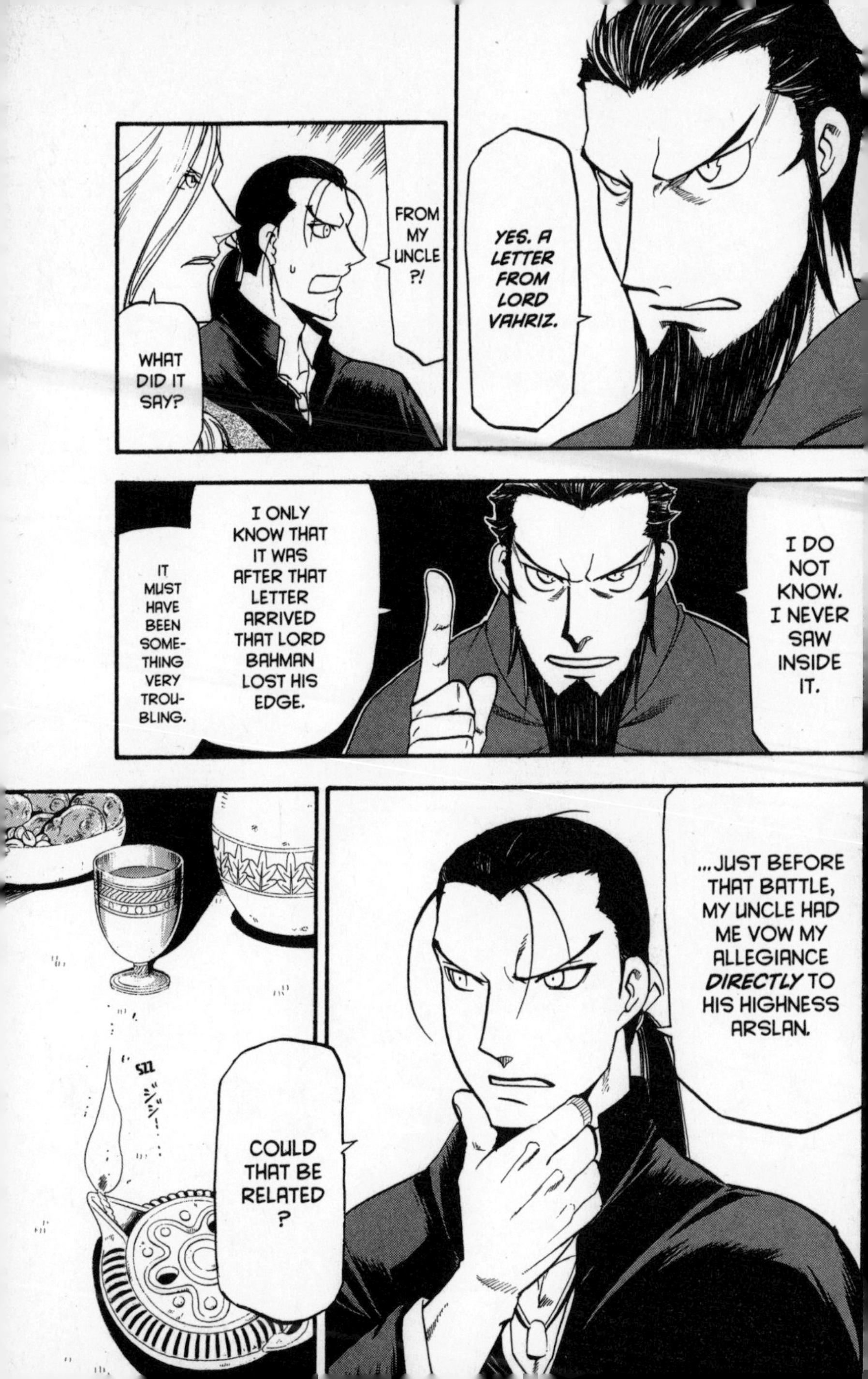
YES. A LETTER FROM LORD VAHRIZ.
FROM MY UNCLE ?!
WHAT DID IT SAY?
I DO NOT KNOW. I NEVER SAW INSIDE IT.
I ONLY KNOW THAT IT WAS AFTER THAT LETTER ARRIVED THAT LORD BAHMAN LOST HIS EDGE.
IT MUST HAVE BEEN SOME-THING VERY TROU-BLING.
...JUST BEFORE THAT BATTLE, MY UNCLE HAD ME VOW MY ALLEGIANCE *DIRECTLY* TO HIS HIGHNESS ARSLAN.
COULD THAT BE RELATED ?

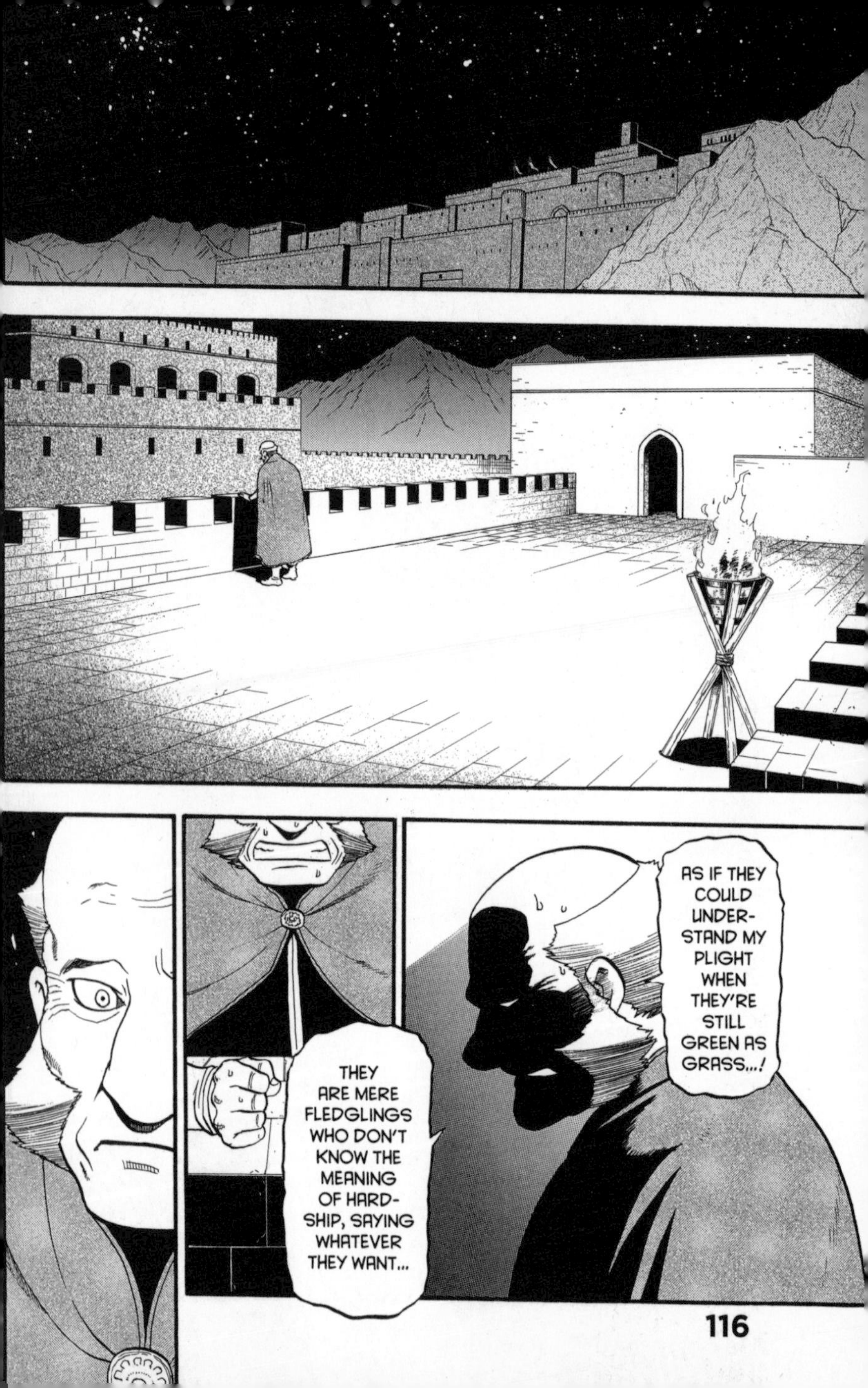
AS IF THEY COULD UNDER-STAND MY PLIGHT WHEN THEY'RE STILL GREEN AS GRASS...!
THEY ARE MERE FLEDGLINGS WHO DON'T KNOW THE MEANING OF HARD-SHIP, SAYING WHATEVER THEY WANT...

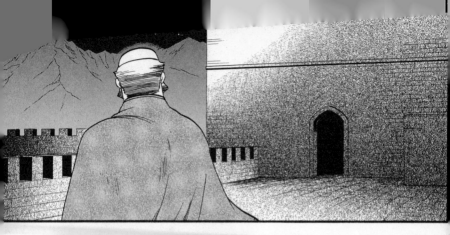

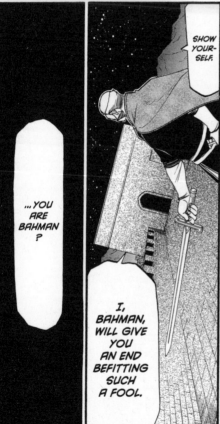

-SWUSH
WHO GOES THERE?
SHOW YOURSELF.
I, BAHMAN, WILL GIVE YOU AN END BEFITTING SUCH A FOOL.
...YOU ARE BAHMAN?

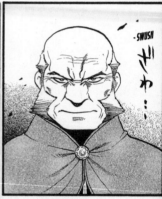

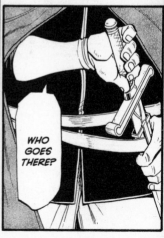

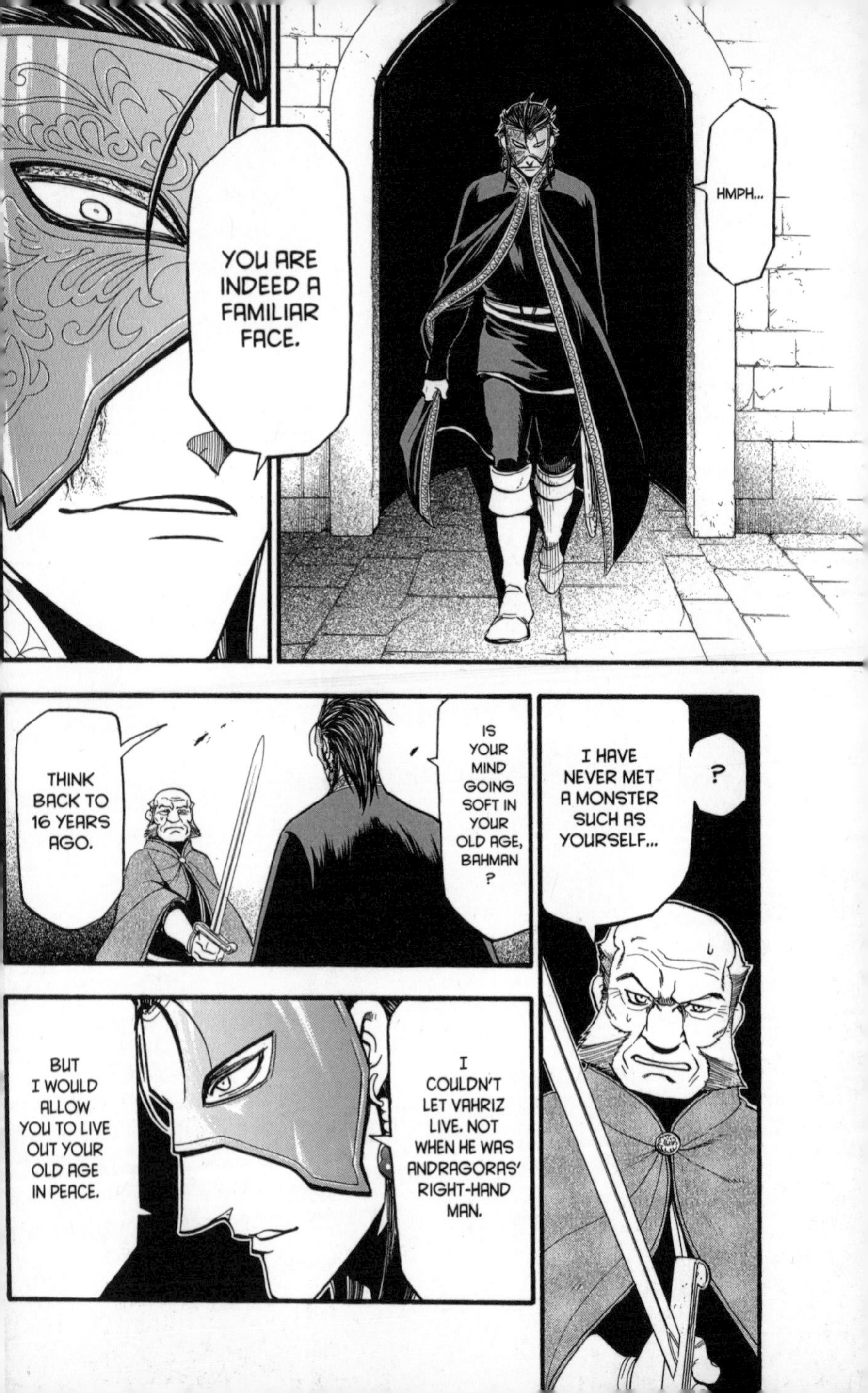
HMPH...
YOU ARE INDEED A FAMILIAR FACE.
?
I HAVE NEVER MET A MONSTER SUCH AS YOURSELF...
IS YOUR MIND GOING SOFT IN YOUR OLD AGE, BAHMAN?
THINK BACK TO 16 YEARS AGO.
I COULDN'T LET VAHRIZ LIVE. NOT WHEN HE WAS ANDRAGORAS' RIGHT-HAND MAN.
BUT I WOULD ALLOW YOU TO LIVE OUT YOUR OLD AGE IN PEACE.

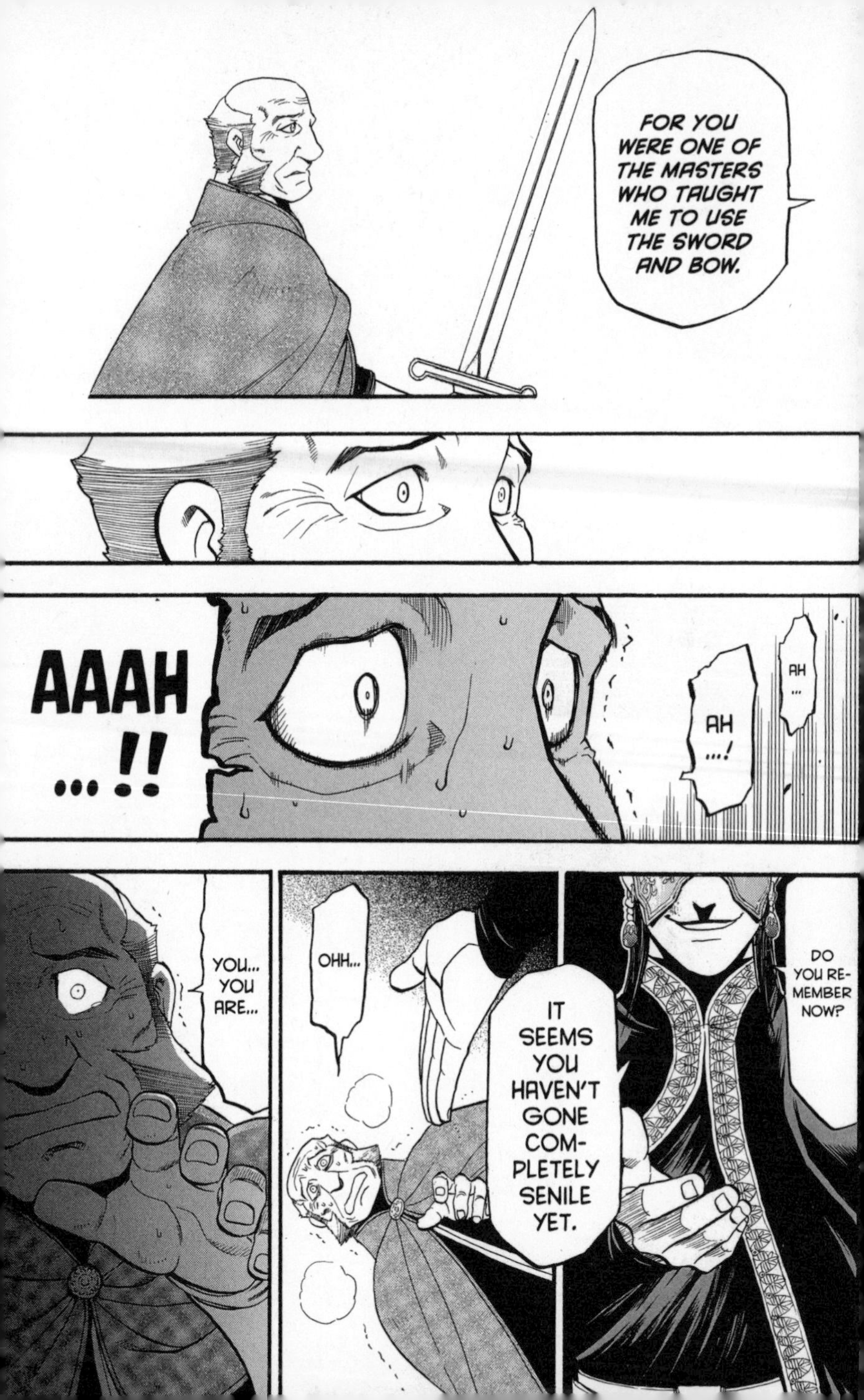
FOR YOU WERE ONE OF THE MASTERS WHO TAUGHT ME TO USE THE SWORD AND BOW.
AH ...
AH ...!
AAAH ...!!
DO YOU RE-MEMBER NOW?
IT SEEMS YOU HAVEN'T GONE COM-PLETELY SENILE YET.
OHH...
YOU... YOU ARE...

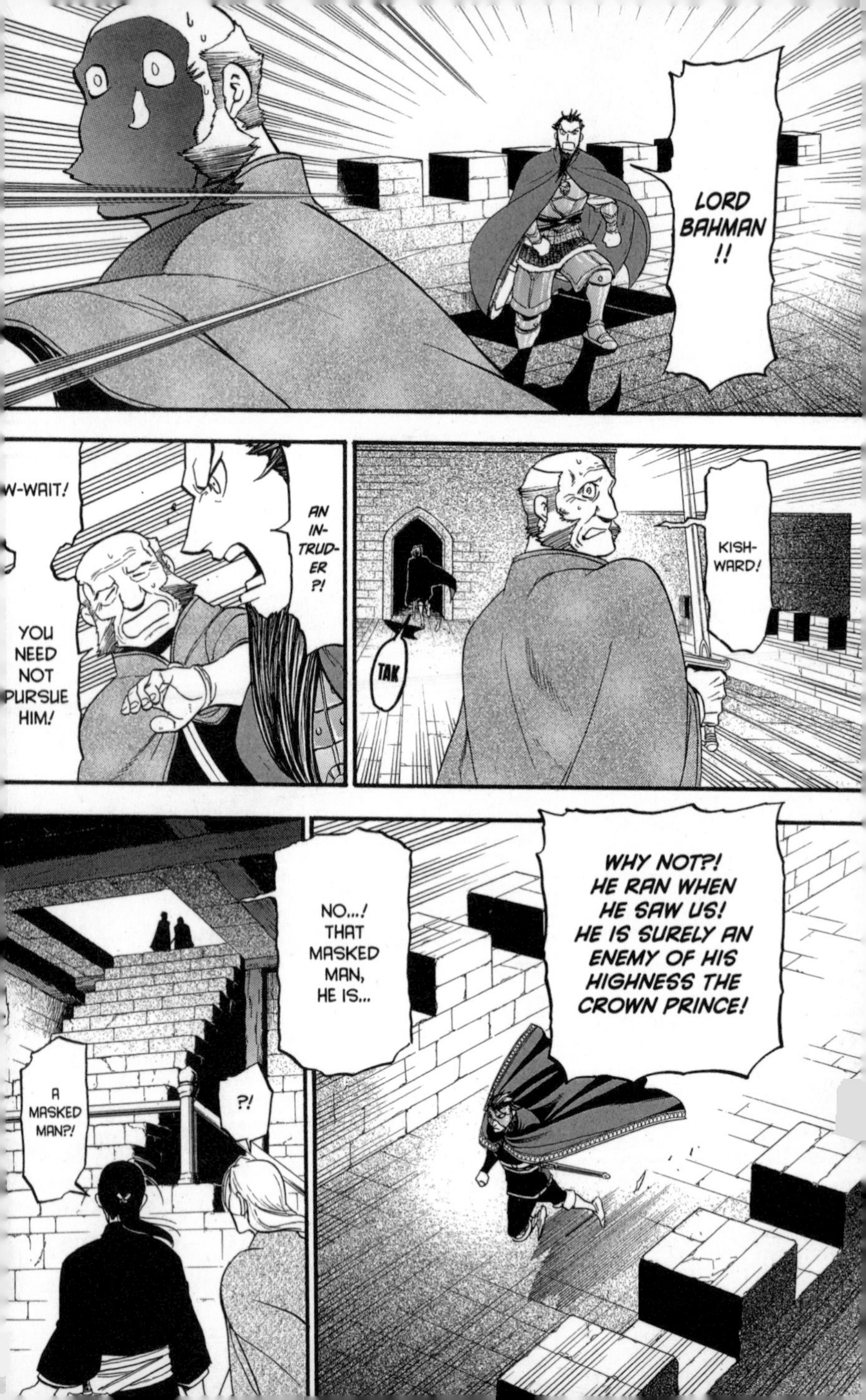
LORD BAHMAN!!
KISH-WARD!
TAK
AN IN-TRUD-ER?!
W-WAIT!
YOU NEED NOT PURSUE HIM!
WHY NOT?! HE RAN WHEN HE SAW US! HE IS SURELY AN ENEMY OF HIS HIGHNESS THE CROWN PRINCE!
NO...! THAT MASKED MAN, HE IS...
?!
A MASKED MAN?!

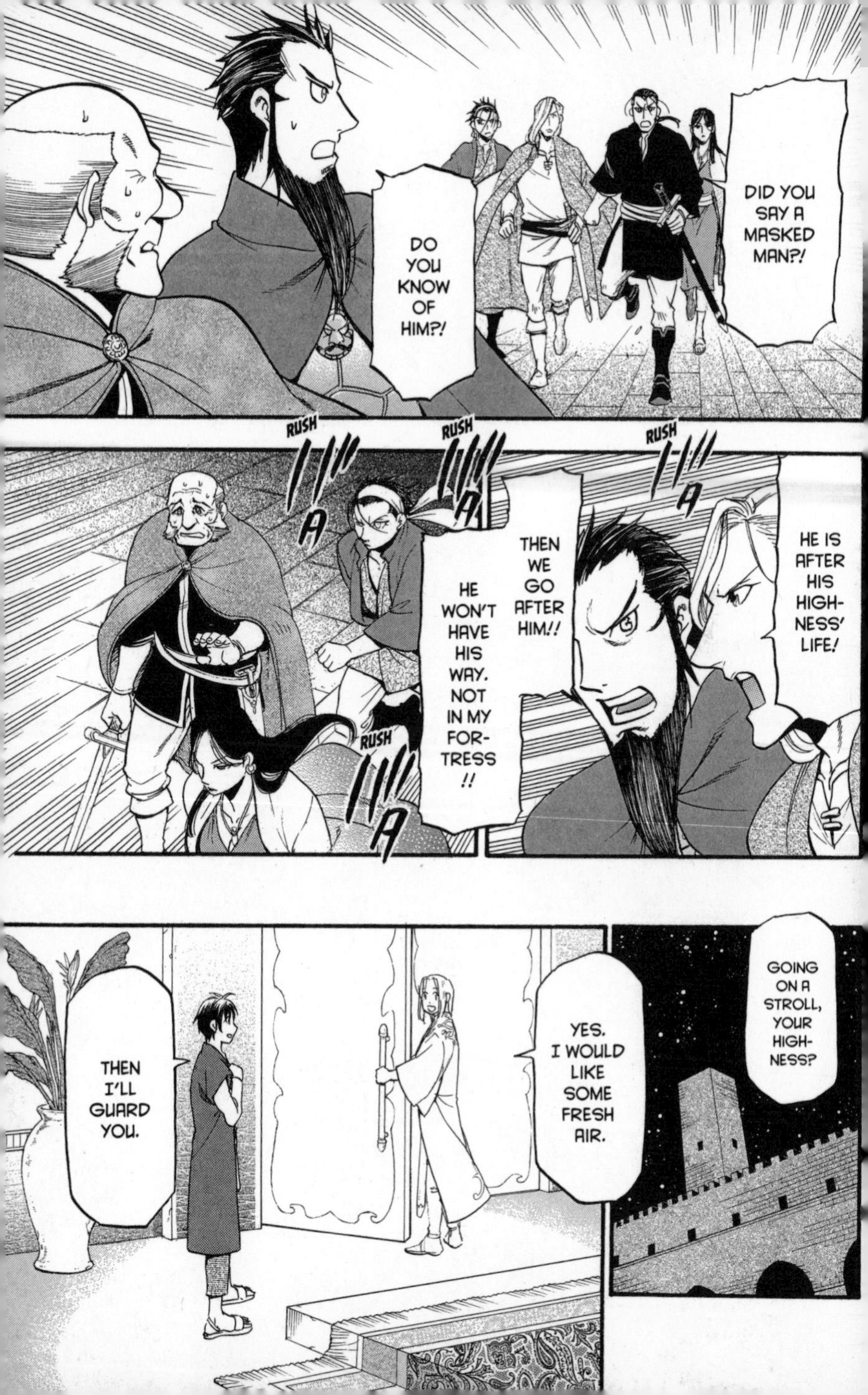
DID YOU SAY A MASKED MAN?!
DO YOU KNOW OF HIM?!
RUSH
HE IS AFTER HIS HIGHNESS' LIFE!
THEN WE GO AFTER HIM!!
HE WON'T HAVE HIS WAY. NOT IN MY FORTRESS!!
RUSH
RUSH
RUSH
GOING ON A STROLL, YOUR HIGHNESS?
YES. I WOULD LIKE SOME FRESH AIR.
THEN I'LL GUARD YOU.

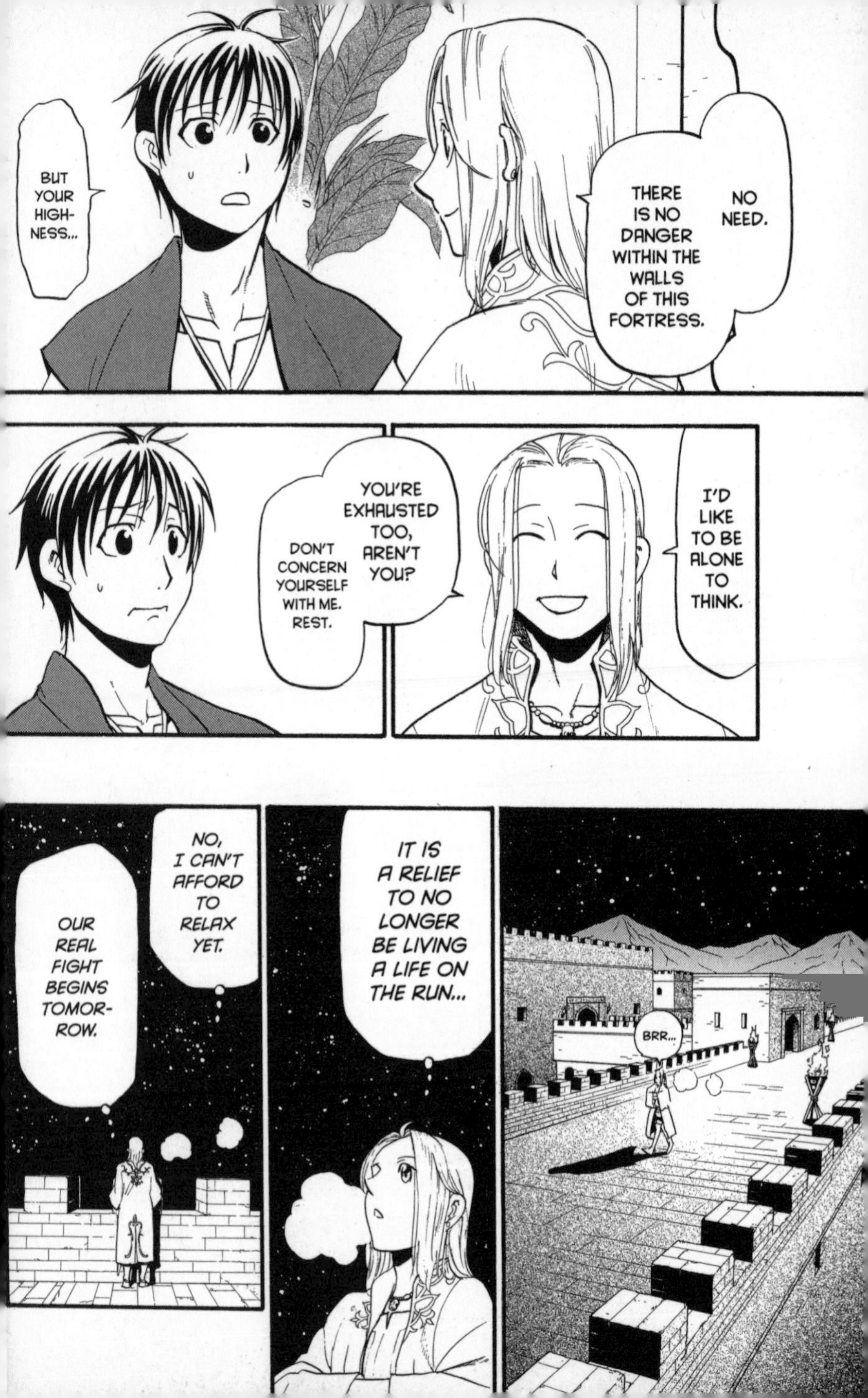
NO NEED.
THERE IS NO DANGER WITHIN THE WALLS OF THIS FORTRESS.
BUT YOUR HIGH-NESS...
I'D LIKE TO BE ALONE TO THINK.
YOU'RE EXHAUSTED TOO, AREN'T YOU?
DON'T CONCERN YOURSELF WITH ME. REST.
BRR...
IT IS A RELIEF TO NO LONGER BE LIVING A LIFE ON THE RUN...
NO, I CAN'T AFFORD TO RELAX YET.
OUR REAL FIGHT BEGINS TOMOR-ROW.

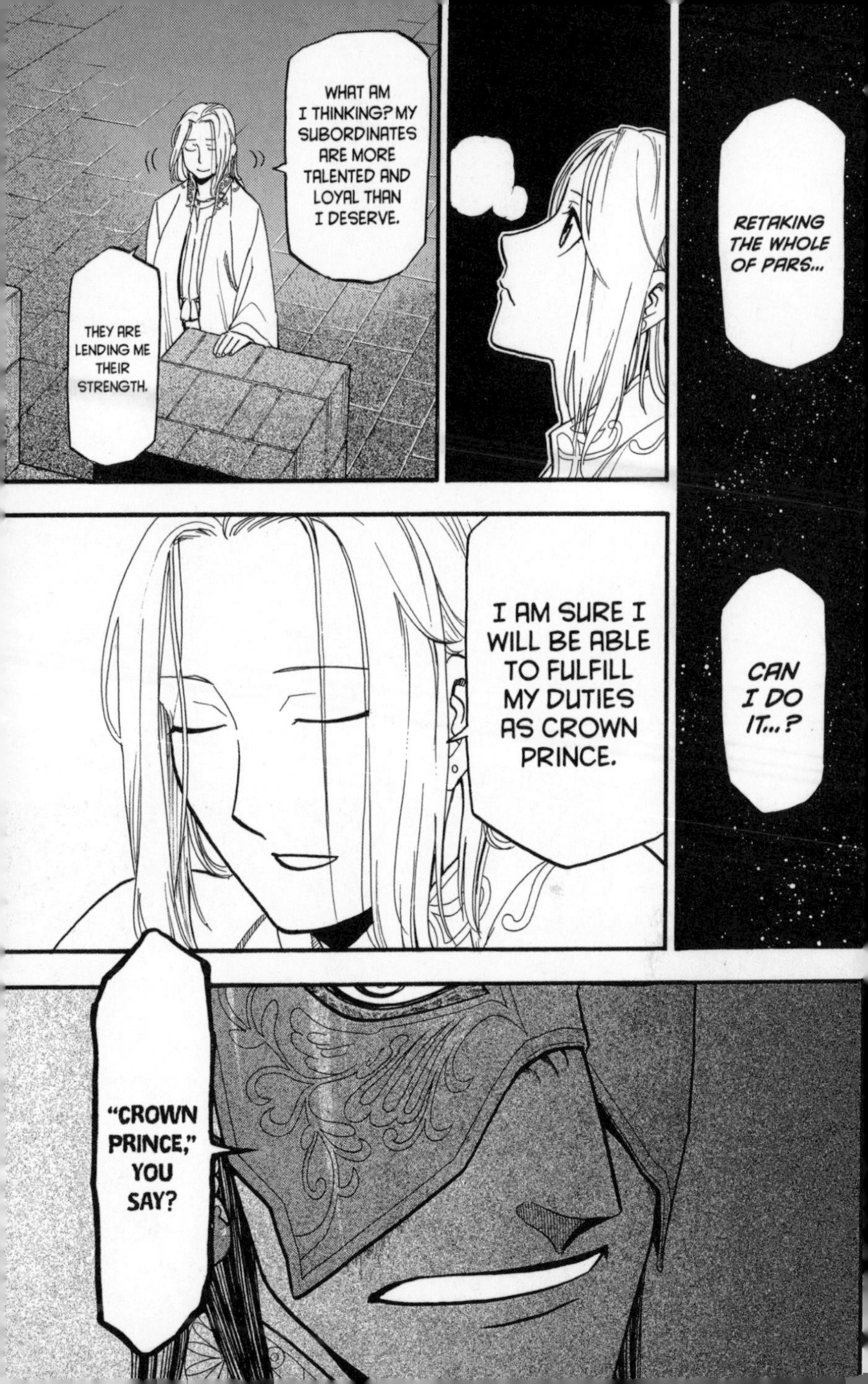
RETAKING THE WHOLE OF PARS...
CAN I DO IT...?
WHAT AM I THINKING? MY SUBORDINATES ARE MORE TALENTED AND LOYAL THAN I DESERVE.
THEY ARE LENDING ME THEIR STRENGTH.
I AM SURE I WILL BE ABLE TO FULFILL MY DUTIES AS CROWN PRINCE.
"CROWN PRINCE," YOU SAY?

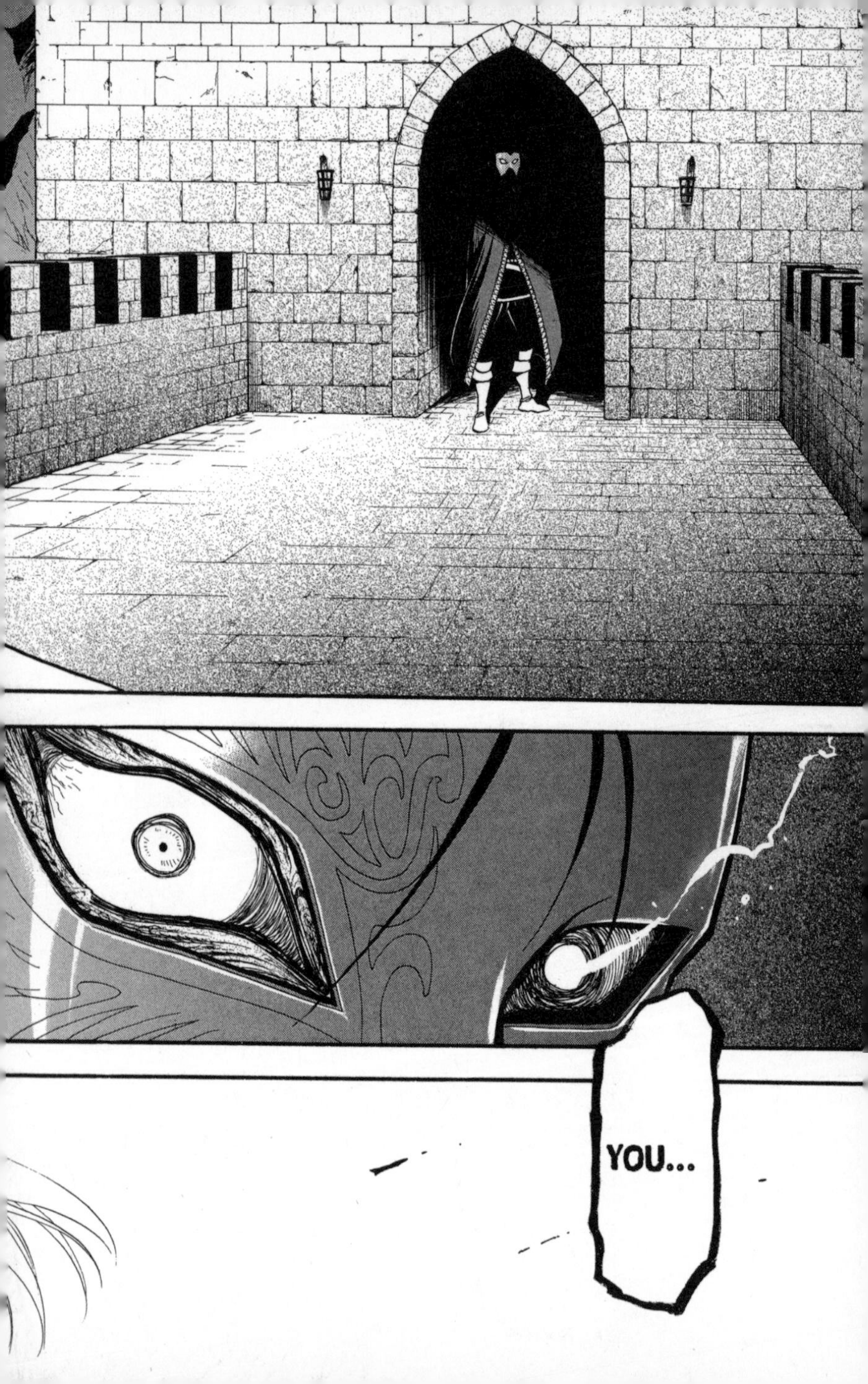
YOU...

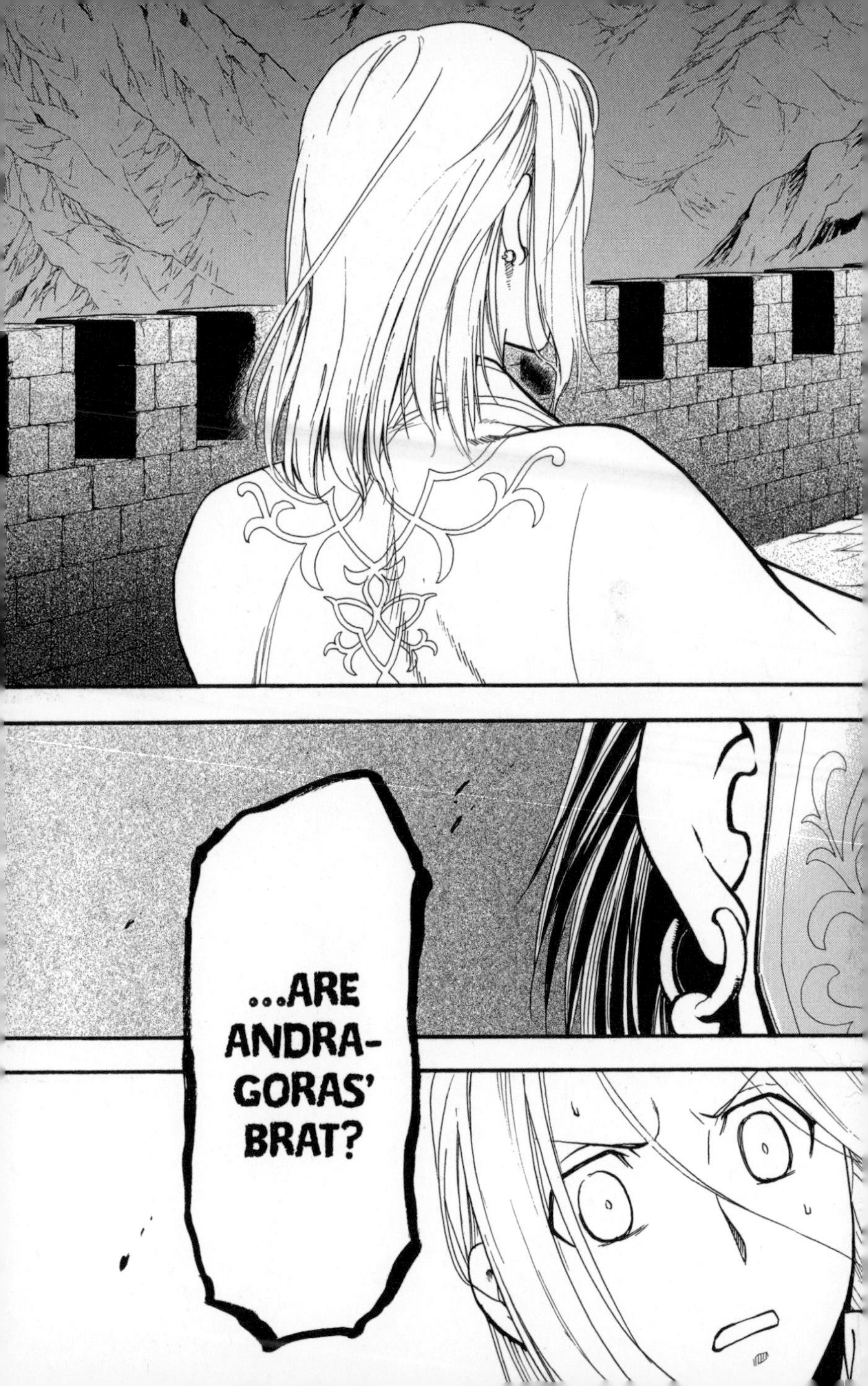
...ARE ANDRA-GORAS' BRAT?

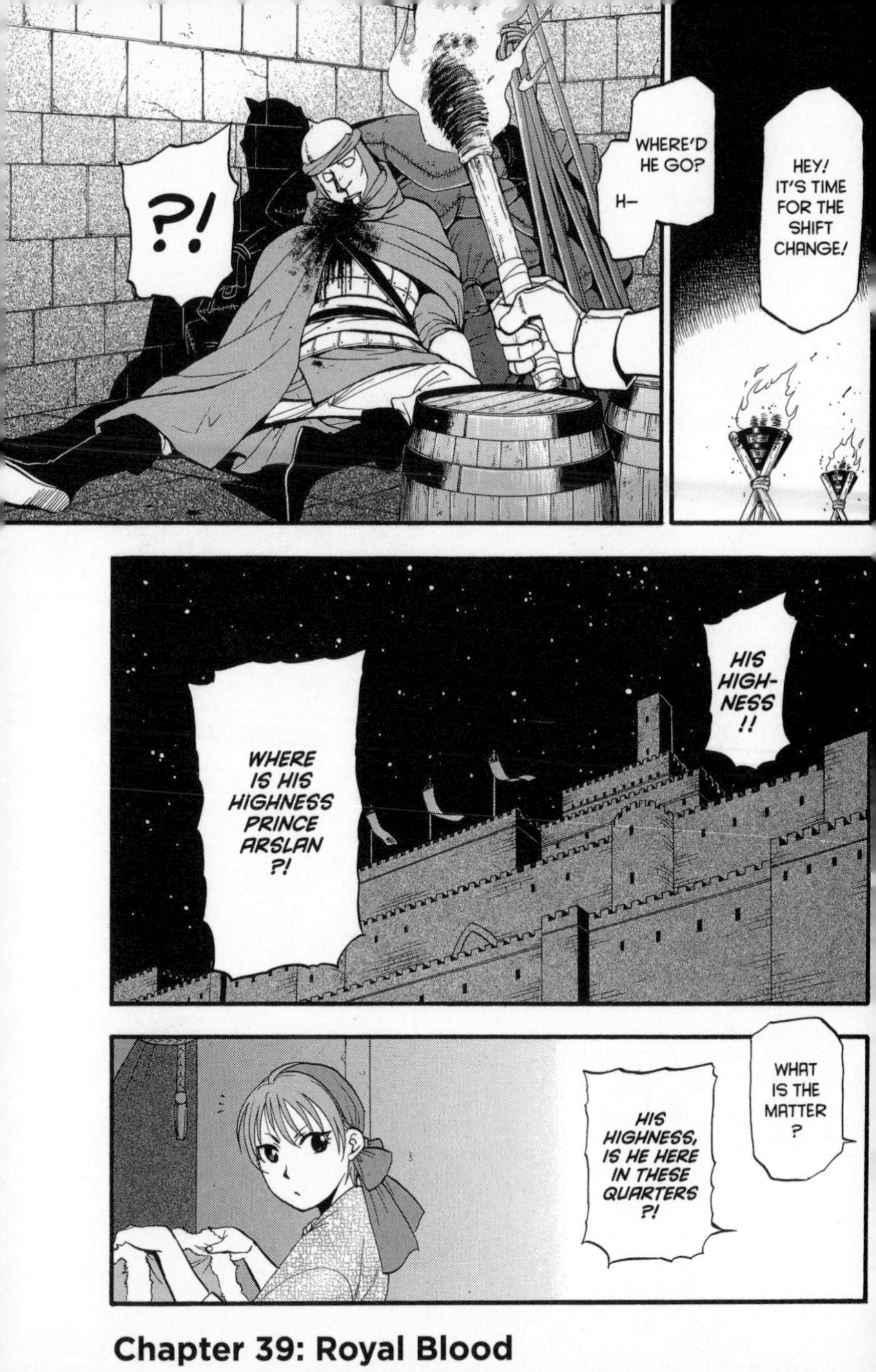
HEY! IT'S TIME FOR THE SHIFT CHANGE!
WHERE'D HE GO?
H–
?!
HIS HIGHNESS !!
WHERE IS HIS HIGHNESS PRINCE ARSLAN ?!
WHAT IS THE MATTER ?
HIS HIGHNESS, IS HE HERE IN THESE QUARTERS ?!

Chapter 39: Royal Blood

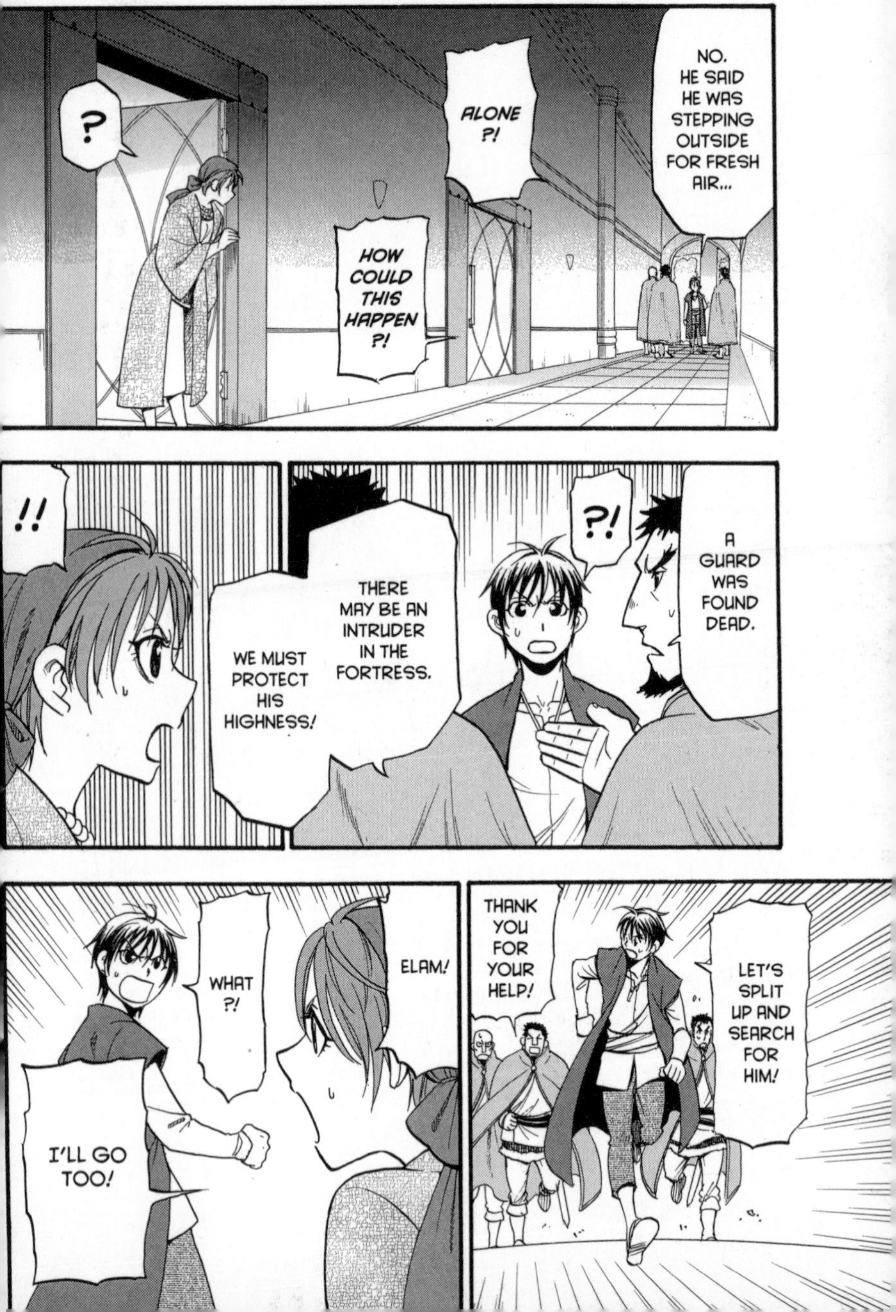
NO. HE SAID HE WAS STEPPING OUTSIDE FOR FRESH AIR...
ALONE ?!
HOW COULD THIS HAPPEN ?!
?
A GUARD WAS FOUND DEAD.
?!
THERE MAY BE AN INTRUDER IN THE FORTRESS.
WE MUST PROTECT HIS HIGHNESS!
!!
LET'S SPLIT UP AND SEARCH FOR HIM!
THANK YOU FOR YOUR HELP!
ELAM!
WHAT ?!
I'LL GO TOO!

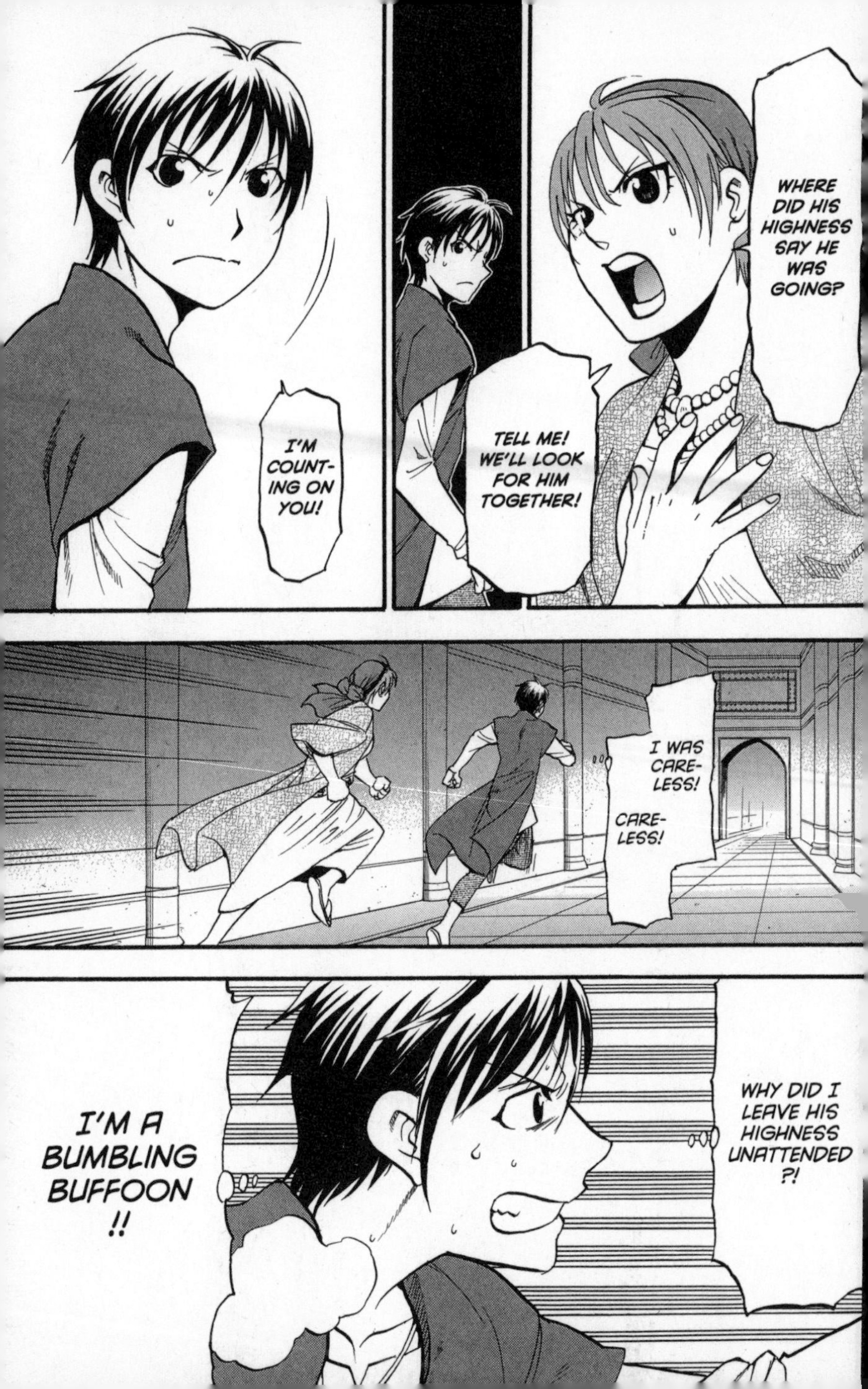
WHERE DID HIS HIGHNESS SAY HE WAS GOING?
TELL ME! WE'LL LOOK FOR HIM TOGETHER!
I'M COUNTING ON YOU!
I WAS CARELESS!
CARELESS!
WHY DID I LEAVE HIS HIGHNESS UNATTENDED?!
I'M A BUMBLING BUFFOON!!

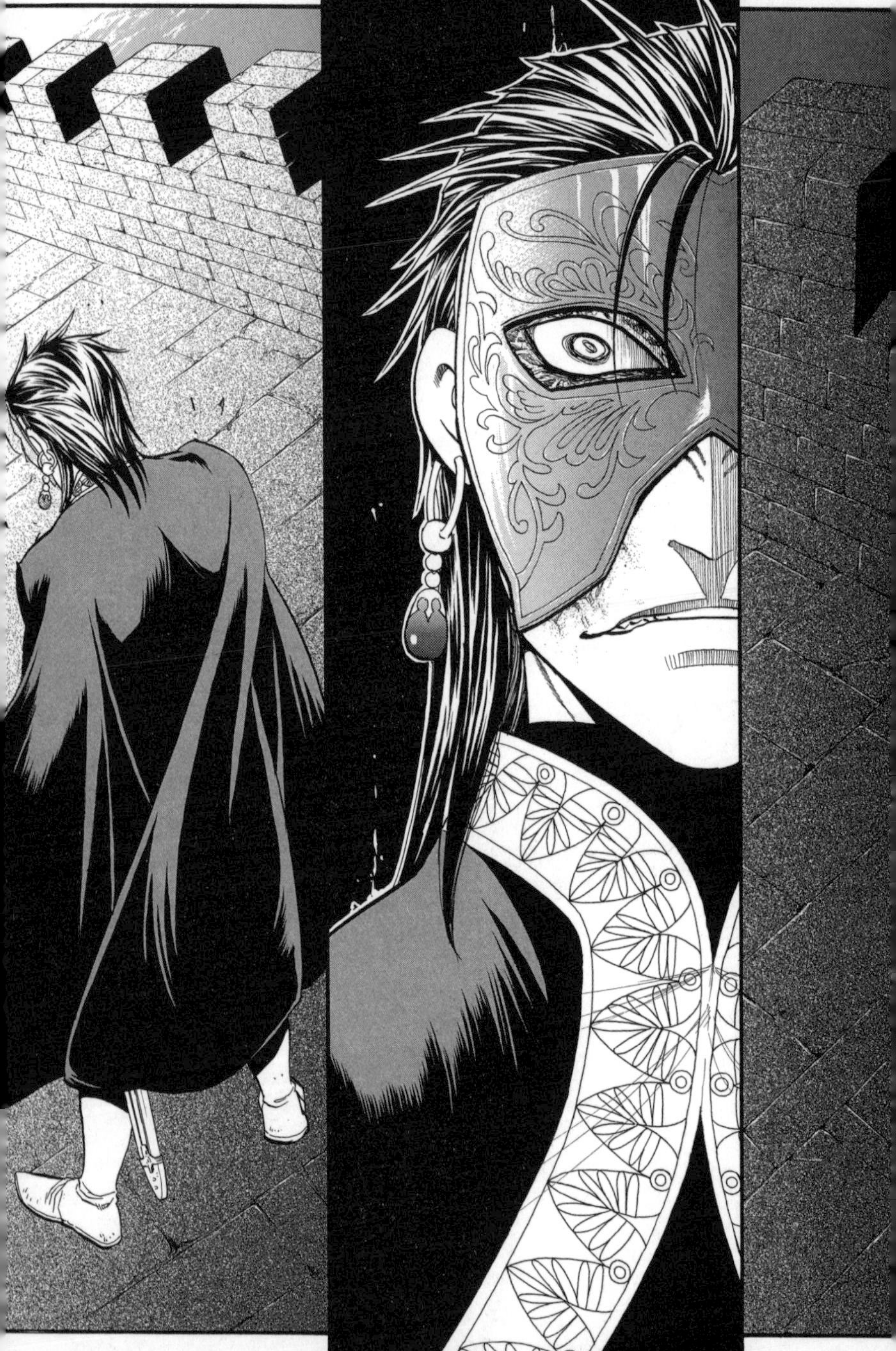

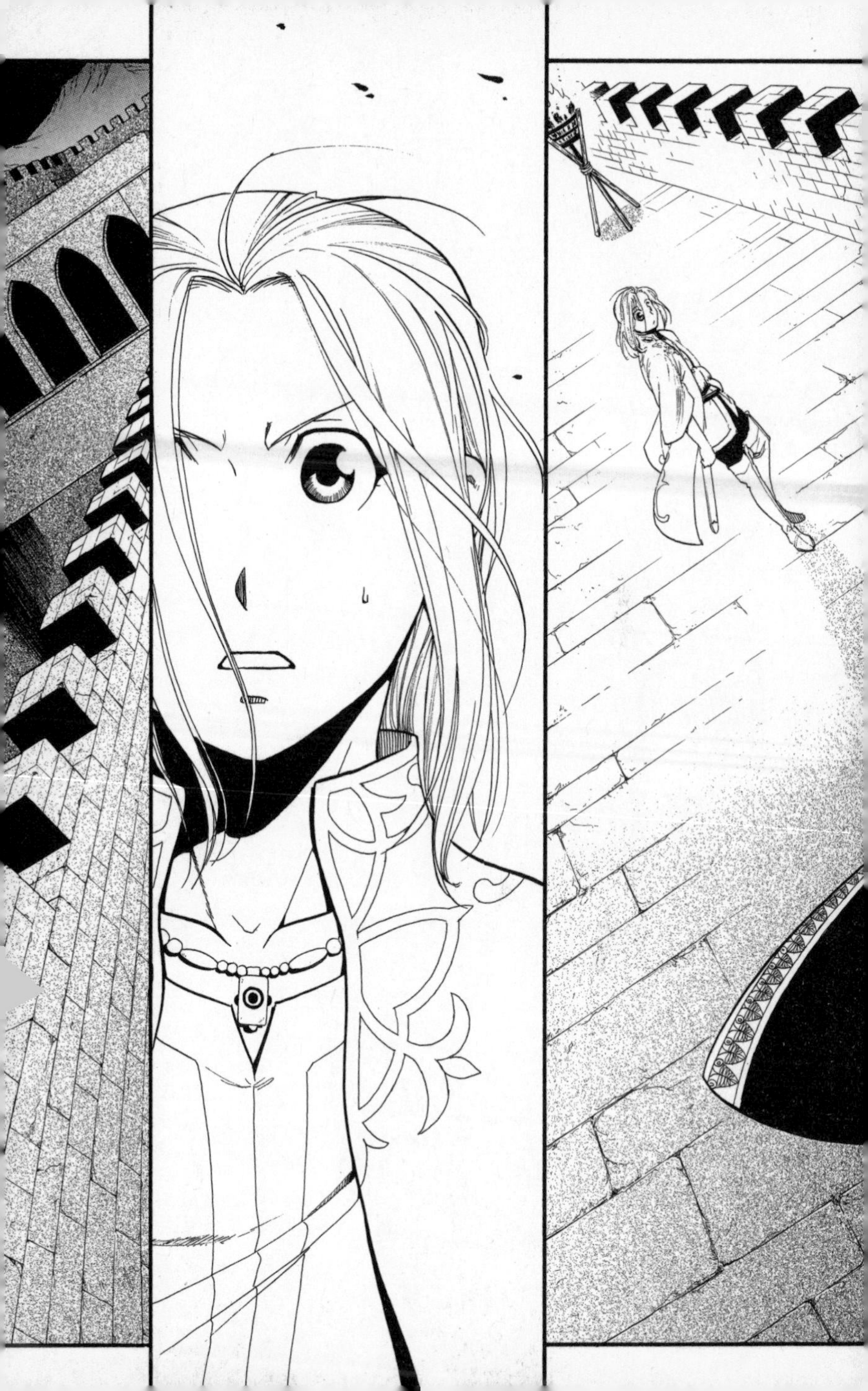

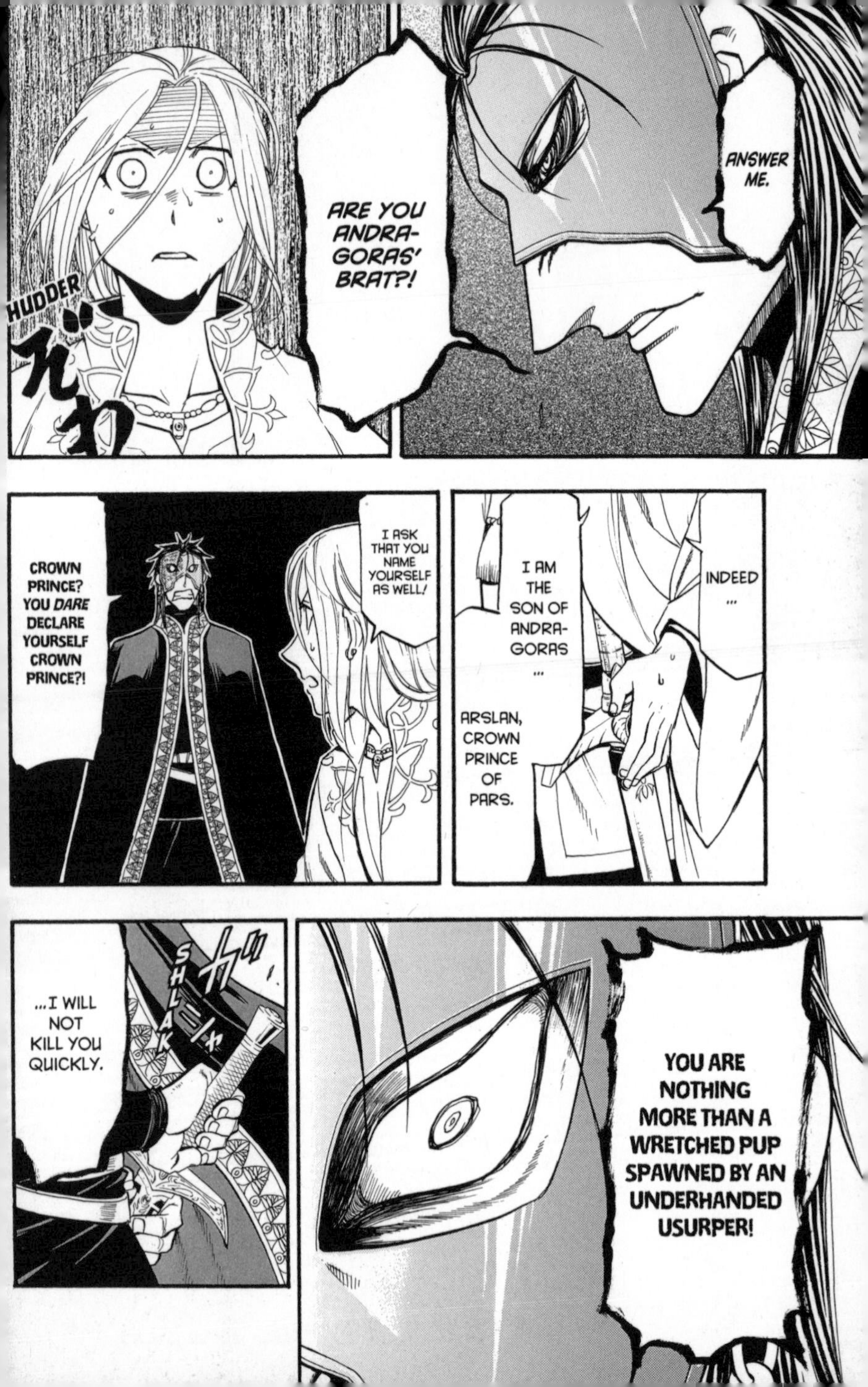
ANSWER ME.
ARE YOU ANDRA-GORAS' BRAT?!
HUDDER
INDEED ...
I AM THE SON OF ANDRA-GORAS ...
ARSLAN, CROWN PRINCE OF PARS.
I ASK THAT YOU NAME YOURSELF AS WELL!
CROWN PRINCE? YOU *DARE* DECLARE YOURSELF CROWN PRINCE?!
YOU ARE NOTHING MORE THAN A WRETCHED PUP SPAWNED BY AN UNDERHANDED USURPER!
SHLAK
...I WILL NOT KILL YOU QUICKLY.

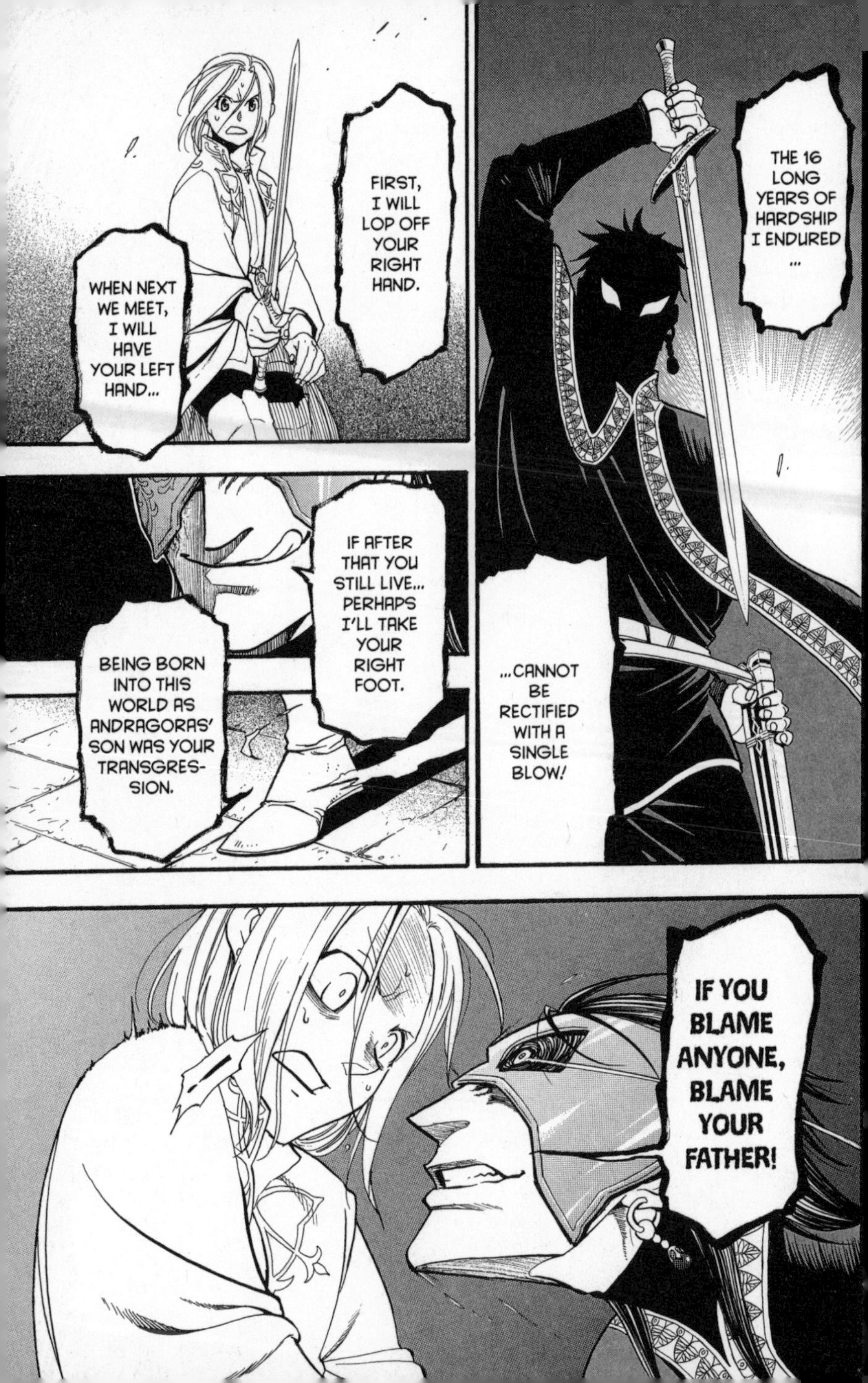
THE 16 LONG YEARS OF HARDSHIP I ENDURED ...
...CANNOT BE RECTIFIED WITH A SINGLE BLOW!
FIRST, I WILL LOP OFF YOUR RIGHT HAND.
WHEN NEXT WE MEET, I WILL HAVE YOUR LEFT HAND...
IF AFTER THAT YOU STILL LIVE... PERHAPS I'LL TAKE YOUR RIGHT FOOT.
BEING BORN INTO THIS WORLD AS ANDRAGORAS' SON WAS YOUR TRANSGRES-SION.
IF YOU BLAME ANYONE, BLAME YOUR FATHER!

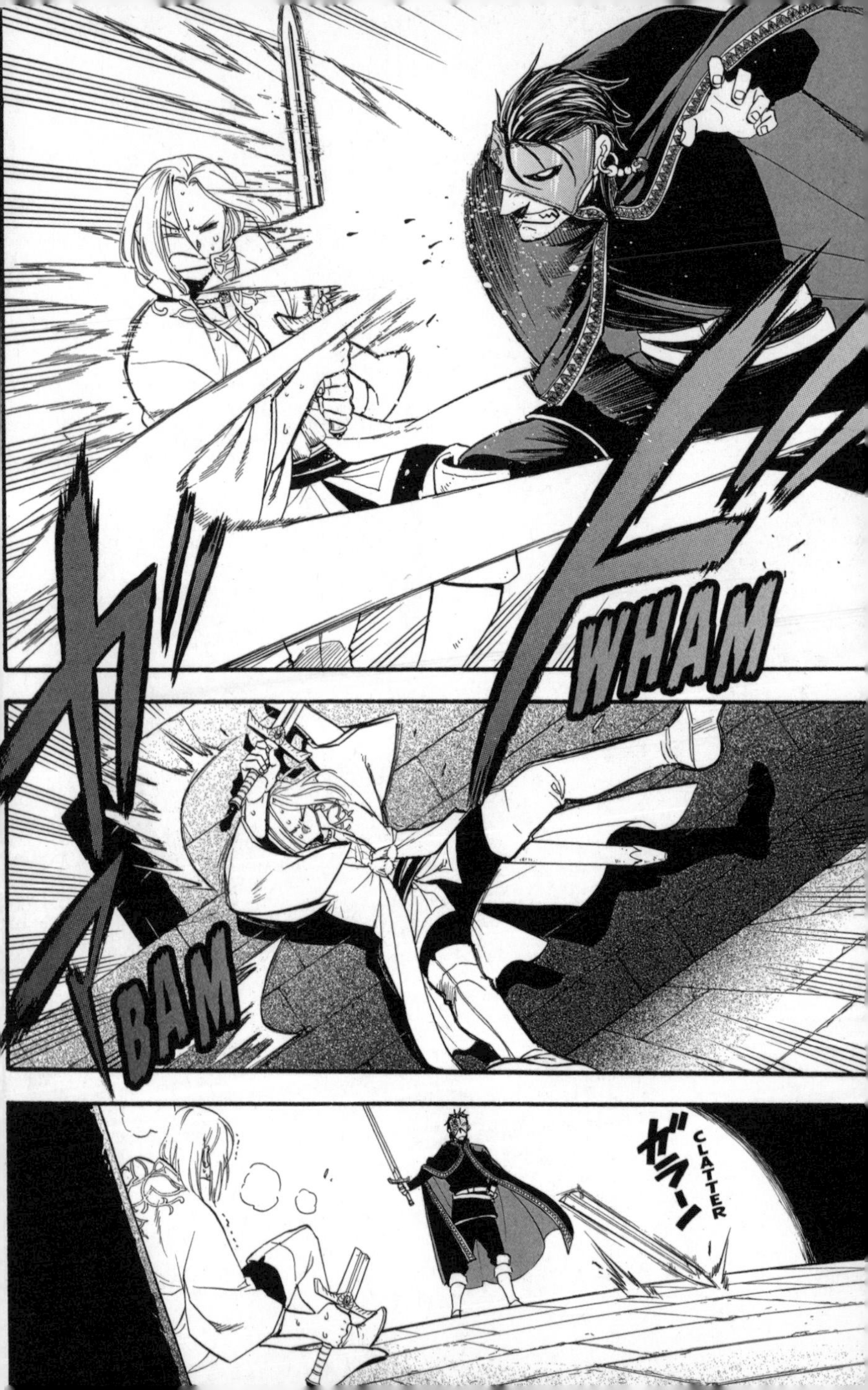
WHAM
BAM
ガラーン
CLATTER

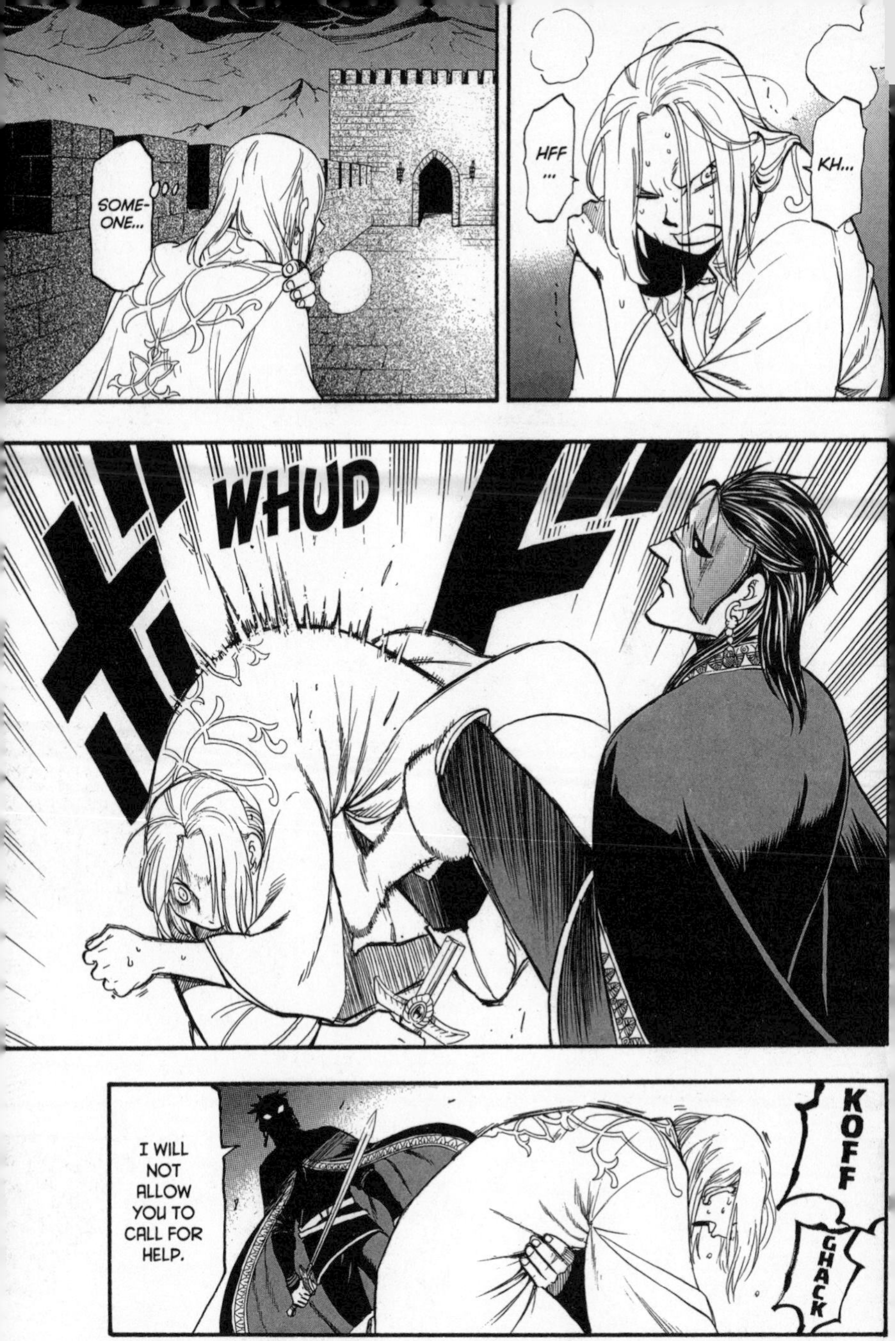
KH...
HFF...
SOME-ONE...
WHUD
KOFF
GHACK
I WILL NOT ALLOW YOU TO CALL FOR HELP.

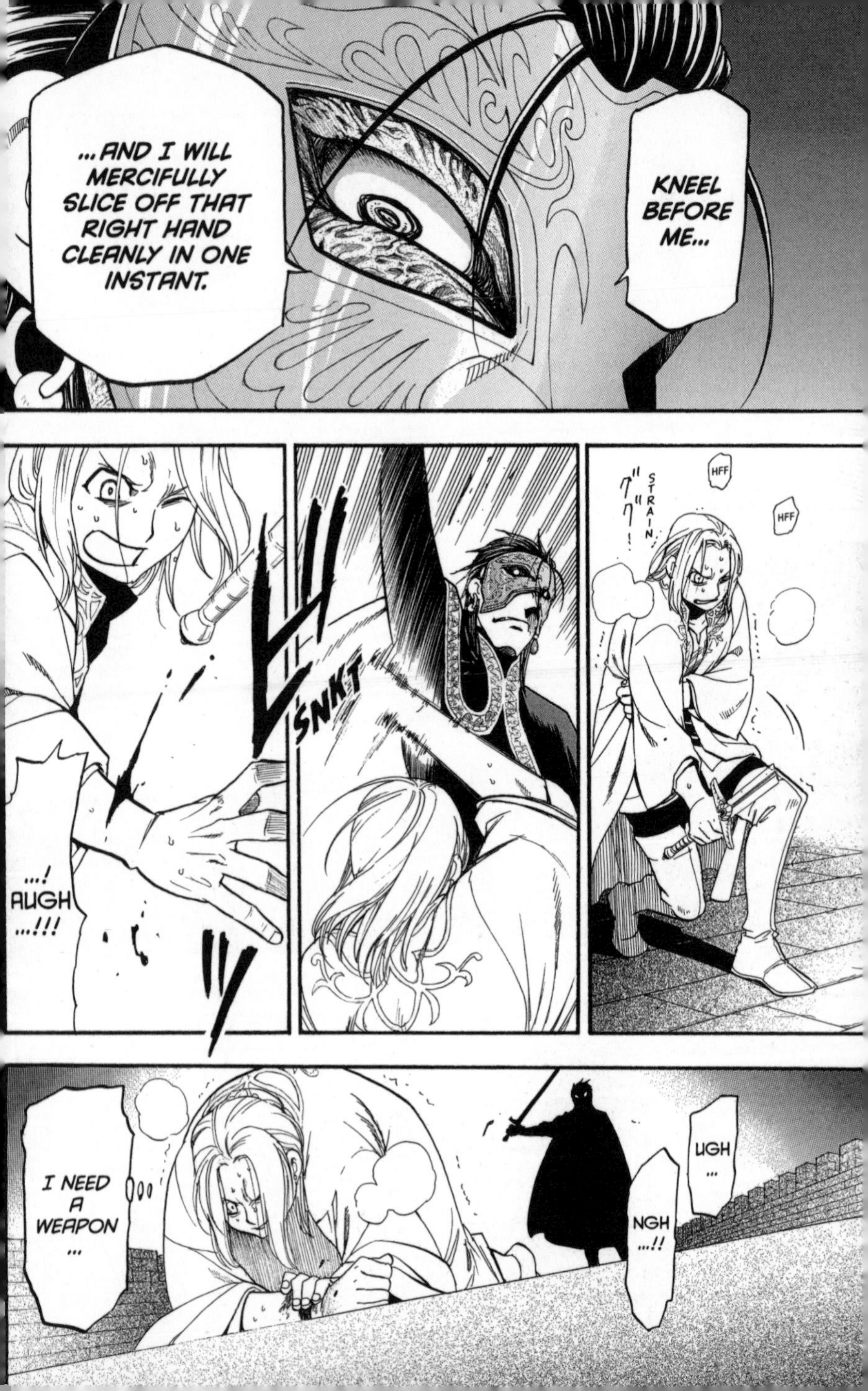
KNEEL BEFORE ME...
...AND I WILL MERCIFULLY SLICE OFF THAT RIGHT HAND CLEANLY IN ONE INSTANT.
STRAIN
HFF
HFF
SNKT
...! AUGH ...!!!
UGH ...
NGH ...!!
I NEED A WEAPON ...

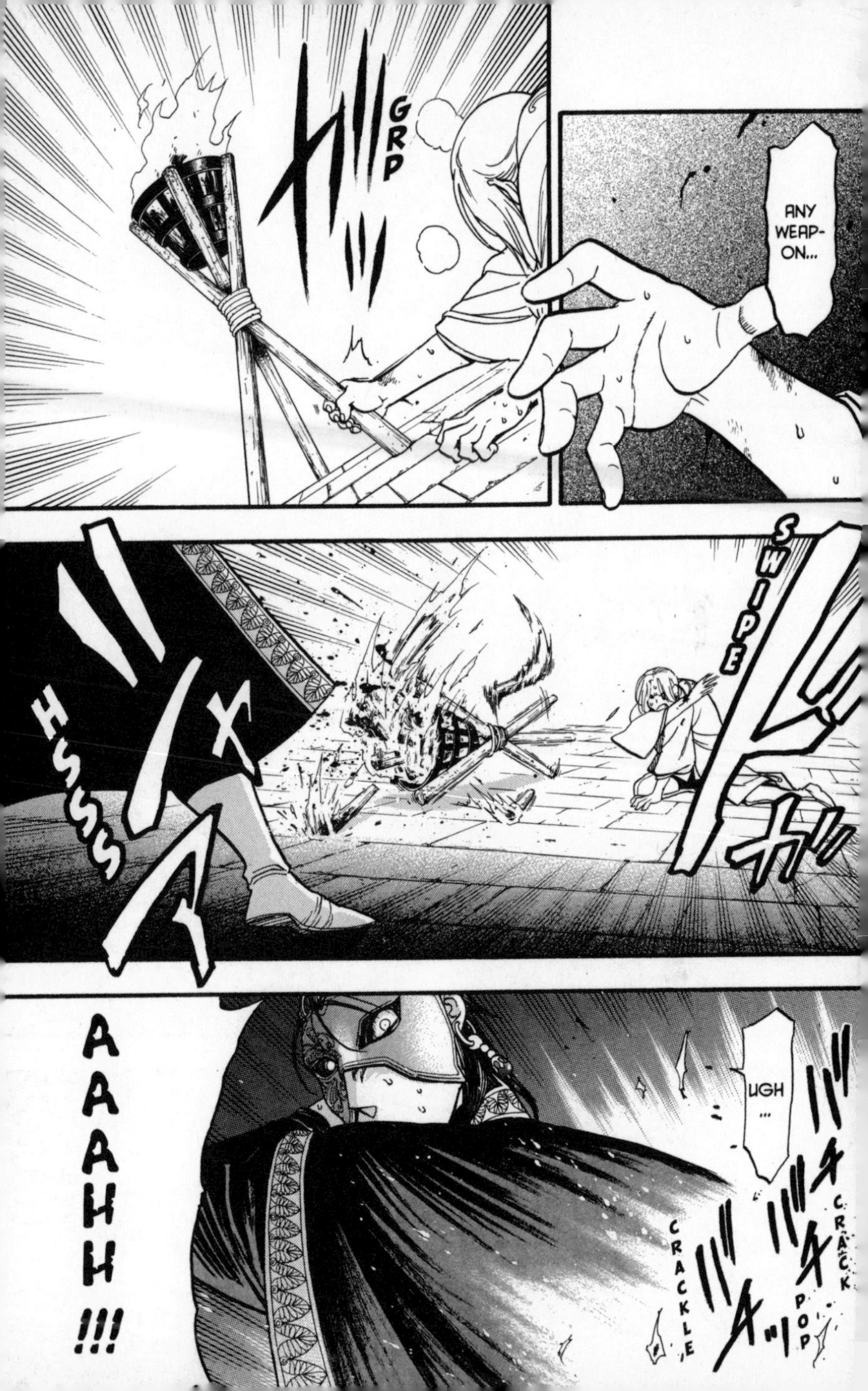

ANY WEAP-ON...
GRP
SWIPE
HSSSS
UGH ...
CRACK
POP
CRACKLE
AAAAHH!!!

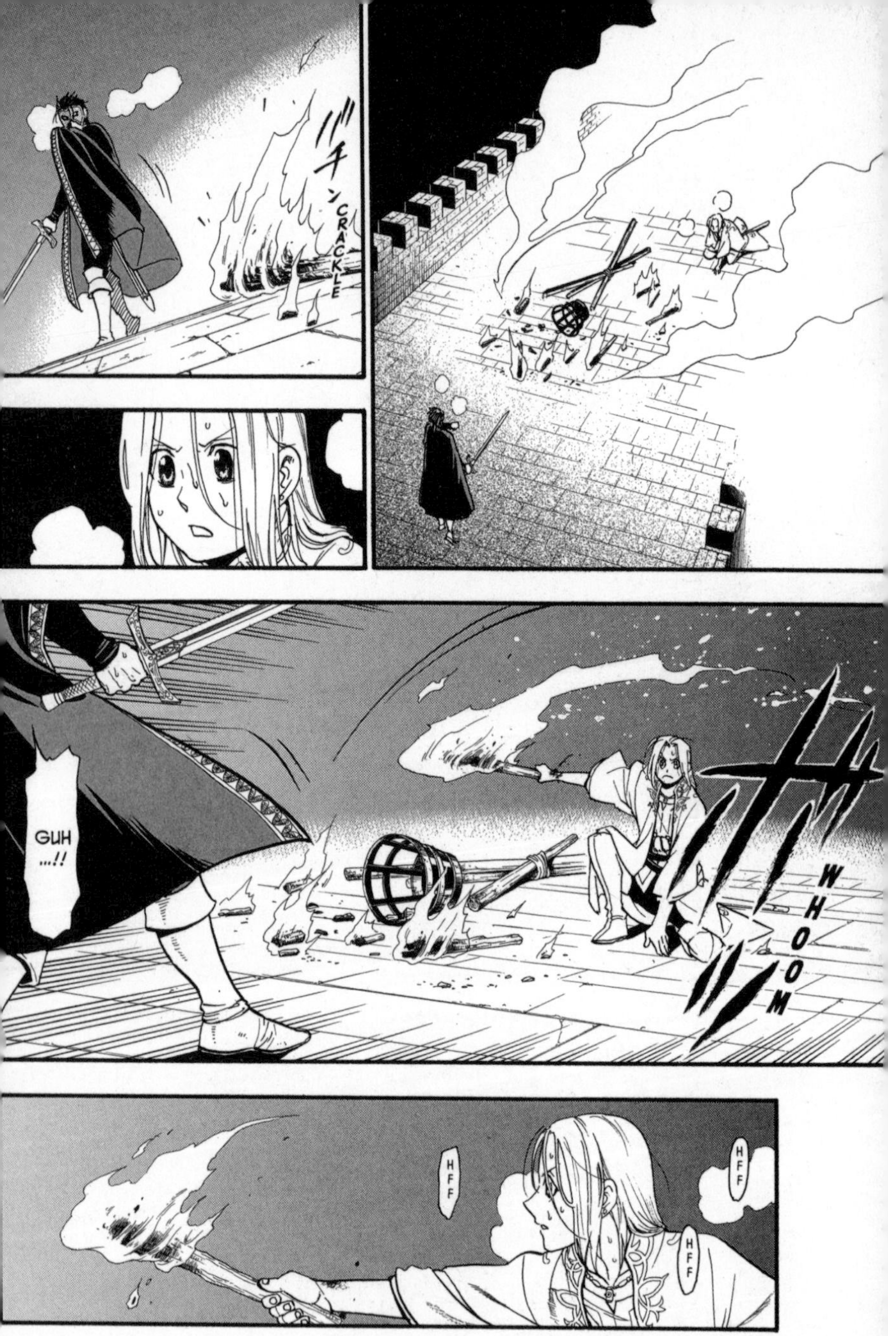
バチン
CRACKLE
WHOOM
GUH ...!!
HFF
HFF
HFF

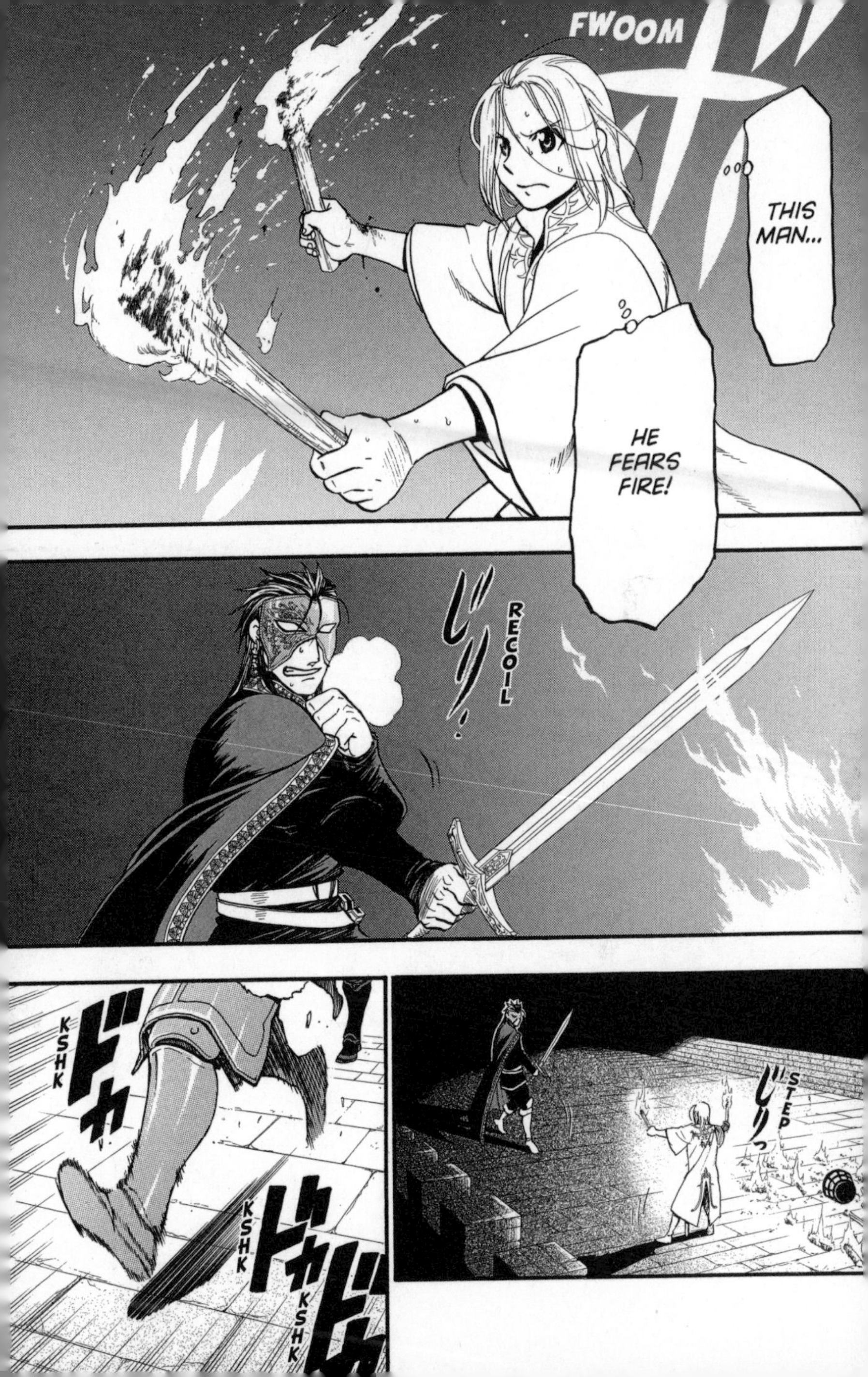
FWOOM
THIS MAN...
HE FEARS FIRE!
RECOIL
STEP
KSHK
KSHK
KSHK

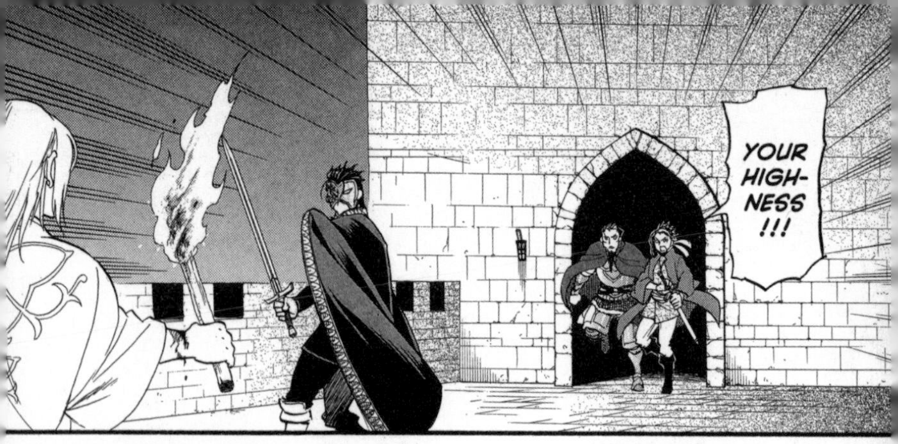
YOUR HIGH-NESS !!!

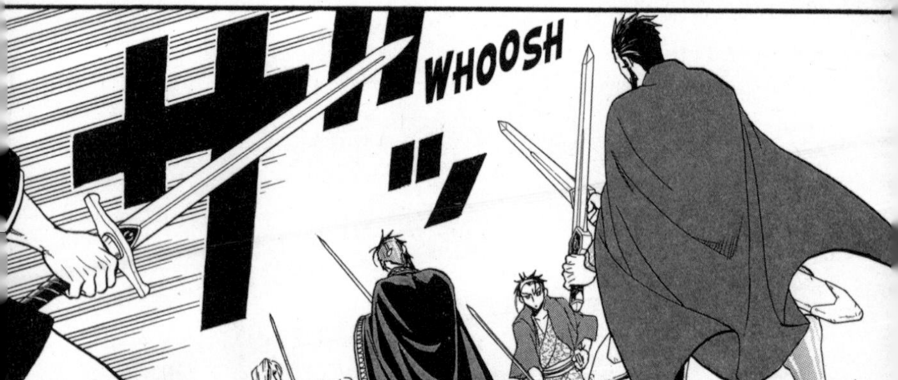
WHOOSH

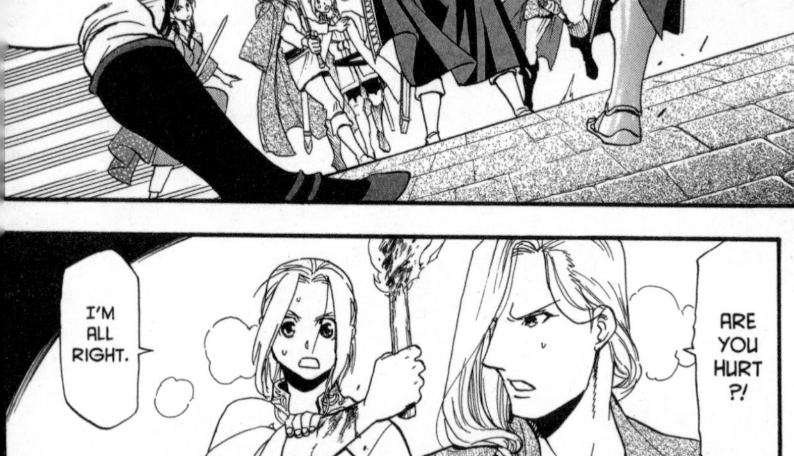
ARE YOU HURT ?!
I'M ALL RIGHT.

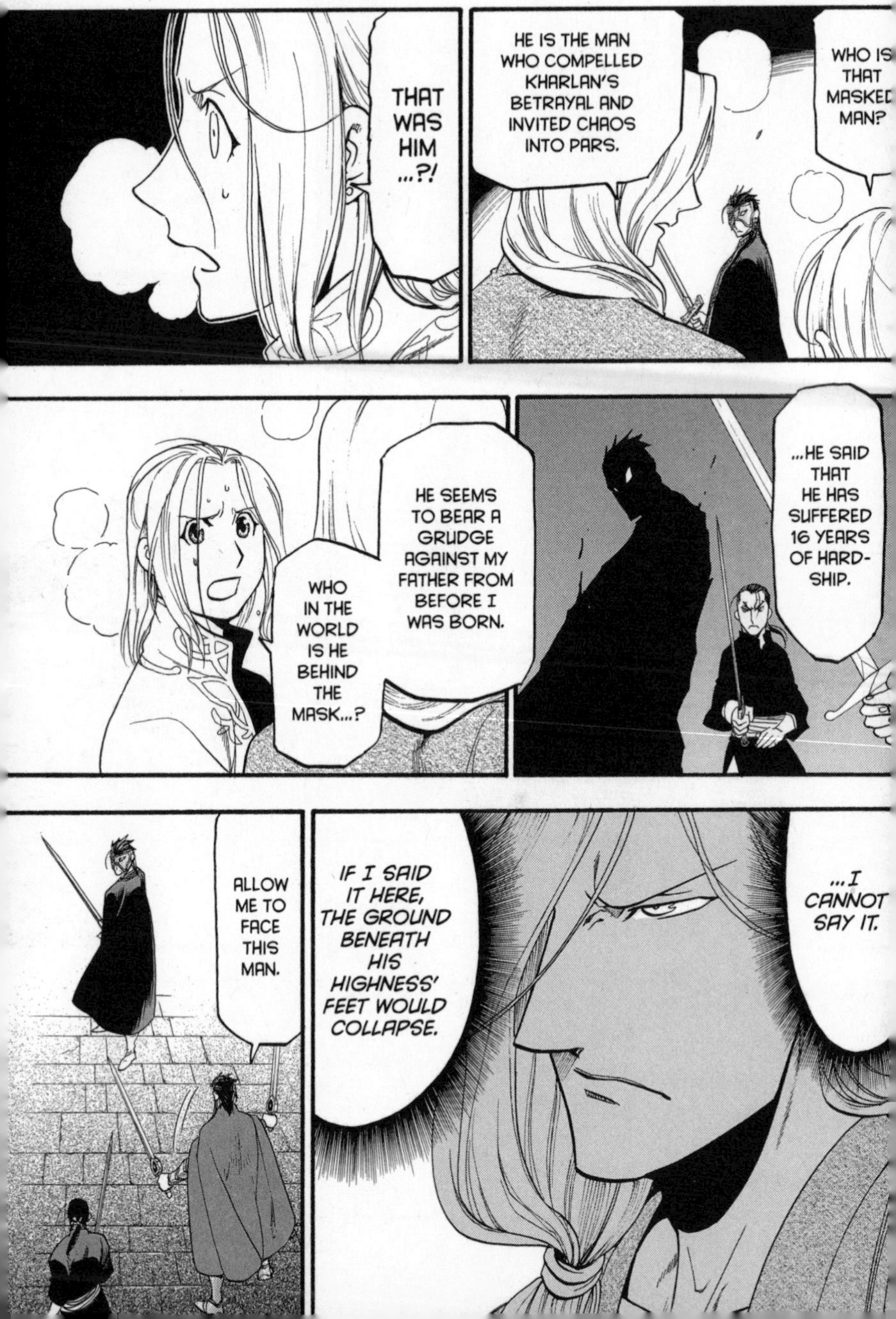
WHO IS THAT MASKED MAN?
HE IS THE MAN WHO COMPELLED KHARLAN'S BETRAYAL AND INVITED CHAOS INTO PARS.
THAT WAS HIM ...?!
...HE SAID THAT HE HAS SUFFERED 16 YEARS OF HARDSHIP.
HE SEEMS TO BEAR A GRUDGE AGAINST MY FATHER FROM BEFORE I WAS BORN.
WHO IN THE WORLD IS HE BEHIND THE MASK...?
...I CANNOT SAY IT.
IF I SAID IT HERE, THE GROUND BENEATH HIS HIGHNESS' FEET WOULD COLLAPSE.
ALLOW ME TO FACE THIS MAN.

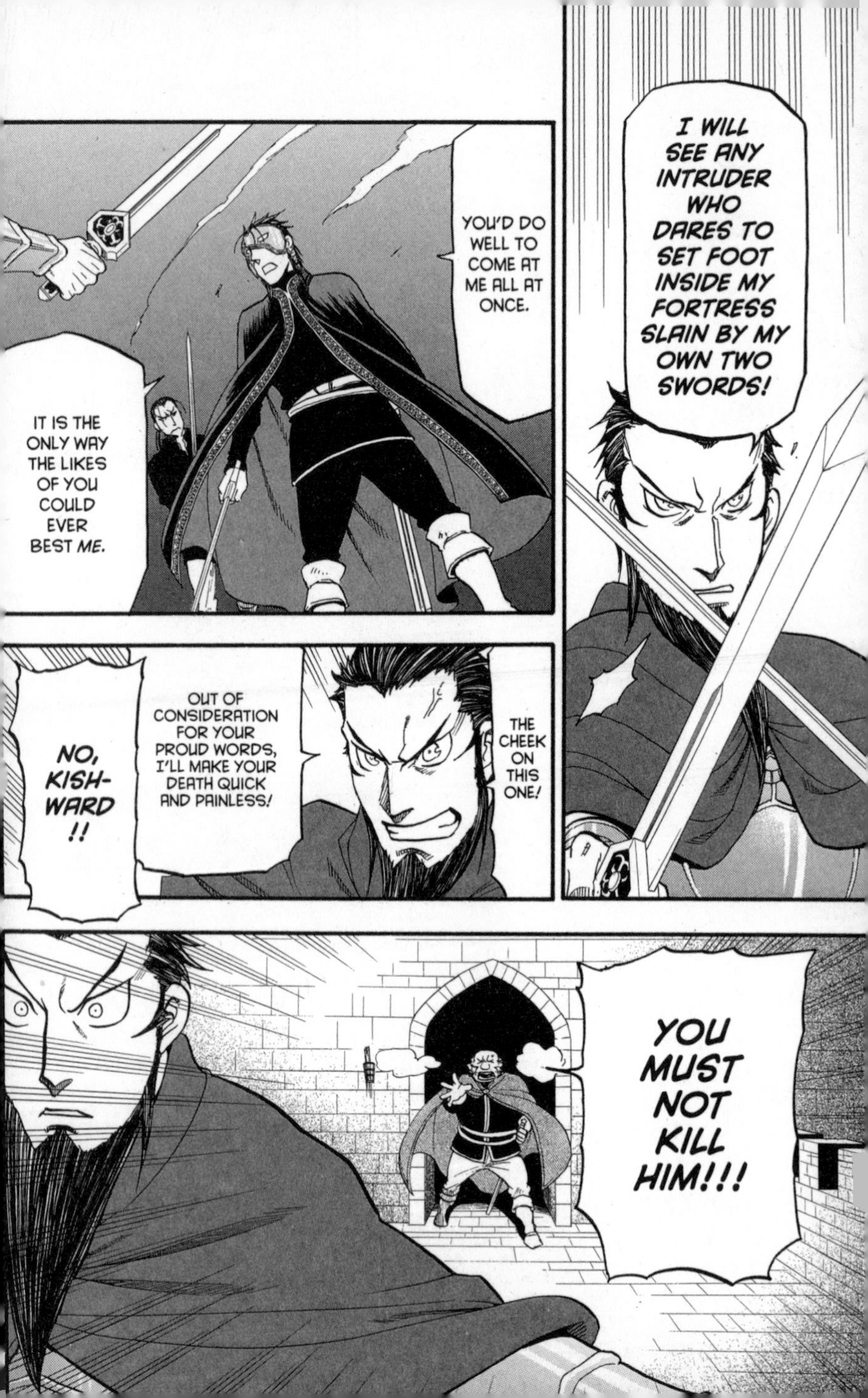
I WILL SEE ANY INTRUDER WHO DARES TO SET FOOT INSIDE MY FORTRESS SLAIN BY MY OWN TWO SWORDS!
YOU'D DO WELL TO COME AT ME ALL AT ONCE.
IT IS THE ONLY WAY THE LIKES OF YOU COULD EVER BEST *ME*.
THE CHEEK ON THIS ONE!
OUT OF CONSIDERATION FOR YOUR PROUD WORDS, I'LL MAKE YOUR DEATH QUICK AND PAINLESS!
NO, KISHWARD!!
YOU MUST NOT KILL HIM!!!

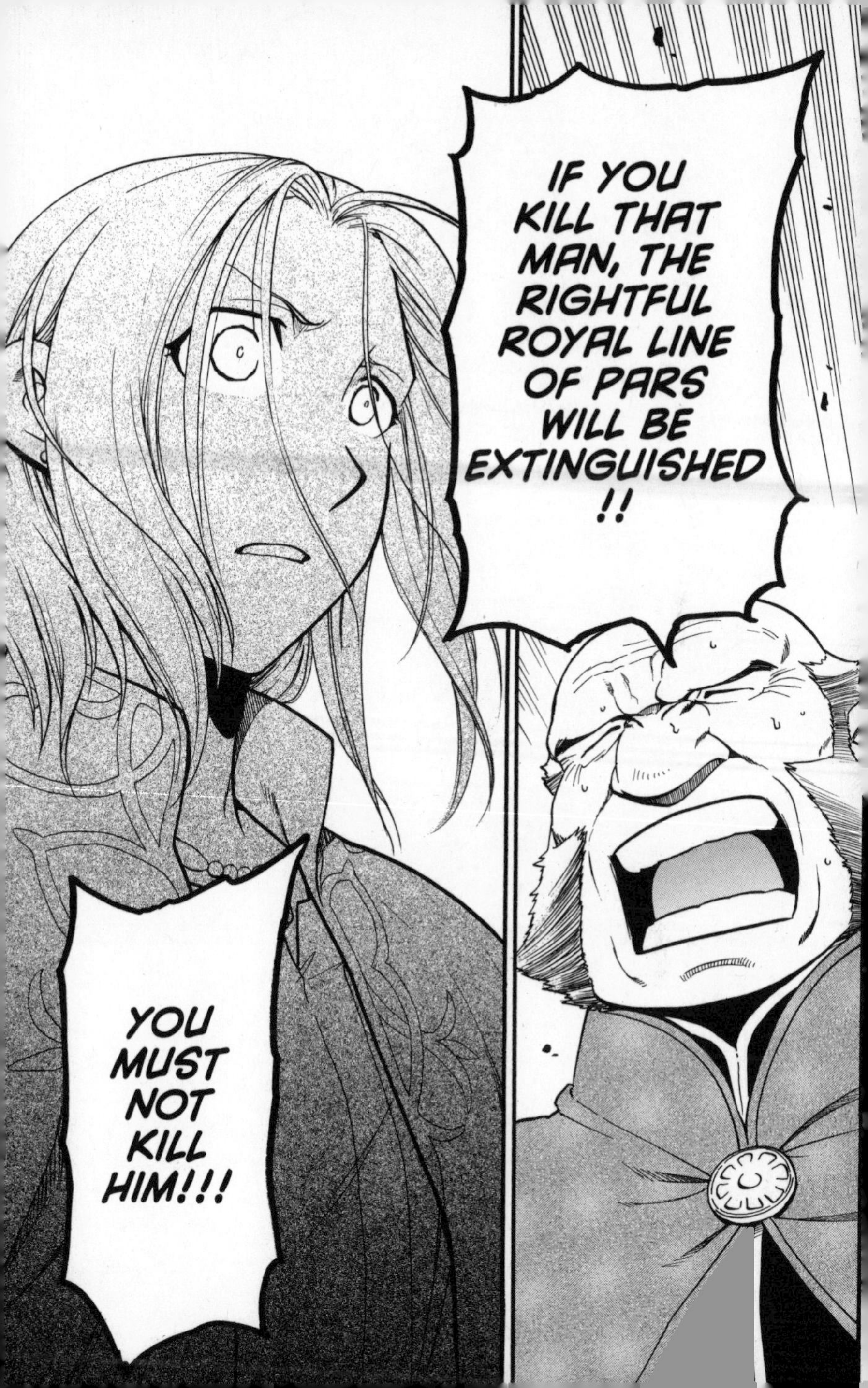
IF YOU KILL THAT MAN, THE RIGHTFUL ROYAL LINE OF PARS WILL BE EXTINGUISHED!!
YOU MUST NOT KILL HIM!!!

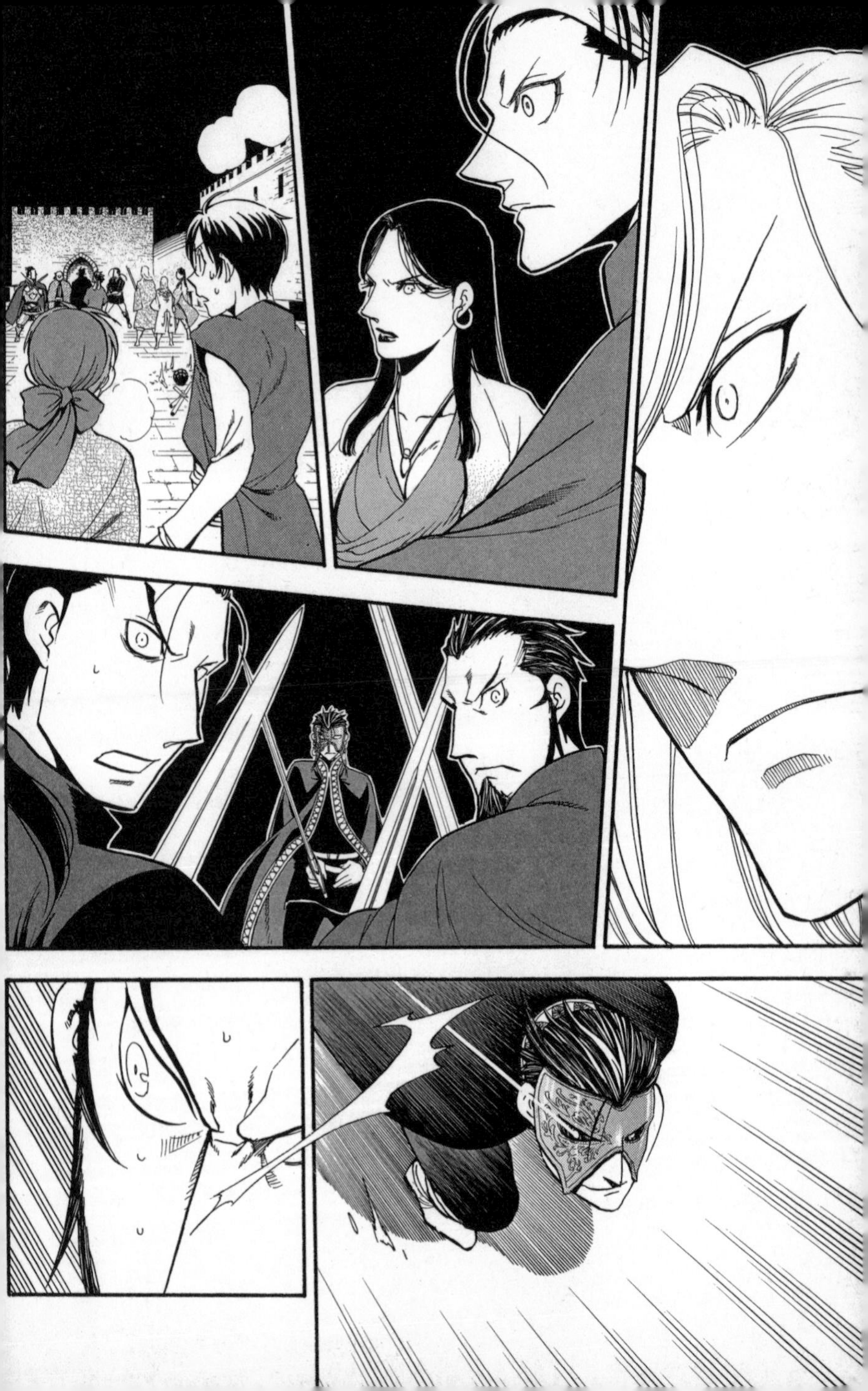

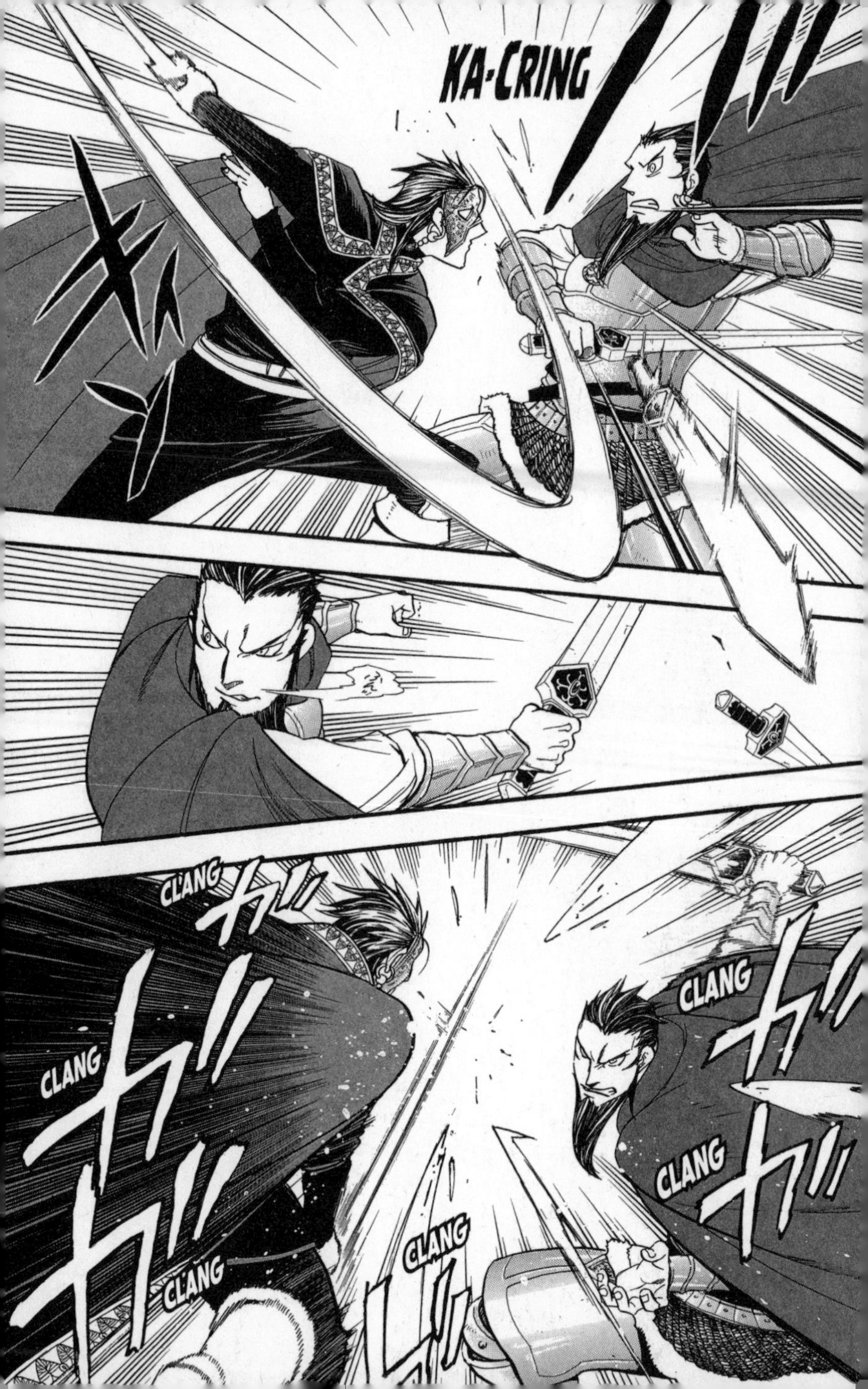
KA-CRING
CLANG
CLANG
CLANG
CLANG
CLANG
CLANG

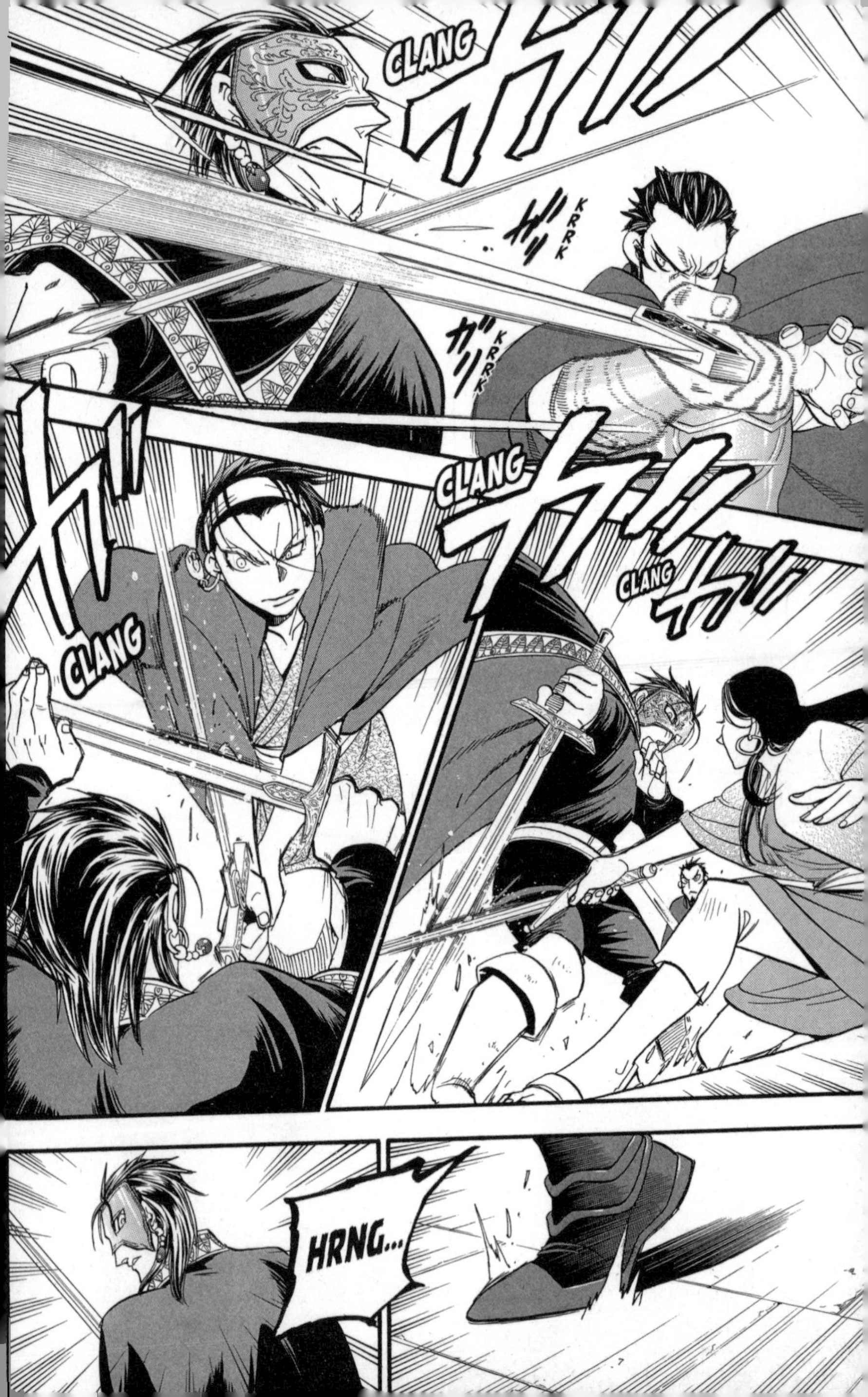
CLANG
KRRK
KRRK
CLANG
CLANG
CLANG
HRNG...

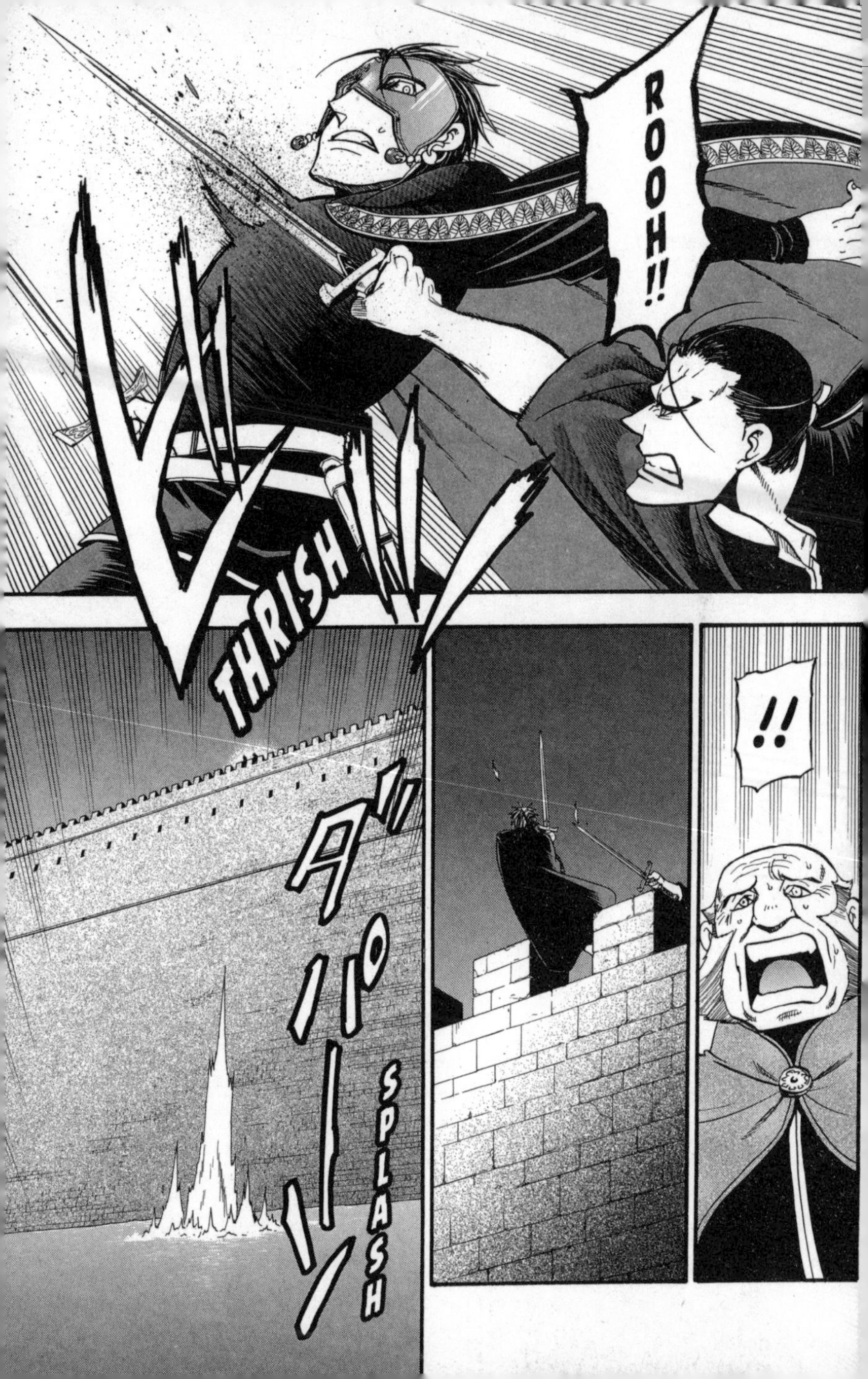
ROOOH!!
THRISH
!!
SPLASH

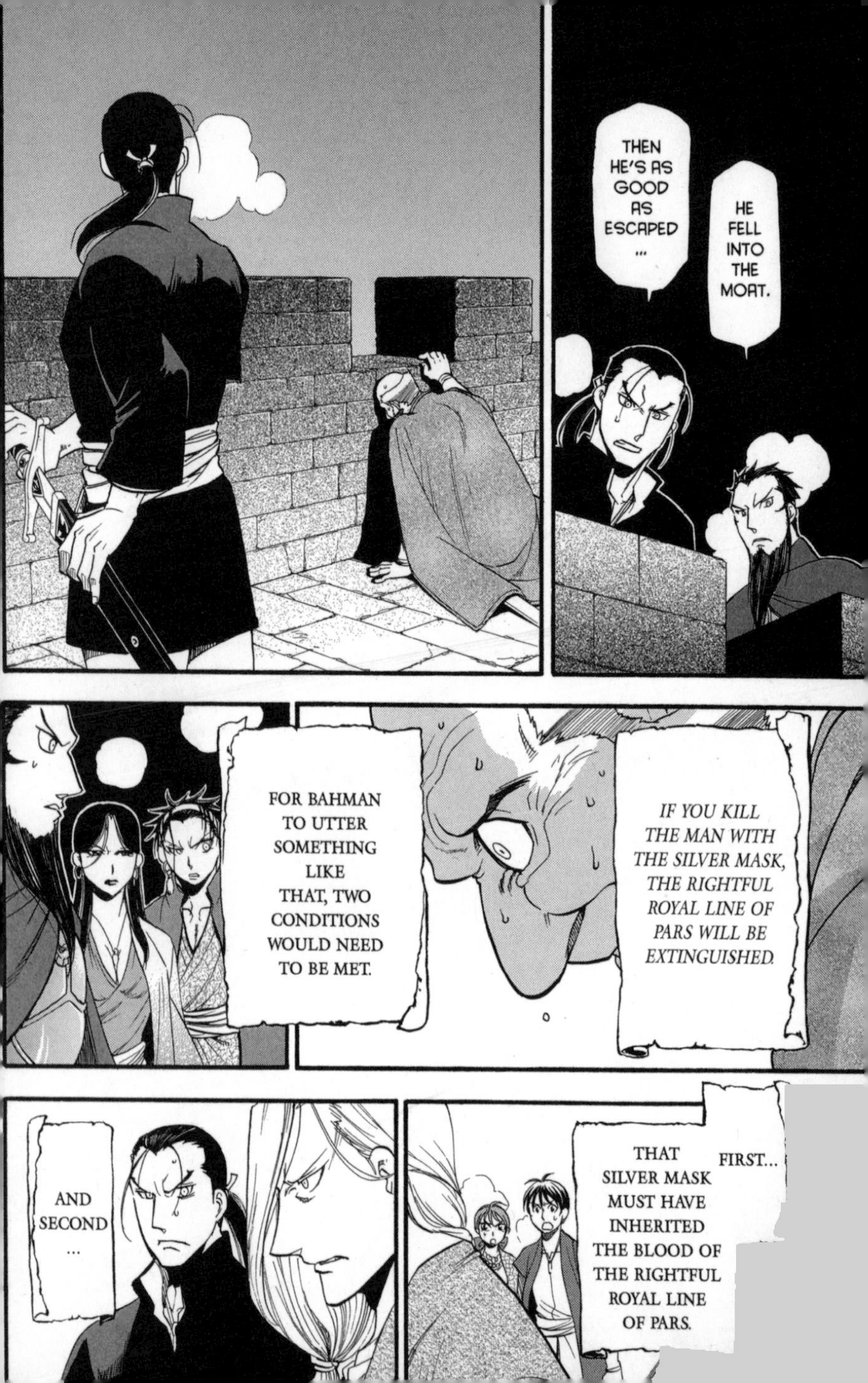
HE FELL INTO THE MOAT.
THEN HE'S AS GOOD AS ESCAPED ...
IF YOU KILL THE MAN WITH THE SILVER MASK, THE RIGHTFUL ROYAL LINE OF PARS WILL BE EXTINGUISHED.
FOR BAHMAN TO UTTER SOMETHING LIKE THAT, TWO CONDITIONS WOULD NEED TO BE MET.
FIRST...
THAT SILVER MASK MUST HAVE INHERITED THE BLOOD OF THE RIGHTFUL ROYAL LINE OF PARS.
AND SECOND ...

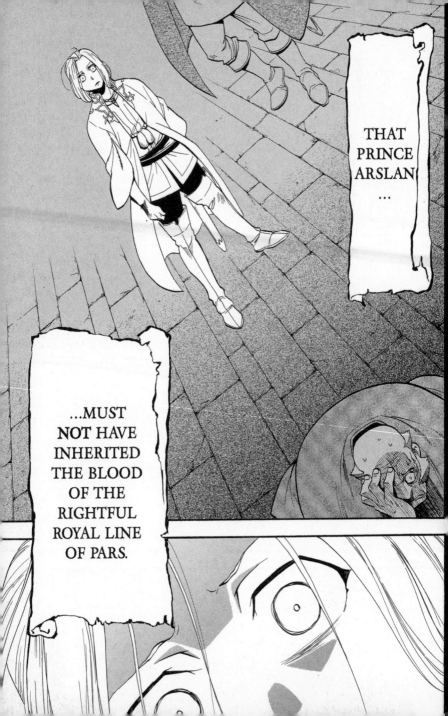

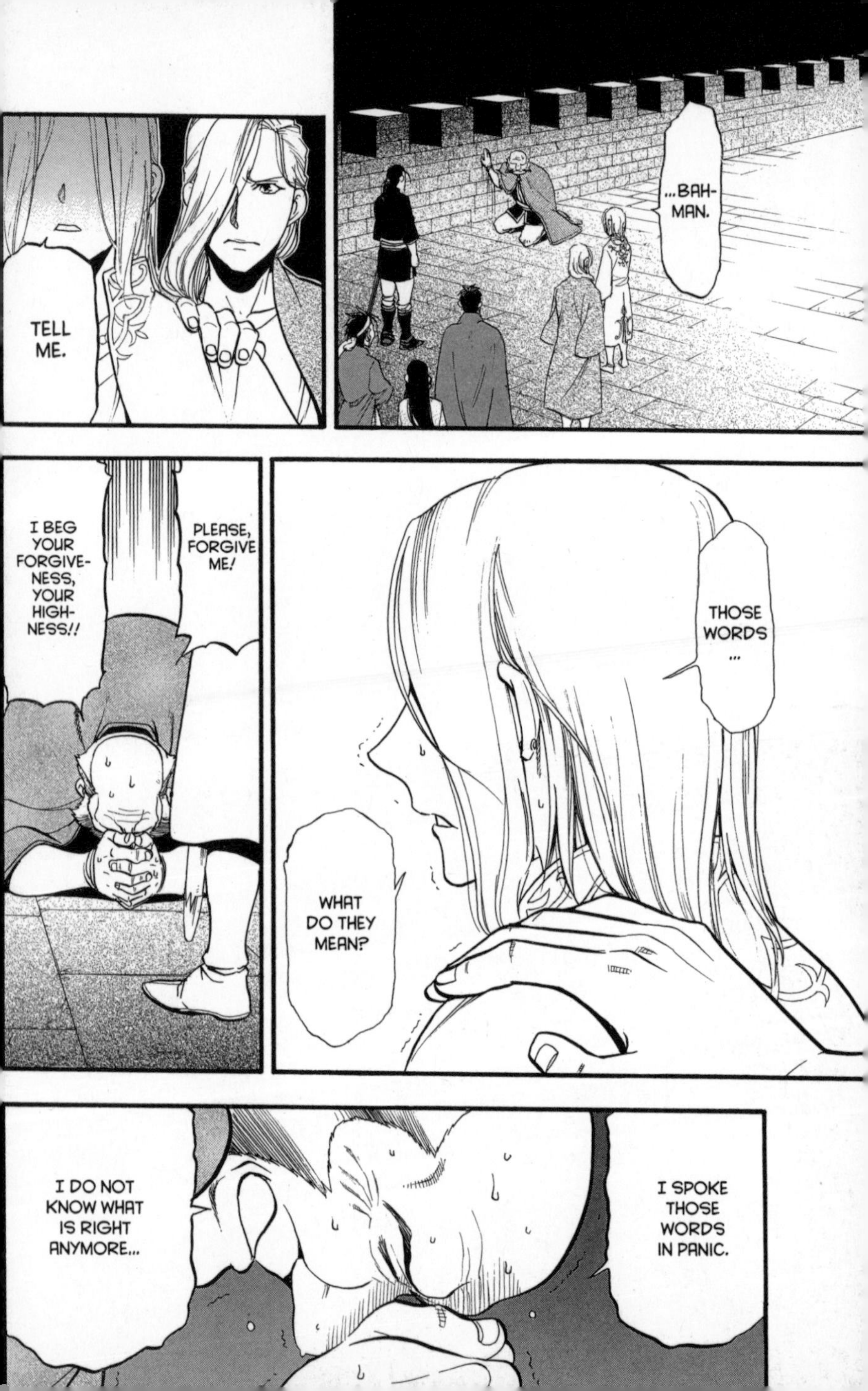
...BAHMAN.
TELL ME.
THOSE WORDS...
WHAT DO THEY MEAN?
PLEASE, FORGIVE ME!
I BEG YOUR FORGIVENESS, YOUR HIGHNESS!!
I SPOKE THOSE WORDS IN PANIC.
I DO NOT KNOW WHAT IS RIGHT ANYMORE...

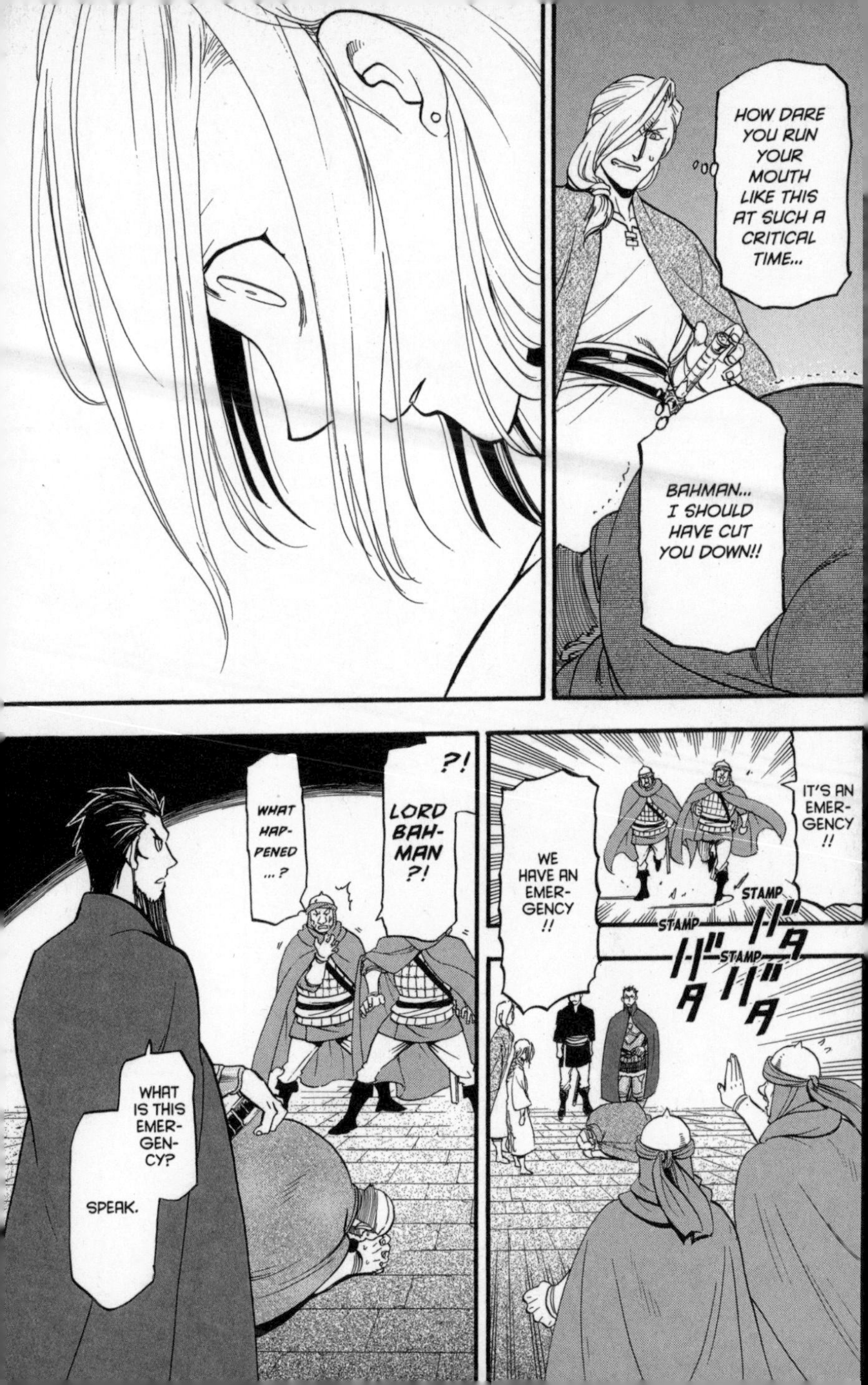
HOW DARE YOU RUN YOUR MOUTH LIKE THIS AT SUCH A CRITICAL TIME...
BAHMAN... I SHOULD HAVE CUT YOU DOWN!!
IT'S AN EMERGENCY!!
WE HAVE AN EMERGENCY!!
STAMP
バタ
STAMP
バタ
STAMP
バタ
?!
LORD BAHMAN?!
WHAT HAPPENED...?
WHAT IS THIS EMERGENCY?
SPEAK.

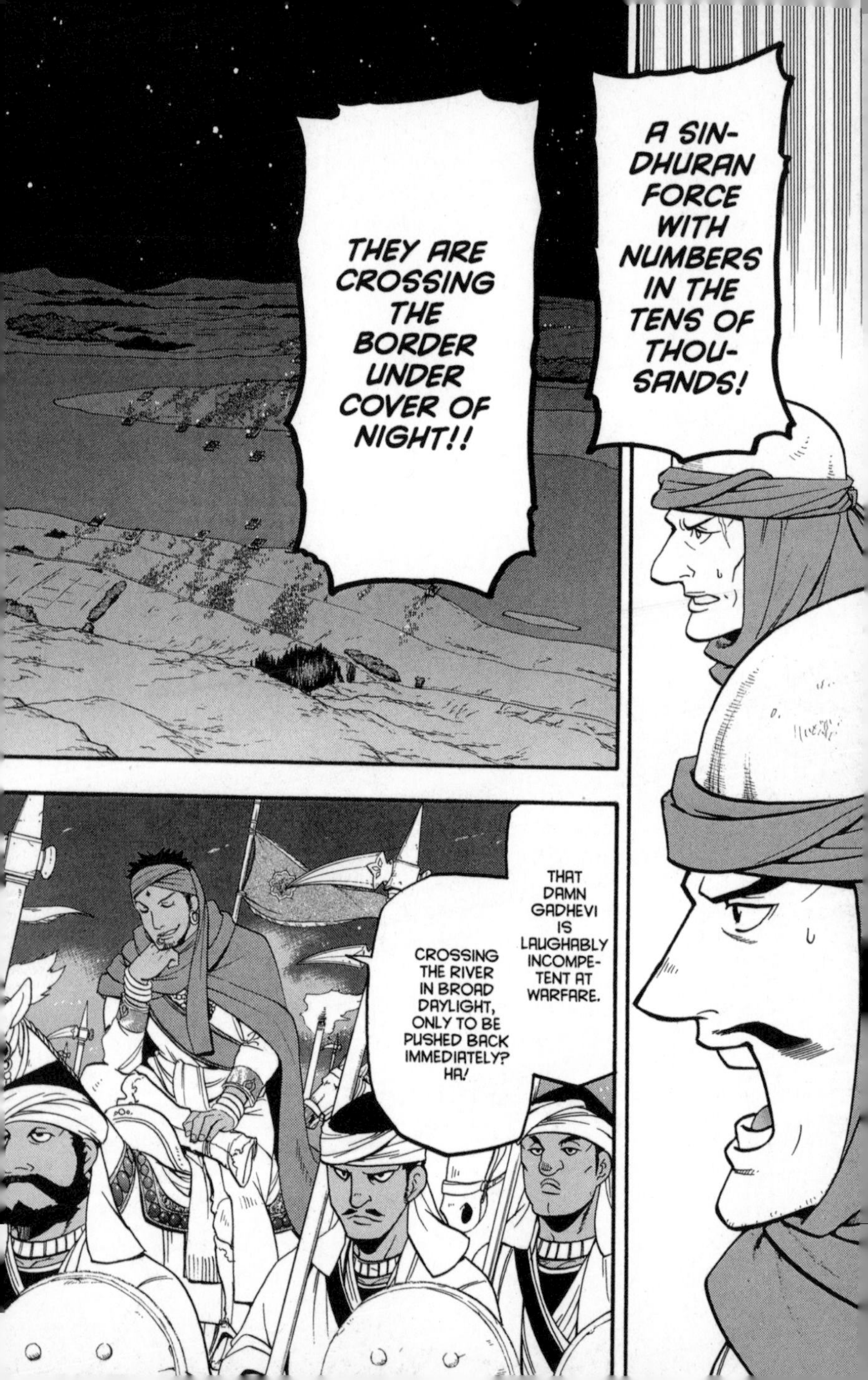
A SIN-DHURAN FORCE WITH NUMBERS IN THE TENS OF THOU-SANDS!
THEY ARE CROSSING THE BORDER UNDER COVER OF NIGHT!!
THAT DAMN GADHEVI IS LAUGHABLY INCOMPE-TENT AT WARFARE.
CROSSING THE RIVER IN BROAD DAYLIGHT, ONLY TO BE PUSHED BACK IMMEDIATELY? HA!

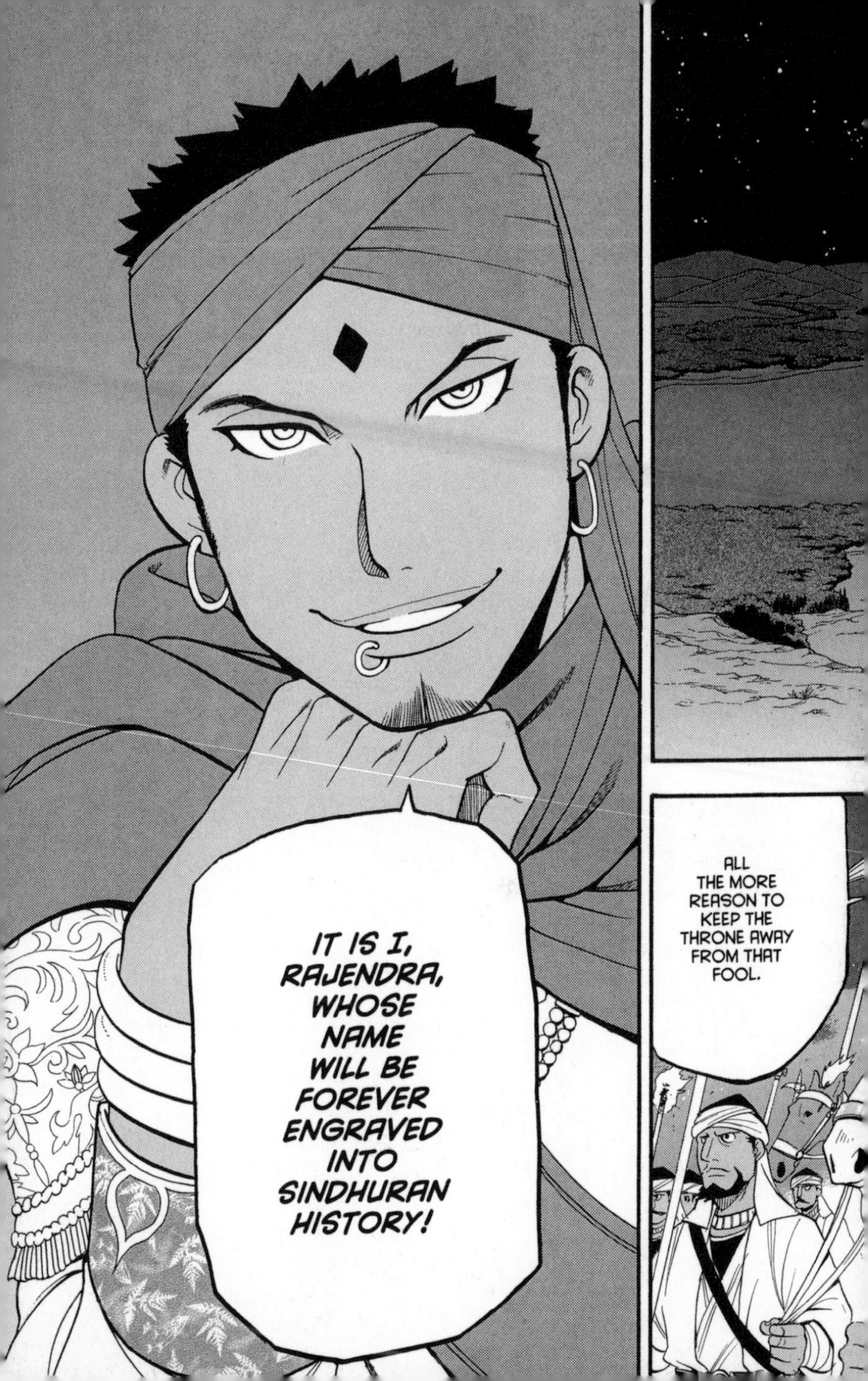
ALL THE MORE REASON TO KEEP THE THRONE AWAY FROM THAT FOOL.
IT IS I, RAJENDRA, WHOSE NAME WILL BE FOREVER ENGRAVED INTO SINDHURAN HISTORY!

THE HEROIC LEGEND OF
ARSLAN

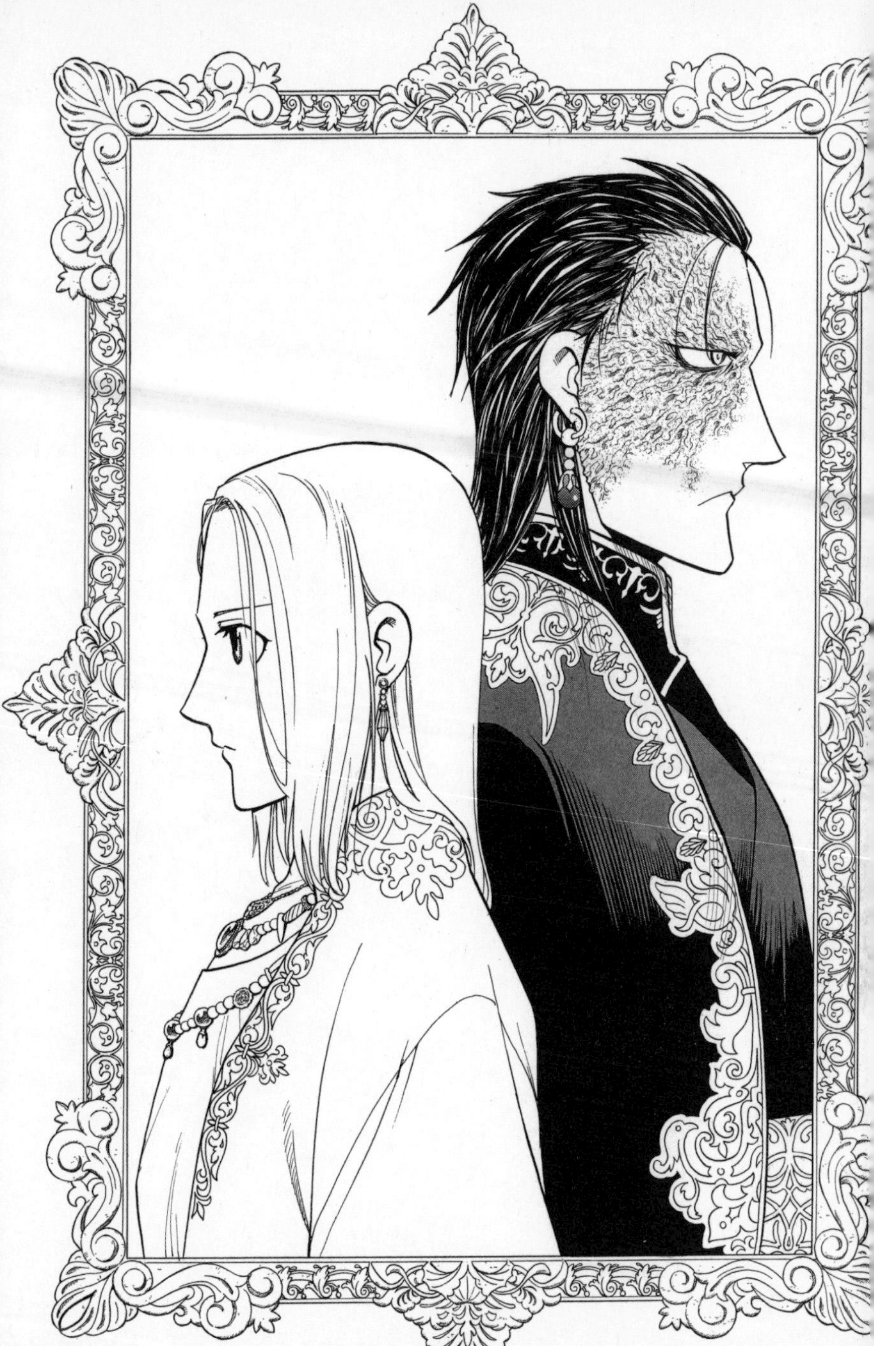

Chapter 40: The Three Principles

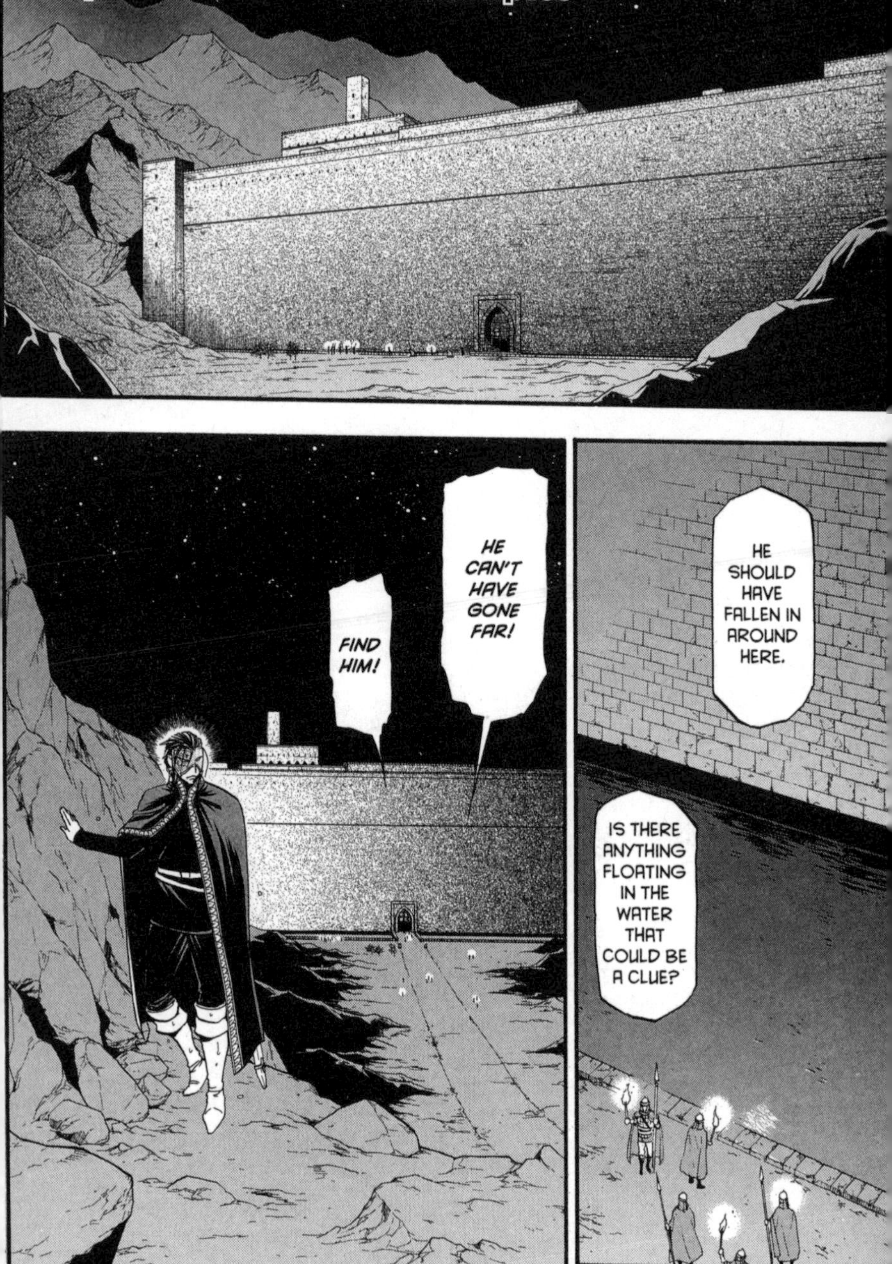
HE SHOULD HAVE FALLEN IN AROUND HERE.
IS THERE ANYTHING FLOATING IN THE WATER THAT COULD BE A CLUE?
HE CAN'T HAVE GONE FAR!
FIND HIM!

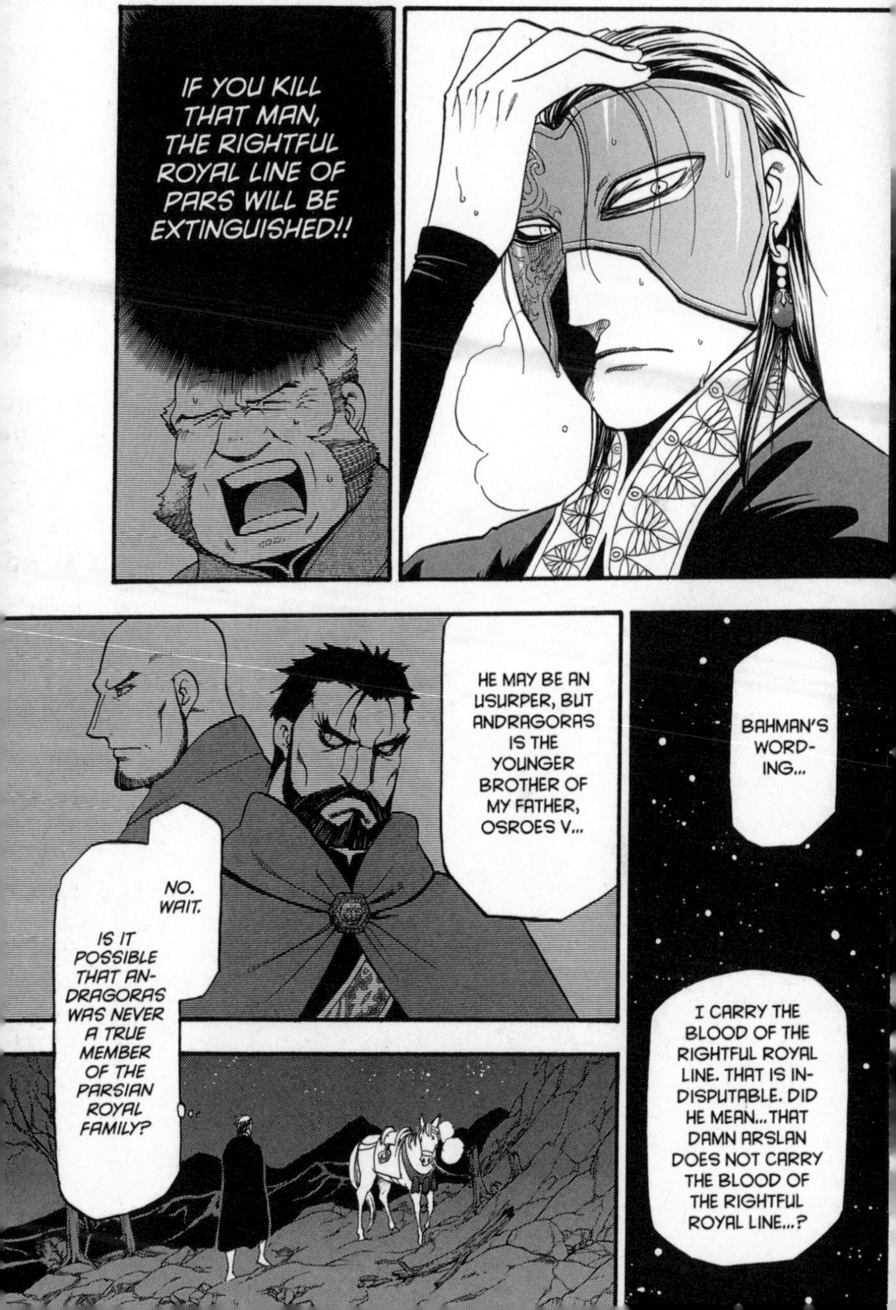
IF YOU KILL THAT MAN, THE RIGHTFUL ROYAL LINE OF PARS WILL BE EXTINGUISHED!!
BAHMAN'S WORD-ING...
I CARRY THE BLOOD OF THE RIGHTFUL ROYAL LINE. THAT IS IN-DISPUTABLE. DID HE MEAN...THAT DAMN ARSLAN DOES NOT CARRY THE BLOOD OF THE RIGHTFUL ROYAL LINE...?
HE MAY BE AN USURPER, BUT ANDRAGORAS IS THE YOUNGER BROTHER OF MY FATHER, OSROES V...
NO. WAIT.
IS IT POSSIBLE THAT AN-DRAGORAS WAS NEVER A TRUE MEMBER OF THE PARSIAN ROYAL FAMILY?

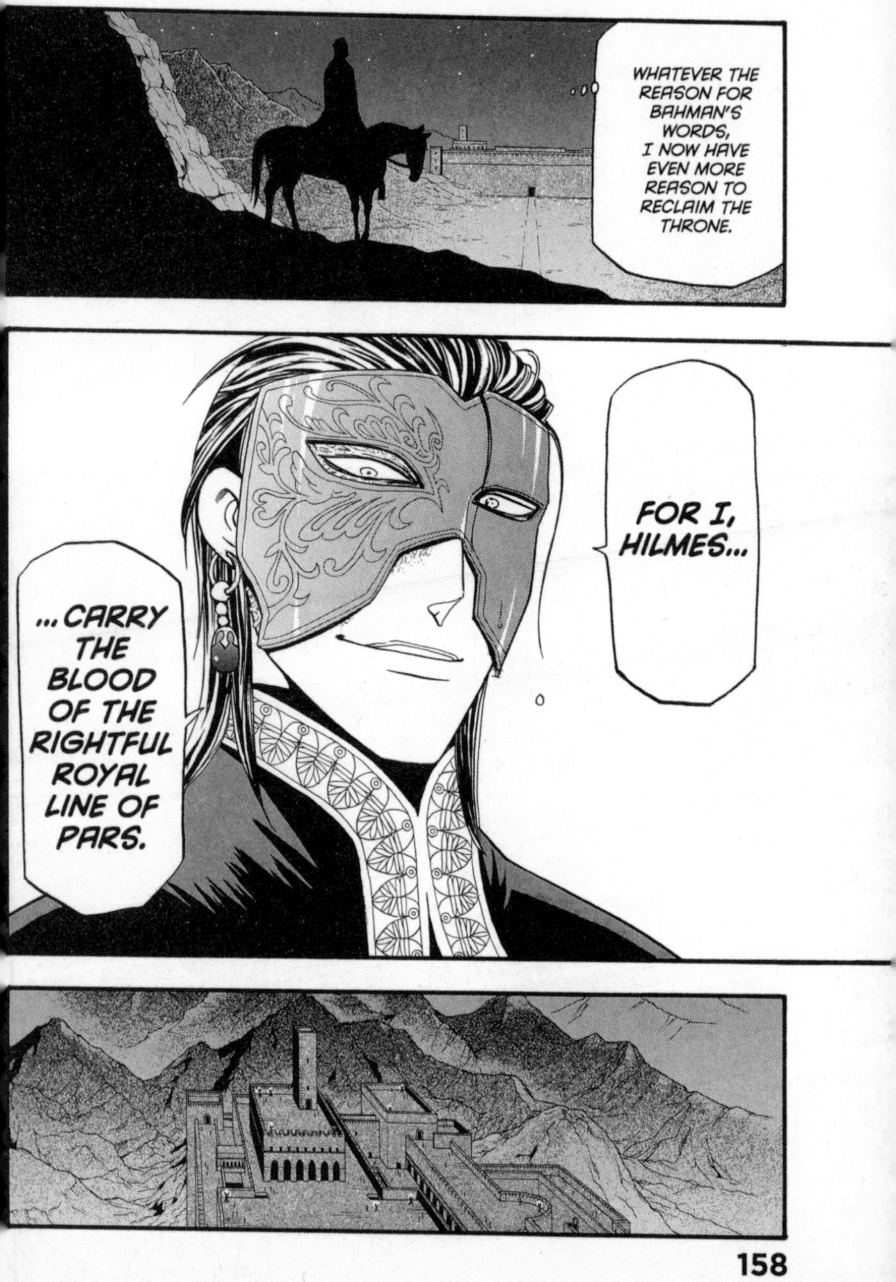
WHATEVER THE REASON FOR BAHMAN'S WORDS, I NOW HAVE EVEN MORE REASON TO RECLAIM THE THRONE.
FOR I, HILMES...
...CARRY THE BLOOD OF THE RIGHTFUL ROYAL LINE OF PARS.

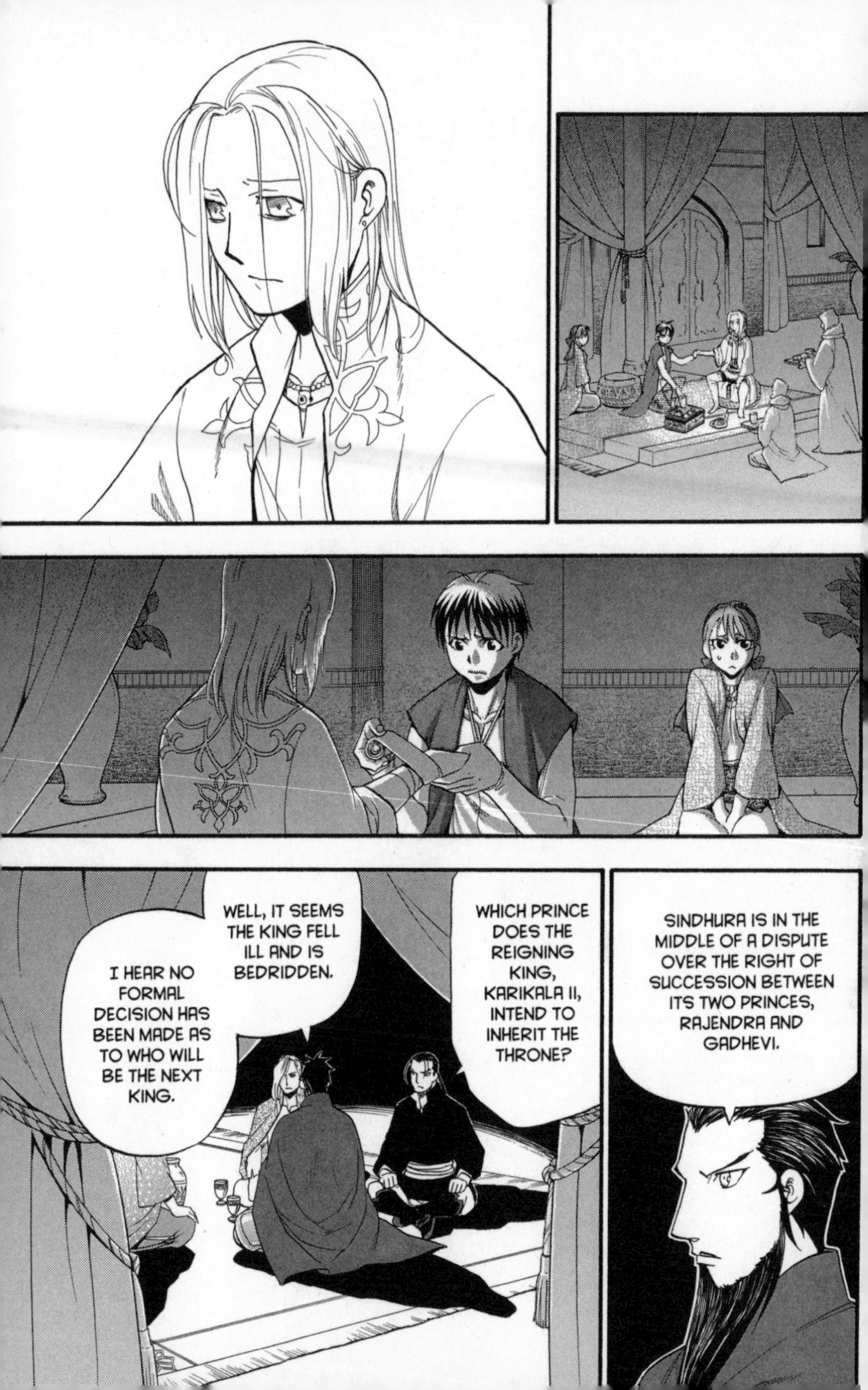
SINDHURA IS IN THE MIDDLE OF A DISPUTE OVER THE RIGHT OF SUCCESSION BETWEEN ITS TWO PRINCES, RAJENDRA AND GADHEVI.
WHICH PRINCE DOES THE REIGNING KING, KARIKALA II, INTEND TO INHERIT THE THRONE?
WELL, IT SEEMS THE KING FELL ILL AND IS BEDRIDDEN.
I HEAR NO FORMAL DECISION HAS BEEN MADE AS TO WHO WILL BE THE NEXT KING.

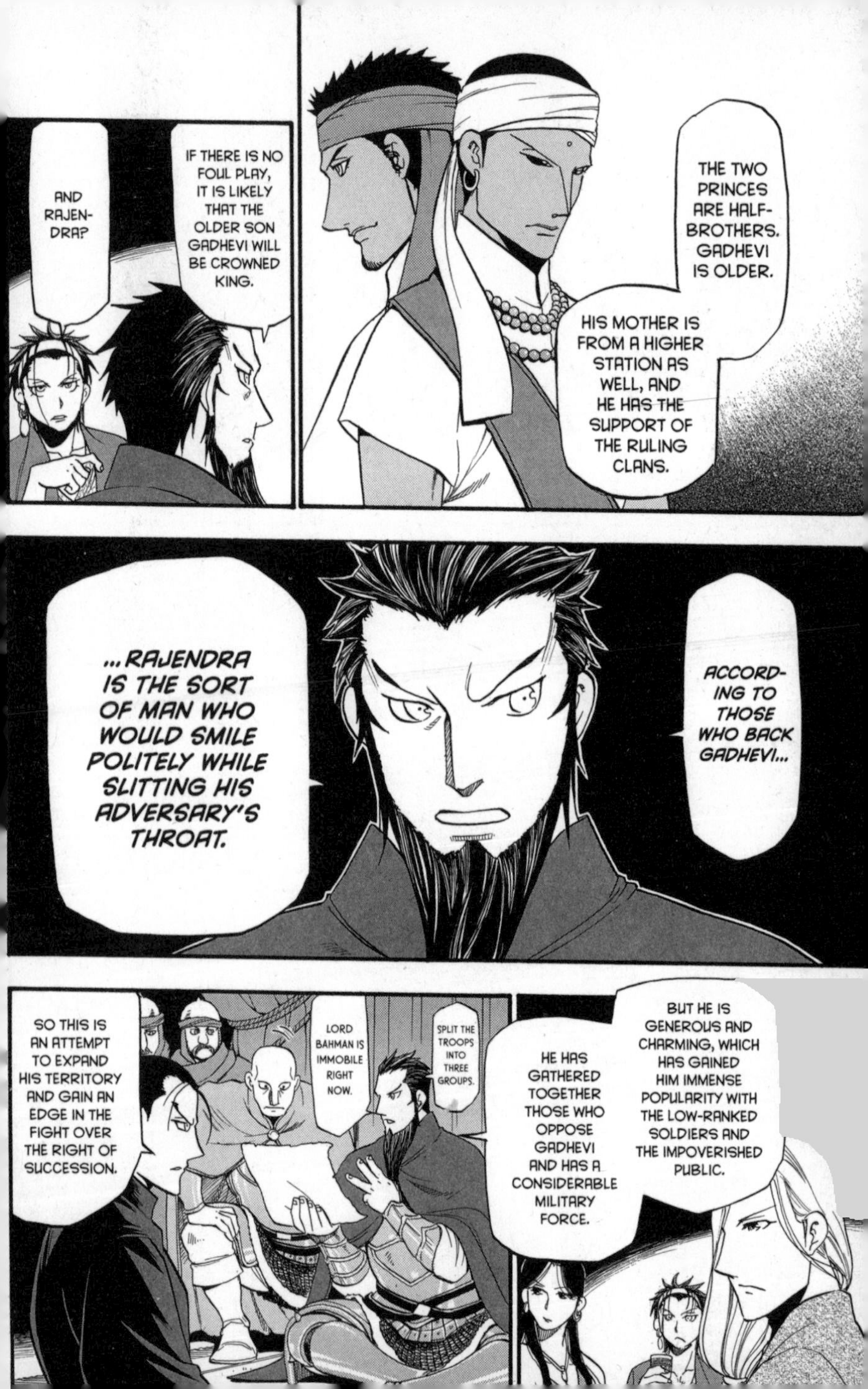
THE TWO PRINCES ARE HALF-BROTHERS. GADHEVI IS OLDER.
HIS MOTHER IS FROM A HIGHER STATION AS WELL, AND HE HAS THE SUPPORT OF THE RULING CLANS.
IF THERE IS NO FOUL PLAY, IT IS LIKELY THAT THE OLDER SON GADHEVI WILL BE CROWNED KING.
AND RAJENDRA?
ACCORDING TO THOSE WHO BACK GADHEVI...
...RAJENDRA IS THE SORT OF MAN WHO WOULD SMILE POLITELY WHILE SLITTING HIS ADVERSARY'S THROAT.
BUT HE IS GENEROUS AND CHARMING, WHICH HAS GAINED HIM IMMENSE POPULARITY WITH THE LOW-RANKED SOLDIERS AND THE IMPOVERISHED PUBLIC.
HE HAS GATHERED TOGETHER THOSE WHO OPPOSE GADHEVI AND HAS A CONSIDERABLE MILITARY FORCE.
SPLIT THE TROOPS INTO THREE GROUPS.
LORD BAHMAN IS IMMOBILE RIGHT NOW.
SO THIS IS AN ATTEMPT TO EXPAND HIS TERRITORY AND GAIN AN EDGE IN THE FIGHT OVER THE RIGHT OF SUCCESSION.

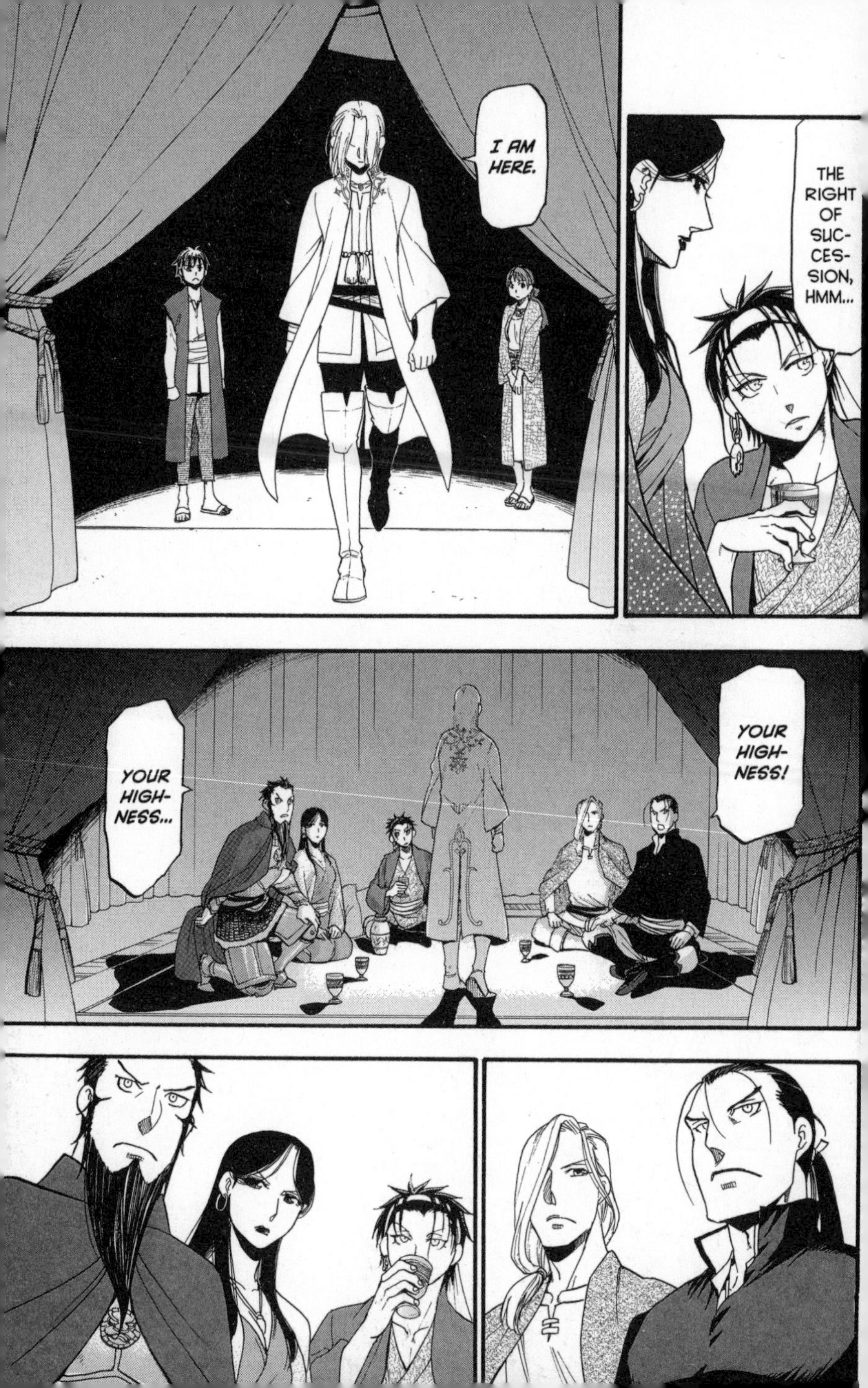
THE RIGHT OF SUCCESSION, HMM...
I AM HERE.
YOUR HIGHNESS!
YOUR HIGHNESS...

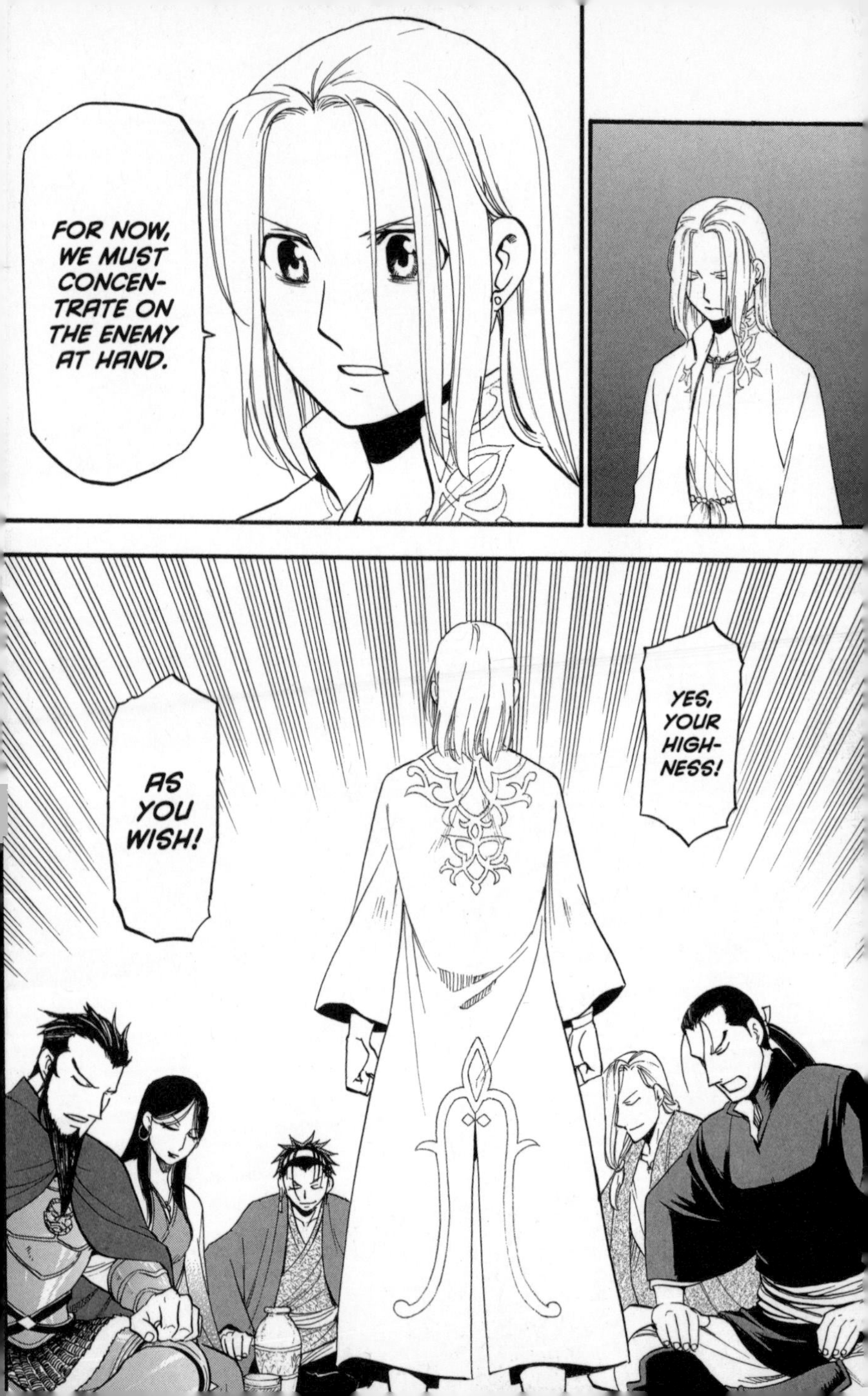
FOR NOW, WE MUST CONCEN-TRATE ON THE ENEMY AT HAND.
YES, YOUR HIGH-NESS!
AS YOU WISH!

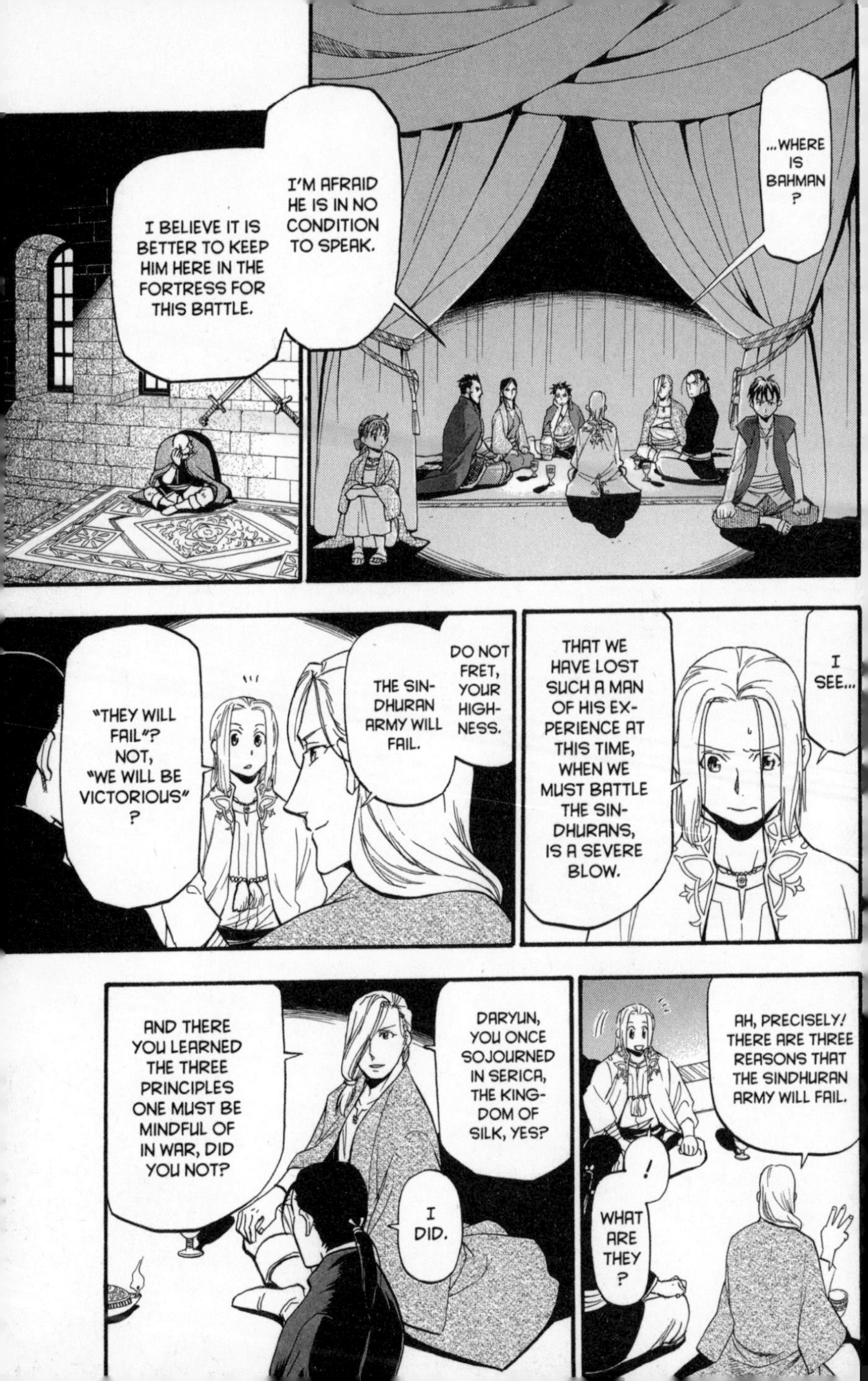
...WHERE IS BAHMAN ?
I'M AFRAID HE IS IN NO CONDITION TO SPEAK.
I BELIEVE IT IS BETTER TO KEEP HIM HERE IN THE FORTRESS FOR THIS BATTLE.
I SEE...
THAT WE HAVE LOST SUCH A MAN OF HIS EX-PERIENCE AT THIS TIME, WHEN WE MUST BATTLE THE SIN-DHURANS, IS A SEVERE BLOW.
DO NOT FRET, YOUR HIGH-NESS.
THE SIN-DHURAN ARMY WILL FAIL.
"THEY WILL FAIL"? NOT, "WE WILL BE VICTORIOUS" ?
AH, PRECISELY! THERE ARE THREE REASONS THAT THE SINDHURAN ARMY WILL FAIL.
!
WHAT ARE THEY ?
DARYUN, YOU ONCE SOJOURNED IN SERICA, THE KING-DOM OF SILK, YES?
AND THERE YOU LEARNED THE THREE PRINCIPLES ONE MUST BE MINDFUL OF IN WAR, DID YOU NOT?
I DID.

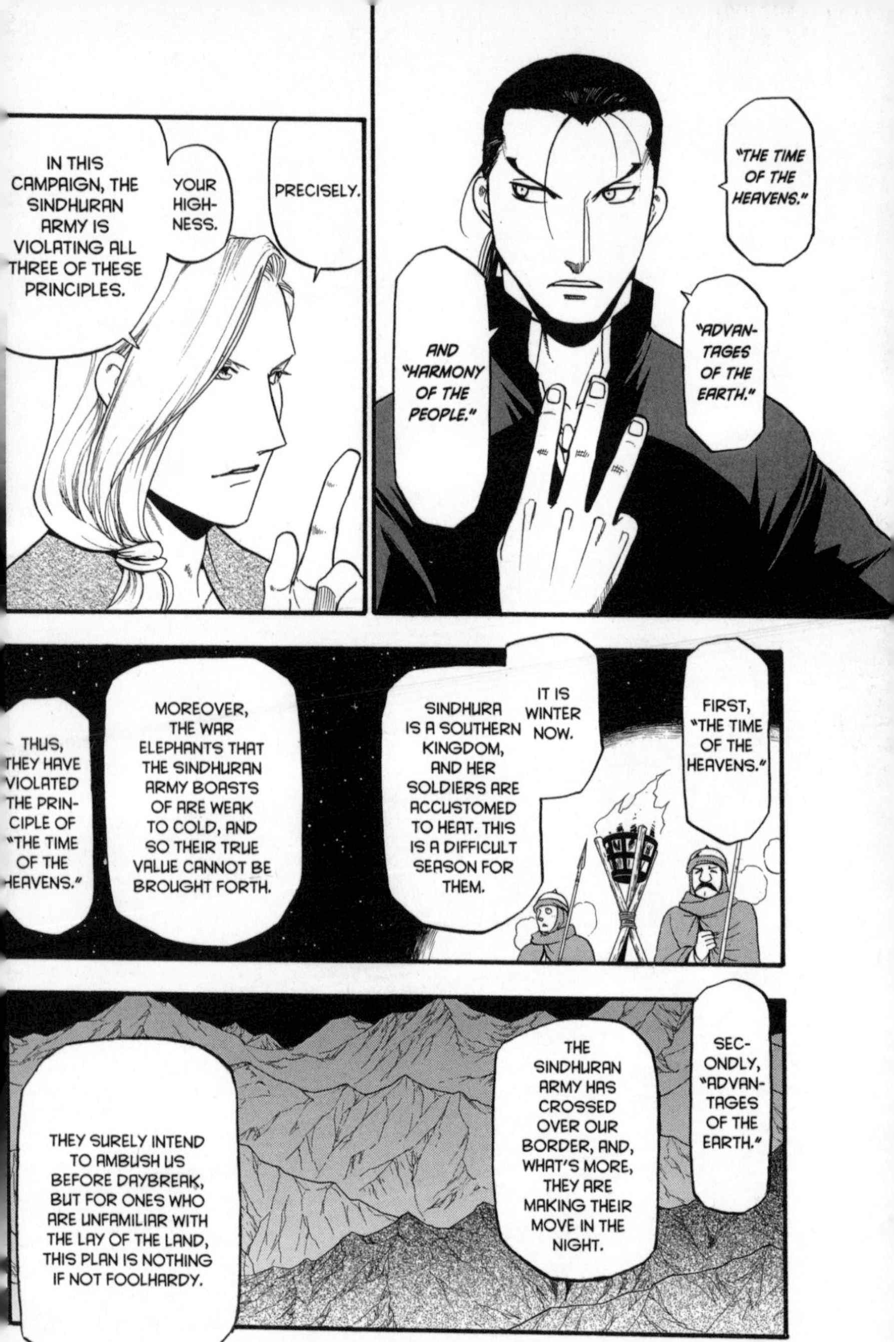
"THE TIME OF THE HEAVENS."
"ADVANTAGES OF THE EARTH."
AND "HARMONY OF THE PEOPLE."
PRECISELY.
YOUR HIGHNESS.
IN THIS CAMPAIGN, THE SINDHURAN ARMY IS VIOLATING ALL THREE OF THESE PRINCIPLES.
FIRST, "THE TIME OF THE HEAVENS."
IT IS WINTER NOW.
SINDHURA IS A SOUTHERN KINGDOM, AND HER SOLDIERS ARE ACCUSTOMED TO HEAT. THIS IS A DIFFICULT SEASON FOR THEM.
MOREOVER, THE WAR ELEPHANTS THAT THE SINDHURAN ARMY BOASTS OF ARE WEAK TO COLD, AND SO THEIR TRUE VALUE CANNOT BE BROUGHT FORTH.
THUS, THEY HAVE VIOLATED THE PRINCIPLE OF "THE TIME OF THE HEAVENS."
SECONDLY, "ADVANTAGES OF THE EARTH."
THE SINDHURAN ARMY HAS CROSSED OVER OUR BORDER, AND, WHAT'S MORE, THEY ARE MAKING THEIR MOVE IN THE NIGHT.
THEY SURELY INTEND TO AMBUSH US BEFORE DAYBREAK, BUT FOR ONES WHO ARE UNFAMILIAR WITH THE LAY OF THE LAND, THIS PLAN IS NOTHING IF NOT FOOLHARDY.

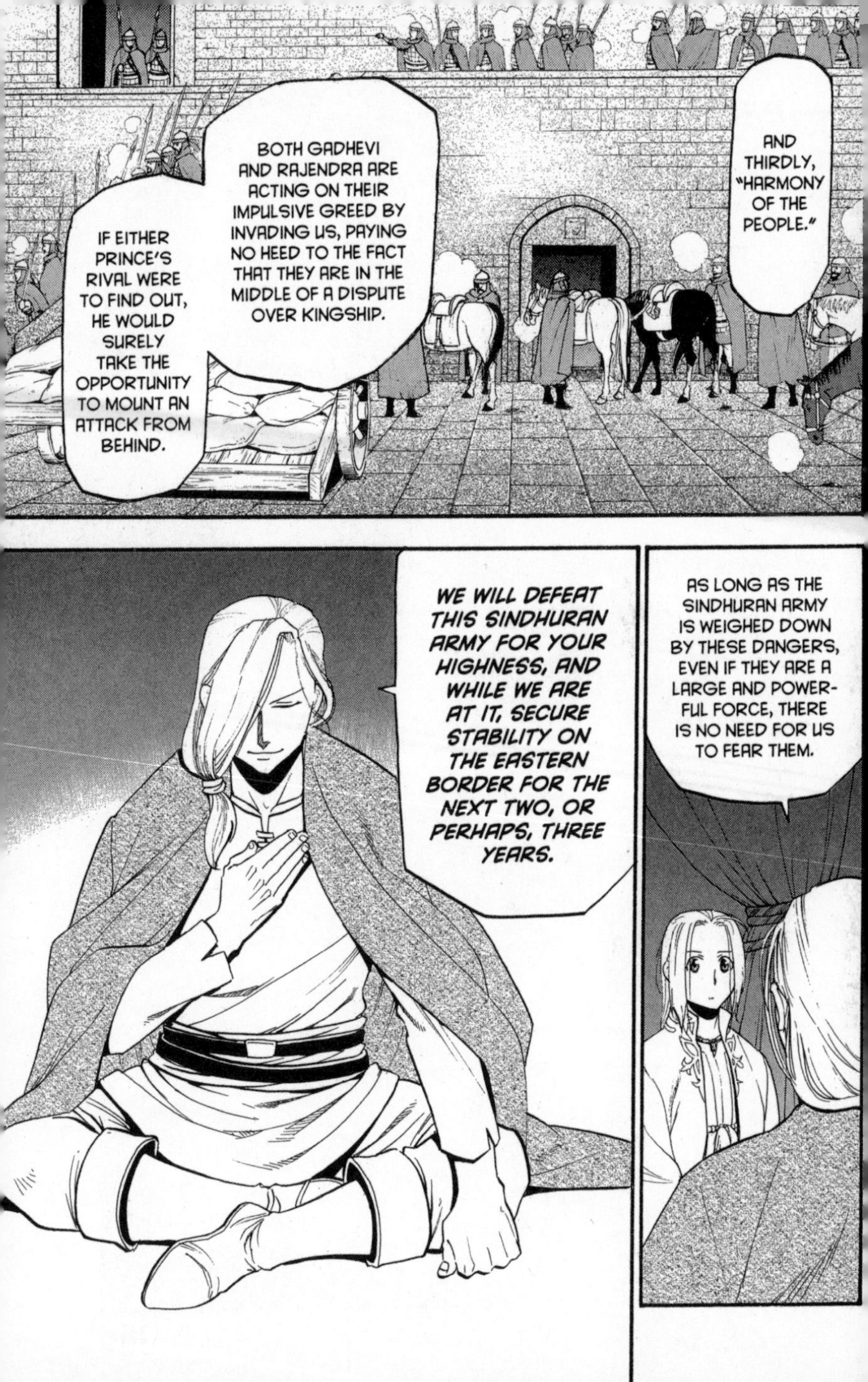
AND THIRDLY, "HARMONY OF THE PEOPLE."
BOTH GADHEVI AND RAJENDRA ARE ACTING ON THEIR IMPULSIVE GREED BY INVADING US, PAYING NO HEED TO THE FACT THAT THEY ARE IN THE MIDDLE OF A DISPUTE OVER KINGSHIP.
IF EITHER PRINCE'S RIVAL WERE TO FIND OUT, HE WOULD SURELY TAKE THE OPPORTUNITY TO MOUNT AN ATTACK FROM BEHIND.
AS LONG AS THE SINDHURAN ARMY IS WEIGHED DOWN BY THESE DANGERS, EVEN IF THEY ARE A LARGE AND POWERFUL FORCE, THERE IS NO NEED FOR US TO FEAR THEM.
WE WILL DEFEAT THIS SINDHURAN ARMY FOR YOUR HIGHNESS, AND WHILE WE ARE AT IT, SECURE STABILITY ON THE EASTERN BORDER FOR THE NEXT TWO, OR PERHAPS, THREE YEARS.

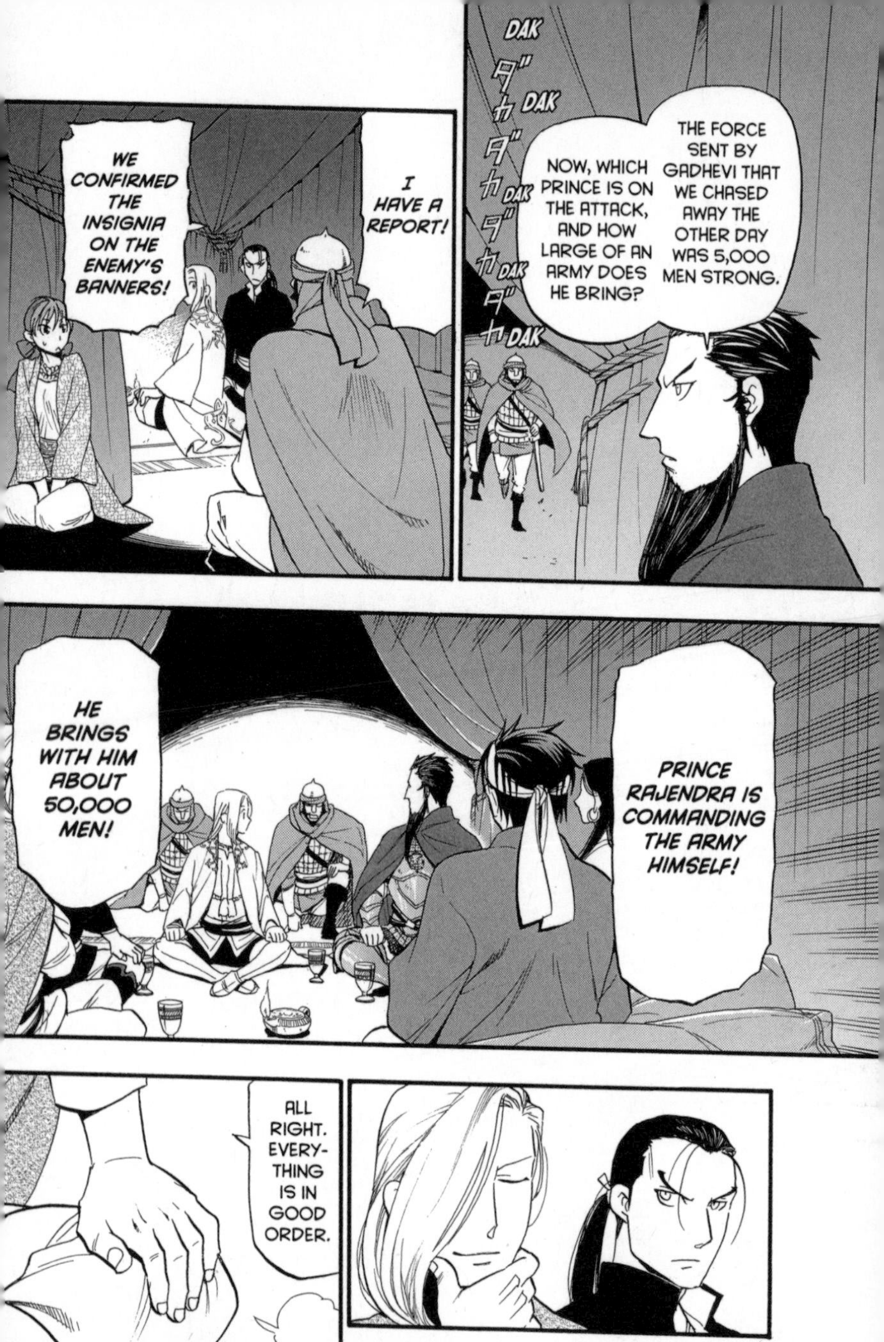
DAK
DAK
DAK
DAK
DAK
THE FORCE SENT BY GADHEVI THAT WE CHASED AWAY THE OTHER DAY WAS 5,000 MEN STRONG.
NOW, WHICH PRINCE IS ON THE ATTACK, AND HOW LARGE OF AN ARMY DOES HE BRING?
I HAVE A REPORT!
WE CONFIRMED THE INSIGNIA ON THE ENEMY'S BANNERS!
PRINCE RAJENDRA IS COMMANDING THE ARMY HIMSELF!
HE BRINGS WITH HIM ABOUT 50,000 MEN!
ALL RIGHT. EVERY-THING IS IN GOOD ORDER.

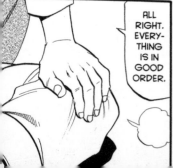

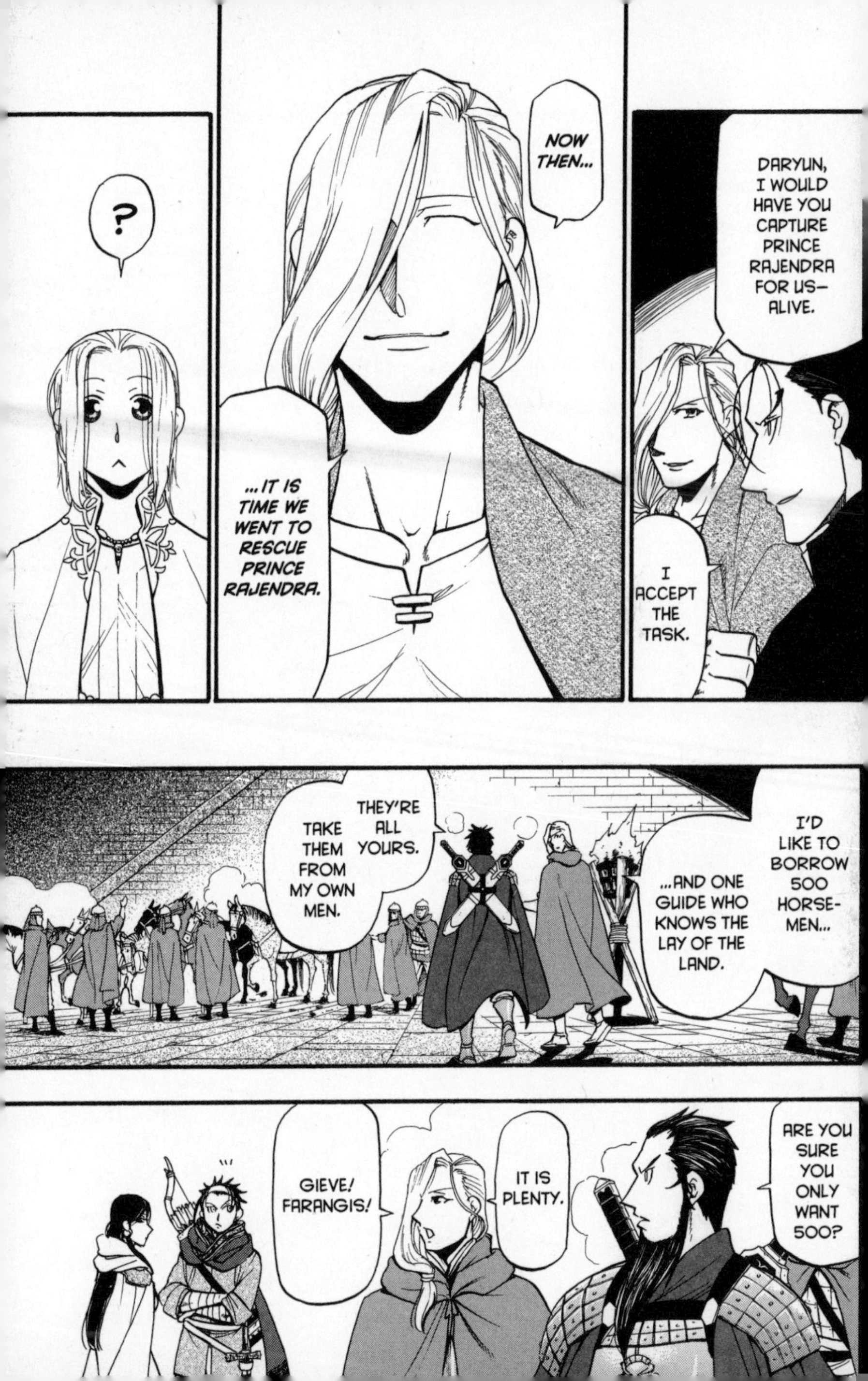
DARYUN, I WOULD HAVE YOU CAPTURE PRINCE RAJENDRA FOR US—ALIVE.
I ACCEPT THE TASK.
NOW THEN...
...IT IS TIME WE WENT TO RESCUE PRINCE RAJENDRA.
?
I'D LIKE TO BORROW 500 HORSEMEN...
...AND ONE GUIDE WHO KNOWS THE LAY OF THE LAND.
THEY'RE ALL YOURS.
TAKE THEM FROM MY OWN MEN.
ARE YOU SURE YOU ONLY WANT 500?
IT IS PLENTY.
GIEVE! FARANGIS!

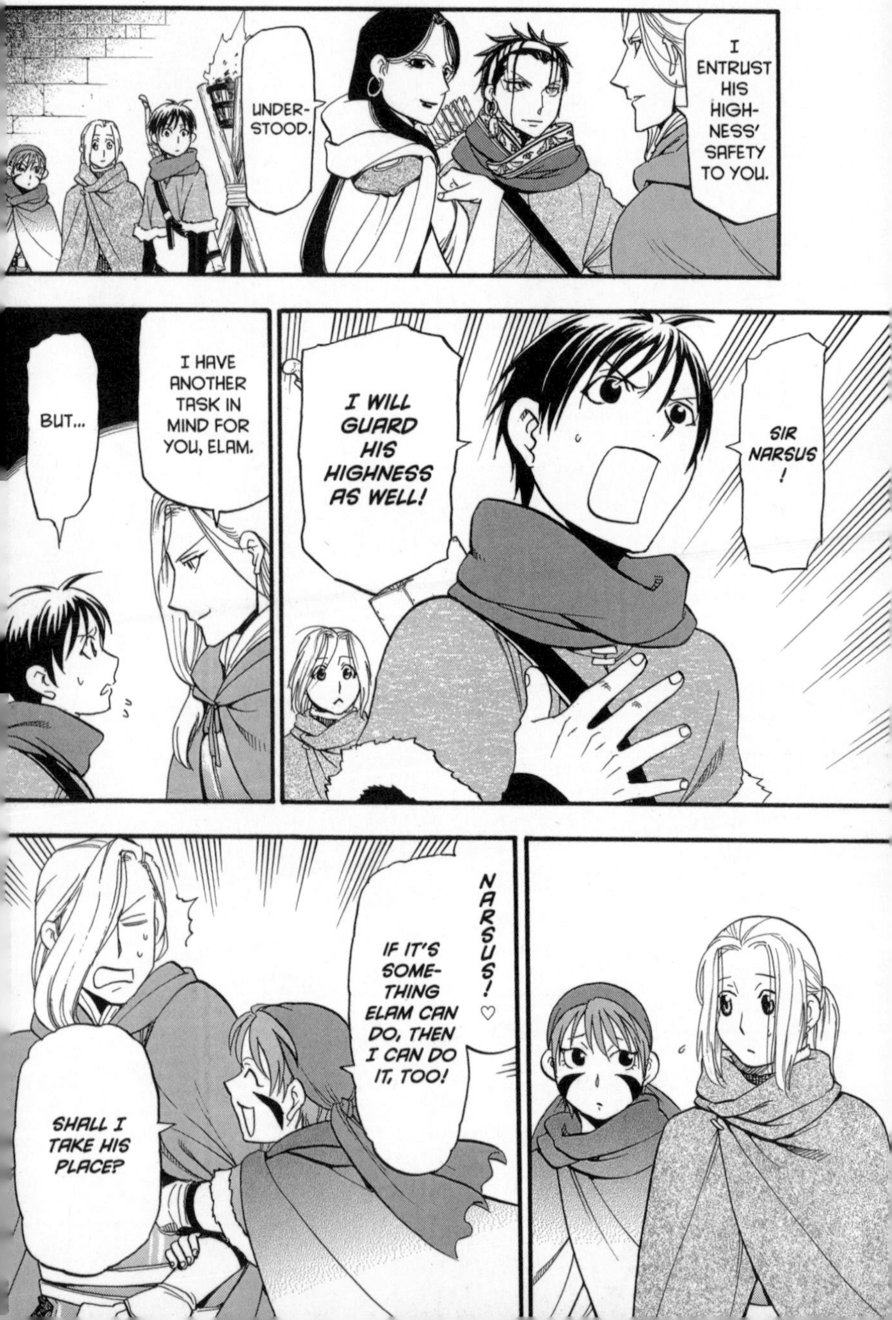
I ENTRUST HIS HIGH-NESS' SAFETY TO YOU.
UNDER-STOOD.
SIR NARSUS!
I WILL GUARD HIS HIGHNESS AS WELL!
I HAVE ANOTHER TASK IN MIND FOR YOU, ELAM.
BUT...
NARSUS!♡
IF IT'S SOME-THING ELAM CAN DO, THEN I CAN DO IT, TOO!
SHALL I TAKE HIS PLACE?

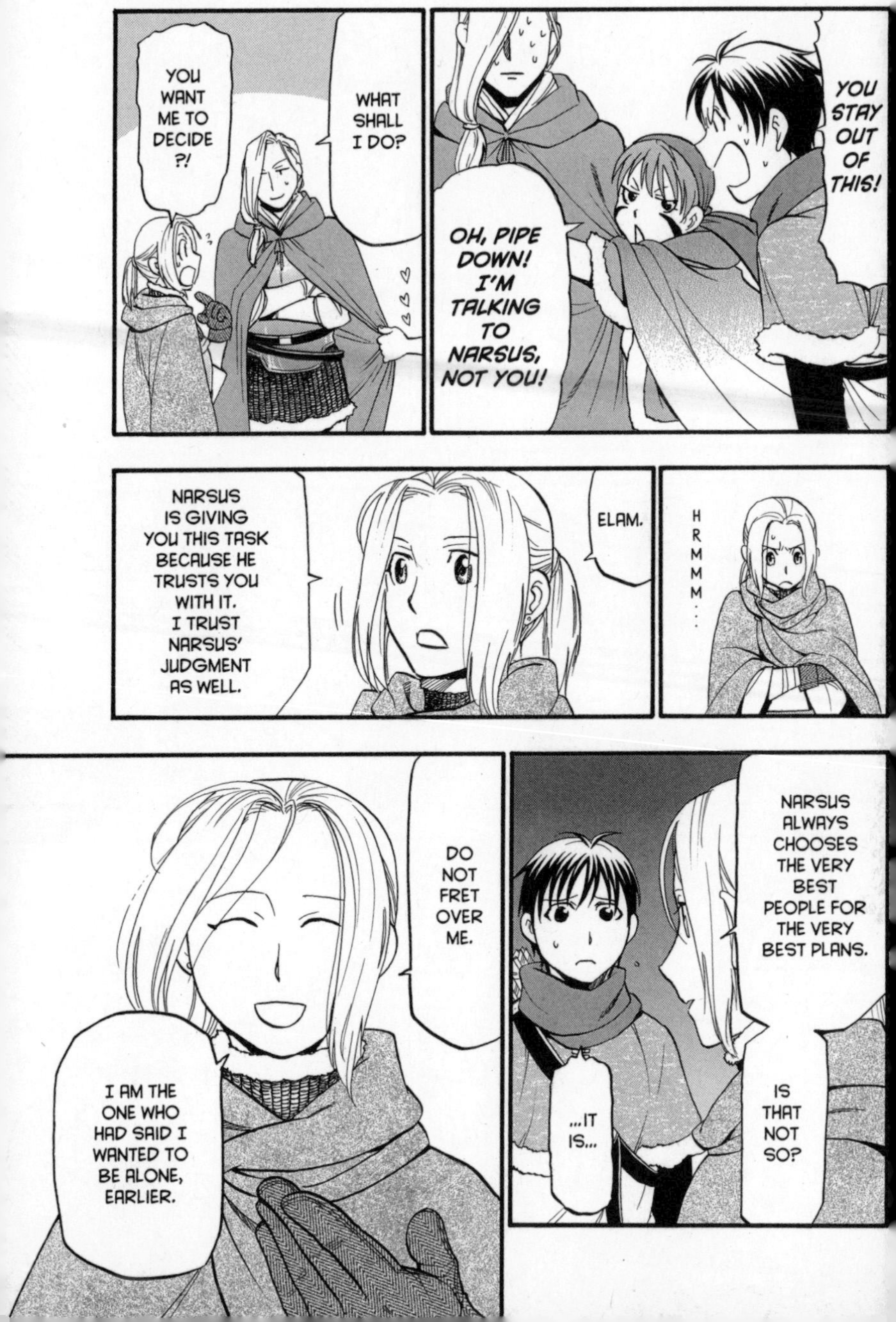
YOU STAY OUT OF THIS!
OH, PIPE DOWN! I'M TALKING TO NARSUS, NOT YOU!
WHAT SHALL I DO?
YOU WANT ME TO DECIDE ?!
HRMMM...
ELAM.
NARSUS IS GIVING YOU THIS TASK BECAUSE HE TRUSTS YOU WITH IT. I TRUST NARSUS' JUDGMENT AS WELL.
NARSUS ALWAYS CHOOSES THE VERY BEST PEOPLE FOR THE VERY BEST PLANS.
IS THAT NOT SO?
...IT IS...
DO NOT FRET OVER ME.
I AM THE ONE WHO HAD SAID I WANTED TO BE ALONE, EARLIER.

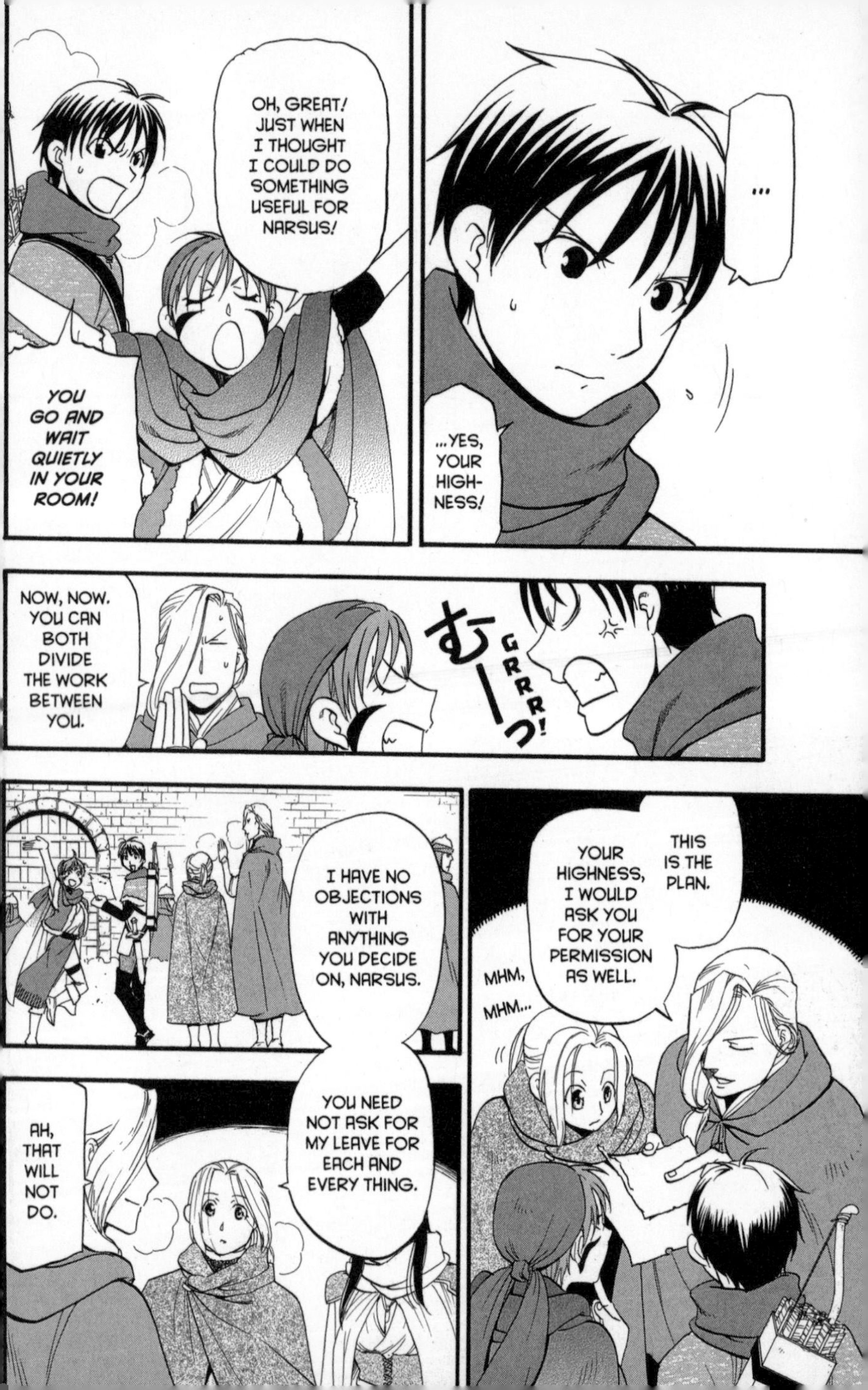
...
...YES, YOUR HIGHNESS!
OH, GREAT! JUST WHEN I THOUGHT I COULD DO SOMETHING USEFUL FOR NARSUS!
YOU GO AND WAIT QUIETLY IN YOUR ROOM!
むーっ GRRR!
NOW, NOW. YOU CAN BOTH DIVIDE THE WORK BETWEEN YOU.
THIS IS THE PLAN.
YOUR HIGHNESS, I WOULD ASK YOU FOR YOUR PERMISSION AS WELL.
MHM, MHM...
I HAVE NO OBJECTIONS WITH ANYTHING YOU DECIDE ON, NARSUS.
YOU NEED NOT ASK FOR MY LEAVE FOR EACH AND EVERY THING.
AH, THAT WILL NOT DO.

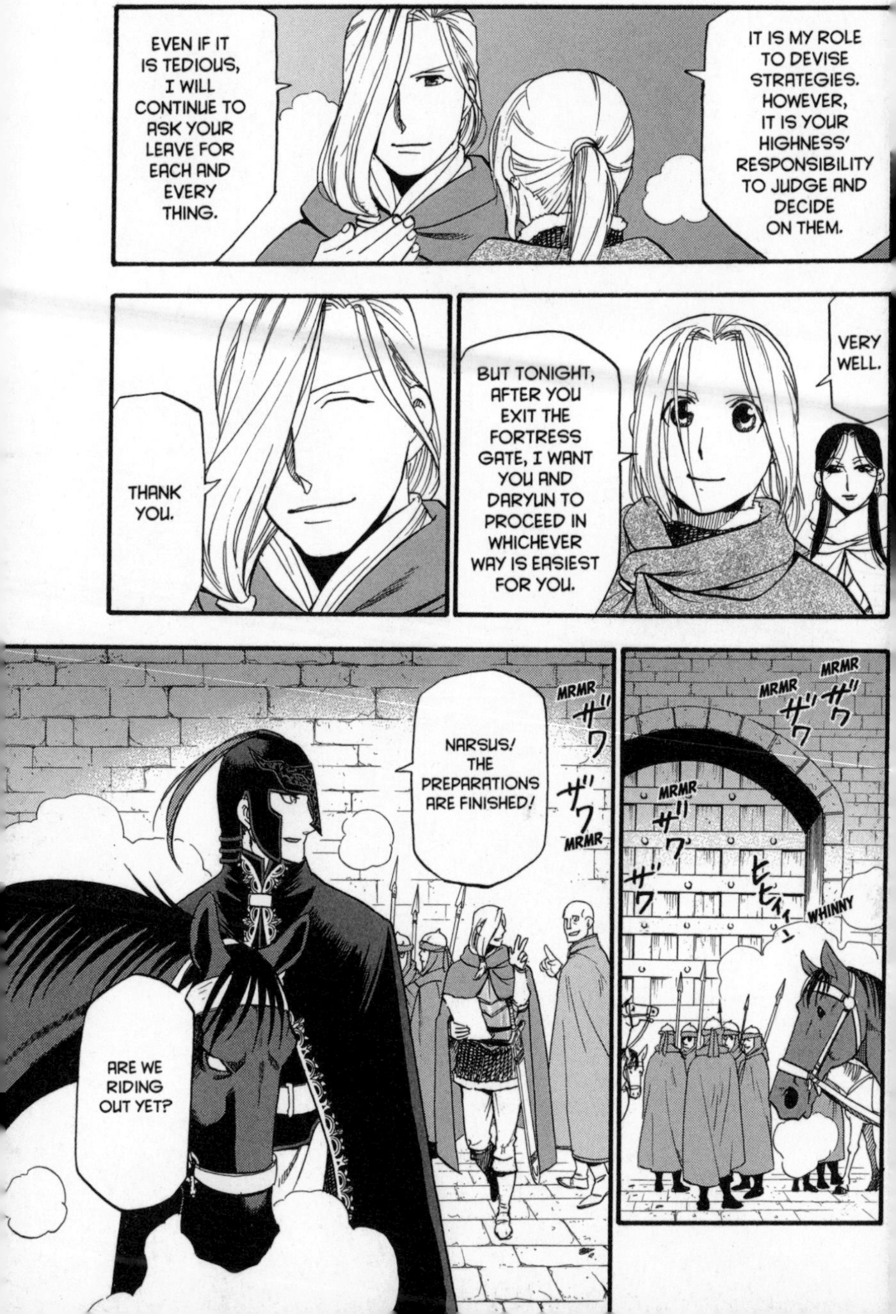
IT IS MY ROLE TO DEVISE STRATEGIES. HOWEVER, IT IS YOUR HIGHNESS' RESPONSIBILITY TO JUDGE AND DECIDE ON THEM.
EVEN IF IT IS TEDIOUS, I WILL CONTINUE TO ASK YOUR LEAVE FOR EACH AND EVERY THING.
VERY WELL.
BUT TONIGHT, AFTER YOU EXIT THE FORTRESS GATE, I WANT YOU AND DARYUN TO PROCEED IN WHICHEVER WAY IS EASIEST FOR YOU.
THANK YOU.
MRMR
ザワ
MRMR
ザワ
MRMR
ザワ
ザワ
ヒヒィィン
WHINNY
MRMR
ザワ
ザワ
MRMR
NARSUS! THE PREPARATIONS ARE FINISHED!
ARE WE RIDING OUT YET?

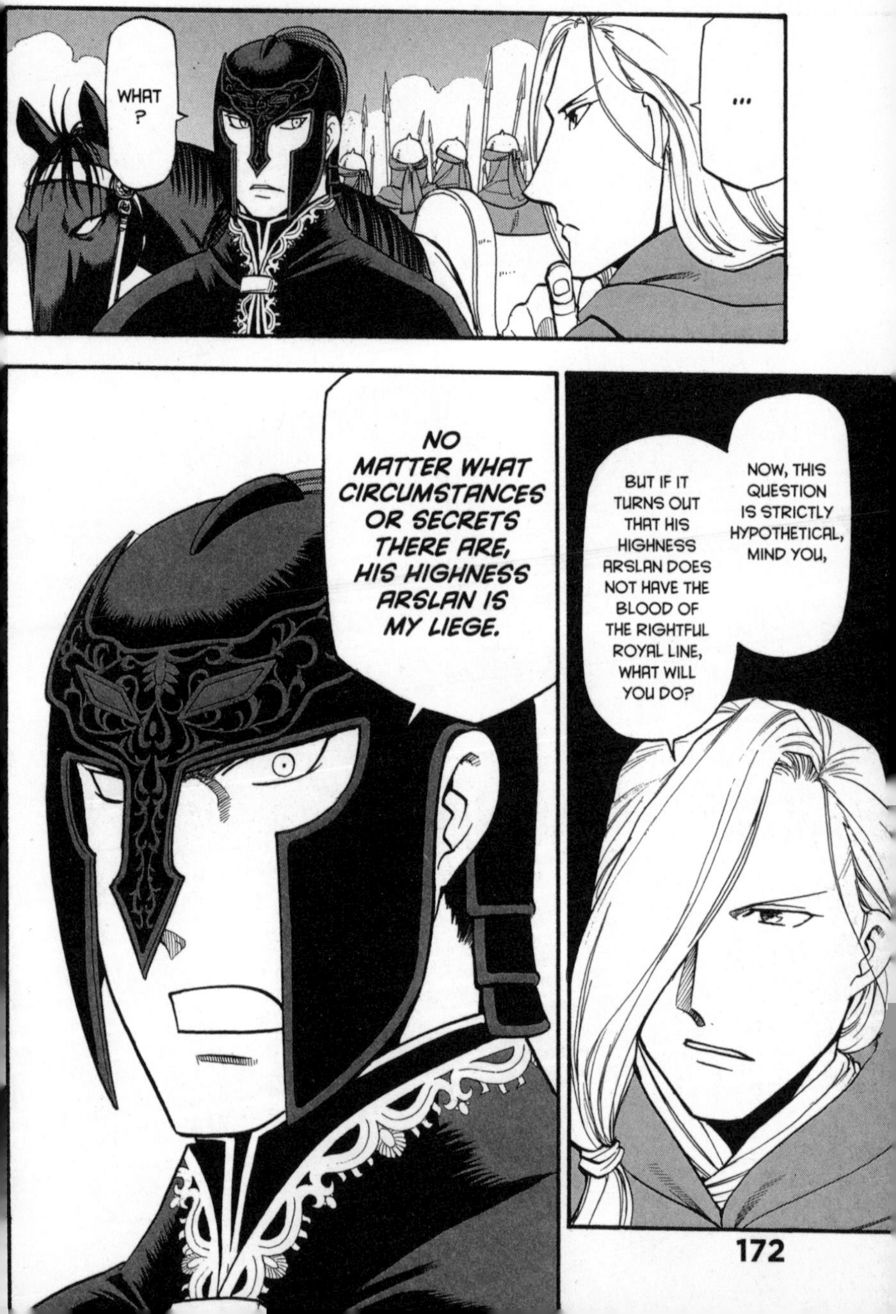
...
WHAT ?
NOW, THIS QUESTION IS STRICTLY HYPOTHETICAL, MIND YOU,
BUT IF IT TURNS OUT THAT HIS HIGHNESS ARSLAN DOES NOT HAVE THE BLOOD OF THE RIGHTFUL ROYAL LINE, WHAT WILL YOU DO?
NO MATTER WHAT CIRCUMSTANCES OR SECRETS THERE ARE, HIS HIGHNESS ARSLAN IS MY LIEGE.

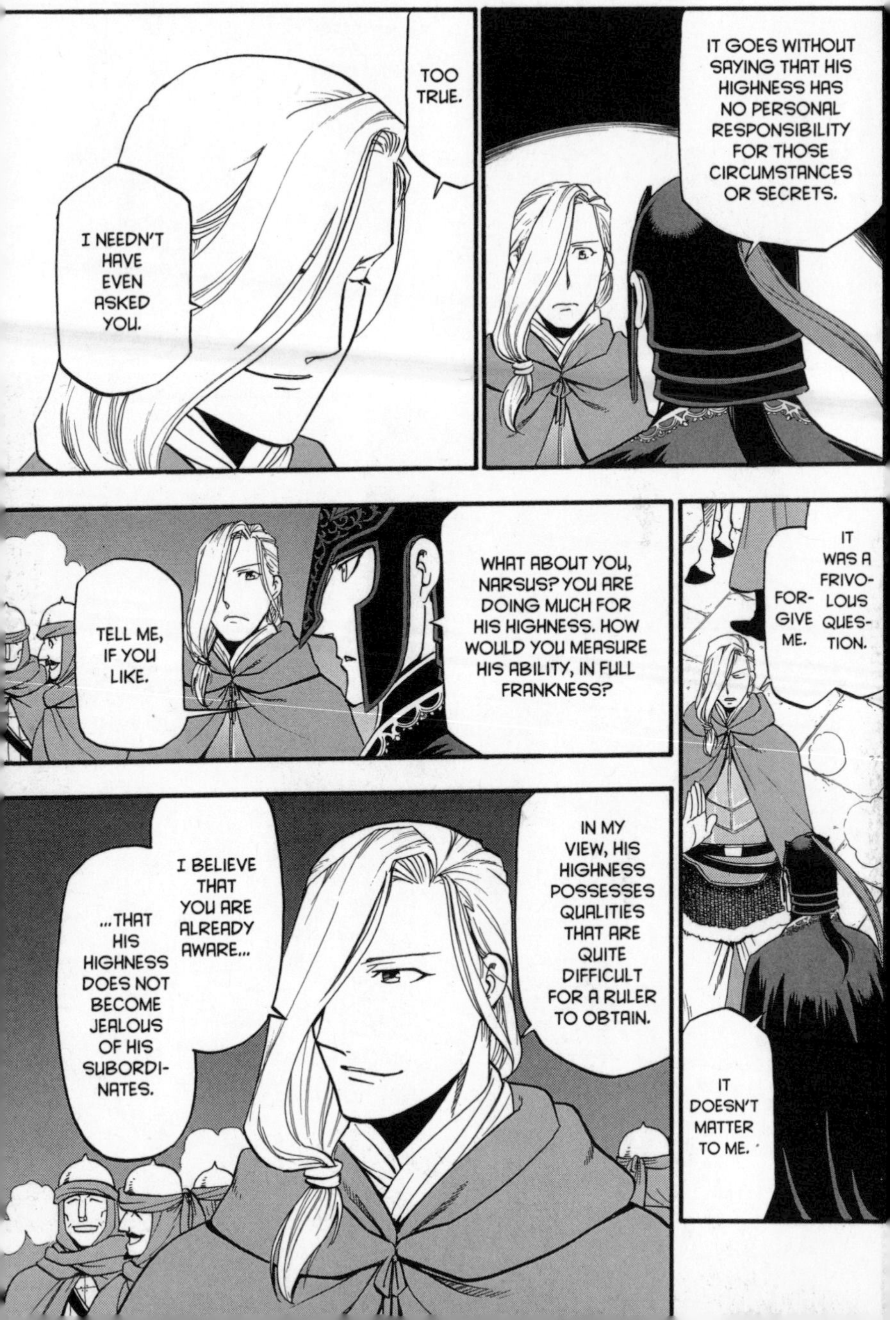
IT GOES WITHOUT SAYING THAT HIS HIGHNESS HAS NO PERSONAL RESPONSIBILITY FOR THOSE CIRCUMSTANCES OR SECRETS.
TOO TRUE.
I NEEDN'T HAVE EVEN ASKED YOU.
IT WAS A FRIVOLOUS QUESTION.
FORGIVE ME.
IT DOESN'T MATTER TO ME.
WHAT ABOUT YOU, NARSUS? YOU ARE DOING MUCH FOR HIS HIGHNESS. HOW WOULD YOU MEASURE HIS ABILITY, IN FULL FRANKNESS?
TELL ME, IF YOU LIKE.
IN MY VIEW, HIS HIGHNESS POSSESSES QUALITIES THAT ARE QUITE DIFFICULT FOR A RULER TO OBTAIN.
I BELIEVE THAT YOU ARE ALREADY AWARE...
...THAT HIS HIGHNESS DOES NOT BECOME JEALOUS OF HIS SUBORDINATES.

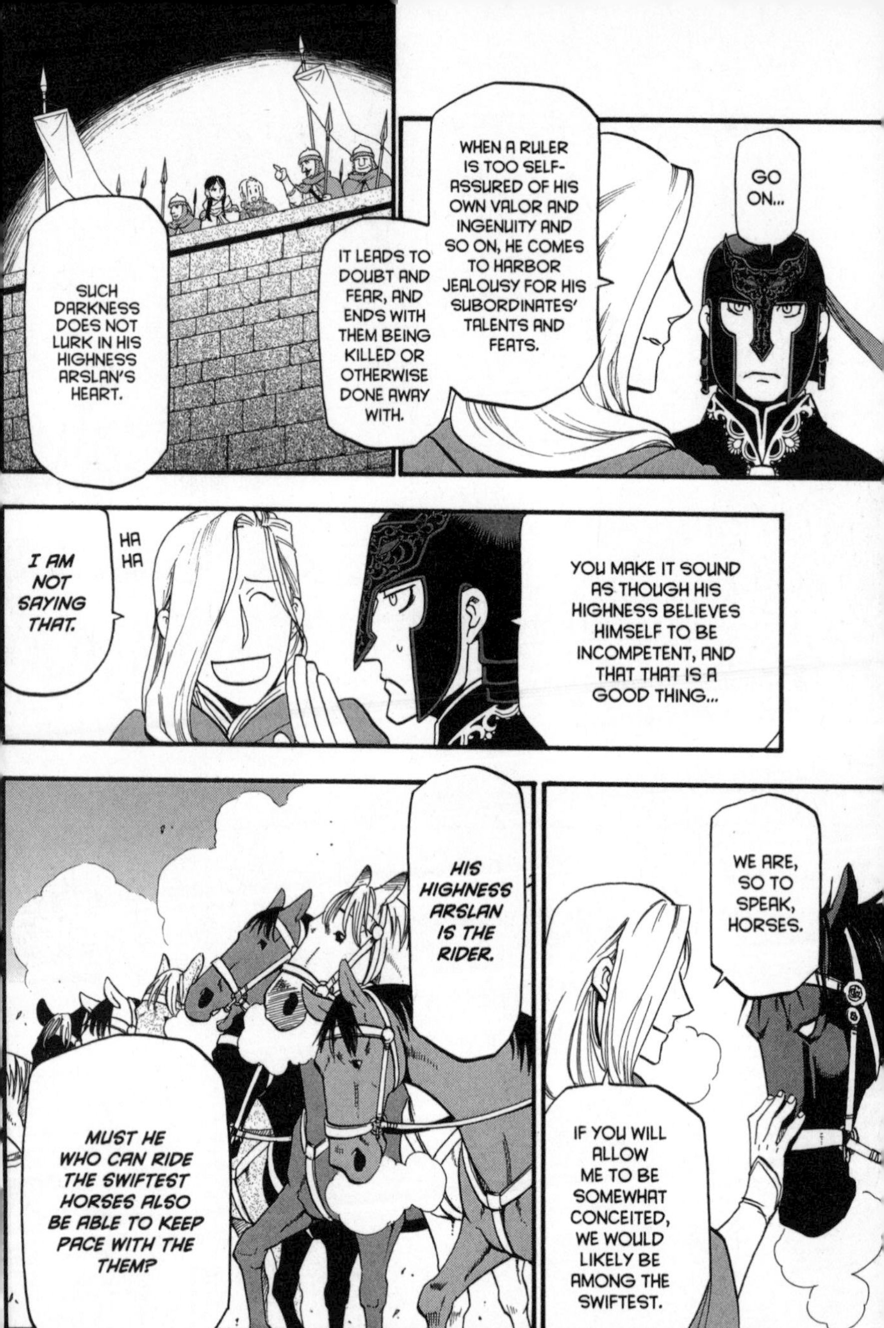
GO ON...
WHEN A RULER IS TOO SELF-ASSURED OF HIS OWN VALOR AND INGENUITY AND SO ON, HE COMES TO HARBOR JEALOUSY FOR HIS SUBORDINATES' TALENTS AND FEATS.
IT LEADS TO DOUBT AND FEAR, AND ENDS WITH THEM BEING KILLED OR OTHERWISE DONE AWAY WITH.
SUCH DARKNESS DOES NOT LURK IN HIS HIGHNESS ARSLAN'S HEART.
YOU MAKE IT SOUND AS THOUGH HIS HIGHNESS BELIEVES HIMSELF TO BE INCOMPETENT, AND THAT THAT IS A GOOD THING...
HA HA
I AM NOT SAYING THAT.
WE ARE, SO TO SPEAK, HORSES.
IF YOU WILL ALLOW ME TO BE SOMEWHAT CONCEITED, WE WOULD LIKELY BE AMONG THE SWIFTEST.
HIS HIGHNESS ARSLAN IS THE RIDER.
MUST HE WHO CAN RIDE THE SWIFTEST HORSES ALSO BE ABLE TO KEEP PACE WITH THE THEM?

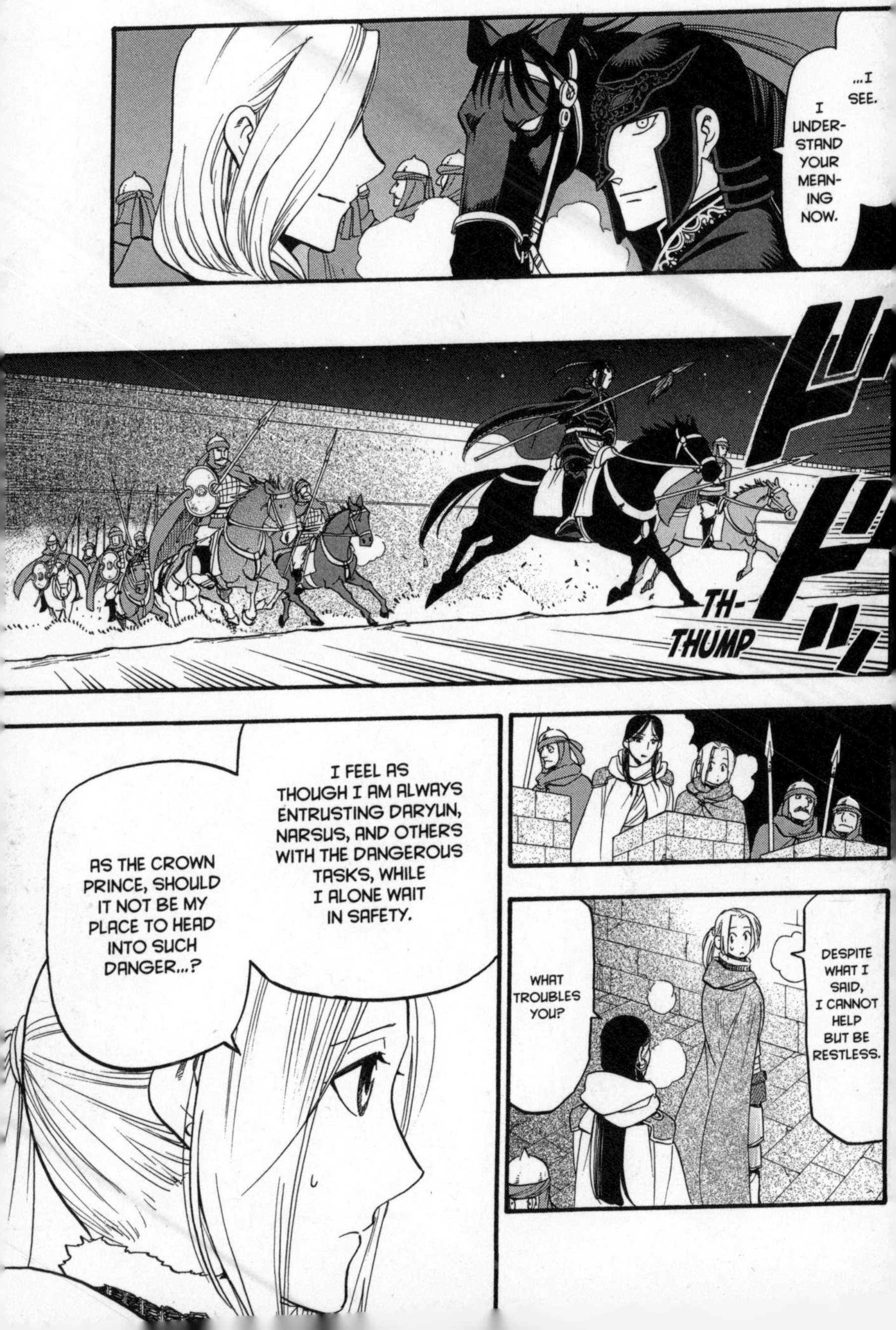
...I SEE.
I UNDERSTAND YOUR MEANING NOW.
TH-THUMP
DESPITE WHAT I SAID, I CANNOT HELP BUT BE RESTLESS.
WHAT TROUBLES YOU?
I FEEL AS THOUGH I AM ALWAYS ENTRUSTING DARYUN, NARSUS, AND OTHERS WITH THE DANGEROUS TASKS, WHILE I ALONE WAIT IN SAFETY.
AS THE CROWN PRINCE, SHOULD IT NOT BE MY PLACE TO HEAD INTO SUCH DANGER...?

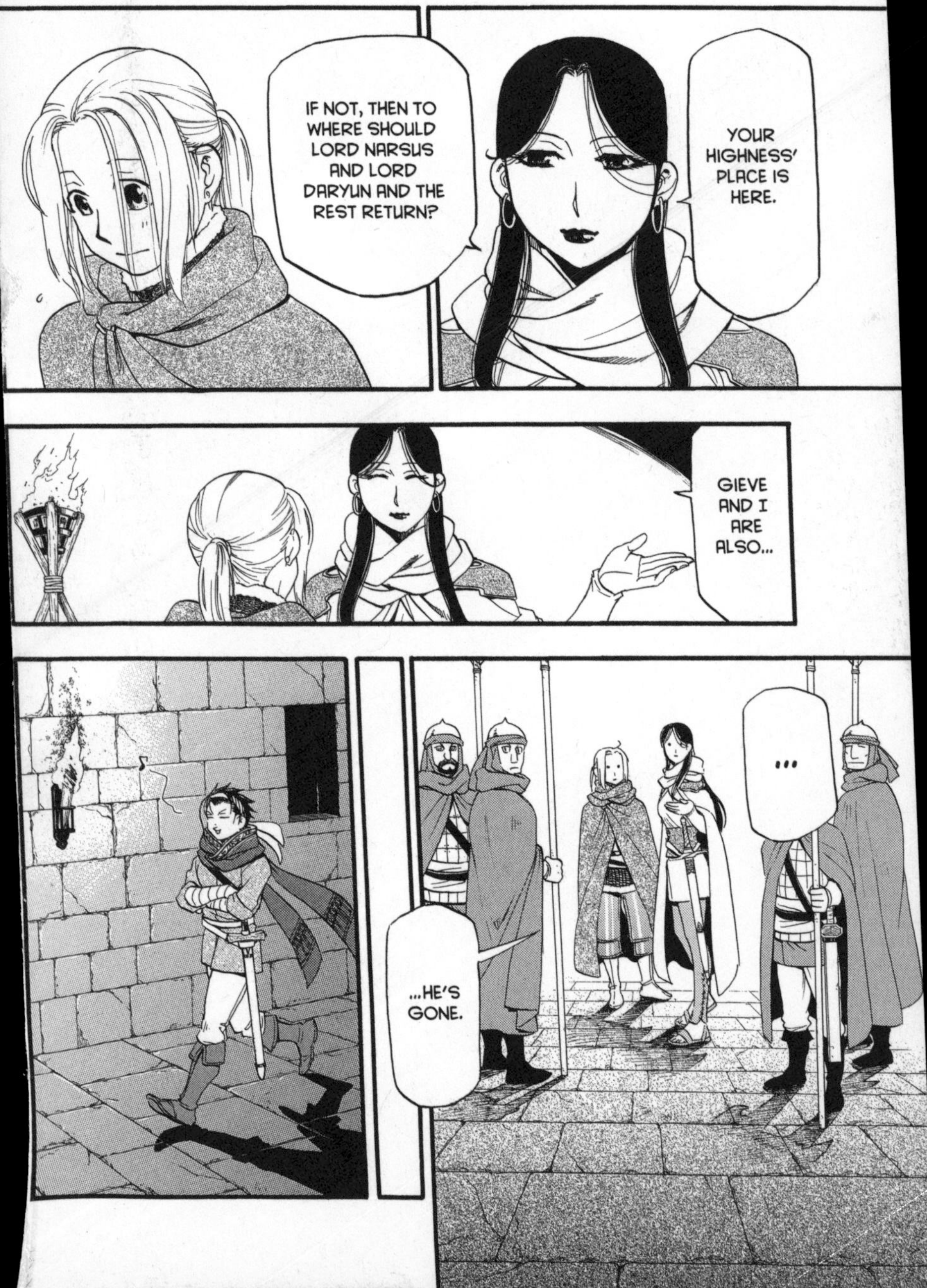
YOUR HIGHNESS' PLACE IS HERE.
IF NOT, THEN TO WHERE SHOULD LORD NARSUS AND LORD DARYUN AND THE REST RETURN?
GIEVE AND I ARE ALSO...
...
...HE'S GONE.

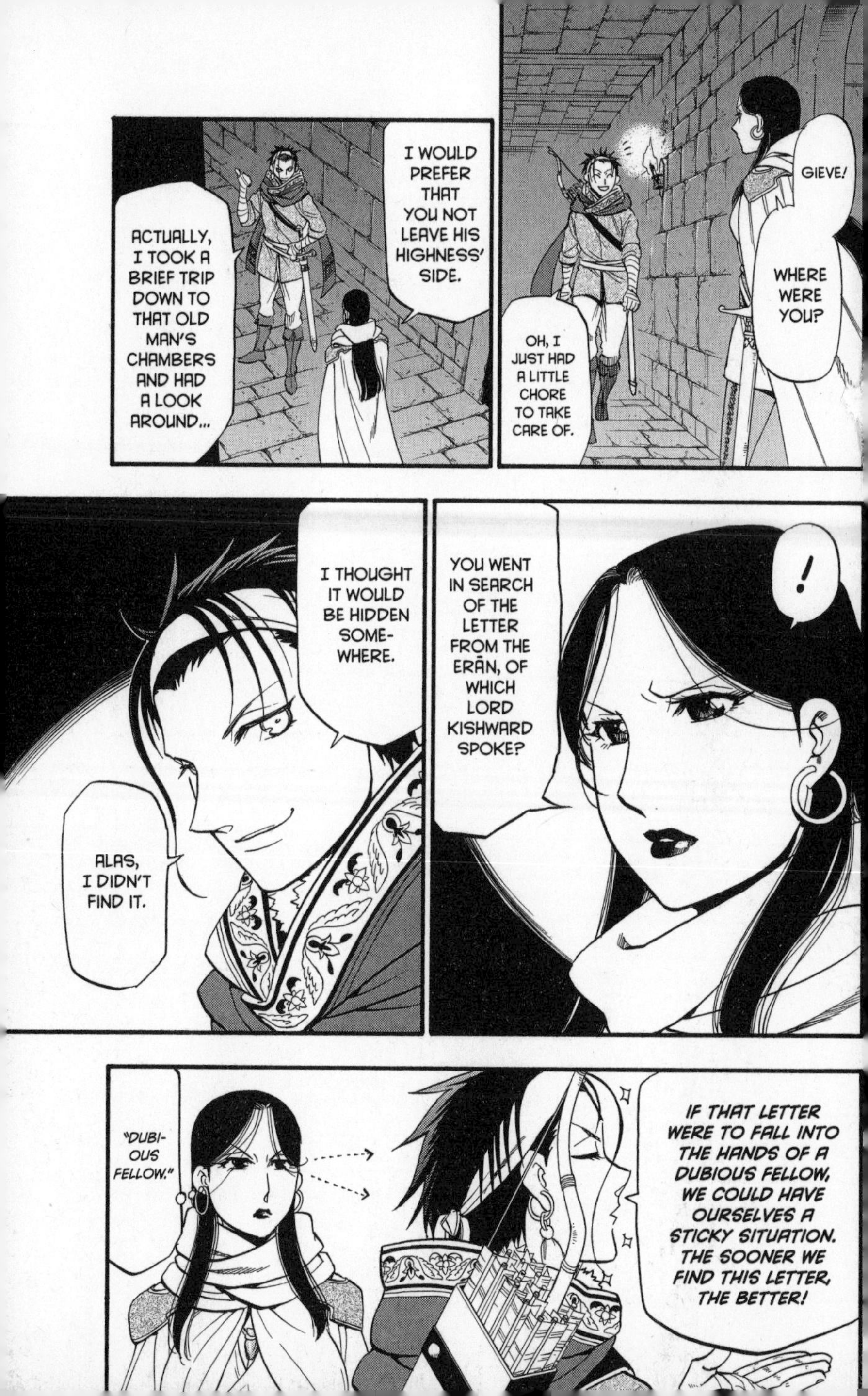
GIEVE!
WHERE WERE YOU?
OH, I JUST HAD A LITTLE CHORE TO TAKE CARE OF.
I WOULD PREFER THAT YOU NOT LEAVE HIS HIGHNESS' SIDE.
ACTUALLY, I TOOK A BRIEF TRIP DOWN TO THAT OLD MAN'S CHAMBERS AND HAD A LOOK AROUND...
!
YOU WENT IN SEARCH OF THE LETTER FROM THE ERĀN, OF WHICH LORD KISHWARD SPOKE?
I THOUGHT IT WOULD BE HIDDEN SOME-WHERE.
ALAS, I DIDN'T FIND IT.
IF THAT LETTER WERE TO FALL INTO THE HANDS OF A DUBIOUS FELLOW, WE COULD HAVE OURSELVES A STICKY SITUATION. THE SOONER WE FIND THIS LETTER, THE BETTER!
"DUBI-OUS FELLOW."

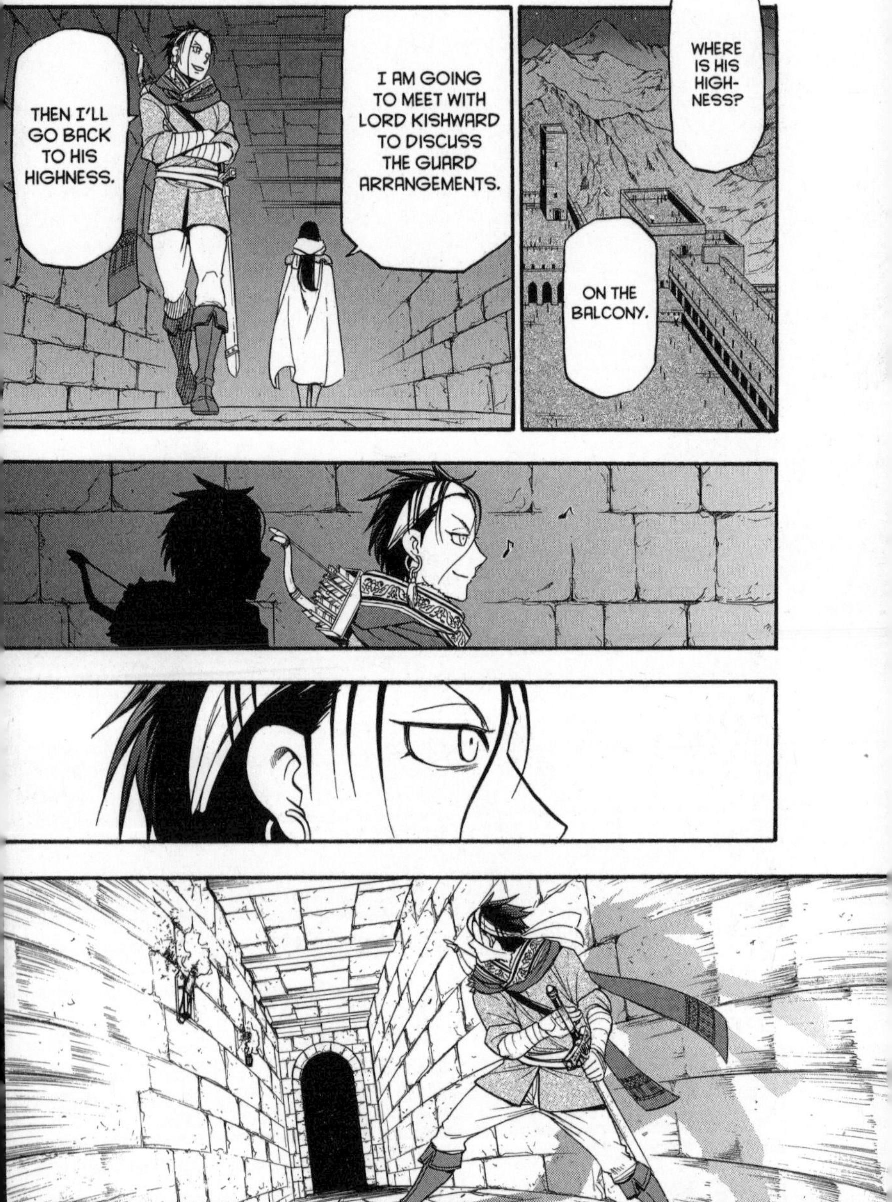
WHERE IS HIS HIGH-NESS?
ON THE BALCONY.
I AM GOING TO MEET WITH LORD KISHWARD TO DISCUSS THE GUARD ARRANGEMENTS.
THEN I'LL GO BACK TO HIS HIGHNESS.

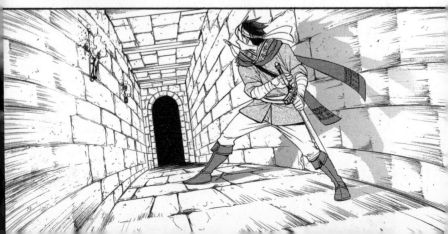

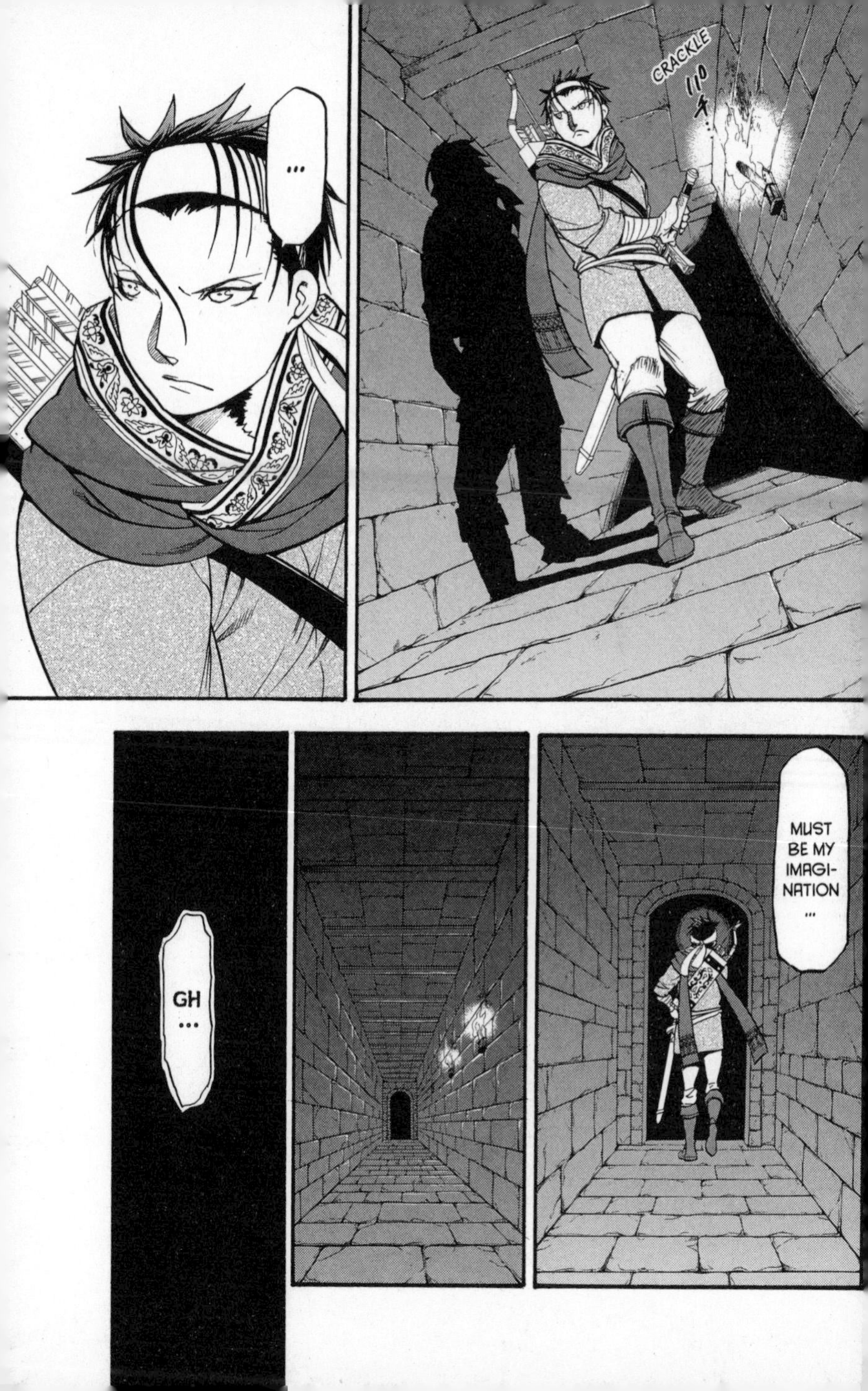
CRACKLE
...
MUST BE MY IMAGINATION ...
GH ...

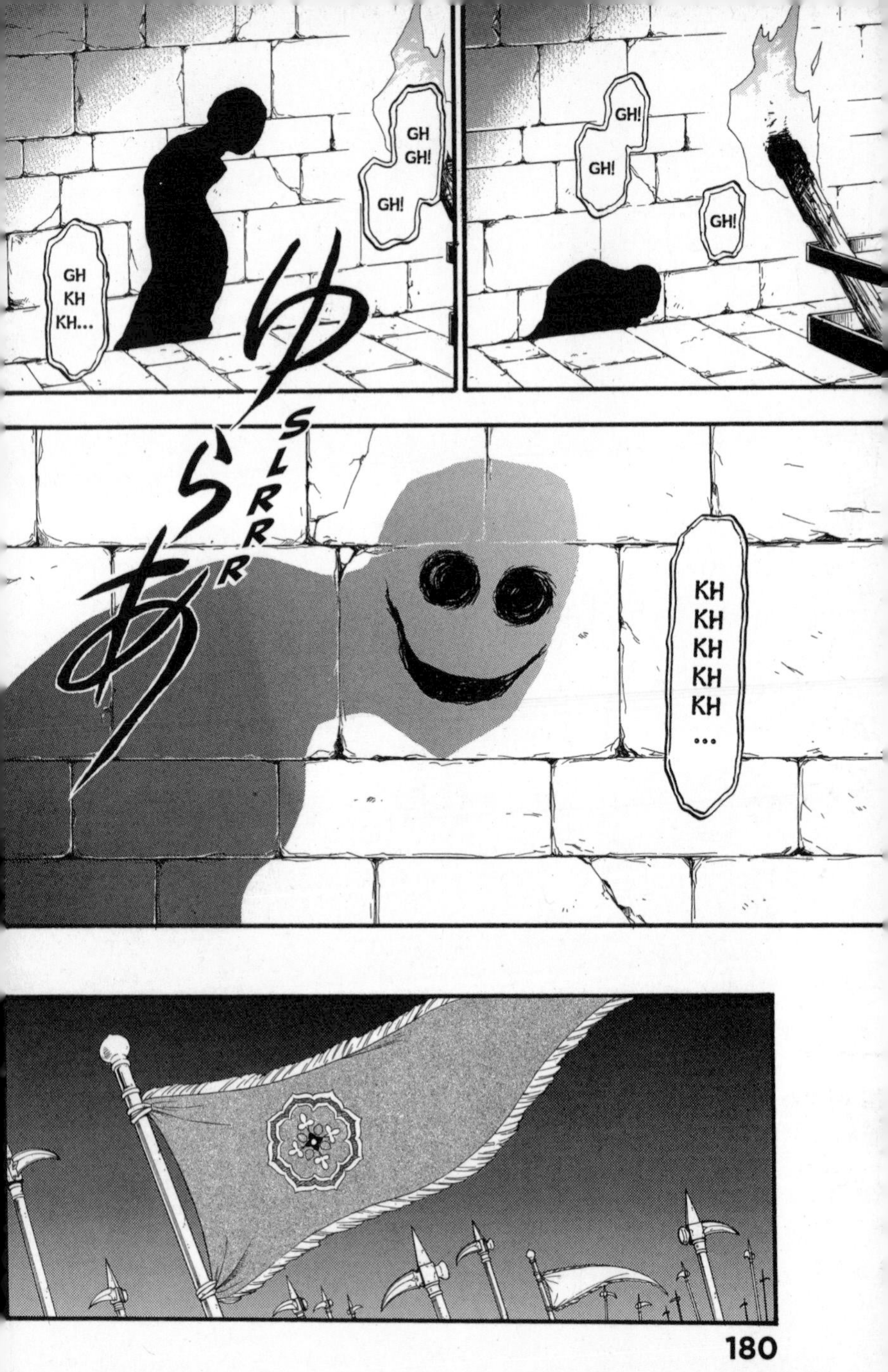
GH! GH!
GH!
GH GH! GH!
GH KH KH...
ゆらあ
SLRRRR
KH KH KH KH KH ...

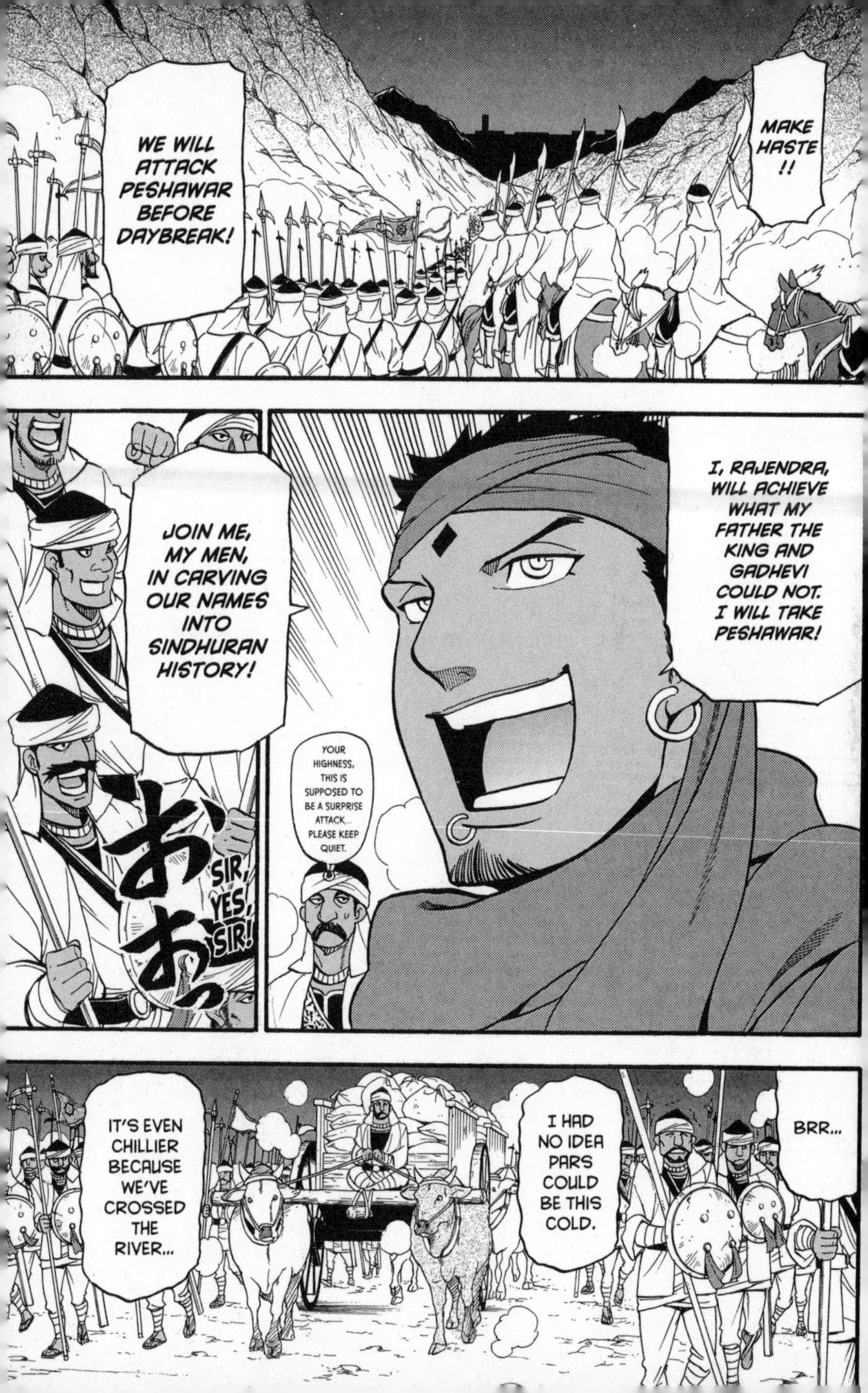
MAKE HASTE !!
WE WILL ATTACK PESHAWAR BEFORE DAYBREAK!
I, RAJENDRA, WILL ACHIEVE WHAT MY FATHER THE KING AND GADHEVI COULD NOT. I WILL TAKE PESHAWAR!
YOUR HIGHNESS, THIS IS SUPPOSED TO BE A SURPRISE ATTACK... PLEASE KEEP QUIET.
JOIN ME, MY MEN, IN CARVING OUR NAMES INTO SINDHURAN HISTORY!
おおっ
SIR, YES, SIR!
BRR...
I HAD NO IDEA PARS COULD BE THIS COLD.
IT'S EVEN CHILLIER BECAUSE WE'VE CROSSED THE RIVER...

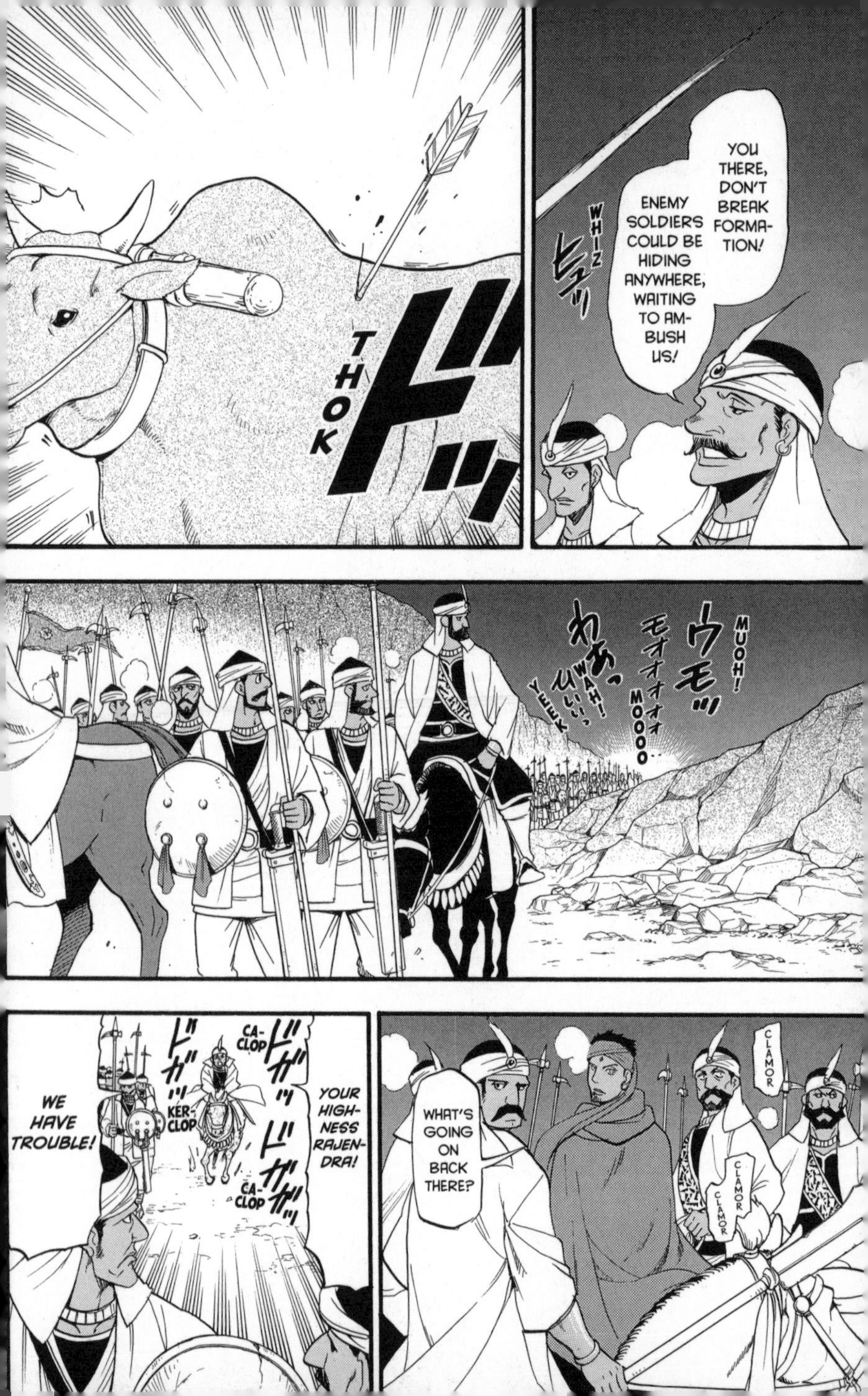
WHIZ
YOU THERE, DON'T BREAK FORMATION!
ENEMY SOLDIERS COULD BE HIDING ANYWHERE, WAITING TO AMBUSH US!
THOK
MUOH!
MOOOO..
WAH!
YEEEK
CLAMOR
WHAT'S GOING ON BACK THERE?
CLAMOR
CLAMOR
CA-CLOP
YOUR HIGHNESS RAJENDRA!
KER-CLOP
CA-CLOP
WE HAVE TROUBLE!

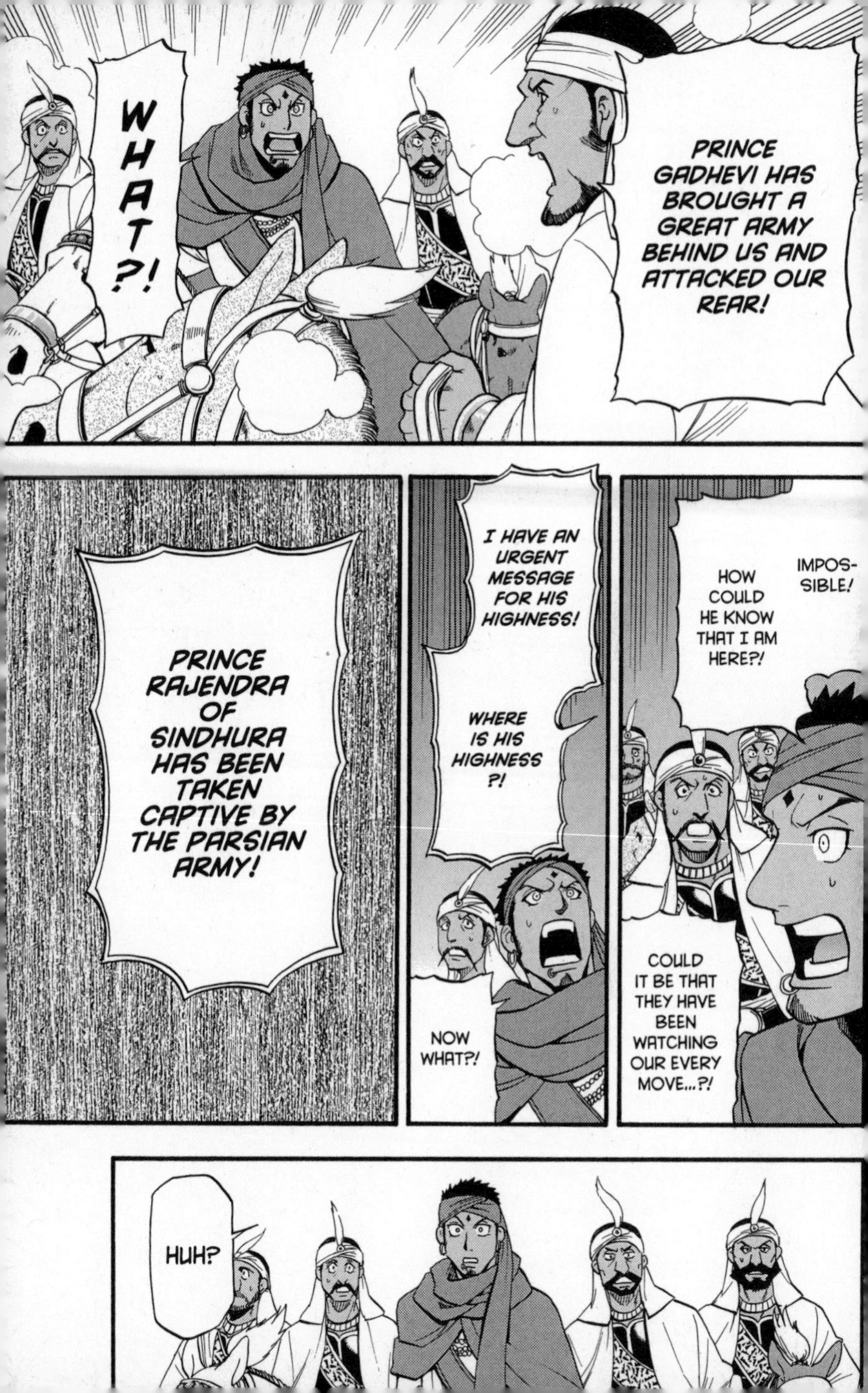
PRINCE GADHEVI HAS BROUGHT A GREAT ARMY BEHIND US AND ATTACKED OUR REAR!
WHAT?!
IMPOSSIBLE!
HOW COULD HE KNOW THAT I AM HERE?!
COULD IT BE THAT THEY HAVE BEEN WATCHING OUR EVERY MOVE...?!
I HAVE AN URGENT MESSAGE FOR HIS HIGHNESS!
WHERE IS HIS HIGHNESS?!
NOW WHAT?!
PRINCE RAJENDRA OF SINDHURA HAS BEEN TAKEN CAPTIVE BY THE PARSIAN ARMY!
HUH?

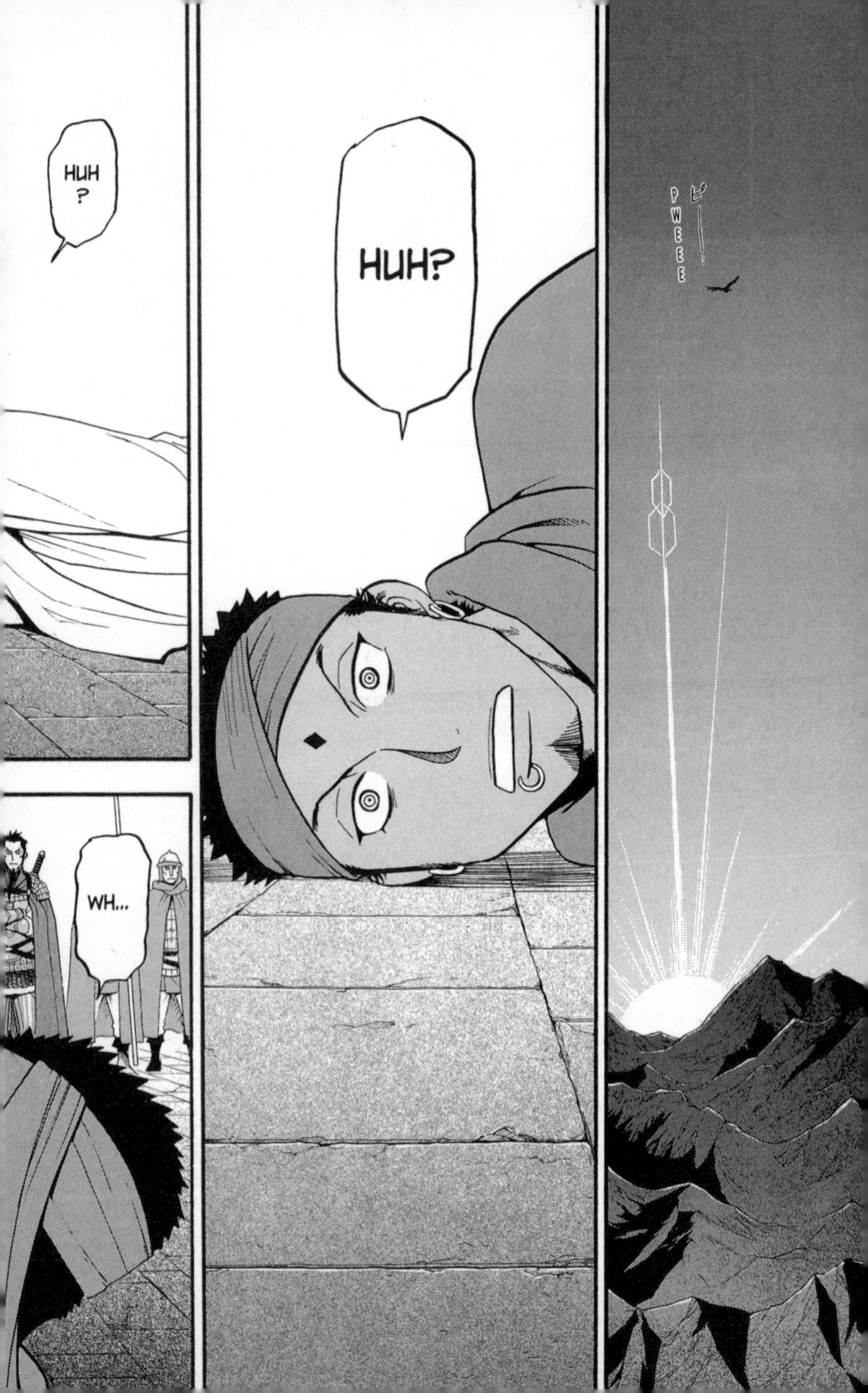
ピー
PWEEE
HUH?
HUH ?
WH...

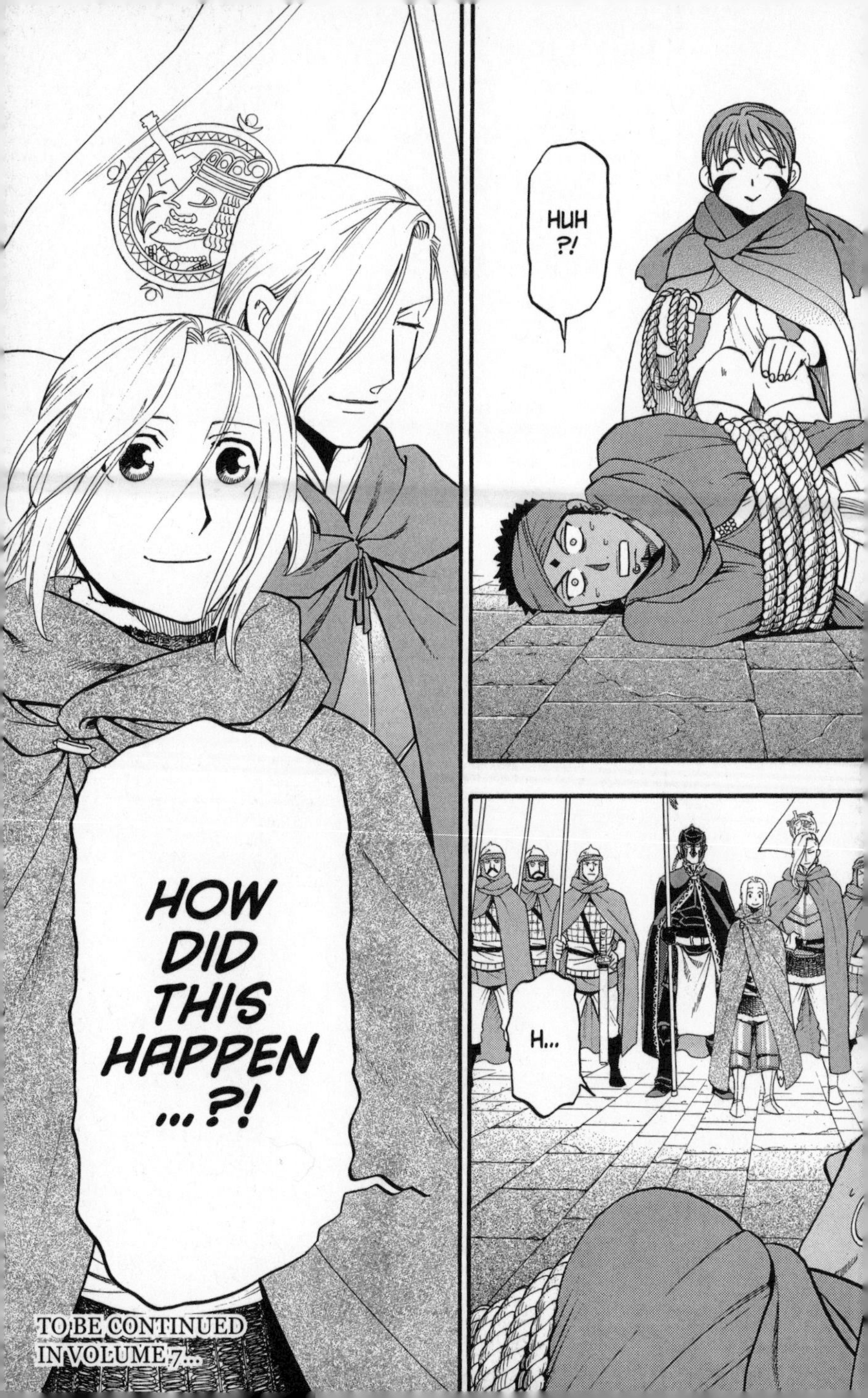
HUH ?!
H...
HOW DID THIS HAPPEN ...?!
TO BE CONTINUED IN VOLUME 7...

THE HEROIC LEGEND OF ARSLAN

TABLE OF CONTENTS

Here are some illustrations that were used for the covers of Bessatsu Shōnen Magazine! Now you can see them in their full, uncovered glory!!

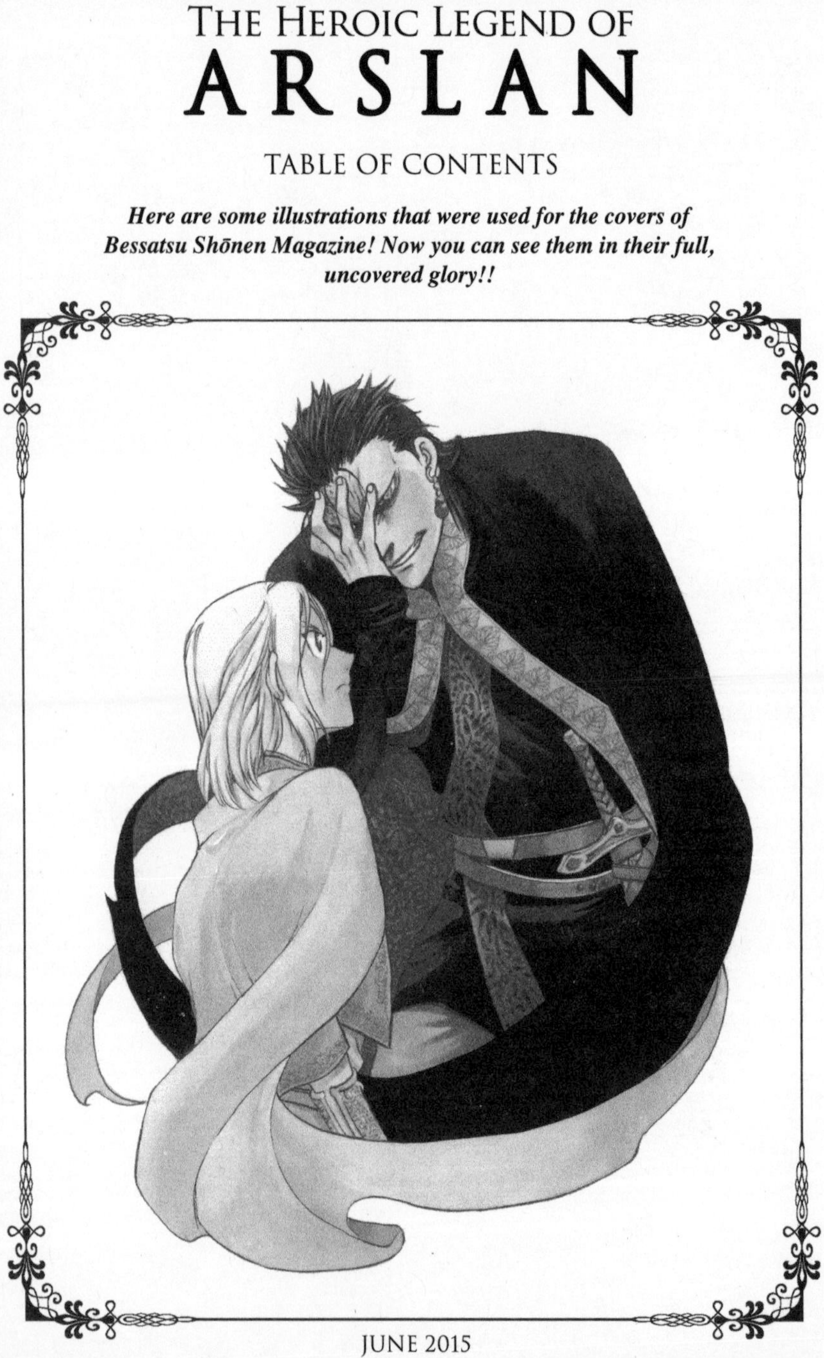

JUNE 2015

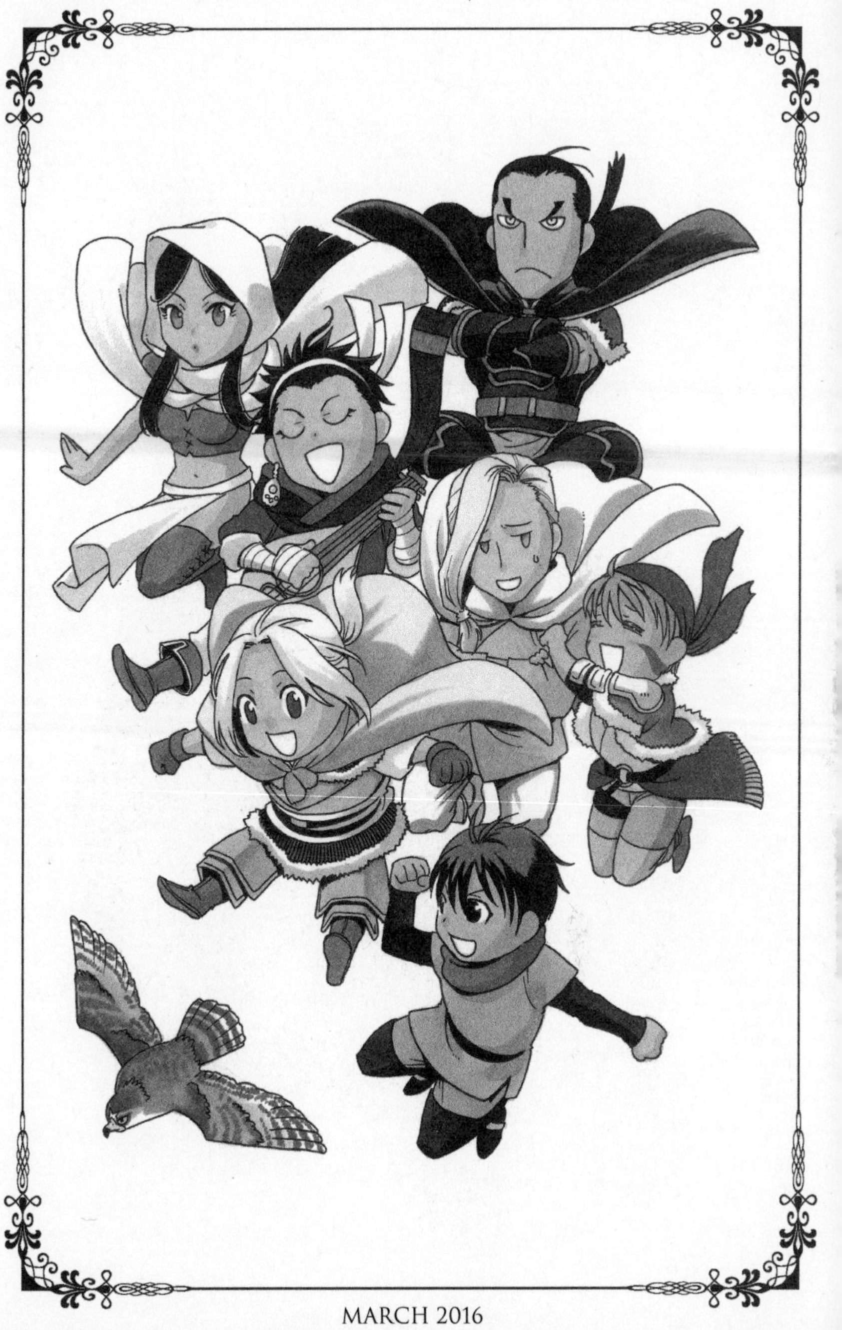

MARCH 2016

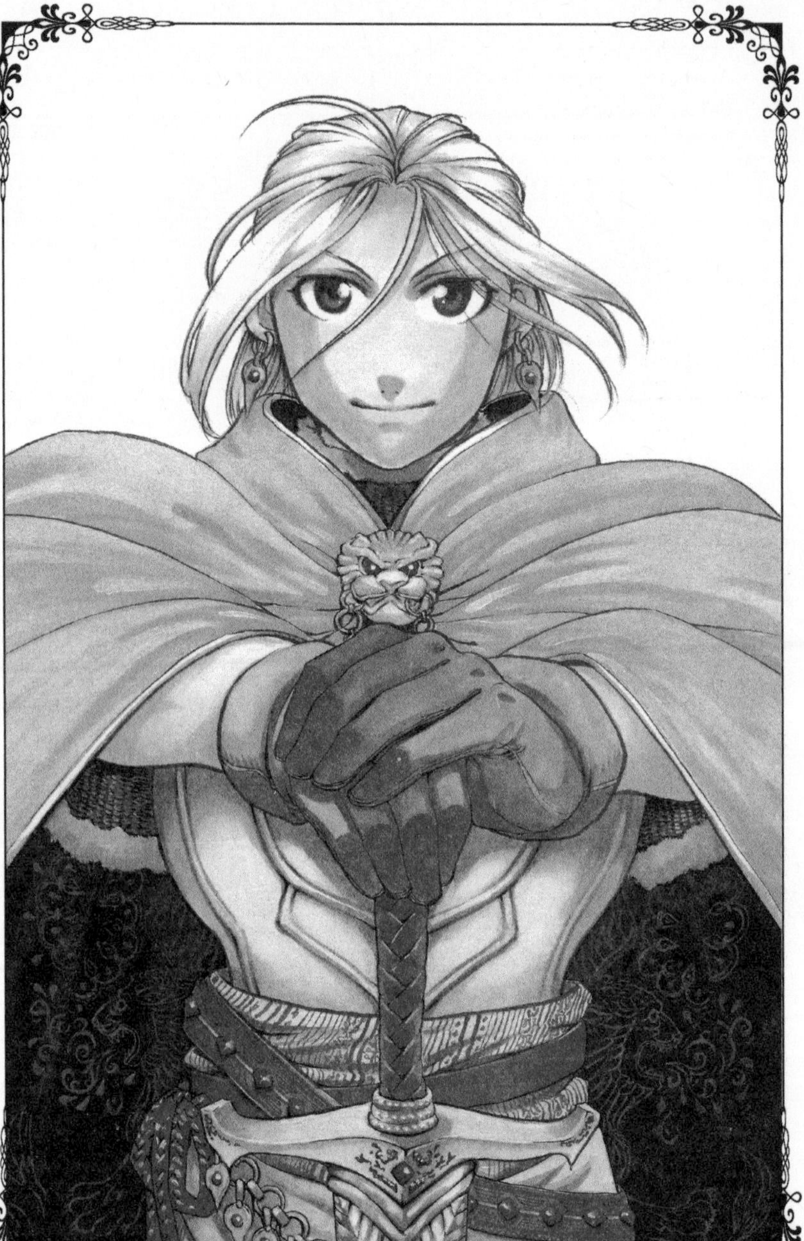

JUNE 2016

THE HEROIC LEGEND OF ARSLAN BONUS GAG MANGA

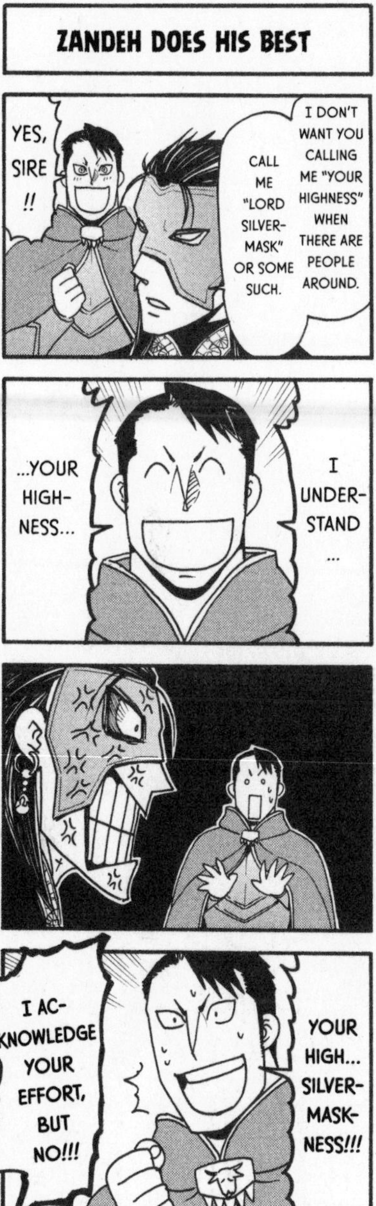
ZANDEH DOES HIS BEST
I DON'T WANT YOU CALLING ME "YOUR HIGHNESS" WHEN THERE ARE PEOPLE AROUND.
CALL ME "LORD SILVER-MASK" OR SOME SUCH.
YES, SIRE !!
I UNDERSTAND ...
...YOUR HIGHNESS...
YOUR HIGH... SILVER-MASKNESS!!!
I ACKNOWLEDGE YOUR EFFORT, BUT NO!!!

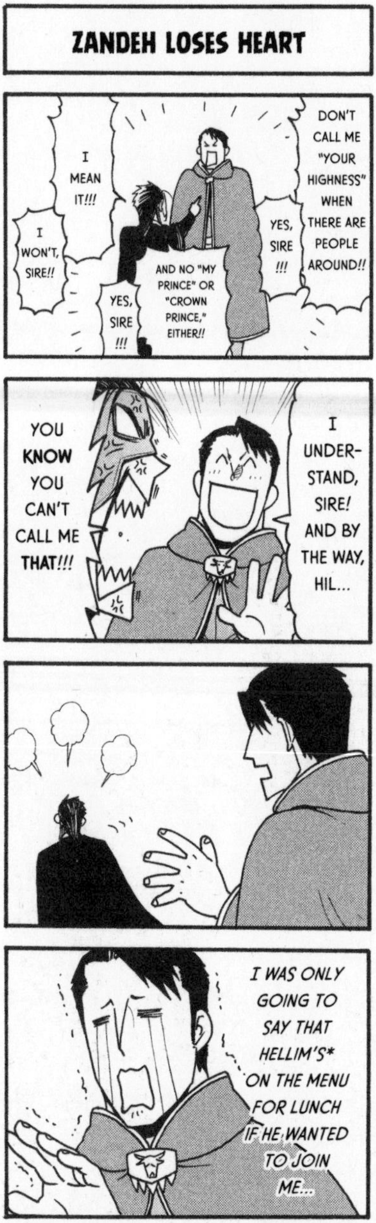
ZANDEH LOSES HEART
DON'T CALL ME "YOUR HIGHNESS" WHEN THERE ARE PEOPLE AROUND!!
YES, SIRE !!!
AND NO "MY PRINCE" OR "CROWN PRINCE," EITHER!!
YES, SIRE !!!
I MEAN IT!!!
I WON'T, SIRE!!
I UNDERSTAND, SIRE! AND BY THE WAY, HIL...
YOU KNOW YOU CAN'T CALL ME THAT!!!
I WAS ONLY GOING TO SAY THAT HELLIM'S* ON THE MENU FOR LUNCH IF HE WANTED TO JOIN ME...

*HELLIM IS THE TURKISH NAME FOR HALLOUMI, A TYPE OF CHEESE THAT ORIGINATED IN CYPRUS. IT MAY OR MAY NOT HAVE ACTUALLY BEEN ON THE MENU; IN THE ORIGINAL JAPANESE, ZANDEH ONLY WANTED TO KNOW IF HILMES (HIRUMESU) WANTED TO JOIN HIM FOR LUNCH.

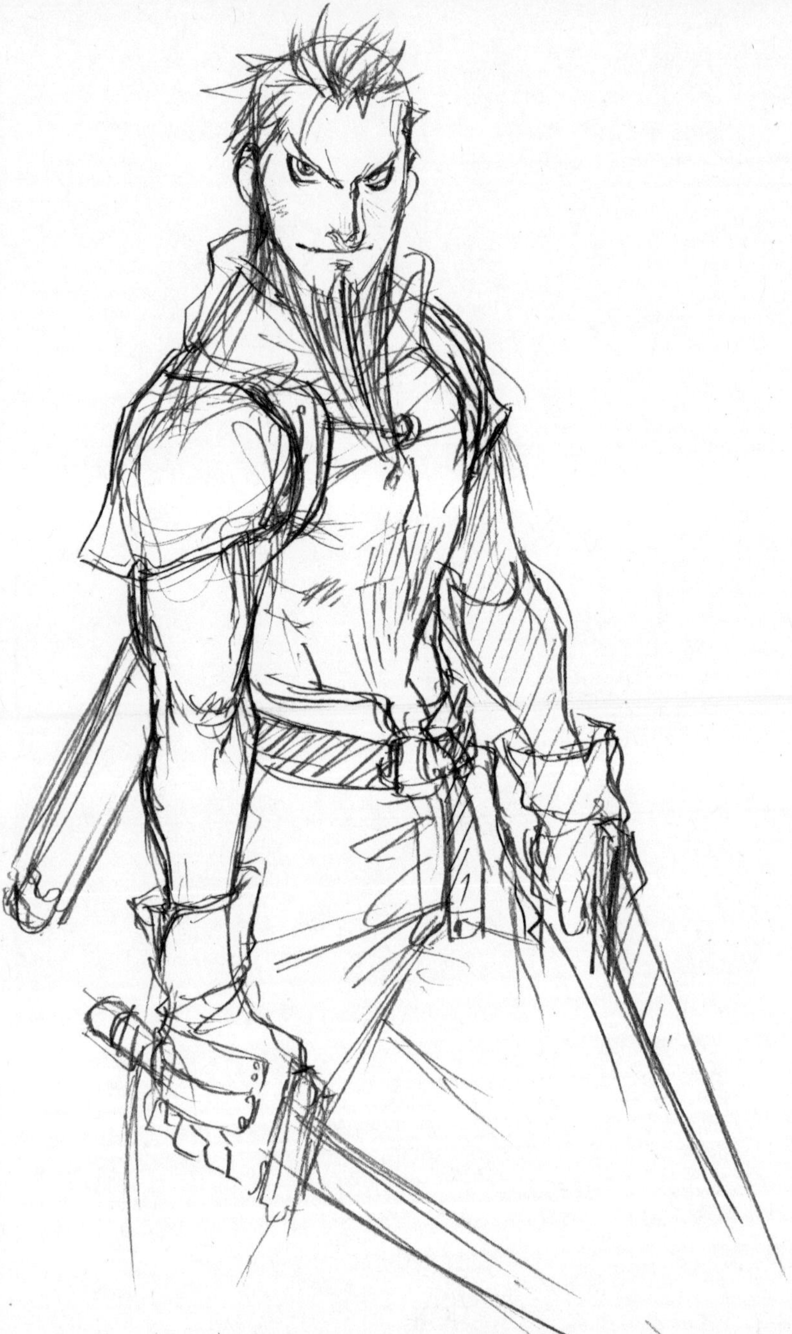

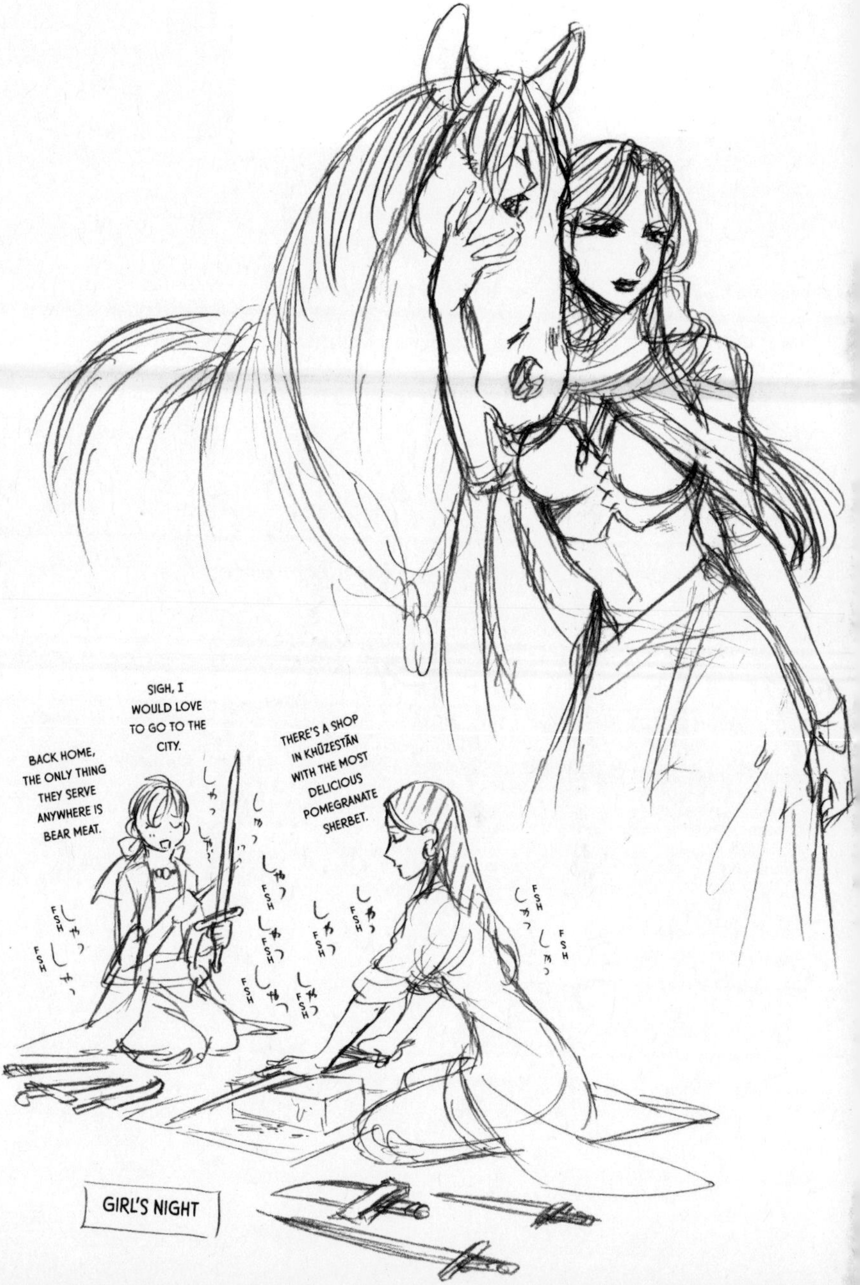
THERE'S A SHOP IN KHŪZESTĀN WITH THE MOST DELICIOUS POMEGRANATE SHERBET.
FSH
FSH
FSH
FSH
FSH
FSH
SIGH, I WOULD LOVE TO GO TO THE CITY.
FSH
FSH
FSH
BACK HOME, THE ONLY THING THEY SERVE ANYWHERE IS BEAR MEAT.
FSH
FSH
GIRL'S NIGHT

The Heroic Legend of Arslan volume 6 is a work of fiction. Names, characters, places, and incidents are the products of the author's imagination or are used fictitiously. Any resemblance to actual events, locales, or persons, living or dead, is entirely coincidental.

A Kodansha Comics Trade Paperback Original.

Published in the United States by Kodansha Comics, an imprint of Kodansha USA Publishing, LLC, New York.

Publication rights for this English edition arranged through Kodansha Ltd., Tokyo.

First published in Japan in 2016 by Kodansha Ltd., Tokyo, as *Arslan Senki* volume 6.

ISBN 978-1-63236-307-7

Printed in the United States of America.

www.kodanshacomics.com

9 8 7 6 5 4 3 2 1

Translation: Amanda Haley
Lettering: James Dashiell
Editing: Ajani Oloye